Africa's Transport Infrastructure

Africa's Transport Infrastructure

Mainstreaming Maintenance and Management

Kenneth Gwilliam
with Heinrich Bofinger, Richard Bullock, Robin Carruthers,
Ajay Kumar, Mike Mundy, Alberto Nogales, and Kavita Sethi

Vivien Foster and Cecilia Briceño-Garmendia,
Series Editors

THE WORLD BANK
Washington, D.C.

© 2011 The International Bank for Reconstruction and Development / The World Bank
1818 H Street NW
Washington DC 20433
Telephone: 202-473-1000
Internet: www.worldbank.org

1 2 3 4 14 13 12 11

This volume is a product of the staff of the International Bank for Reconstruction and Development / The World Bank. The findings, interpretations, and conclusions expressed in this volume do not necessarily reflect the views of the Executive Directors of The World Bank or the governments they represent.

The World Bank does not guarantee the accuracy of the data included in this work. The boundaries, colors, denominations, and other information shown on any map in this work do not imply any judgement on the part of The World Bank concerning the legal status of any territory or the endorsement or acceptance of such boundaries.

ISBN: 978-0-8213-8456-5
eISBN: 978-0-8213-8605-7
DOI: 10.1596/978-0-8213-8456-5

Library of Congress Cataloging-in-Publication Data
Gwilliam, K. M.
    Africa's transport infrastructure / Kenneth Gwilliam.
        p. cm. — (Africa development forum series)
    Includes bibliographical references and index.
    ISBN 978-0-8213-8456-5 — ISBN 978-0-8213-8605-7 (electronic)
    1. Transportation—Africa. 2. Infrastructure (Economics)—Africa. I. Title.
    HE282.A2G87 2011
    388.096—dc22

                                                                    2010047211

Cover photo: Arne Hoel, World Bank
Cover design: Debra Naylor, Washington, D.C.

Contents

Boxes

Figures

About the AICD

This study is a product of the Africa Infrastructure Country Diagnostic (AICD), a project designed to expand the world's knowledge of physical infrastructure in Africa. The AICD provides a baseline against which future improvements in infrastructure services can be measured, making it possible to monitor the results achieved from donor support. It also offers a more solid empirical foundation for prioritizing investments and designing policy reforms in the infrastructure sectors in Africa.

The AICD was based on an unprecedented effort to collect detailed economic and technical data on the infrastructure sectors in Africa. The project produced a series of original reports on public expenditure, spending needs, and sector performance in each of the main infrastructure sectors, including energy, information and communication technologies, irrigation, transport, and water and sanitation. The most significant findings were synthesized in a flagship report titled *Africa's Infrastructure: A Time for Transformation*. All the underlying data and models are available to the public through a Web portal (http://www.infrastructureafrica.org), allowing users to download customized data reports and perform various simulation exercises.

The AICD was commissioned by the Infrastructure Consortium for Africa following the 2005 G-8 Summit at Gleneagles, which flagged the importance of scaling up donor finance to infrastructure in support of Africa's development.

The first phase of the AICD focused on 24 countries that together account for 85 percent of the gross domestic product, population, and infrastructure aid flows of Sub-Saharan Africa. The countries were Benin, Burkina Faso, Cape Verde, Cameroon, Chad, Democratic Republic of Congo, Côte d'Ivoire,

Ethiopia, Ghana, Kenya, Lesotho, Madagascar, Malawi, Mozambique, Namibia, Niger, Nigeria, Rwanda, Senegal, South Africa, Sudan, Tanzania, Uganda, and Zambia. Under a second phase of the project, coverage was expanded to include the remaining countries on the African continent.

Consistent with the genesis of the project, the main focus was on the 48 countries south of the Sahara that face the most severe infrastructure challenges. Some components of the study also covered North African countries to provide a broader point of reference. Unless otherwise stated, therefore, the term "Africa" is used throughout this report as a shorthand for "Sub-Saharan Africa."

The AICD was implemented by the World Bank on behalf of a steering committee that represents the African Union, the New Partnership for Africa's Development (NEPAD), Africa's regional economic communities, the African Development Bank, and major infrastructure donors. Financing for the AICD was provided by a multidonor trust fund to which the main contributors were the Department for International Development (United Kingdom), the Public Private Infrastructure Advisory Facility, Agence Française de Développement, the European Commission, and Germany's Kreditanstalt für Wiederaufbau (KfW). The Sub-Saharan Africa Transport Policy Program and the Water and Sanitation Program provided technical support on data collection and analysis pertaining to their respective sectors. A group of distinguished peer reviewers from policy-making and academic circles in Africa and beyond reviewed all of the major outputs of the study to ensure the technical quality of the work.

Following the completion of the AICD project, long-term responsibility for ongoing collection and analysis of African infrastructure statistics was transferred to the African Development Bank under the Africa Infrastructure Knowledge Program (AIKP). A second wave of data collection of the infrastructure indicators analyzed in this volume was initiated in 2011.

THE WORLD BANK

Series Foreword

The Africa Infrastructure Country Diagnostic (AICD) has produced continent-wide analysis of many aspects of Africa's infrastructure challenge. The main findings were synthesized in a flagship report titled *Africa's Infrastructure: A Time for Transformation*, published in November 2009. Meant for policy makers, that report necessarily focused on the high-level conclusions. It attracted widespread media coverage feeding directly into discussions at the 2009 African Union Commission Heads of State Summit on Infrastructure.

Although the flagship report served a valuable role in highlighting the main findings of the project, it could not do full justice to the richness of the data collected and technical analysis undertaken. There was clearly a need to make this more detailed material available to a wider audience of infrastructure practitioners. Hence the idea of producing four technical monographs, such as this one, to provide detailed results on each of the major infrastructure sectors—information and communication technologies (ICT), power, transport, and water—as companions to the flagship report.

These technical volumes are intended as reference books on each of the infrastructure sectors. They cover all aspects of the AICD project relevant to each sector, including sector performance, gaps in financing and efficiency, and estimates of the need for additional spending on investment, operations, and maintenance. Each volume also comes with a detailed data appendix—providing easy access to all the relevant infrastructure indicators at the country level—which is a resource in and of itself.

In addition to these sector volumes, the AICD has produced a series of country reports that weave together all the findings relevant to one particular country to provide an integral picture of the infrastructure situation at the national level. Yet another set of reports provides an overall picture of the state of regional integration of infrastructure networks for each of the major regional economic communities of Sub-Saharan Africa. All of these papers are available through the project web portal, http://www.infrastructureafrica.org, or through the World Bank's Policy Research Working Paper series.

With the completion of this full range of analytical products, we hope to place the findings of the AICD effort at the fingertips of all interested policy makers, development partners, and infrastructure practitioners.

Vivien Foster and Cecilia Briceño-Garmendia

About the Authors

The lead author, Ken Gwilliam, retired from the post of economic adviser to the transport sector of the World Bank in 2002. During a decade in that role, he was the author of Bank policy documents and papers on transport strategy (Sustainable Transport, 1996), urban transport (Cities on the Move, 2002) and transport and air pollution (Air Pollution from Mobile Sources, 2004). Prior to this, he was professor of transport economics and director of university transport research institutes in the United Kingdom (University of Leeds) and the Netherlands (Erasmus University Rotterdam). He was for six years a director of the British National Bus Company, editor of the *Journal of Transport Economics and Policy*, and a member of numerous British and European committees and commissions.

Henrich Bofinger is an air transport specialist consulting with the World Bank in Africa.

Dick Bullock is a rail specialist consulting with the World Bank in Africa.

Robin Carruthers, now retired, was a Lead Transport Economist at the World Bank with a special focus on multimodal sectorwide planning.

Ajay Kumar is a Lead Transport Economist with the Africa Region of the World Bank and has been leading the practice on urban transportation issues.

Mike Mundy is a ports specialist with Ocean Shipping Consultants working across Africa.

Alberto Nogales is a roads specialist consulting with the World Bank in Africa.

Kavita Sethi is a senior transport economist with the Africa Region of the World Bank.

Acknowledgments

This book was authored by Kenneth Gwilliam, under the overall guidance of series editors Vivien Foster and Cecilia Briceño-Garmendia. All the Africa Infrastructure Country Diagnostic (AICD) transport work was undertaken in the framework of a partnership with the Sub-Saharan Africa Transport Policy Program.

The book draws upon a number of background papers that were prepared by World Bank staff and consultants, under the auspices of the AICD. Excluding the chief author, key contributors to the book on a chapter-by-chapter basis were as follows.

Chapter 2

Contributors
Rodrigo Archondo Callao, Kavita Sethi, Vivien Foster, Alberto Nogales, Supee Teravaninthorn, Gael Raballand

Key AICD Source Documents
"The Burden of Maintenance: Roads in Sub-Saharan Africa," Background Paper 14, AICD

"Transport Prices and Costs in Africa: A Review of the Main International Corridors," Working Paper 14, AICD

Chapter 3

Contributors
Richard Bullock, Mapapa Mbangala, Pierre Pozzo di Borgo, Lucien Andre Aegerter

Key AICD Source Document
"Railways in Sub-Saharan Africa," Background Paper 11, AICD

Chapter 4

Contributors
Heinrich Bofinger, Charles Schlumberger

Key AICD Source Document
"Challenges to Growth in Africa's Air Transport Industry," Background Paper 16, AICD

Chapter 5

Contributors
Mike Mundy, Andrew Penfold, Bradley Julian, Michel Luc Donner, C. Bert Kruk

Key AICD Source Document
"Beyond the Bottlenecks: Ports in Sub-Saharan Africa," Background Paper 8, AICD

Chapter 6

Contributors
Ajay Kumar, Fanny Barrett

Key AICD Source Document
"Stuck in Traffic: Urban Transport in Africa," Background Paper 1, AICD

Chapter 7

Contributors
Robin Carruthers, Ranga Rajan Krishnamani, and Siobhan Murray

Key AICD Source Document
"Improving Connectivity: Investing in Transport Infrastructure in Sub-Saharan Africa," Background Paper 7, AICD

Chapter 8

Contributors
Cecilia Briceño-Garmendia, William Butterfield, Chuan Chen, Jacqueline Irving, Astrid Manroth, Nataliya Pushak, Afua Sarkodie, Karlis Smits

Key AICD Source Document
"Financing Public Infrastructure in Sub-Saharan Africa: Patterns, Issues, and Options," Background Paper 15, AICD

Chapter 9

Contributors
Bruce Thompson, Kavita Sethi

Key AICD Source Documents
The largest collection of primary data was in the roads sector where two consulting firms carried out the AICD data collection in the field for 40 countries:

- Africon in association with InfraAfrica, led by Paul Lombard, covered mostly anglophone countries, and
- Tecsult Inc., led by Denis Baron, collected data from most francophone countries.

Among the many World Bank staff who helped set up arrangements for data collection, we would particularly like to thank Alain Labeau, Anil Bhandari, and Supee Teravaninthorn, AFTTR Coordinators; and Pauline de Curieres de Castelnau, AFTTR Program Assistant, all based in Washington, DC; Alexandre Dossou, Senior Transport Specialist based in the Democratic Republic of Congo; Aguiratou Savadogo-Tinto, Senior Transport Specialist based in Burkina Faso; Ibou Diouf, Senior Transport Specialist based in Côte d'Ivoire; John Kobina Richardson, Transport Specialist based in Ghana; Kingson Khan Apara, Senior Transport Specialist based in Gabon; and Lavite Victorio Ocaya, Senior Highway Engineer based in Uganda. None of the research would have been possible without the generous collaboration of government officials in the key sector institutions of each country, as well as the arduous work of local consultants who assembled the information in a standardized format.

The data were analyzed using the ROad Network Evaluation Tools (RONET) model designed, developed, and adjusted to satisfy the specific needs of the AICD study by Rodrigo Archondo, Senior Highway Engineer, World Bank. We would particularly like to thank David Luyimbazi (Uganda), Godwin Brocke (Ghana), Atanásio Mugunhe (Mozambique), and Joseph Lwiza (Tanzania), from the road agencies that applied the RONET model in the four initial countries where the model was tested.

Seabury ADG gave access to the basic data on which much of the air transport service analysis is based. The AICD also used and adapted Institutional Data collected by the Sub-Saharan Africa Transport Policy Program (SSATP), as well as many SSATP publications referred to in the text. Mustapha Benmmaamar, Senior Transport Specialist, is particularly thanked for his contribution in this respect.

The book benefited from widespread peer review by colleagues within the World Bank, notably Michel Donner, C. Bert Kruk, Pierre Pozzo di Borgo, and Kavita Sethi. The external peer reviewer for this volume, Bruce Thompson, provided constructive and thoughtful comments. Alberto Nogales, Carolina Dominguez, and Nataliya Pushak prepared statistical and graphic materials both for the text and the appendixes. The comprehensive editorial effort of Steven Kennedy is much appreciated.

Abbreviations

AADT	annual average daily traffic
AC	asphalt concrete
ACCO	Association des Chauffeurs du Congo
ACI	Airports Council International
ACSA	Airports Company South Africa
ADC	Aeroports du Cameroun
ADG	Airline Data Group
ADS-B	automatic dependent surveillance-broadcasts
AfDB	African Development Bank
AGETU	Agence de Gestion des Transports Urbains (urban transport agency)
AICD	Africa Infrastructure Country Diagnostic
AMU	Arab Maghreb Union
ANS	air navigation services
ASECNA	Agence pour la Sécurité de la Navigation Aérienne en Afrique et à Madagascar
ATC	air traffic control
ATRACO	Association pour le Transport Commun
BAG	Banjul Accord Group
BR	Botswana Railway

BRT	bus rapid transit
c/ntkm	cents/net tonne-kilometer
c/pkm	cents/passenger-kilometer
CAA	civil aviation authority
CAPEX	capital expenditure
CCFB	Companhia dos Caminhos de Ferro da Beira (Beira Railway Company)
CDN	Corredor de Desenvolvimento do Norte
CEAR	Central East African Railways Company
CEMAC	Economic and Monetary Community of Central Africa
CETUD	Conseil Exécutif des Transports Urbains de Dakar (Executive Council of Dakar Urban Transport)
CFCO	Chemin de fer Congo-Océan
CFM	Caminhos de Ferro de Moçambique
CFMK	Chemins de Fer Matadi Kinshasa
CICOS	Commission Internationale du Bassin Congo-Oubangui-Sangha
COMESA	Common Market for Eastern and Southern Africa
COSCAPS	Cooperative Development of Operational Safety and Continuing Airworthiness Programme
DARCOBOA	Dar es Salaam Commuter Buses Owners Association
DDD	Dakar Dem Dikk
DRCTU	Direction de la Régulation et du Contrôle du Transport Urbain (Directorate of Traffic Regulation and Urban Transport)
EAC	East African Community
ECOWAS	Economic Community of West African States
EDIFACT	Electronic Data Interchange for Administration, Commerce, and Transport
EU	European Union
FAA	Federal Aviation Administration (United States)
FCE	Fianarantsoa Côte Est Railway
GDP	gross domestic product
GIS	geographic information system
GPRTU	Ghana Private Road Transport Union
GPS	global positioning system
HDM-4	Highway Development and Management Model
IATA	International Air Transport Association
IASA	International Aviation Safety Assessment
ICAO	International Civil Aviation Organization

ICTSI	International Container Terminal Services Inc.
IDA	International Development Association
IFI	international financial institution
ILS	instrumented landing system
IMF	International Monetary Fund
IMO	International Maritime Organization
IOSA	IATA Operational Safety Audit
Ircon	Indian Railways Construction Corporation
ISPS	International Ship and Port Facility Security
ISSG	Industry Safety Strategy Group
IT	information technology
KBS	Kenya Bus Service
km	kilometer(s)
km^2	square kilometer(s)
km/hr	kilometers per hour
KRC	Kenya Railways Corporation
LAMATA	Lagos Metropolitan Area Transport Authority
LIC	low-income country
LPI	logistics performance index
m^2	square meter(s)
MIC	middle-income country
mm	millimeter(s)
MMT	Metro Mass Transit Ltd. (Ghana)
MVOA	Matatu Vehicle Owners Association
NPV	net present value
NRSC	national road safety council
ntkm	net tonne-kilometer
NURTW	National Union of Road Transport Workers
OCBN	Organisation Commune Benin-Niger des Chemins de Fer et des Transports (Benin-Niger Railway and Transport Organization)
ODA	official development assistance
OECD	Organisation for Economic Co-operation and Development
O&M	operations and maintenance
ONATRACOM	Office National de Transport en Commun
OPEX	operating expenditure
PIARC	World Road Association
pkm	passenger-kilometer
PMU	project management unit

PPI	Private Participation in Infrastructure
PPIAF	Public-Private Infrastructure Advisory Facility
PPP	public-private partnership
PROTOA	Progressive Transport Owners Association
PSO	public service obligation
PV	present value
RAI	Rural Accessibility Index
REC	regional economic community
ROCKS	Road Costs Knowledge System
RONET	Road Network Evaluation Tool
rpkm	revenue passenger-kilometer
RSZ	Railway Systems of Zambia
RVRC	Rift Valley Railways Consortium
SAA	South African Airways
SACU	Southern African Customs Union
SADC	Southern African Development Community
SARCC	South Africa Rail Commuter Corporation
SCCF	Société Camerounaise des Chemins de Fer
SEFICS	Société d'Exploitation Ferroviaire des Industries Chimiques du Sénégal
SETRAG	Société Transgabonnaise
SICTA	Société Ivoirienne de Contrôle Techniques Automobiles et Industriels
SNCC	Societe Nationale de Chemins de Fer Congolais (Congolese National Railways)
SNTMVCI	Syndicat National des Transportent de Marchandes et Voyageurs de Côte d'Ivoire
SOCATUR	Société Camerounaise de Transports Urbains
SOFIB	Société Ferroviaire Ivoiro-Burkinabè
SOLAS	Safety of Life at Sea Convention
SOTRA	Société de Transport Abidjanais
SOTRACO	Société de Transport en Commun
SOTUC	Societé de Transports Urbains du Cameroun
SSATP	Sub-Saharan Africa Transport Policy Program
ST	surface treatment
STUC	Société des Transports Urbains du Congo
SUMATRA	Surface and Marine Transport Regulatory Authority
TEU	twenty-foot equivalent unit
TRC	Tanzania Railways Corporation
TU	traffic unit

UNCTAD	United Nations Conference on Trade and Development
UNECA	United Nations Economic Commission for Africa
UPETCA	Union des Propriétaires de Taxis Compteurs d'Abidjan
URC	Uganda Railways Corporation
UTODA	Uganda Taxi Operators and Drivers Association
WACEM	West African Cement Company
WAEMU	West African Economic and Monetary Union
WBI	World Bank Institute
WGI	Worldwide Governance Indicators
YD	Yamoussoukro Decision
ZR	Zambia Rail

CHAPTER 1

The Legacy of History

This book is about transport in Africa, where Africa is defined to exclude the six countries and one disputed territory generally called North Africa (Algeria, the Arab Republic of Egypt, Libya, Morocco, Sudan, Tunisia, and Western Sahara). What is often referred to as Sub-Saharan Africa will be referred to here as Africa. The main purpose of this book is to assess the factors that affect the performance of Africa's transport infrastructure. While the book is not about geography or political history, a brief review of the fortuities of natural resource endowment and the vicissitudes of history is necessary to understand the current state of transport infrastructure and the distortions of transport operations.

Political History: Colonialism and Independence

Africa's rich natural endowment of diamonds, gold, and other mineral deposits was the attraction that eventually led the industrial powers of Europe to colonize the continent. Later, oil became an even more valuable prize. Though these resources are concentrated in a broad band of states in Central and West Africa, other countries not formally classified as resource rich, such as South Africa, also have substantial mineral resources. In many parts of the continent, agricultural products such as rubber, coffee, cocoa, and cotton also have high export potential. While the colonial powers exploited Africa's rich resources, most of its population remained dependent on subsistence agriculture.

By 1945, the whole of the continent—with the exception of Ethiopia and Liberia—had been colonized by one European state or another, with the Union of South Africa gaining independence in 1910. Belgium, France, Great Britain, Italy, Portugal, and, in a smaller way, Spain, all had a stake in Africa—as Germany had until the end of World War I. While World War II did not change the basic face of colonial Africa, it renewed European powers' interest in developing their colonies as sources of materials for the war effort. During this period, many transport facilities were built, primarily for the exploitation and export of natural resources. More recently, China's investment in railways has been motivated by that country's need to secure supplies of scarce minerals critical to its growth.

The European powers adopted radically different approaches to the political structures of their colonies. Belgium and Portugal did not permit any political activity at all in their territories. Great Britain governed each of its 14 territories separately, allowing a degree of self-determination on internal matters in some. France viewed the African colonies as an integral and indissoluble part of metropolitan France, with entirely parallel political systems and processes. Whatever the system of administration, pressure for independence grew rapidly in the post–World War II years until, eventually, the winds of change swept across the colonial territories. The Belgian Congo gained independence in 1960, and by the end of 1968, all the British and French colonies were independent. Portugal withdrew from Angola and Mozambique by 1975. In many cases, the leaders of the independence movements became heads of the newly formed states.

Precolonial African societies have been described by Meredith (2005, 154) as "a mosaic of lineage groups, clans, villages, chiefdoms, kingdoms and empires with shifting and indeterminate frontiers and loose allegiances." He argues that colonial administrators actually oversimplified and hence accentuated ethnic distinctions in their zeal to classify indigenous populations for administrative purposes. The countries that emerged at independence were to a large extent the artificial constructs of colonialism, through which tribal divisions became more deeply entrenched. Many subsequent civil conflicts, such as that in Rwanda, were in part the result of this emphasis on the identification and manipulation of tribal groupings. In the early days of independence, many had expected that the interests of nation building would supersede ethnic divisions and lead to greater union. Instead, ethnic divisions increasingly dominated and fractured the political processes of many countries, including Ghana, Nigeria, and, saddest of all, Rwanda.

The independence process itself had significant effects on the political shape of Africa. After France's initial expulsion from Guinea, to which it reacted by withdrawing all resources and support, France shifted to a policy of restructuring before liberating its African colonies. Both French West Africa and French Equatorial Africa were split into multiple independent countries with the intent of maintaining French interest and influence on the continent. Given the historical association of the colonies with metropolitan France, and given the experience that a number of African politicians had obtained in French government, this strategy did in fact perpetuate strong French influence in a number of countries, such as Côte d'Ivoire.

The initial stages of each country's independence were critical. The most significant consequence of the new order was the emergence in many countries of a one-party system. While this system was initially defended as appropriate for nation building in states with multiple ethnic communities, many of the liberators became dictators.

Many new national leaders adopted the theories of Marx and Lenin, though not all interpreted socialism the same way. In Ghana, President Kwame Nkrumah saw the path of development in terms of rapid industrialization; in Tanzania, President Julius Nyerere saw it in terms of agricultural self-sufficiency. Most new leaders, however, shared the belief that the state should direct economic activity, implying strict government control, if not full ownership, of most productive sectors.

A Consequence of History: A Distorted Transport Sector

This political history has had profound economic consequences for the transport sector, bequeathing a legacy of structural and institutional distortions from which it has still not completely escaped. Several component elements of distortion can be identified.

Networks were incomplete. Colonialism was about the exploitation of natural resources. Colonial government administration was typically settled in a capital city, often a port, and had little concern for inland passenger transport. The infrastructure it developed was usually limited to whatever was deemed necessary for the export of minerals or agricultural products. Only the links between the port and the material source (which might be in one of the neighboring landlocked countries) were of prime interest. The result was that transport networks were extensive in linking ports and distant sources rather than intensive in giving good network coverage to the whole of the territory.

Rail development was emphasized. For heavy, bulk movements over long distances, rail transport was usually believed to have a comparative advantage over other modes—particularly road transport. So major investments were made in ports and rail systems. Moreover, because speed was not essential, the rail systems were built to modest technical specifications, with the consequence that once roads began to be developed, the railways were not well equipped to compete in the more time-sensitive passenger transport markets.

Systems were distorted by national fragmentation. Independence was accompanied by national fragmentation—a deliberate policy in the case of the former French colonies. Such radical political subdivision of already small postcolonial economies took a heavy toll on the welfare of African citizens (Collier and Venables 2008). In the private sector, subdivision frustrated scale economies and skewed the structure of the overall economy toward peasant agriculture. In the public sector, the small scale raised the cost of public goods. The fragmentation of countries also resulted in some wasteful investment as small countries developed their own ports and transit corridors to neighboring landlocked countries. The duplication could be very costly, as in the case of Guinea (box 1.1).

These difficulties are exacerbated by mutual suspicions, which prevent sensible economic collaboration. In the transport sector, the previously integrated railway administrations of Mali and Senegal and of Burkina Faso and Côte d'Ivoire were separated, to the detriment of all four countries. Cross-border transport is particularly affected by such separations. Some of these problems have been overcome. The joint concessioning of separated railways has enabled them to be operated once again as unitary systems. And the creation of regional economic communities has enabled the development of some sound regional policies—especially with respect to the liberalization of international air transport. But there is still much to do to overcome these difficulties.

State enterprises were excessive and inefficient. The commitment of many of the new leaders to Marxism has already been noted. Unfortunately, almost without exception these leaders had unrealistic expectations of what could be achieved with state ownership or control. Price controls and other populist impositions starved governments of cash and eventually drove many of the enterprises into decline or bankruptcy. Many of the experiments with state ownership failed because of politicized management, with senior management appointments made on the basis

Box 1.1

The Economic Costs of Political Fragmentation:
The Case of Guinea

The recent discovery of large iron ore deposits in Guinea by Rio Tinto Zinc raises important and difficult issues common in the postcolonial context. The exploitation of the deposits evidently requires investment in a mine, but the pertinent issue is the investment needed in transport infrastructure. A railway already links the deposit to a deepwater port, Buchanan, a legacy from the age of empires. But Buchanan is in Liberia, and the government of Guinea does not want to find its work captive to administrative holdups by the Liberian government. It has therefore insisted that the transport of the iron ore be done entirely within Guinea, which requires the construction of a new dedicated railway and deepwater port. This decision has more than doubled the total investment needed for the project, adding around $4 billion.[1] Evidently, these additional costs will be passed on to the people of Guinea. The government has agreed with Rio Tinto Zinc to absorb them through a reduced flow of royalty payments. The decision is also costly for the people of Liberia: the port of Buchannan is losing what may prove to be a key opportunity for a scale economy.

Source: Collier and Venables 2008.

of political support or tribal and family membership, rather than on the basis of technical and managerial competence. The transport sector was not unique in this respect, as even the most ambitious of the industrialization programs failed.

Corruption was rife. The wish to control Africa's rich natural resources was the major driver of colonialism. Independence redirected the gains not to the national populace but to its political leaders. In practice, one-party rule in Africa resulted in repression of minorities and extreme exploitation of national wealth by rulers. Control of the extraction and export of raw materials proved a major source of wealth for those who governed postcolonial Africa, as well as the root cause of several regional wars. A large proportion of the proceeds from developing mineral reserves was conspicuously consumed by the rulers and their close associates at home or went into their bank accounts abroad. Meanwhile, domestic economies benefited little. A preparatory document for the African Union draft convention on corruption in September 2002 estimated that corruption cost

Africa $148 billion per year, more than 25 percent of the continent's gross domestic product (GDP) (African Union 2002). The corruption that will later be identified as a major source of inefficiency in the transport system is thus an expression of a general political malaise rather than anything specific to the transport sector.

Civil wars were common. Military overthrow of corrupt civilian administrations rarely eliminated the corruption (World Bank 1989). Spurred by events in Eastern Europe, many countries returned to multiparty politics in the early 1990s, but doing so rarely eliminated corruption, and in several cases it unleashed historic ethnic hatreds in genocidal frenzies. By 2000, there were more than 10 major conflicts going on in Africa, and more than one-fifth of the total population lived in war-torn countries. These "fragile states" are among the poorest of nations and often have the worst transport facilities, as transport links, particularly railways and bridges, are prime targets in civil wars.

The sector was poorly prepared for urbanization. This poor preparation had a number of root causes. The emphasis on rail rather than road development meant that urban road systems were often inadequate in density, badly constructed, and poorly maintained. The poor management of the state or municipal bus companies, together with attempts to maintain uneconomically low fares without any compensating subsidies, destroyed many of the conventional bus companies. The lack of adequate urban regulatory institutions meant that the informal sector services that emerged were effectively subject only to self-regulation by operators' associations, which acted primarily in operators' rather than passengers' interests.

The Outcome: High Costs, Poor Service, and Reduced Trade

Inland transport costs in Africa are much higher than those in any other region of the world. The United Nations Conference on Trade and Development estimated that international transport costs faced by African countries, at 12.6 percent of the delivered value of exports, were more than twice as high as the world average of 6.1 percent (UNCTAD 2003). The United Nations Economic Commission for Africa put the average at 14 percent of the value of exports—and higher still for the landlocked countries such as Malawi (56 percent), Chad (52 percent), and Rwanda (48 percent)—compared with 8.6 percent for all developing countries (UNECA 2004). Moreover, freight moves slowly and uncertainly. Naudé and Matthee (2007) estimate that the reduction in trade resulting from this transport performance could be well in excess of 20 percent.

Why is performance so bad? Mainly because political and economic conditions in Africa have prevented the development of the type of modern logistical systems that have fostered trade and economic growth in the industrial world. The following aspects of logistics performance are encapsulated in the World Bank's Logistics Performance Index (LPI):

- Efficient clearance of customs and other border-control agencies
- High-quality information technology systems
- Easy and affordable arrangement of shipments
- Competence among transport operators, customs brokers, and so on
- Ability to track and trace shipments
- Adequate infrastructure (local transportation, terminal handling, warehousing)
- On-time arrival

Individual country performance is illustrated in map 1.1, which shows that, with the exception of South Africa, African countries south of the Sahara perform very poorly on aggregate. Looking at the separate components of the index makes clear that all countries except South Africa performed poorly not only on infrastructure quality but also on all the main aspects of logistics competence.

Map 1.1   World Logistics Performance Index

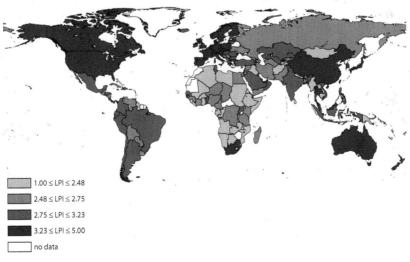

1.00 ≤ LPI ≤ 2.48

2.48 ≤ LPI ≤ 2.75

2.75 ≤ LPI ≤ 3.23

3.23 ≤ LPI ≤ 5.00

no data

Source: World Bank 2010.
Note: LPI = logistics performance index; 1 is the minimum and 5 the maximum score.

Several of these components relate to the efficiency of transport infrastructure in meeting the demands of tightly organized trading chains. The strength of those trading chains can be no greater than that of their weakest links, usually the interchanges. The weaknesses are partly physical—for example, in cases where there is a missing connection between the modes or infrastructure needed for transshipment. They are partly institutional—as in cases where responsibility for the interchanges does not fall clearly with one agency or another. And they are partly operational—as when government's interest in collecting taxes and duties, or staff's interest in collecting bribes, slows down movement and drives up costs.

The port-rail connection is the first major weakness. The comparative advantage of using rail over roads for long-distance transport of time-insensitive commodities means that railways depend heavily on international trade. Good rail-port connections are essential to complete the journey of goods overseas, but such connections are often inhibited by conflicts between rail and port authorities over control of rail movements in port areas; except in South Africa, inland transport and supporting facility investments are poorly aligned with port development. The stripping and stuffing of containers in port areas also creates inland transport congestion in many ports. It is no accident that some of the most successful lines in Africa perform well in national corridors where specialized rail and port facilities are vertically integrated (for example, the South African Transnet Freight Rail coal and ore lines and the Gabonese manganese ore line).

Links among complementary rail systems are also essential. Some railway organizations have already created such links. The binational railways in Burkina Faso–Côte d'Ivoire and Mali–Senegal offer the prospect of freer movement, as does the involvement of the same contractor in contiguous railways (the NLPI role in the route from South Africa through Zimbabwe to Zambia) or the same concessionaire (Central East African Railways Company in Malawi and Mozambique). But these arrangements also create local monopolies that can use predatory practices to increase profits, as in the case of the Zambian treatment of Congolese copper exports (see chapter 3 of this book). In East Africa, joint concessioning of railways is part of a World Bank–funded corridor, including the reform of border-crossing arrangements. Some countries are now trying to develop coordinated corridor systems, as in the Ghana Gateway and Maputo corridors.

Whatever the mode of transport, however, the most serious impediments are administrative. For road transport, the regulation and market structures of the road freight industry, rather than the quality of road infrastructure, are the binding constraints on international corridors (Teravaninthorn and Raballand 2008). Third-party logistics, which have played such a large role in increasing production and distribution efficiency in industrialized countries, are still poorly developed in Africa. Customs and transshipment improvements are also central to corridor improvement. Some landlocked countries already have bonded warehouses at ports in West Africa. Concessionaires are also speeding transit, such as through the Sitarail intermodal terminal proposal in Ouagadougou, the Zambia Rail company customs bond at Victoria Falls, and the planned Madarail bonded container terminal near Antananarivo. There is scope for a regional program on trade facilitation similar to the successful effort in southeastern Europe, which was catalyzed by the prospect of entry into the European Union.

Transport in Africa is also very unsafe. Vehicles and infrastructure are poorly maintained. Failures of governance accentuate the problem, as policing is corrupt and laws are not enforced. Over the past two decades, life in general has been precarious and violence prevalent. In such circumstances, transport safety is not an obvious priority. It is therefore not surprising that all modes of transport, in particular road and air, have extremely poor safety records. While the nature and causes of incidents differ between these two sectors—as will be discussed in more detail—neither mode has a developed safety culture.

As with so many aspects of transport in Africa, the problem is deeply embedded in the continent's recent troubled history. General social stabilization should help, but deeply ingrained attitudes are difficult to change. Unless such attitudes are overcome, no amount of infrastructure development is likely to bring about much improvement.

The necessity of transport infrastructure for economic development is taken as axiomatic. But transport infrastructure in Africa is judged insufficient for achieving this end in two important senses. First, and most obviously, the region is found to be quantitatively underendowed compared with other regions of the world. Its road system is less dense, its rail system built to lower standards, its ports ill-equipped for the development of containerization, and its air transport system lacking in adequate air traffic control and navigation services. Second, the region's physical infrastructure is not accompanied by good transport service; that is, the infrastructure is not well maintained, managed, or operated. Hence, it is not only in physical terms but also in governance that transport infrastructure in Africa is insufficient.

Country Diversity and Uneven Economic Performance

Despite similarities in their postcolonial political history and problems, Africa's many countries face diverse economic conditions. Understanding that structural differences in economies and institutions affect countries' growth and financing challenges as well as their economic decisions (Collier and O'Connell 2006), this book categorizes the nations studied into four types to organize much of the discussion (map 1.2).

Map 1.2   A Country Typography of Sub-Saharan Africa

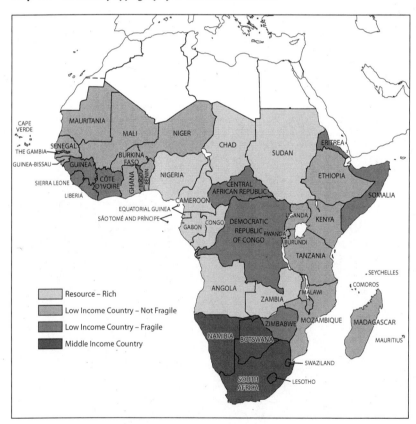

Source: Briceño-Garmendia, Smits, and Foster 2009.

The categories shown in map 1.2 are defined as follows:

- *Middle-income* countries have GDP per capita in excess of $745 but less than $9,206. Examples include Cape Verde, Lesotho, and South Africa (World Bank 2010).
- *Resource-rich* countries are low-income countries whose behaviors are strongly affected by their endowment of natural resources (Collier and O'Connell 2006). These countries typically depend on minerals, petroleum, or both. A country is classified as resource rich if primary commodity rents exceed 10 percent of the GDP. South Africa is not classified as resource rich, using this criterion.
- *Low-income, fragile* states face particularly severe development challenges, such as weak governance, limited administrative capacity, violence, or the legacy of recent conflict. Countries that score less than 3.2 on the World Bank's Country Policy and Institutional Performance Assessment (WBI 2004) belong to this group. Some 14 African countries are in this category.
- *Low-income, nonfragile* states are those that have GDP per capita below $745 and are neither resource rich nor fragile.

Table 1.1 shows how all the countries in the study are categorized and also notes whether they are coastal or landlocked.

The most significant feature of Africa is that it has a much larger proportion of low-income countries than the rest of the developing world. An important element of this poverty is that nearly one-third of African countries are classified as low-income, fragile states that have recently suffered from major political and economic trauma. But even its resource-rich countries have an average GDP per capita that is only 70 percent of that of the lower-middle-income developing countries in the rest of the world (table 1.2).

African countries share some common economic features. Thirty-seven percent of their populations lives in cities, with little variation among the four country types. Agriculture accounts for about a third of the GDP, on average, again with relatively little variation among the country types. But other features are not shared so equally: for example, the share of land available for agriculture varies from a low of 29 percent for the low-income, fragile states to 63 percent for the middle-income countries. The trade share of GDP ranges even more widely, from 120 percent for low-income countries to 39 percent for the low-income, fragile states (World Bank 2009).[2] Together with

Table 1.1 Typology of Countries

Resource-rich	Low-income, nonfragile	Low-income, fragile	Middle-income	Alternative classification for low-income countries	
				Low-income, coastal	Low-income, landlocked
Angola	Benin	Burundi	Botswana	Benin	Burkina Faso
Cameroon	Burkina Faso	Central African Republic	Cape Verde	Comoros	Burundi
Chad	Ethiopia	Comoros	Lesotho	Côte d'Ivoire	Central African Republic
Congo, Rep.	Ghana	Congo, Dem. Rep.	Mauritius	Eritrea	Congo, Dem. Rep.
Equatorial Guinea	Kenya	Côte d'Ivoire	Namibia	Gambia, The	Ethiopia
Gabon	Madagascar	Eritrea	Seychelles	Ghana	Malawi
Nigeria	Malawi	Gambia, The	South Africa	Guinea	Mali
Sudan	Mali	Guinea-Bissau	Swaziland	Guinea-Bissau	Niger
	Mozambique	Guinea		Kenya	Rwanda
	Niger	Liberia		Liberia	Uganda
	Rwanda	São Tomé and Príncipe		Madagascar	Zambia
	Senegal	Sierra Leone		Mozambique	Zimbabwe
	Tanzania	Togo		São Tomé and Príncipe	
	Uganda	Zimbabwe		Senegal	
	Zambia			Sierra Leone	
				Tanzania	
				Togo	

Source: Classification as proposed in IMF (2007), except for Sudan, which was added for completeness.

Table 1.2 Basic Characteristics of African Countries vs. World's Other Developing Countries

	Africa					Rest of the world		
	Total	Resource-rich	Low-income, nonfragile	Low-income, fragile	Middle-income	Low-income	Lower-middle-income	Upper-middle-income
Number of countries	48	9	15	15	9	13	44	39
GDP per capita, PPP (constant 2005 US$)	843	930	342	269	4,850	421	1,337	5,329
Population (millions)	763	239	324	143	56	423	3,300	874
Land area (millions of km²)	23.6	7.6	8.5	4.9	2.7	3.7	25.5	43.3
Total GDP (constant 2005 US$ billions)	643	222	111	39	271	178	4,413	4,655
Urban population as share of total (%)	34.9	45.5	23.8	34.5	55.8	28.9	38.7	74.7
Trade as share of GDP (%)	69.8	82.7	59.7	84.7	61.3	75.9	68.1	58.2
Agricultural land as share of total land (%)	44.0	48.3	42.5	29.3	63.3	38.8	49.8	28.1

Source: Carruthers, Krishnamani, and Murray 2009.
Note: km² = square kilometer; PPP = purchasing power parity.

geographic and climatic features, these similarities and differences—which are even greater when individual countries are considered—contribute to the varying needs for and costs of transport infrastructure.

A New-Millennium Renaissance

Fortunately, the portents are not all ominous. The advent of democracy in South Africa in 1994 acted as a catalyst for some change. The launch of the New Partnership for Africa's Development by a group of 15 African states in 2001 and the replacement of the Organization of African Unity by the African Union in 2002 heralded a commitment not only to more democratic political processes but also to multilateral action as a means of achieving and maintaining them. The Clinton initiative in 1998 and the Commission for Africa report in 2005 reflected the supportive Western attitude. Hopefully, these mark the beginnings of a political renaissance.

Partly as a consequence of these developments there has been at least a minor renaissance in Africa's economy. From 2004 to 2008, it expanded by more than 5 percent every year—the first time in more than 45 years that such a growth rate had been sustained over a long period.[3] In 2008, the overall growth rate was 5.4 percent despite the global economic downturn (World Bank 2009). These figures suggest the emergence of an economic renaissance.

The outlook for the immediate future is also promising in spite of the poor world economic climate. Admittedly, weaker external demand and lower commodity prices will take a toll. In particular, declines in demand in key external markets are likely to lead to a negative trend in the contribution of trade to GDP growth, with an impact on international transport demand, particularly for shipping services (discussed in chapter 5). Official development assistance flows may also slow, which is of particular significance when considering how fast backlogs in capital investment can be overcome, as discussed in chapter 8. Nevertheless, growth is forecast to slow only to 3.5 percent overall. This is partly because the African economies are not well integrated into the international financial system. Hence the direct effects of the global financial and economic crisis were considered likely to be limited in the African economies, according to a World Bank Global Economic Prospects review in mid-2009 (World Bank 2009).

In summary, Africa has inherited from its history a distorted and relatively poor transport infrastructure, which it has neither managed nor maintained well. It has been heavily dependent on official development assistance for much of its transport spending but has nonetheless achieved substantial economic growth and has prospects for more. Against this background, the book now moves on to discuss the major modes of transport.

Notes

1. Throughout the book, monetary values are given in U.S. dollars unless otherwise specified.
2. Trade share of GDP measures the importance of trade to an economy. Merchandise trade as a share of GDP is the sum of merchandise exports and imports divided by the value of GDP, all in current U.S. dollars. According to the World Bank (2009), the highest ratio in 2005 was that of Singapore, with a value of 368, while Hong Kong, China, had a value of 333. Equatorial Guinea and Liberia ranked fourth and fifth with values of 285 and 253.
3. The main exception was South Africa, which grew by only 3.4 percent and appeared to be facing weaker demand for its exports (World Bank 2009).

References

African Union. 2002. "Draft African Convention on Preventing and Combating Corruption." Document prepared at the Ministerial Conference of the African Union, Addis Ababa, September 18–19.

Briceño-Garmendia, C., K. Smits, and V. Foster. 2009. "Financing Public Infrastructure in Sub-Saharan Africa: Patterns, Issues and Options." Africa Infrastructure Country Diagnostic Background Paper 15, World Bank, Washington, DC.

Carruthers, R., R. R. Krishnamani, and S. Murray. 2009. "Improving Connectivity: Investing in Transport Infrastructure in Sub-Saharan Africa." Africa Infrastructure Country Diagnostic Background Paper 7, World Bank, Washington, DC.

Collier, P., and S. A. O'Connell. 2006. "Opportunities and Choices." In *The Political Economy of Economic Growth in Africa 1960–2000*, ed. B. J. Ndulu, S. A. O'Connell, J.-P. Azam, R. H. Bates, A. K. Fosu, J. W. Gunning, and D. Njinkeu. Cambridge: Cambridge University Press.

Collier, P., and A. Venables. 2008. "Trade and Economic Performance: Does Africa's Fragmentation Matter?" Paper presented at the Annual Bank Conference in Development Economics, World Bank, Washington, DC, May 28.

IMF (International Monetary Fund). 2007. *World Economic Outlook*. Washington, DC: IMF.

Meredith, M. 2005. *The State of Africa*. London: Free Press.

Naudé, W., and M. Matthee. 2007. "The Significance of Transport Costs in Africa." UNU Policy Brief 5, United Nations University–World Institute for Development Economics Research, Helsinki.

Teravaninthorn, S., and G. Raballand. 2008. *Transport Prices and Costs in Africa: A Review of the Main International Corridors*. Washington, DC: World Bank.

UNCTAD (United Nations Conference on Trade and Development). 2003. *Efficient Transport and Trade Facilitation to Improve Participation by Developing Countries in International Trade*. Geneva: UNCTAD.

UNECA (United Nations Economic Commission for Africa). 2004. *Assessing Regional Integration in Africa*. New York: UNECA.

WBI (World Bank Institute). 2004. *Building State Capacity in Africa: New Approaches, Emerging Lessons*. Washington, DC: WBI.

World Bank. 1989. *From Crisis to Self-Sustainable Growth*. Washington, DC: World Bank.

———. 2009. *Global Economic Prospects*. Washington, DC: World Bank.

———. 2010 Logistics Performance Index (software). Washington, DC: World Bank. http://go.worldbank.org/88X6PU5GV0.

CHAPTER 2

Roads: The Burden of Maintenance

Roads dominate the transport sector in most African countries, carrying 80 to 90 percent of passenger and freight traffic. Moreover, they are the only means of access to most rural communities. This dominance is achieved despite the fact that the density of the region's network is lower, both per person and per square kilometer of land area, than that of other world regions. The condition of the road system is also poor by international standards.

Nevertheless, the fiscal burden of the road network per capita is relatively high—a consequence of the combination of low population density and low gross domestic product (GDP) per capita. In these difficult circumstances, the provision of secure funding for road maintenance and efficient implementation of that maintenance are critical to the effectiveness of the sector. While reforms in both of these areas over the past 15 years have improved performance, there is much left to do.

In addition, road use needs to be efficient. Unfortunately, much remains to be done in this area also. The road freight industry is heavily cartelized and controlled, and yields high profits despite high costs. Road passenger transport—particularly in urban areas—has suffered from counterproductive fare regulation, with the result that most service is now provided by an informal sector that is largely self-regulated.

This chapter analyzes more fully the nature and performance of the African road networks and their main commercial user, the road freight sector.[1] It is based on three data sources: (i) a comprehensive road network survey undertaken specifically for the Africa Infrastructure Country Diagnostic (AICD), (ii) an institutional database prepared and maintained as part of the Sub-Saharan Africa Transport Policy Program (SSATP), and (iii) a fiscal cost study undertaken as part of the AICD (appendix 2a).

The basic country data—including land area, population, GDP, vehicle fleet, and transport fuel consumed—are shown in appendix 2b. Two kinds of country typologies are used to facilitate the presentation of the results. The first relates to factors completely exogenous to the road sector but that could nonetheless be expected to influence it significantly. These factors include macroeconomic circumstances (countries are classified as middle-income, low-income, or resource-rich; or as low-income and aid-dependent),[2] geography (coastal, landlocked, or island), and terrain (flat and arid versus rolling and humid). The second set of factors relates to policy variables, which are completely endogenous to the road sector. These factors include institutions (namely whether the country has a road fund, a road agency, or both) and funding mechanisms (for example, the existence of a fuel levy and the level at which it is set).

The Road Network

The size of the classified road network, including the main roads and secondary network, is estimated to be 1,052,000 kilometers (km). Together with an unclassified network of 492,000 km and an urban road network of about 193,000 km, this makes an estimated total network of 1,735,000 km (appendix 2c).

Strategic Roads: Serving International Transit Corridors

Relatively few international road transport corridors play a crucial role in maintaining the economies of the landlocked countries of Africa. Of these, the main international trade corridors that connect the landlocked countries of each subregion to their respective ports are widely considered the most important. Some $200 billion worth of imports and exports per year move along these key corridors, which have a combined length of little more than 10,000 km (table 2.1).

For Central Africa, regional transport is dominated by two road and rail corridors, which link the port of Douala in Cameroon with Chad

Table 2.1   Overview of Africa's Key Transport Corridors for International Trade

Corridor	Length (km)	Roads in good condition (%)	Trade density (US$ million/km)	Implicit speed (km/hour)	Freight tariff (US$/tonne-km)
Western	2,050	72	8.2	6.0	0.08
Central	3,280	49	4.2	6.1	0.13
Eastern	2,845	82	5.7	8.1	0.07
Southern	5,000	100	27.9	11.6	0.05

Source: Adapted from Teravaninthorn and Raballand (2008).
Note: Implicit speed includes time spent stationary at ports, border crossings, and other stops.

(serving cotton and oil exports) and the Central African Republic (serving logging exports).

For West Africa, there are several potential gateways (in Benin, Côte d'Ivoire, Ghana, Guinea, Senegal, and Togo) serving the landlocked countries of Burkina Faso, Mali, and Niger. But the closing of the international routes from Abidjan as a consequence of the crisis in Côte d'Ivoire has meant that most of the traffic now goes through ports in Benin, Ghana, Togo, and with Burkina Faso also becoming a transit country for Mali. Some 50 percent of the import traffic to Burkina Faso is now routed through Lomé, Togo, and 36 percent through Tema, Ghana.

In East Africa, 80 percent of trade flows originate or terminate outside the region, despite the creation of the East African Community (EAC). Mombasa is the main port for the region, handling more than 13 million tonnes of freight per year and serving not only Kenya and Uganda but also Burundi, the Democratic Republic of Congo, and Rwanda through the northern corridor. The central corridor from Dar es Salaam also serves the Democratic Republic of Congo as well as being an alternative for Zambia.

In southern Africa, there are four significant trade routes. The main route, the north-south corridor from Durban, serves as an intraregional trade route linking Zambia, southeastern Democratic Republic of Congo, and western Malawi with Botswana, Zimbabwe, and South Africa. The alternate routes through Beira, Walvis Bay, and Dar es Salaam, although closer to parts of the region, suffer relative to the north-south corridor from Durban, because of the latter's superior road infrastructure, better port equipment, and lower maritime rates.

The idea of creating a comprehensive continental road system in Africa—the Trans-African Highway network—was formulated in 1970 as part of a political vision for pan-African cooperation. As envisioned, the system would consist of nine main corridors with a total length of

59,100 km. In any event, national governments have not committed the financing needed to make this network a reality. While many of the roads already exist as elements of national highway networks, almost half of the 50,000 km that could be used is in poor condition. About 70 percent is currently paved, but 25 percent has either an earth surface or is not developed at all. Most of the missing links are concentrated in Central Africa. When the status of the concept was reviewed in 2003, it was found that of nine proposed links in the network, only one, Cairo–Dakar, was near complete (African Development Bank 2003). It was estimated that the costs of completing the whole network would be over $4 billion. At that price the network's future looks dubious.

National Classified Roads: Too Sparse

The spatial density of roads in Africa is low by international standards. The country-weighted average is 109 km of classified roads and 149 km of all roads per 1,000 square kilometers (km/1,000 km^2) of land area, with median values of 57 and 82, respectively. With the exception of Mauritius, which has 993 km/1,000 km^2, the classified road densities range between 10 (Mauritania) and 296 (The Gambia).

For density per capita, the average total classified network density is 2.5 km per 1,000 people, and the median value is 1.5. But there is huge variation, with total network density as low as 0.5 km per 1,000 people in Burundi and Rwanda and as high as 21.0 in sparsely populated Namibia (appendix 2d). Overall, about one-quarter of the networks are designated as primary, one-quarter secondary, and one-half tertiary, with unclassified networks about equal to the tertiary. At one extreme, Lesotho, Namibia, and South Africa have around 50 km of primary roads per million people, while at the other extreme, Niger and Uganda have more than 1,000 km of primary roads per million people. The variation in secondary road densities is lower, with most countries having secondary network densities of between 10 km and 100 km per million (figure 2.1).

In terms of road space per vehicle, the number of kilometers of classified road per 1,000 vehicles ranges from 950 in the Central African Republic to only 11 in Nigeria, with a country-weighted average value of 152 and a median value of 82 km per 1,000 vehicles.

The proportion of road that is paved also varies greatly (see appendix 2e). While on average 64 percent of primary roads and 17 percent of all classified roads are paved, the richer countries such as South Africa and Botswana have a higher proportion paved. But three countries (the Central African Republic, Chad, and the Democratic Republic of Congo)

Figure 2.1 Range of Primary and Secondary Road Densities

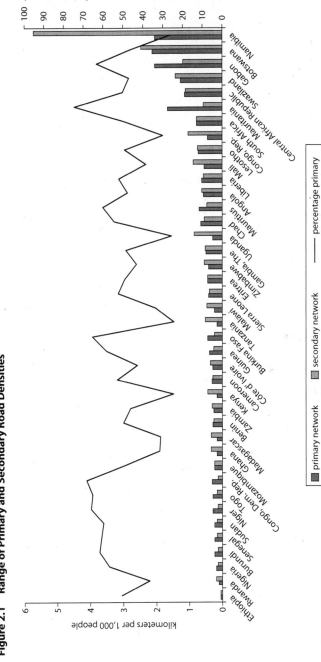

Source: Tabulation by A. Nogales based on data from Gwilliam and others 2009.

have less than 20 percent of their primary network paved, and more than one-quarter of the countries have 10 percent or less of their total road network paved.

Rural Transport Infrastructure: Critical to Agriculture

Rural transport infrastructure consists of more than designated and mapped roads. In rural areas, people and vehicles move across myriad unclassified and unrecorded paths and tracks. The size of the rural network is thus difficult to determine. But it is estimated that Africa has about 1 million km of designated rural roads (either tertiary or unclassified), whose replacement value is estimated at $48 billion, together with a network of undesignated rural roads, tracks, paths, and footbridges, which may be one and a half to two times as extensive as the local government road networks.

In most countries, the majority of rural network kilometers are captured by the official tertiary network. But in a number of cases—including Benin, Ethiopia, and Rwanda—less than one-third of the rural network is classified. Figure 2.2 shows the huge variation in the density of this rural road network as well as the relative weight of classified tertiary roads. The density of rural roads (tertiary and unclassified) ranges from 0.1 km per 1,000 people in the Democratic Republic of Congo to 21.6 in Namibia, with a mean of 2.6 km and a median of 1.2 km. Burkina Faso, Namibia, and South Africa stand out as having extensive rural networks relative to their populations. A low density of rural roads limits access to agricultural production, which accounts for one-third of the region's GDP and 40 percent of its export revenues.

The Region's Roads in an International Context

Africa has a much lower spatial density of roads than any other region of the world (figure 2.3). It has only 204 km of roads per 1,000 km^2 of land area, with only one-quarter paved, while the world average is 944 km/1,000 km^2, with over half paved. The spatial density of Sub-Saharan Africa's roads is less than 30 percent that of South Asia, where half of the roads are paved, and only 6 percent that of North America, where two-thirds are paved.

To some extent, this low spatial density reflects the low population densities of Africa. Sub-Saharan Africa has a total road network of 3.40 km per 1,000 people, compared with a world average of 7.07 km (figure 2.4). The road density with respect to population in Sub-Saharan Africa is actually slightly higher than that of South Asia, which has 3.19 km of

Figure 2.2   Range of Tertiary and Unclassified Road Densities

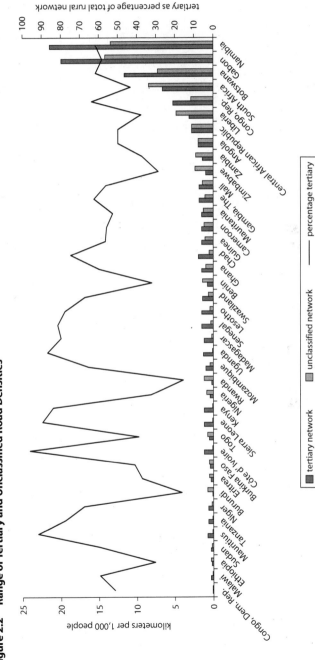

Source: Tabulation by A. Nogales based on data from Gwilliam and others 2009.

Figure 2.3   Spatial Density of Road Networks in World Regions

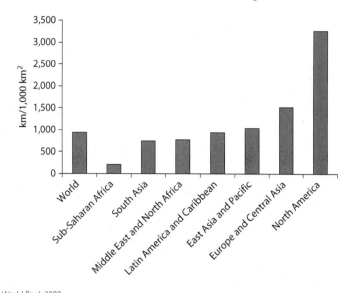

Source: World Bank 2009.

Figure 2.4   Total Road Networks per Capita in World Regions

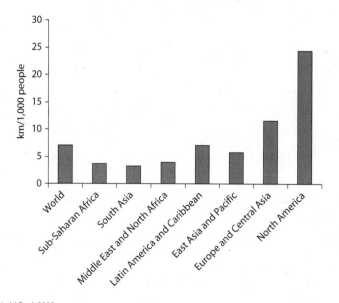

Source: World Bank 2009.

roads per 1,000 people, and only slightly lower than that of the Middle East and North Africa, which has 3.88 km per 1,000 people. But the paved road length in Sub-Saharan Africa, 0.79 km per 1,000 people, still remains less than half of that of South Asia and only about one-fifth of the world average.

Moreover, given low GDP, the fiscal burden of maintaining this limited road network is significantly higher than elsewhere (figure 2.5). Sub-Saharan Africa has a total road network of 6.55 km per $1 million, compared with South Asia's 5.32 and a world average of 3.47. The North American equivalent value, 0.79 km per $1 million, is just over a tenth that of Sub-Saharan Africa.

With respect to paved roads, Africa has a network of 1.12 km per million dollars of GDP, which is only slightly higher than the world average of 0.98, and less than South Asia's average of 2.67. Table 2.2 compares the paved road networks of the AICD countries with those of other lower-income and lower-middle-income countries of the world. It shows that lower-income countries in Africa have lower levels of paved roads per capita, per square kilometer, and per GDP per capita than other low-income countries in the world. While African low-income countries have lower average population densities than low-income countries in the rest

Figure 2.5   Total Road Network as Share of GDP in World Regions

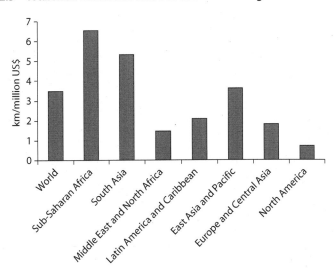

Source: World Bank 2009.

Table 2.2   Cross-Regional Comparison of Paved Road Infrastructure in Low-Income Countries

Paved roads	Units	Africa	Rest of world
Density by area	km/1,000 km²	10.7	37.3
Density by population	km/1,000 people	269.1	700.7
Density by GDP per capita	km/US$ billion	663.1	1,210.0

Source: Carruthers, Krishnamani, and Murray 2009.

of the world (70 per km² compared with 125), the relative disparity in the proportion of paved roads is substantially greater than this (10.7 km per 1,000 km² compared to 37.3 km).

Road Traffic Volumes: Manageable . . . for Now

Traffic volumes in Africa are relatively low by international standards (appendix 2f). The annual average daily traffic on roads in the primary network ranges from only 50 vehicles in the Democratic Republic of Congo and the Republic of Congo to over 7,000 in Mauritius and slightly less in South Africa. The country-weighted average is 1,198 and the median 829. Of the larger countries, only Nigeria and South Africa have heavy average volumes on the main road network (figure 2.6). Such low volumes effectively preclude the possibility of financing roads from tolls in most countries. Volumes on the secondary networks range from 746 vehicles per day in Nigeria to less than 30 in seven countries, with a country-weighted mean of 185 and a median value of 126.

Traffic is heavily concentrated on the main road network (see appendix 2g). In most countries, at least 90 percent of reported traffic on the classified network is carried on the main networks, which typically comprise centrally administered primary networks plus secondary networks. But in a handful of countries (Malawi, Nigeria, South Africa, and Uganda), only the primary network is centrally administered.

Rural networks typically carry very low levels of traffic, amounting to no more than 10 percent of overall traffic on the classified network (figure 2.7).

In a handful of countries, the rural network plays a more prominent role, capturing more than 20 percent of traffic—namely, in Ethiopia, Malawi, and Nigeria. But with the exception of Nigeria, the absolute volumes of traffic on the rural network are very low, averaging around 30 vehicles per day. Fourteen countries have an average daily traffic rate of fewer than 10 vehicles on their tertiary networks (appendix 2h). The

Figure 2.6 Volume of Traffic Carried on Main Network

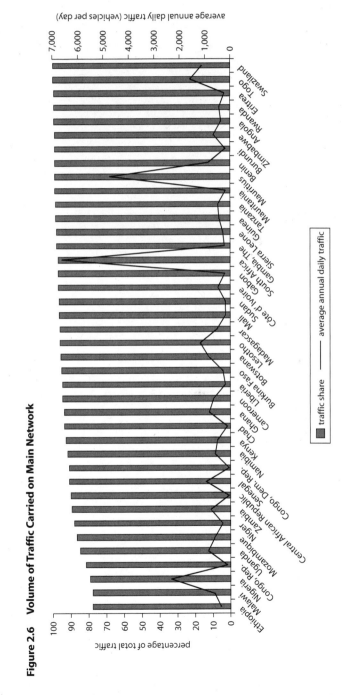

Source: Tabulation by A. Nogales based on data from Gwilliam and others 2009.

Figure 2.7   Volume of Traffic Carried on Rural Network

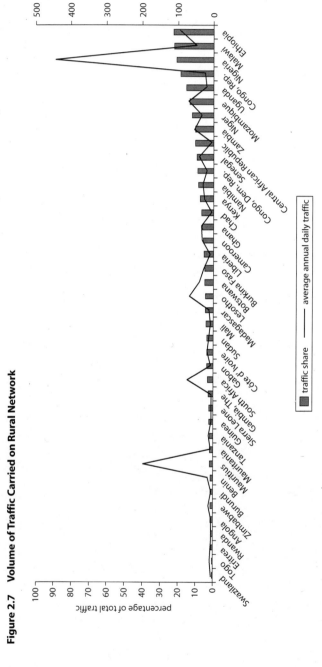

Source: Tabulation by A. Nogales based on data from Gwilliam and others 2009.

highest average for the tertiary network is in Mauritius, with 200 vehicles per day.

Road Infrastructure Performance

Ideally, the performance of the road infrastructure should be measured in terms of the speed, cost, and safety of traffic using it. However, as detailed measurement of these variables is not available, the measured condition of roads is used instead as a proxy.

Condition of Main Roads: Poor, but Improving

Road condition is the primary indicator of the performance of a road management system. In the AICD study, link-by-link data were collected on the quality of the sample countries' main road networks (managed by the central government or affiliated agency) and rural networks (managed by local governments) (see appendix 2i). A three-way quality classification was used: good, fair, and poor. "Poor" designates roads in need of rehabilitation. The data on the rural networks are less reliable than those on the main road networks, as subnational field visits were not made.

Figure 2.8 shows huge variation in the percentage of main roads in good condition but slightly less variation in the percentage of main roads in good or fair condition. On average, about 43 percent of the main networks are in good condition, a further 31 percent are in fair condition, and the remaining 27 percent are in poor condition.[3] The percentage in good condition ranges from 4 percent in the Republic of Congo to 90 percent in South Africa. But the percentage in good or fair condition covers a narrower range, from 27 percent in the Republic of Congo to 98 percent in South Africa. In five countries, more than 50 percent of the primary network is in poor condition (Democratic Republic of Congo, Republic of Congo, Guinea, Senegal, and Togo), while in six (mostly middle-income) countries, less than 10 percent of the primary network is in poor condition (Burkina Faso, Mauritius, Namibia, South Africa, Swaziland, and Tanzania).

Of particular interest are the trends in road quality over time. Unfortunately, time-series data on road conditions are extremely limited. An early detailed review of new, "second-generation" road funds showed improvements in outcomes for the five countries (Benin, Ethiopia, Ghana, Malawi, and Zambia) for which road condition data were available (Gwilliam and Kumar 2003). More recent trends in road conditions have also been broadly positive. But there are only very limited data

Figure 2.8   Distribution of Road Network Length across Condition Classes

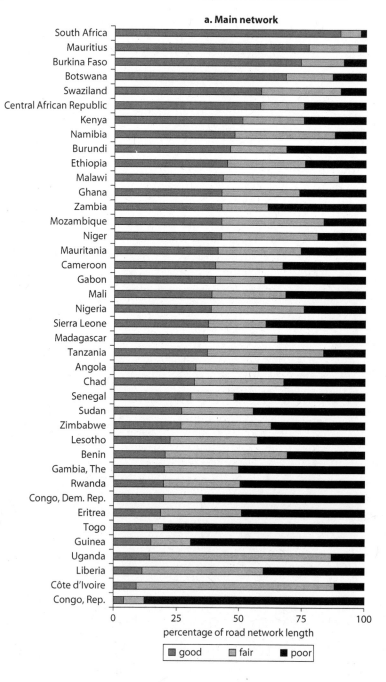

a. Main network

percentage of road network length

■ good   ☐ fair   ■ poor

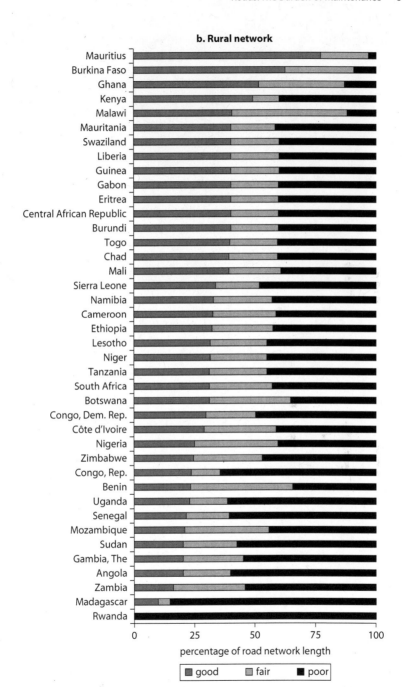

b. Rural network

Mauritius
Burkina Faso
Ghana
Kenya
Malawi
Mauritania
Swaziland
Liberia
Guinea
Gabon
Eritrea
Central African Republic
Burundi
Togo
Chad
Mali
Sierra Leone
Namibia
Cameroon
Ethiopia
Lesotho
Niger
Tanzania
South Africa
Botswana
Congo, Dem. Rep.
Côte d'Ivoire
Nigeria
Zimbabwe
Congo, Rep.
Benin
Uganda
Senegal
Mozambique
Sudan
Gambia, The
Angola
Zambia
Madagascar
Rwanda

0   25   50   75   100

percentage of road network length

■ good   ■ fair   ■ poor

Source: Tabulation by A. Nogales based on data from Gwilliam and others 2009.

available on road quality trends, collected by the SSATP for a sample of 16 countries between 2004 and 2007. While some of the figures for 2004 depend heavily on local engineers' judgments (as opposed to independent technical assessments), and subsequent changes in classification reduce the reliability and comparability of the data, overall, many countries appear to have made substantial progress in improving the quality of their main road networks. Half of the sample increased the percentage of main roads in good or fair condition by more than 10 points—and more than 30 points in a number of cases (table 2.3). Only in a handful of cases has there been a significant deterioration in quality (Côte d'Ivoire, Ghana, Guinea, and Lesotho). In the case of Côte d'Ivoire, this can be attributed to the general collapse of services associated with political unrest. Furthermore, the gap between the best and worst performers has been closing over time, from 90 percentage points in 2004 to around 50 percentage points in 2007.

The asset value of the classified road networks—in their current condition, as a percentage of the asset value of the same networks in entirely good condition—can be assessed with the Road Network Evaluation Tool (RONET) data analysis. The value of this indicator is strongly influenced

Table 2.3   Trends in Road Condition, 2004–07

	% of roads in good or fair condition		
	August 2004	September 2007	Change to good or fair (percentage points)
Madagascar	30	75	+45
Mali	44	80	+36
Burundi	5	40	+35
Tanzania	50	69	+19
Benin	75	93	+18
Chad	30	48	+18
Niger	57	72	+15
Kenya	57	67	+10
Cameroon	60	65	+5
Ethiopia	62	65	+3
Malawi	63	65	+2
Mozambique	70	72	+2
Guinea	66	62	−4
Ghana	65	60	−5
Côte d'Ivoire	60	50	−10
Lesotho	96	80	−16

Sources: SSATP 2004, 2007.

by the condition of the paved road networks, since these have a much higher replacement cost per kilometer than the unpaved networks. The range runs from a minimum of 62 percent for Togo to a maximum of 94 percent for Mauritius, with the majority of countries having scores in the 80 to 90 percent range (figure 2.9). These findings indicate that countries are sensibly focusing their efforts on maintaining their high-value paved networks in good or fair condition.

Quality of Rural Roads: Generally Poor

As might be expected, the condition of the rural networks is substantially lower than that of the main road networks (figure 2.10). On a country-weighted average, about 33 percent of the tertiary road networks are in good condition, a further 23 percent are in fair condition, and the remaining 44 percent are in poor condition. The percentage in good condition ranges from zero in Rwanda to 77 percent in Mauritius. Only four countries have more than 70 percent of their tertiary networks in good or fair condition (Burkina Faso, Ghana, Malawi, and Mauritius); the average is 56 percent and the median is 54 percent. There is a fairly strong correlation between the quality of the main road networks and the quality of the rural road networks in a given country (figure 2.11). This correlation suggests that there is a country effect, with competence in main network management carrying over into the rural networks.

One way of assessing the performance of a rural network is to consider the level of accessibility it offers to rural inhabitants. This measure is encapsulated in the Rural Accessibility Index (RAI), which measures the proportion of the rural population within a two-kilometer walking distance of an all-season road (World Bank 2007a). Based on household survey evidence analyzed for 20 countries in Africa, the RAI has an average value of less than 40 percent (World Bank 2007b), compared with an average of 94 percent for richer borrowing country members of the World Bank.

Estimating the RAI is possible using a geographic information system (GIS) model of Africa's road network and the geographical distribution of population (figure 2.11). The average value of the estimated RAI was even lower than the surveyed value—only 22 percent for the 24 countries in the sample. Countries such as Ethiopia, Niger, Sudan, and Zambia show particularly low estimated RAI—under 20 percent. Even Namibia, with its extensive rural network, reaches an RAI of just over 20 percent. If one uses the same GIS model, it is possible to calculate how many kilometers of additional tertiary roads would need to be built to reach a 100 percent

Figure 2.9   Road Asset Value as Percentage of the Potential Maximum

Source: Tabulation by A. Nogales based on data from Gwilliam and others 2009.

Figure 2.10   Correlation between Percentage of Main and Rural Roads in Good Condition

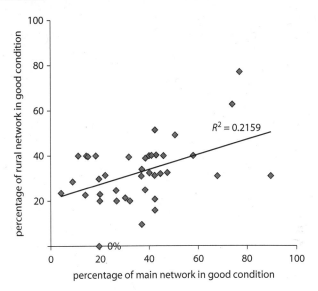

Source: Calculation by A. Nogales based on data from Gwilliam and others 2009.

Figure 2.11   Estimated RAI from Current Network and Percentage of Expansion Needed to Reach 100 Percent RAI

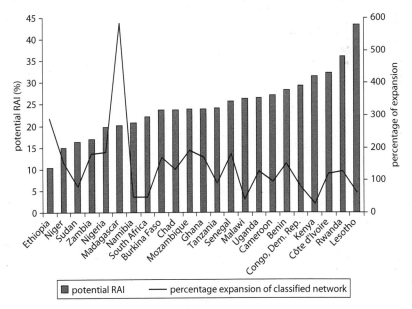

Source: Tabulation by A. Nogales based on data from Gwilliam and others 2009.
Note: RAI = Rural Accessibility Index.

target for the RAI. When these additional kilometers are expressed as a percentage of the current classified network, the results are striking (figure 2.12). Even in the best cases, the classified road network would need to grow in length by around 50 percent, and in most cases it would need to double or even triple in length. Madagascar, evidently an outlier, would need to increase the length of its current classified road network sixfold to attain 100 percent rural accessibility.

Isolated rural areas may not be able to realize their full agricultural potential. Hence, another way of assessing the rural network is to look at the extent to which it provides adequate access to high-value agricultural land. For exploration of this effect, estimates by the United Nations Food and Agriculture Organization were compared with actual and potential crop production, using GIS maps. The ratio, indicating the extent of realized agricultural potential, was then plotted against the degree of remoteness (figure 2.12).

For most countries, exploitation of potential (for many crops such as cotton, maize, and coffee) was highest in zones between two and five hours' travel time from the nearest large town. Beyond this zone, the ratio of actual production to potential dropped off sharply (the startling outlier in this graph being Namibia). The reason the highest production is not closer to the towns is that in areas close to towns, agricultural production is

Figure 2.12   Accessibility and Agricultural Production

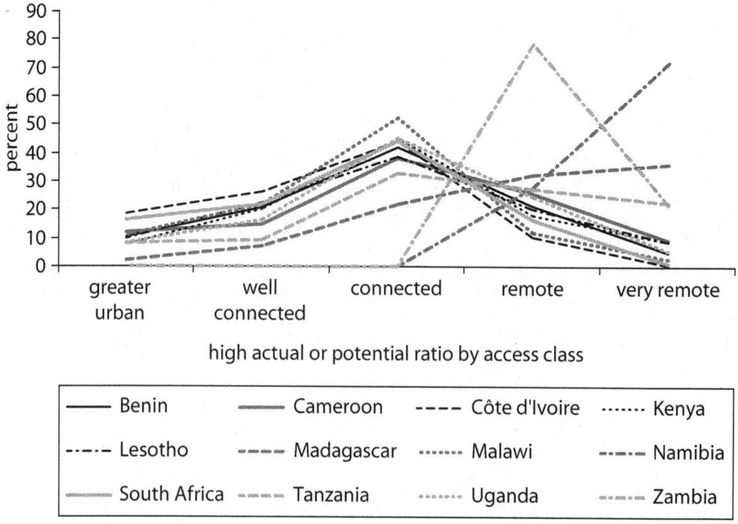

Source: Carruthers, Krishnamani, and Murray 2009.

either limited to, or concentrated on, food crops not included in the survey. Lack of accessibility thus appears to be limiting the exploitation of agricultural potential in poorer countries with less-dense road networks. This concept is further developed and applied in chapter 7.

Road Safety: An Urgent Problem

Road safety is a very serious problem in most African countries. Road accident statistics, even those for fatalities, are difficult to obtain, and recent studies have depended on extrapolations from recorded death numbers (see appendix 2j). Nevertheless, it is believed that Africa has 10 percent of the world's road fatalities with only 4 percent of the world's vehicle fleet. In the early years of the new millennium, nearly 3,000 people per year were killed on Kenyan roads. This translates to approximately 68 deaths per 1,000 registered vehicles, which is 30 to 40 times greater than in highly motorized countries. Road traffic crashes are the third-leading cause of death after malaria and HIV/AIDS and present a major public health problem in terms of morbidity, disability, and associated health care costs.

The gravity of the road safety problem has now been recognized by governments. At a Pan-African Road Safety Conference, held in Accra in February 2007, government delegates resolved in a joint declaration to make road safety a national health and transport priority and to seek funding for a set of positive actions. These included, among other things, strengthening prehospital and emergency services; mainstreaming safety considerations in road programs; collecting reliable road accident statistics; and enacting and implementing national legislation to counter driving under the influence of alcohol, speeding, not using helmets, driving unsafe vehicles, and using mobile phones when driving. Some countries have already taken action: Ghana has established a National Road Safety Council, with subsidiary regional bodies; Uganda has established a Road Safety Education Program; and the South African province of KwaZulu-Natal has launched a comprehensive road safety campaign. Yet in the many nations without an institution dedicated to this issue, it seems that road safety will continue to be ignored.

Institutions: Ongoing Reforms

Over the past decade, most countries in Africa have followed a consistent path of institutional reform in the road sector. Most countries have a formal transport policy statement, and many have a long-term investment program. More than 80 percent of the countries studied have adopted formal sector policies, although most of these policies have not been reviewed in the past five years. Just over 60 percent of countries have a long-term road investment program, in most cases instituted only recently. Such programs, however, depend heavily on foreign aid and cheaply borrowed finance rather than on dedicated and reliable domestic income streams.

The central focus of road sector reforms over the past decade has been institutional reform to improve the availability of funds for road maintenance and the capacity to execute public works (appendix 2k). Through initiatives such as the SSATP, country governments and development partners have largely come to agree on the establishment of or increase in road funds to provide ring-fenced revenues for road maintenance based on a user charge implemented through fuel levies. A review of the performance of second-generation road funds in Africa (Benmaamar 2006) found that while they were steadily improving, their effectiveness was impeded by the inefficiency with which resources were used by the implementing agencies. A second area of action has therefore concerned the establishment of independent road agencies with strong capabilities for the execution of public works (Pinard 2009).

These reforms have implications for the line transport ministries, the functions of which should shift from execution to overall supervision. Other institutions of importance include the rural administrations, which are responsible for at least the classified part of the rural road networks, often without any reliable source of funding. The regional economic communities have a lesser role—they are primarily concerned with coordinating country actions related to both infrastructure and operations in the transit corridors.

Second-Generation Road Funds: Getting Results

The aim of establishing second-generation road funds is to improve the condition of the road stock by better funding and more professional management of road maintenance. The philosophy is that road users would be willing to pay increased charges for road use if they were assured that the funds generated would be used for improved maintenance. Eighty percent of the initial sample of 24 countries have already introduced road funds, and others are in the process of doing so.

Seven design features characterize a "good" second-generation road fund. First, it is important to establish a strong legal basis for road fund operations as a protection against ad hoc political interference. Such a basis ideally entails a concise enabling law supported by published regulations specifying how the fund is to be managed. Fifteen (60 percent) of the sample countries with road funds have such founding legislation; the rest have relied on decrees. But the quality of the legislation is not uniformly high: a review in 2004 concluded that many of the funds were poorly designed, with limited administrative or financial autonomy and inadequate auditing provisions.

Second, the functions of road funding and road service provisions should be separated, with both undertaken by autonomous agencies. The creation of autonomous road agencies for public works execution has generally lagged behind that of road funds. At present, about 65 percent of the countries with quasi-independent road funds also have an independent implementation agency, with implementation undertaken in other countries by departments of the relevant central ministry.

Third, the fund should be financed by user charges entirely independent of any fuel taxes that may meet general revenue purposes. About 80 percent of the sample countries have established road user charges, typically in the form of fuel levies. But in many cases, the fuel levy is set well below the level needed to cover the maintenance costs arising from wear and tear of the network by road users, let alone contribute to funding the rehabilitation backlog (figure 2.13).

Figure 2.13   Fuel Levy Relative to Optimal Requirements for Maintenance and Rehabilitation

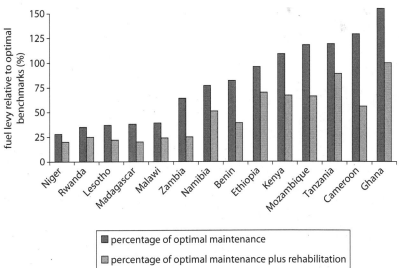

Sources: SSATP 2007; Briceño-Garmendia, Smits, and Foster 2009.

In practice, the fuel levy varies widely across countries, from 3 cents per liter in Lesotho to 16 cents per liter in Tanzania (figure 2.14, panel a). Moreover, the fuel levy collection rate also varies substantially. Four countries (Ghana, Niger, Rwanda, and Tanzania) collect only about half of the fuel levy revenue that should go to the road fund. The problems responsible for the shortfall range from widespread tax evasion in Tanzania to administrative problems in the transfer of revenues from the collection agency to the road fund in Rwanda (figure 2.14, panel b). In some cases (notably Ethiopia and Madagascar), the ratio of actual funding to estimated

Figure 2.14   Average Fuel Levy across Countries with Second-Generation Road Funds, 2007

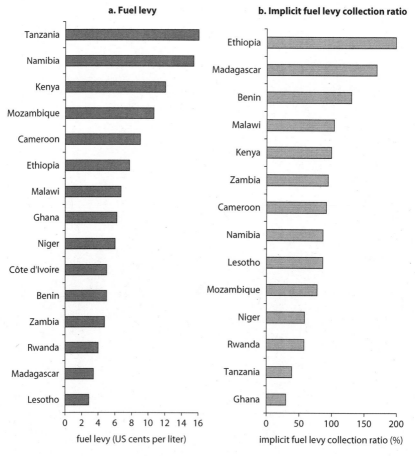

Source: SSATP 2007; Briceño-Garmendia, Smits, and Foster 2009.

fuel levy revenue is well above 100 percent, indicating substantial central government transfers to the road fund. In several cases (Benin, Côte d'Ivoire, Ethiopia, Gabon, and Zambia), the fund is dependent on budget allocations for more than 75 percent of its resources. Few road boards have effective power to adjust fuel levies in line with changing maintenance requirements, because of residual controls by the ministry of finance over the level of fuel levies.

Fourth, road user charges should be transferred directly to the road fund without passing through the government budget. Channeling of fuel levy revenues through the budget increases the risk that the revenues may be diverted to finance other public expenditures. Just over 50 percent of the sample countries with road funds successfully channel a high percentage (that is, at least 75 percent) of their fuel levy revenues directly to the road fund. In other cases, direct channeling covers a very low proportion of fuel levy revenues (less than 25 percent) or none at all, making the resource base for road funds much more vulnerable to diversion.

Fifth, user representation on the road fund board helps to strengthen accountability. It also allows users to make direct trade-offs between the level of user charges and the quality of the road network. With the exception of Malawi, all the countries with road funds have established independent road fund boards. But half of the boards still have a majority of government representation, with the chairman and executive secretaries usually being political appointees.

Sixth, to reduce discretion in fund allocation, clear and explicit rules for the allocation of funds to different types of expenditures are needed. About 60 percent of the road funds surveyed have established percentage allocations for dividing funds among different portions of the road network, although the chosen allocations differ substantially across countries (figure 2.15). On average, about 60 percent of the resources go to the main road network. Around half of the countries are allocating at least 20 percent of the road fund resources to the rural road network. Overhead typically accounts for no more than 6 percent of road fund revenues, even though the number of professional staff members employed varies widely, from only 6 in Niger to 48 in Kenya (the large size of the staff in Djibouti is due to the fact that employees are also involved in collecting transit fees).

Seventh, independent technical and financial auditing and public reporting of the road fund activities help to strengthen accountability (Heggie and Vickers 1998). About 80 percent of the countries with road

Figure 2.15   Overview of Road Fund Allocation Rules

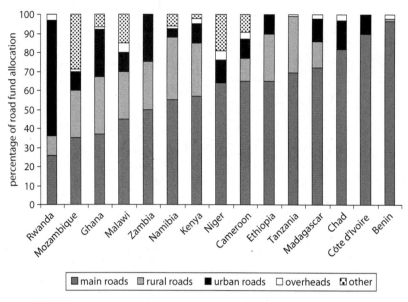

Source: SSATP 2007.

funds report that auditing procedures are in place. In most cases, these cover both technical and financial auditing and take place on an annual basis. But the quality of these audit processes is dubious in some countries. The prevalence of financial auditing is somewhat higher than that of technical auditing.

The SSATP Road Maintenance Initiative policy matrix shows that the prevalence of each of these criteria differs significantly (figure 2.16, panel a) and that the overall score for road fund design also varies widely across countries (figure 2.16, panel b). On average, the road funds in the sample countries meet 65 percent of the defining criteria for second-generation road funds. There is a broad performance range, from countries such as Tanzania, Namibia, and Kenya that fulfill 100 percent of the criteria to countries such as Benin and Burkina Faso that appear to capture well below 50 percent of them.

Another important achievement of road funds has been to stabilize, increase, and improve the predictability of maintenance expenditures. The volatility of road fund expenditures (measured by calculating the standard deviation around the trend line) was shown to be only half that of expenditures arising from external funding and one-third that of central

Figure 2.16   Evaluation of Road Fund Reforms

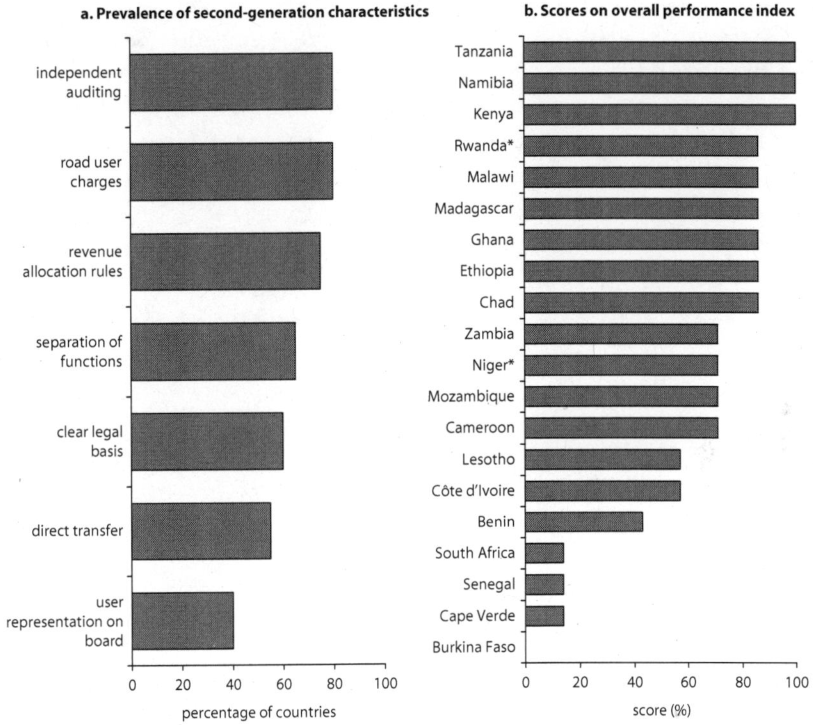

a. Prevalence of second-generation characteristics

b. Scores on overall performance index

Source: SSATP 2007.
* = based on incomplete information.

government allocations in time-series data over the period 2001–05. Moreover, the volatility of road fund expenditures appears to be lower in countries that have made efforts to ensure the independence of their road funds and have increased the proportion of revenues channeled directly into the funds.

Road Agency Performance: Lagging Behind

In many countries, the weaknesses of traditional maintenance by force account are now well recognized. It was initially thought that the problems associated with timely and cost-effective implementation of public works contracts could be solved by reforming and restructuring the road departments housed in the line ministries for the sector. But restructuring of road departments has not had the expected beneficial impact on road project implementation, in part because too many constraints still prevent the full use of existing technical capacity. One important constraint has been staff skills and leadership. The economic growth in the region over the past decade has increased the demand for engineers in the private sector, which has attracted better-qualified staff with higher salaries. But road departments typically lack employees with the skills needed to review the design, costs, and work under various contracts. This situation prolongs the contracting process and may be a reason for the recent escalation in the unit costs of road construction.

For those reasons, current thinking focuses on moving the responsibility for managing implementation out of the traditional civil service structure into an independent agency. About two-thirds of the sample of countries in the SSATP survey have already established some sort of independent, commercialized roads agency, and a number of others are in the process of doing so. But only a third of these have private sector representation on their boards. Levels of autonomy vary from full responsibility for road network management to limited responsibility for the execution of road maintenance programs defined by the roads department or ministry of roads.

A recent study by Pinard (2009) identified two quite different institutional forms, namely (i) a roads agency, which, though a legal entity, is not independent of its ministry, and (ii) a roads authority, which is essentially an independent legal identity. Pinard compared the two types in terms of their institutional characteristics (a combination of their legal foundation, composition, powers, and processes) and their performance. He found that paved road conditions were better under the independent authorities, a trend he attributed largely to the authorities' greater autonomy. But even with an authority, problems remain. Most road authorities are still not able to pay market-based wages—staff salaries are typically 60 to 80 percent of those for similar jobs in the private sector—making staff recruitment and retention difficult. Many road authorities fulfill aspects of the "supplier" function and undertake varying amounts of noncore activities, which reduces their focus on managing performance. Many are unable to operate their road asset management systems to produce reliable outputs in terms of optimal network strategies and programs. This deficiency suggests that more aspects of data collection and system operation should be contracted out to competent consultants, though both the number and the capacity of local consultants and contractors are limited in a number of countries. Hence, although road authorities are improving governance, attracting skilled staff and ensuring continuous collection of reliable data remain a challenge.

In about half of the sample countries, more than 80 percent of maintenance work was contracted out. This approach was strongly, though not exclusively, associated with the presence of a road agency in the country. Contractors were typically paid directly by the road fund, usually in fewer than 30 days for undisputed bills; however, in Burundi, Ghana, and Kenya, the average payment time was 90 days in 2006. Improved contract management and disbursement arrangements have resulted in a 10 to 20 percent reduction in road maintenance costs per kilometer in Ethiopia, Ghana, and Zambia.

An associated development has been the establishment of performance-based contracts with the private sector for road maintenance on a longer-term, multiyear basis. Such contracts have been made possible by the greater security of road maintenance revenues resulting from the establishment of second-generation road funds. They are advantageous in that they provide a strong incentive for contractors to undertake effective maintenance activities and to reduce expenditure uncertainties for the road fund. But it is already clear that the benefits of shifting road work from force account to private performance-based contracting depend on the existence of an efficient and competitive road-contracting industry, a transparent process of selecting contractors, and an ability to negotiate and manage the contracts effectively (Stankevich, Qureshi, and Queiroz 2005). In particular, ensuring that trucks are not overloaded is important for the implementation of long-term performance contracts.

Rural Road Administration: The Orphaned Sector

In many countries, the responsibility for the rural segment of the network is devolved to the local level (Malmberg Calvo 1998). There are two distinct administrative categories of rural transport infrastructure, namely, *local government roads* and *community roads and tracks*. The former are designated as the responsibility of the appropriate local government unit; the latter have no formal owner. While community facilities may have been built by nongovernmental organizations or even by foreign-aid agencies, they tend to be neglected if they have not been formally assigned to any agency for their subsequent maintenance. For example, a Zambian nongovernmental organization built 1,000 km of roads during the early 1990s as part of a drought-relief effort, but the roads have deteriorated badly because no institution is legally responsible for them.

Sources for financing local government roads are usually very limited. Local governments mobilize only modest revenues of their own, the main sources often being market and business taxes. Intergovernmental transfers are usually the main source of domestic funding for local governments. Three main problems result from relying on the central budget for funding maintenance of rural roads. First, throughout most of Africa, less than 5 percent of aggregate public sector revenue is generally made available to rural governments. Second, general budgets rarely allocate adequate funds for maintaining main roads, much less rural roads. Third, capital and recurrent allocations to local governments are usually not fungible, and the allocation for recurrent expenditures may barely cover the salary expenditures of the local rural road unit. Moreover, such transfers are dictated by the budget cycle, so they are unlikely to provide an adequate and timely source of funding. Adequate and steady funding of local government road maintenance is more likely to come from a dedicated road fund, as long as the road fund law expressly states that the fund accepts responsibility for local roads.

Local government networks tend to be small, often too small to attract the interest of competent consulting firms to manage their maintenance. In Madagascar, the average network size for a local government is 140 km; in Cameroon and Nigeria, 180 km; and in Tanzania and Zambia, 280 km. But a network size of 500 to 2,000 km is usually required to justify employing an engineer. Joint services committees of local authorities may achieve economies of scale in procurement, but they usually require substantial technical assistance from central ministries or from regional offices of a main-roads authority. In countries with an autonomous authority over the main roads, local governments may contract this authority to manage roads on their behalf or to assist with planning and procurement. Private sector capacity and capabilities can also be mobilized by contracting out physical works or even key management functions to local consultants. Specialized contract management agencies known as AGETIPs are common in Francophone Africa—for example, in Madagascar, Mali, Niger, and Senegal. These agencies manage and use private consultants and contractors on behalf of the public authority and perform all the necessary functions of contract preparation, implementation, and supervision.

Some countries centralize the technical responsibility for rural roads. This practice has the advantage of enabling better technical support, but because the central authority often operates independent of the local government structure, it is usually poorly connected to local needs and developments. In principle, a central coordinating unit for local government roads should be able to perform as well as a central government rural-roads department. In practice, however, such coordinating units for local government roads are weak, as they were in Tanzania and Zambia in the late 1990s.

A comprehensive study of road administrations in three countries (Mexico, Uganda, and Zambia) has found that decentralization has yielded few of the expected advantages (Robinson and Stiedl 2001). Several factors contributed to this outcome: lack of local government powers to exercise political influence, insufficient financial resources, lack of management capability, and lack of accountability mechanisms at the local level. It was concluded that countries contemplating decentralization were most likely to benefit from the "devolved and delegated" model (local government is the owner, with a parastatal or private sector administrator working under contract) or the centralized road fund model. These options were not mutually exclusive. For example, a joint services committee may use private consultants, hired through a contract management agency. The best option for managing local government roads depends on many local factors, including the size of the authority, the nature of the network for which it is responsible, and the competence of the sector or higher-level public authority units.

Community infrastructure faces particular problems. Community contributions in cash and in kind (usually labor) are suitable primarily for community roads and paths. But contributions in kind may produce relatively inefficient labor, making other sources of money necessary. Strategically designed cost-sharing arrangements for local government roads and community roads may stimulate resource mobilization at all levels and increase the proportion of the networks receiving regular maintenance. Well-structured donor financing through rural road projects or through social funds or rural infrastructure funds can assist investment in community-level infrastructure as well. Cost-sharing arrangements may also be effective in maintaining community roads. Many local authorities in Africa have more roads to maintain than they can afford. Achieving effective community management is often impeded by lack of technical know-how. Communities in Africa therefore need technical advice (for instance, on road design and standards, appropriate materials, and work planning) and managerial advice (in areas such as financial accounting, contract management, and procurement) so that they can effectively perform the responsibilities that come with ownership of roads and paths.

Road Spending: A Problem of Execution

It is important to recognize the distinction between road funding (the process of budget allocation) and road spending (the actual execution of the budget). These can differ substantially, either because delays in the budget process leave too little time for execution within the fiscal year or because of lack of capacity in the road construction sector.

The percentage of national income actually spent in the road sector in the initial AICD sample countries, taking into account all budget and extrabudgetary channels (such as road funds), has been estimated in the AICD fiscal costs study (Briceño-Garmendia, Smits, and Foster 2009). This analysis shows that, on average, the sample countries devote 1.8 percent of their GDP to the road sector (figure 2.17). This is within the 1 to 2 percent range of expenditures found in those countries around the world with already well-developed infrastructure and GDP growth rates of 2 to 3 percent, but it is below the levels found in a number of fast-growing countries that have made intensive efforts to upgrade transport

Figure 2.17   Average Annual Expenditures on Road Transport by Country, 2001–05

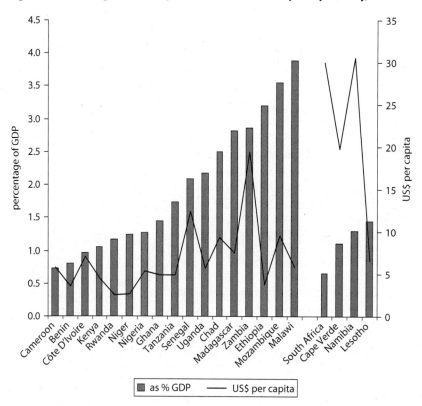

Source: Briceño-Garmendia, Smits, and Foster 2009.

infrastructure. For example, Brazil, India, the Republic of Korea, and the former Soviet Union all invested between 2 to 3 percent of their GDP in transport infrastructure during the 1980s, while between 2000 and 2002, Korea, Malaysia, and Thailand were investing 1.7 percent to 1.9 percent of their GDP and achieving GDP growth rates between 4 and 6 percent. Thus, while the African expenditure effort is not far below that achieved in many developing countries, it does fall short of that associated with very high rates of economic growth.

Average spending on roads in Africa varies from less than 1 percent of the GDP in South Africa to almost 4 percent in Malawi. The highest income shares are found in the poorest countries. For the middle-income countries in the sample, spending tends to be clustered around 1 percent of the GDP, but in all countries, the absolute values remain small, at around $7 per capita per year for low-income countries and $22 per capita per year for middle-income countries. Virtually all road expenditure is in the public sector. Even in the future, the relatively modest traffic volumes projected for most corridors mean that the scope for privately funded toll roads is limited (box 2.1).

The same aggregate information on road expenditure can also be expressed as a rate per kilometer of main road network (again, composed of roads managed by the central government). In most countries, the main network comprises the primary and secondary networks, but in a few cases it is limited to the primary network. On average, the African countries investigated in the fiscal costs study spent just over $9,000 per kilometer of main road (table 2.4). But spending levels in low-income countries are more than 50 percent higher per kilometer than spending levels in the middle-income countries, with resource-rich, low-income countries spending slightly more than aid-dependent ones. Landlocked countries and islands spend substantially more per kilometer than what is spent by coastal nations, which may be attributable to higher costs of importing materials and services. Countries with rolling terrain and humid conditions, which tend to accelerate road deterioration, show somewhat higher levels of spending than countries with flat terrain and arid conditions. Some of the observed outcomes are paradoxical. For example, countries with road agencies seem to spend substantially less than those without them, irrespective of whether they have road funds, and those countries with low fuel levies actually spend substantially more on roads than those with no or high fuel levies. To resolve those paradoxes, one must look further into the composition of the spending and the sources from which it is financed.

Box 2.1

Road Concessions in Africa

Only 10 African toll road projects are recorded for the years since 1990 in the World Bank's Private Participation in Infrastructure (PPI) database. These include eight projects in South Africa alone, one an international road corridor connecting South Africa to Mozambique. The other two projects involve the construction of bridges over the Abidjan Lagoon in Côte d'Ivoire and the Limpopo River in Zimbabwe. The projects are quite evenly divided among greenfield projects, concession contracts, and lease contracts.

Overall, only 1,600 km of Africa's total classified road network of 1.2 million km have been contracted out to the private sector under a medium- or long-term management arrangement. The total cumulative private sector investment committed under these projects amounts to $1.6 billion, barely 20 percent of the estimated annual investment needed in Africa's road sector ($7.6 billion).

The potential for toll road concessions in Africa remains limited because of the relatively low traffic flows in the region. Based on the AICD sample of countries, only 8 percent of the region's road network (that is, less than 9,000 km) has traffic levels in excess of 10,000 vehicles per day, which is the threshold to make toll road concessions economically viable. Some 86 percent of those viable kilometers are concentrated in South Africa, and a further 8 percent are in Nigeria. A number of other countries have up to 100 km of paved road at this traffic level, but many others do not reach this level of traffic in any segment of their paved road network.

Source: Author, based on World Bank 2008a.

Capital Investment: More than a Fair Share of Spending

A strong capital bias is evident in road sector spending. Analysis of African road needs suggests that about half of road sector spending should go to capital projects and the other half to maintenance of existing assets. In reality, about two-thirds of spending is allocated to capital projects in the 19 countries studied (figure 2.18).

The bias is most pronounced in low-income countries, those with challenging geographical environments, and those without road funds or fuel levies. There is a very striking difference between the middle-income countries, which devote only 25 percent of their road spending to capital projects, and the low-income countries, which devote around 70 percent to capital projects (table 2.5).

Table 2.4   Average Annual Expenditures per Kilometer of Main Road by Country Category, 2001–05

Country characteristics	Average annual spending on roads (US$ per km)	Country characteristics	Average annual spending on roads (US$ per km)
Income level		*Institutions*	
Middle-income	6,050	Road fund and road agency	7,112
Low-income, aid-dependent	8,823	Road fund only	9,793
Low-income, resource-rich	9,551	Road agency only[a]	6,053
Geography		*Financing*	
Coastal	7,014	Low fuel levy	9,458
Island	13,302	High fuel levy	8,117
Landlocked	9,984	No fuel levy[a]	7,153
Topography			
Flat and arid	7,977		
Rolling and humid	9,518		

Source: Briceño-Garmendia, Smits, and Foster 2009.
a. South Africa is excluded from this group.

Figure 2.18   Percentage of Road Spending Allocated to Capital Projects

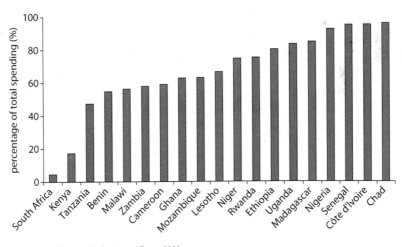

Source: Briceño-Garmendia, Smits, and Foster 2009.

To some extent, this difference may reflect the fact that the low-income countries are still developing transport networks, whereas the middle-income countries have already established their basic transport platform and can devote themselves predominantly to maintenance.

Table 2.5   Percentage of Road Spending Allocated to Capital Projects, by Country Category

Country characteristics	Spending for capital projects (as % of all road spending)	Country characteristics	Spending for capital projects (as % of all road spending)
Income level		*Institutions*	
Middle-income	25	Road fund and road	58
Low-income, aid-	68	agency	
dependent		Road fund only	64
Low-income,	77	Road agency only [a]	86
resource-rich		*Financing*	
Geography		Low fuel levy	72
Coastal	53	High fuel levy	45
Island	85	No fuel levy [a]	85
Landlocked	74		
Topography			
Flat and dry	58		
Rolling and humid	72		

Source: Briceño-Garmendia, Smits, and Foster 2009.
a. South Africa is excluded from this group.

Countries facing difficult geographic and topographic conditions also show evidence of a stronger bias toward capital expenditure. Countries with road funds show a lower degree of capital bias than those without, irrespective of whether they have independent road agencies or not. Countries with high fuel levies show no evidence of capital bias.

Even these relatively high levels of capital expenditure understate the true extent of capital bias in road spending. The reason is that, on average, only around 70 percent of budgeted capital spending is actually executed within the corresponding budgetary cycle due to weaknesses and delays in the public procurement process. These delays prevent contracts from being awarded and completed within the 12-month budget cycle (figure 2.19).

There are substantial and systematic variations in budget execution across countries and country groupings. Budget execution ranges from 25 percent in Benin to over 100 percent in South Africa (table 2.6).

There are also systematic differences across country categories. Middle-income countries perform substantially better than low-income countries, and countries with road funds and fuel levies perform substantially better than those without. There is also a striking difference in favor of countries with rolling, humid terrain relative to those facing flat, arid

Figure 2.19   Capital Budget Execution Ratios

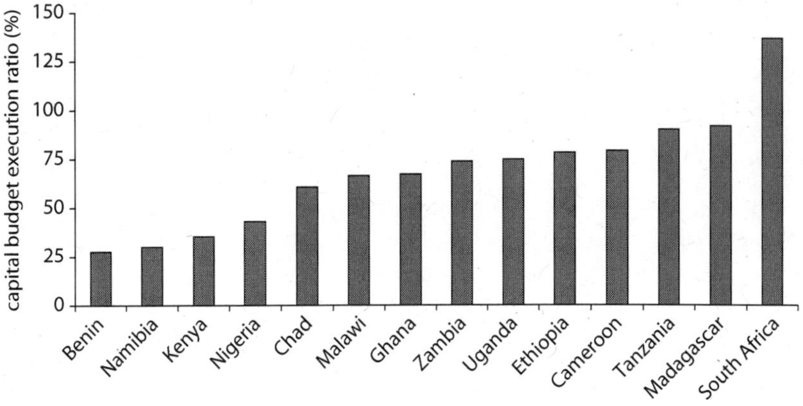

Source: Briceño-Garmendia, Smits, and Foster 2009.

Table 2.6   Capital Budget Execution Ratios, by Country Category

	Percentage		Percentage
Macroeconomy		*Institutions*	
Middle-income	83	Road fund and road agency	66
Low-income, aid-dependent	67	Road fund only	64
Low-income, resource-rich	61	Road agency only[a]	43
Geography		*Financing*	
Coastal	64	Low fuel levy	65
Island	92	High fuel levy	62
Landlocked	71	No fuel levy[a]	59
Topography			
Flat and dry	63		
Rolling and humid	78		

Source: Briceño-Garmendia, Smits, and Foster 2009.
a. South Africa is excluded from this group.

conditions, perhaps indicating the greater urgency of road works in the former setting.

Above average capital expenditure on roads may be justified by large rehabilitation backlogs. Using the RONET model, it is possible to produce detailed estimates of the requirements for rehabilitating each country's road network, taking into account the current distribution of network conditions and working toward a target of clearing the current rehabilitation backlog within a reasonable period of time. On that basis, the rehabilitation requirements can be compared with the current levels of capital expenditure to determine whether these are high enough to eliminate the rehabilitation backlog within a five-year period (figure 2.20). Negative numbers indicate that the current levels of expenditures are not sufficient to eliminate the backlog. It is important to note that this calculation is only illustrative and is based on the assumption that the entire capital budget is devoted to network rehabilitation.

While rehabilitation usually dominates capital spending, some upgrading of road categories and addition of new roads does occur. Although the available data do not make it possible to know the exact split, the calculation in table 2.7 is helpful in indicating whether current levels of capital expenditure would be high enough to address the rehabilitation problem if they were fully allocated to rehabilitation works. In fact, only in half the countries is capital spending high enough to reasonably address rehabilitation backlogs. In the other half, capital spending has fallen well below what is needed to clear rehabilitation backlogs. Chad and Ethiopia stand out as countries undergoing very large road investment programs, including major works to upgrade road categories and extend the reach of the networks. In these cases, spending is two to three times the level needed to clear rehabilitation backlogs. Countries with both a road fund and a road agency seem to show the highest margin of capital spending

Figure 2.20   Deviation of Capital Expenditure from Expenditure Required to Meet Rehabilitation Requirements within a Five-Year Period

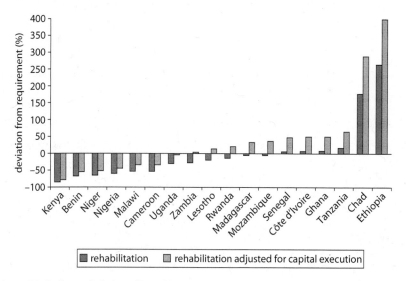

Source: Briceño-Garmendia, Smits, and Foster 2009.

Table 2.7   Capital Expenditure as Percentage of Rehabilitation Needs, by Country Category

Percentage deviation of actual annual total capital expenditure from expenditure necessary to eliminate accumulated rehabilitation needs over a period of five years

	Percentage		Percentage
Macroeconomy		*Institutions*	
Middle-income	−6	Road fund and road agency	60
Low-income, aid-dependent	−3	Road fund only	−19
Low-income, resource-rich	22	Road agency only[a]	−27
Geography		*Financing*	
Coastal	−21	Low fuel levy	−5
Island	−4	High fuel levy	24
Landlocked	30	No fuel levy[a]	−28
Topography			
Flat and arid	−7		
Rolling and humid	13		

Source: Briceño-Garmendia, Smits, and Foster 2009.
a. South Africa is excluded from this group.

over rehabilitation requirements. Resource-rich, low-income countries, landlocked countries, and countries with high fuel levies also tend to show capital spending that is somewhat higher than rehabilitation needs.

Failure to execute the budget is common. Budgeted capital spending is typically 40 percent higher than what countries actually succeed in spending. Hence if rehabilitation requirements are compared to an estimate of budgeted (versus actual) capital spending, the funding situation looks somewhat more positive, with the percentage of countries able to meet their rehabilitation requirements within a reasonable time period increasing from one-half to two-thirds. Thus, improving capital budget execution is an important first step toward clearing rehabilitation backlogs.

Public investment in roads is highly dependent on flows of aid, which can be volatile. It is not always possible to trace with precision the items on the public investment budget that are financed by official development assistance. The limited evidence available indicates a heavy dependence on foreign funding, which ranges from just over 50 percent in Senegal to almost 90 percent in Rwanda (figure 2.21). The volatility of official development assistance flows contributes to the volatility of public investment in the sector. Thus, the very high ratios of road investment to GDP in Chad in 2003–05, in Tanzania in 2000, and in Madagascar in 2004–05 were all associated with short-lived surges in aid.

Figure 2.21   Foreign Funding as Percentage of Capital Spending

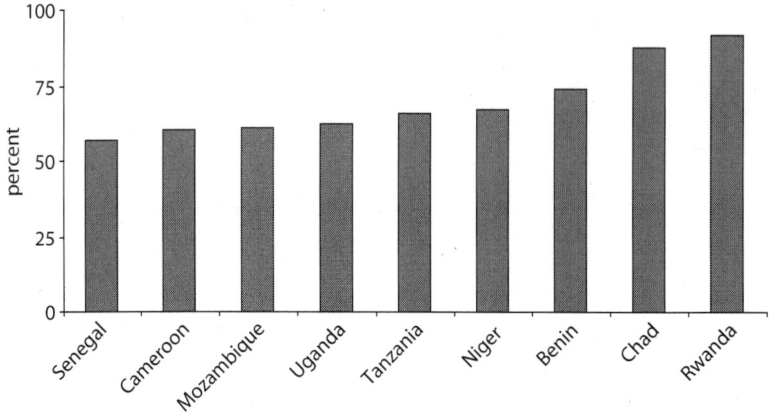

Source: Briceño-Garmendia, Smits, and Foster 2009.

Higher construction standards result in slower deterioration rates and lower annual maintenance costs. They also counteract, to some extent, the adverse effects of vehicle overloading, which is rife. As noted above, the AICD data already show a negative correlation between capital and maintenance expenditures as well as the underfunding of maintenance expenditures. Given the reduction in operation costs per tonne-km as vehicle loadings increase, it may be sensible for countries to jointly reconsider their policies on construction standards and vehicle axle weights.

Maintenance Expenditures: Squeezed

There appears to be a trade-off between levels of capital expenditure and levels of maintenance expenditure, shown by the large negative correlation (−0.33) between the level of maintenance expenditure per kilometer of the main network and the level of capital expenditure per kilometer (figure 2.22). This can be plausibly explained. On the one hand, countries that spend too little on maintenance will end up with larger rehabilitation liabilities, often resulting in the need for emergency works to restore the functionality of critical infrastructure. On the other hand, countries with large investment programs may have fewer resources left over to address road maintenance needs. The latter scenario is worrisome because if high capital spending comes at the expense of lower maintenance expenditure, then the condition of the network will only deteriorate further over time.

Figure 2.22   Relationship between Capital Spending and Maintenance Spending per Kilometer of Main Network

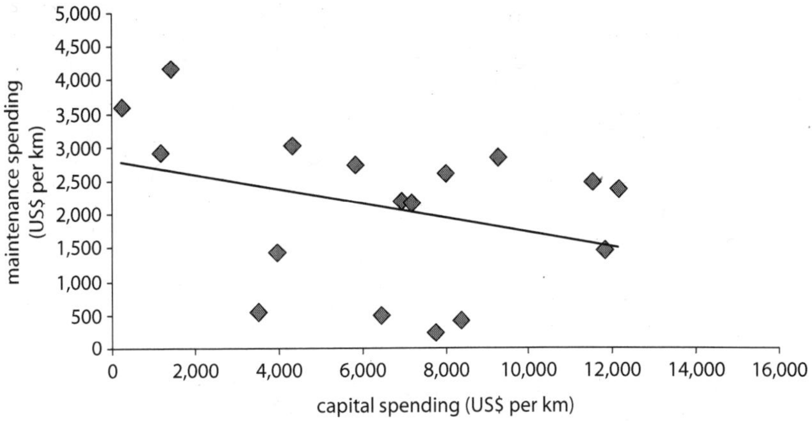

Source: Briceño-Garmendia, Smits, and Foster 2009.

There is huge variation in maintenance expenditure efforts, both across countries and across rural and main road networks. For the main road networks, the range extends from barely $200 per kilometer in Chad to over $6,000 per kilometer in Zambia. For the rural road networks, the range extends from barely $20 per kilometer in Chad to more than $3,000 per kilometer in Lesotho (figure 2.23). On average, countries are spending $1,100 per kilometer on rural networks and about double that amount, or $2,200 per kilometer, on the main networks. Indeed, some countries are spending more on maintenance per kilometer for their rural networks than other countries are spending on maintenance per kilometer for their main road networks—as is the case with Tanzania and Madagascar. Overall, the correlation between maintenance efforts on main networks and those on rural networks is positive and high (0.36) across countries, which is to say that countries that tend to spend larger amounts on main network maintenance also tend to spend larger amounts on rural network maintenance and vice versa.

For a comparison of countries, two different standards were hypothesized (appendix 2I). The "custom" standard assumes that all primary roads are kept in good condition and secondary roads in fair condition, with other roads allowed to be in poor condition. The "optimal" standard links the standard to be achieved to the traffic volume on any network, with the total maintenance budget optimized to reduce total system operating and maintenance costs.

Figure 2.23   Average Maintenance Spending across Different Parts of the Network (US$ per km)

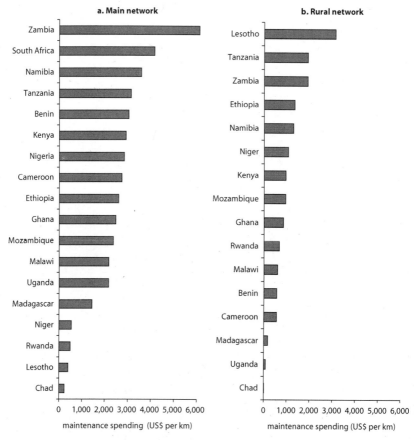

Source: Briceño-Garmendia, Smits, and Foster 2009.

Even more important than the absolute spending is the comparison between spending and requirements. If one uses the RONET, it is possible to produce detailed estimates of the routine and periodic maintenance requirements needed to preserve each country's road network to the custom standard (appendix 2m) or to the optimal standard (appendix 2n), taking into account the current distribution of network conditions. It is important to note that this calculation is based on the assumption that the entire maintenance budget is spent on maintenance works at efficient unit costs. The results of this comparison are shown in figure 2.24 for the custom standard. Appendixes 2o and 2p show the distribution of expenditure by type of work for these two standards to be achieved.

Figure 2.24   Deviation of Actual Maintenance Expenditure from That Required to Attain Custom Standard of Maintenance

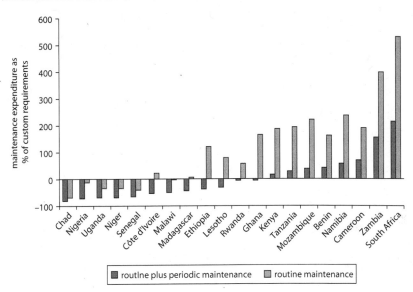

Sources: Briceño-Garmendia, Smits, and Foster 2009; calculation by A. Nogales based on data from Gwilliam and others 2009.

This exercise shows that half of the countries are not devoting adequate resources to routine and periodic maintenance of the main road networks. In countries such as Chad, Niger, Nigeria, Senegal, and Uganda, maintenance spending comes to less than half the norm requirements. Moreover, around a quarter of the countries are not devoting enough resources to cover even routine maintenance activity.

Table 2.8 shows that underspending on maintenance to the custom standard is evident in the low-income countries (particularly the resource-rich countries) and in countries with difficult geographical environments and terrain. Middle-income countries tend to spend substantially above the maintenance norm. Of the six countries not covering even routine maintenance, two were without road funds and levies. Among countries with fuel levies, those with high levies did substantially better than those with low ones.

The network preservation costs estimated by the RONET, including both maintenance and rehabilitation for the entire classified network, can be compared to the GDP to gauge their overall affordability at the country level (figure 2.25). The estimated average annual cost of preserving the classified road network lies in the range 0.2 to 4.1 percent of GDP.

Table 2.8   Actual Maintenance Expenditure as Percentage of Expenditure Required for Custom Maintenance Standard, by Country Category

Country characteristics	Maintenance spending (as % of requirement)	Country characteristics	Maintenance spending (as % of requirement)
Income level		*Institutions*	
Middle-income	80	Road fund and road	−11
Low-income, aid-dependent	−12	agency	
		Road fund only	−3
Low-income, resource-rich	−28	Road agency only[a]	−69
		Financing	
Geography		Low fuel levy	−19
Coastal	20	High fuel levy	28
Island	−45	No fuel levy[a]	−69
Landlocked	−24		
Topography			
Flat and arid	12		
Rolling and humid	−24		

Source: Briceño-Garmendia, Smits, and Foster 2009.
Note: Numbers in the table indicate the percentage deviation of actual maintenance expenditure from amount required for custom standard of maintenance.
a. South Africa is excluded from this group.

Most countries lie in the range of 0.5 to 2.0 percent of GDP per year. Only three countries (Central African Republic, Liberia, and Zimbabwe) are estimated to need expenditures in excess of 2.5 percent of GDP per year. Overall, these numbers do not look very high compared to the data on real historic expenditure reported above. The RONET calculations are based on efficient unit costs, however, and hence are probably an underestimation of the actual expenditure needs.

Road Work Costs: The Toll of Inflation

Available data, though limited, indicate that, on average, maintenance costs in Africa, at $2,160 per kilometer, are higher than the worldwide average of $2,024 per kilometer and twice as high as those in South and East Asia. These data suggest that routine maintenance is somewhat less effectively performed in Africa than in other regions (table 2.9).

Moreover, there has been a marked increase in unit costs in recent years, large enough to undermine the adequacy of road funding. A recent unit cost study, undertaken as part of the AICD (Gwilliam and others 2009), analyzed data from bills for 115 recently completed donor-funded

Figure 2.25 Aggregate Requirements over a 20-Year Period for Preserving the Road Networks as Percentage of the Current Annual GDP

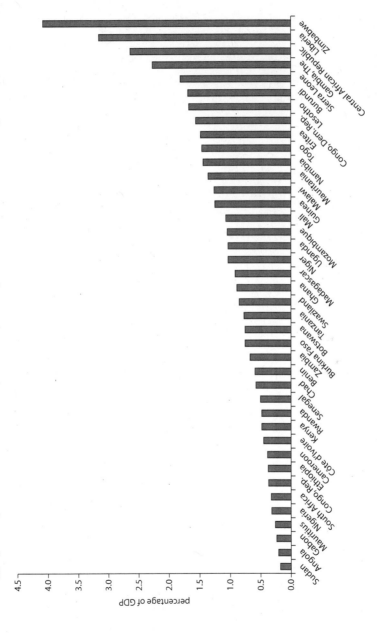

Source: Calculation by A. Nogales based on data from Gwilliam and others 2009.

Table 2.9   Recent Estimates of Unit Costs of Road Maintenance and Rehabilitation

| | World Bank ROCKS database[a] | | AICD unit cost study |
$ per km	Other developing regions	Africa	Africa
Routine maintenance	2,000	2,200	—
Periodic maintenance	43,000	54,000	158,000
Rehabilitation	191,000	162,000	300,000

Sources: World Bank 2008b; calculation by A. Nogales based on data from Gwilliam and others 2009.
Note: — = not available.
a. ROCKS = Road Costs Knowledge System

road contracts in Africa. The unit costs from this study are two to three times as high as those found in the World Bank road cost database, ROCKS (World Bank 2008b). As a result, a number of donors are finding that their road projects experience cost overruns ranging from 20 to 120 percent relative to expectations based on initial engineering designs. Those cost increases, if general, are large enough to seriously affect the adequacy of road sector maintenance and rehabilitation expenditure.

A more detailed investigation of cost overruns identifies three explanatory factors. First, a lack of effective competition—defined as having a price spread of no more than 10 percent among the three lowest bidders—is strongly associated with the presence of cost overruns in road maintenance and rehabilitation contracts. Second, since 2002 and especially since 2005, prices for the basket of items that are key inputs into road construction (such as bitumen, cement, steel, aggregates, and so on) have increased 60 to 100 percent. Third, significant delays in project implementation (which are not uncommon) are also associated with greater cost overruns, in part because they lead to greater exposure to other inflationary influences. The study concluded that cost overruns were the result of increased input costs against a growing demand for contracting in an environment of generally low competition for contracts. Hence, action is required to develop more competitive domestic markets for engineering contracting services.

In view of the mounting upward pressure on road costs, it is relevant to ask whether any savings can be achieved by choosing alternative road technologies at the design stage. Key questions are whether the road surface type and condition are well aligned with the traffic volumes carried by each road, and whether the technologies used are the most cost-effective for delivering a particular type of surface. The RONET analysis shows a strong positive correlation between traffic levels and road surface type (that is, paved or unpaved), close to 0.7, although the correlation between traffic levels and road condition is much weaker, ranging from 0.2 to 0.4.

A minimum of 300 vehicles per day is widely accepted as the traffic threshold that makes paving of roads economically viable, and it is possible to compare actual traffic levels against this benchmark. Paved roads with traffic volumes below the threshold have been potentially overengineered, while unpaved roads with high volumes are potentially underengineered.

On this criterion, there is some evidence of substantial overengineering in the main road networks, and much less of underengineering (figure 2.26). On average across countries, about 30 percent of the main networks appear to be overengineered and about 10 percent underengineered, suggesting a scope for significant cost savings by better aligning surface types with traffic volumes. Nevertheless, the variation across countries is huge. At one extreme, in Nigeria, almost 30 percent of the main road networks appear to be underengineered and only a minimal share are overengineered. At the other extreme, in Zambia, more than 60 percent of the main networks look to be overengineered. There are several possible explanations for overengineering. It may reflect a past expectation of high traffic growth that has not been realized, or a present expectation of high traffic growth in the near future. More commonly, however, it reflects political pressures (especially where cheap funding has been available) or a hope that maintenance performance, presently underfunded, will improve before periodic maintenance is required.

On the rural network, the key traffic threshold is 30 vehicles per day, widely considered to be the minimum required to justify gravelling of roads. According to the minimum, 15 percent of the rural network length appears to be underengineered, meaning that a gravel surface is warranted (figure 2.27). At one extreme, in Burkina Faso, Ethiopia, Ghana, Lesotho, Mozambique, and Niger, 30 to 50 percent of the rural networks may be underengineered. At the other extreme, countries such as Chad, Rwanda, South Africa, Tanzania, and Uganda offer no evidence of underengineering. The results show no evidence of overengineering on the rural networks, implying no real scope for related cost savings.

Further economies in road network costs could be made by adapting design standards to local conditions. Standards and warrants need continuous adjustment in light of materials availability and development. In turn, designs should take into account the local climate, natural materials available in the area, and traffic load and volume. In many cases, sealing gravel at traffic thresholds of less than 100 vehicles per day is economically

Figure 2.26 Extent of Over- and Underengineering on Main Road Networks

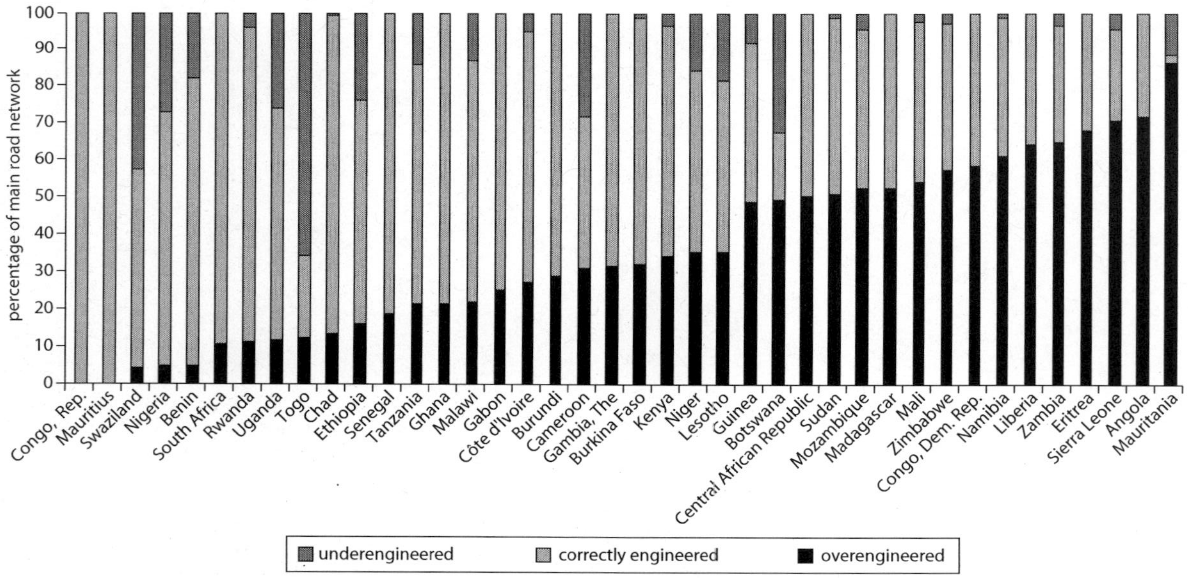

Source: Calculation by A. Nogales based on data from Gwilliam and others 2009.

Figure 2.27 Extent of Over- and Underengineering on Rural Road Networks

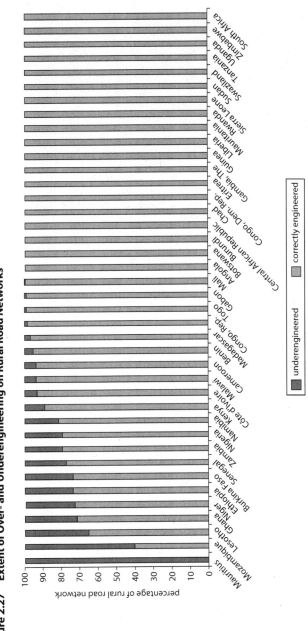

Source: Calculation by A. Nogales based on data from Gwilliam and others 2009.

justifiable even though the conventional standard is 200 vehicles per day. Sealed gravel roads have a black surface like any bitumen road. Typically, life-cycle cost savings would be on the order of 30 to 50 percent over 20 years compared with traditional surface treatments. The reduced cost of construction is achieved through reduced earthworks, reduced haulage distances for construction materials, reduced need for material processing, and reduced surfacing costs because of use of locally available materials. Pavement life is also increased because of reduced pavement deflection as pavement layers are compacted.

Geometric standards also need review in light of the improvement of road materials. Prior to 2001, the de facto standard adopted in most Southern African Development Community (SADC) countries was the 1965 Policy on Geometric Design of Rural Highways—which did not cater specifically to low-volume roads—issued by the American Association of State Highway and Transportation Officials. More recently, the SADC has recognized that to minimize total transport costs, road improvements should be designed to meet the lowest practicable standards (without unduly impairing safety requirements).

Recognizing the shortcomings of using guidelines from developed countries, the United Kingdom's Transport Research Laboratory has published a series of Overseas Road Notes (TRL 2001) with more appropriate guidelines for developing countries. Guidelines have also been developed in Africa for use either nationally, for example, in South Africa (Transpotek 2001), or regionally (Pinard, Gourlay, and Greening 2003). The challenge is to apply existing designs and standards in a flexible manner to fit the parameters of the local environment and to do so safely and economically. To that end, the recent SADC guidelines offer advice on the implementation of low-volume sealed roads (SADC 2003).

Labor-based methods have been an important part of the strategy to improve rural transport infrastructure in Africa over the past 35 years. These methods not only produce gravel roads of equal quality to those produced using equipment-based methods but also generate rural employment in a cost-effective manner. Nevertheless, these methods have not been applied on a large scale, often because of contractors' reluctance to adopt them (Stock 1996). First, contractors believe the cost of learning this new technology is high. Second, it has been argued that the cost of managing large labor forces makes labor-based methods more expensive than equipment-based methods. Unit-rate cost comparisons of labor-based and equipment-based methods, therefore, cannot predict firm behavior. Small firms appear more open to using labor-based methods than large firms because they can supervise their sites more closely and increase worker productivity and control truancy more easily. Moreover, unlike large firms, small firms that wish to use equipment-based methods face high variable costs: they either own older, less-efficient equipment with high maintenance costs or must rent equipment at a high cost.

Decentralization of responsibilities and improved financial management are essential for labor-based maintenance to work effectively. A review of experience gained under the Rural Travel and Transport Program in 1996 identified these as the two key reforms necessary to mainstream labor-based programs (Stock and de Veen 1996). Improved financial management is needed to ensure that funds flow adequately and laborers are paid on time, and decentralization is needed to streamline payment procedures and strengthen stakeholders' support of programs. These factors would need to be accompanied by strong government commitment, effective labor laws, appropriate design standards and training, and a suitable delivery mechanism.

One way of assessing the burden of road maintenance at the country level is to look at the capital value of the road stock as a percentage of GDP (figure 2.28). In most countries, road networks are worth less than 30 percent of GDP. But some very poor countries (such as Malawi, Mozambique, Niger, and Zimbabwe), and countries with an exceptionally low population density (such as Namibia), have networks that are worth significantly more than that. It is in such countries that the fiscal burden of maintenance is likely to be particularly high.

Identifying the Main Influences on Road Quality

A key question is the extent to which road network quality is determined by economic and geographic fundamentals or can be influenced by policy variables.

GDP *per capita* has a significant statistical impact on the condition of main roads but, curiously, none whatsoever on the condition of rural networks. Overall, differences in the GDP alone explain 33 percent of the variation in road quality observed across countries. Nevertheless, both for main and rural roads there is a very wide range of network conditions across countries in the low-income bracket (with GDP per capita of less than $1,000 per year). Within the low-income class, the percentage of main roads in good condition ranges from 9 percent in Côte d'Ivoire to 74 percent in Burkina Faso. Similarly, the percentage of rural roads in good condition in the low-income countries ranges from 0 percent in Uganda to 63 percent in Burkina Faso.

Figure 2.28 Road Asset Value as Percentage of GDP

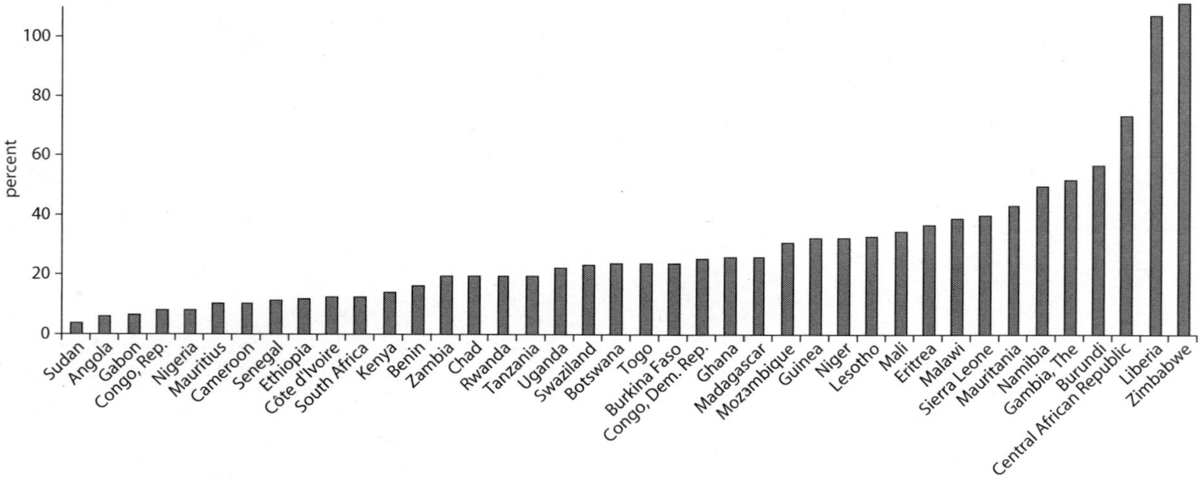

Source: Calculation by A. Nogales based on data from Gwilliam and others 2009.

Geographic conditions also have a major impact on road conditions. In particular, countries with wetter and more mountainous terrain face substantially higher costs of road construction and maintenance than do those with flat and arid terrain. A high rainfall level greatly accelerates the process of road deterioration, requiring frequent and more intensive maintenance interventions, and thus stretching the limited road sector budgets. A composite index is created that indicates the percentage of a country's national territory that is steep, moderately steep, or rolling *and* has rainfall in excess of 600 millimeters per year. The climate-terrain index shows a significant correlation with the quality of both main networks and rural networks, though the correlation is stronger in the case of rural roads (figure 2.29).

Vehicle overloading is without doubt one of the main influences on road quality. For example, as engineers estimate damage to road surfaces to be proportional to the fourth power of the axle weight, a road designed for a load of 9 tonnes per axle will incur 35 percent more damage per axle when the overload is only 10 percent. The aggregate cost of overloading for South Africa was estimated at $90 million a year in 1998. Many governments are trying to take action to reduce this cost. Kenya has attempted to ban heavy vehicles (through limiting the number of axles rather than the axle loads) and, in 2009, announced the intention of imposing heavy fines for overloading on owners rather than drivers. The South African Department of Transport drafted a National Overload Strategy in 2009, and there have been efforts within the regional economic communities to harmonize rules on overloading.

Previous attempts to control overloading have not been successful, however. Control measures in Kenya have been challenged in the courts. While transit traffic can be controlled on entry to a country, domestic traffic is more difficult to control. Evasion by truckers has been extensive and systematic, aided by corrupt enforcement, sometimes at a high level. For example, Trans-African Concessions, which runs the motorway between Maputo and Witbank in South Africa, has complained that the Mozambican police and the National Road Administration are not doing enough to stop overloading of trucks on this road.

Given the practical difficulties of adjusting trucks to the roads, it may be sensible to consider the converse policy of adjusting the roads to the trucks. The economies of scale of heavier trucks are compelling, and a carrier has strong incentives to load his vehicle to the maximum. Studies in the mid-1980s showed that the savings in operating costs when trucks are allowed to carry 12–15 tonnes per single axle, rather than the usual

Figure 2.29   Relationship between Road Networks in Poor Condition and the Climate-Terrain Index

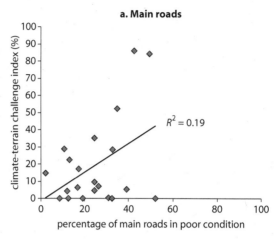

a. Main roads

$R^2 = 0.19$

climate-terrain challenge index (%)

percentage of main roads in poor condition

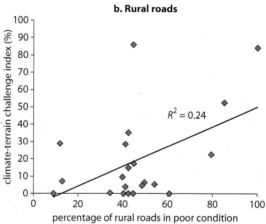

b. Rural roads

$R^2 = 0.24$

climate-terrain challenge index (%)

percentage of rural roads in poor condition

Source: Gwilliam and others 2009.

8–10 tonnes, far outweigh the extra cost of constructing or repaving roads to bear the heavier load (World Bank 1988). This finding implies that on all but lightly used road networks, stronger pavement is economically justified. Moreover, as the worst offenders are usually dump trucks hauling the densest of cargo—crushed stone, sand, gravel, cement—specific, targeted regulations requiring multiaxle vehicles for these businesses might be a more enforceable policy.

The problem is that upgrading a whole network designed for relatively low-axle loads could be extremely expensive. In summary, though vehicle overloading adversely impacts road conditions, this does not necessarily imply that restricting vehicle size is the appropriate policy response. Requiring large vehicles to have multiple axles is one alternative. Recognizing that axle-load limits are difficult to enforce, a policy emphasis on strengthening roads to achieve the operating cost savings associated with very heavy vehicles is another. Detailed analysis of this long-term strategic decision should be a high priority.

Institutional arrangements also matter. Countries with *both* a road fund *and* a road agency have 20 percent more of their main and rural road networks in good or fair condition than countries without these two elements. The quality of the road fund institutions, as measured by a road fund quality index devised for this study, also has a substantial and significant effect on the percentage of the main road networks in good condition but not on the quality of the rural road networks (figure 2.30).

In countries with high fuel levies, an additional 10 percent of the main road networks and an additional 5 percent of the rural road networks are in good or fair condition. (But there is no clear ranking of countries with low fuel levies versus no fuel levies at all.) As might be expected, the level of maintenance expenditures shows strong correlation with the quality of the main networks but not with that of the rural networks (figure 2.31).

Policy choices on road institutions and funding levels thus have a material impact on the quality of the main road networks. Countries with both road funds and road agencies, as well as those with high fuel levies and relatively high maintenance expenditures, seem to reap the benefits and have a higher proportion of their main road networks in good or fair condition. But these variables have a much weaker impact on the quality of the rural road networks. This situation may reflect deficiencies in the accuracy of data on spending and road quality for the rural networks, or it may reflect the fact that rural network management is driven by institutions and resource allocations at the local level, and thus does not adequately reflect national policy.

Freight Transport: Too Expensive

Freight transport services are very important to the African economies, many of which are dependent on exports of relatively low value-for-weight goods to world markets. Unfortunately, empirical studies carried

Figure 2.30   Relationship between Road Networks in Good Condition and Their Score on the Road Fund Quality Index

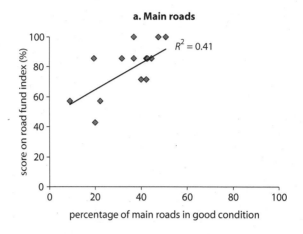

a. Main roads

$R^2 = 0.41$

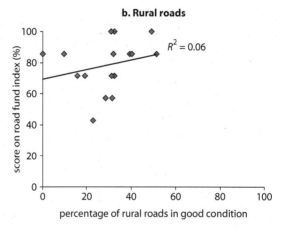

b. Rural roads

$R^2 = 0.06$

Source: Gwilliam and others 2009.

out since the mid-1990s have consistently demonstrated that transport prices in Africa are higher than in other regions. Rizet and Hine (1993) estimated that prices of road freight transport in Cameroon, Côte d'Ivoire, and Mali were six times those in Pakistan. A later study (Rizet and Gwet 1998) demonstrated that for distances up to 300 km, unit costs of road transport were 40 to 100 percent higher in Africa than in Southeast Asia. Transport charges for landlocked African countries have been shown to range from 15 to 20 percent of import costs, a rate that is

Figure 2.31   Relationship between Road Networks in Good Condition and Maintenance Expenditures

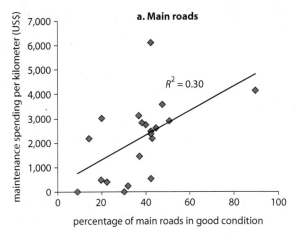

a. Main roads

$R^2 = 0.30$

percentage of main roads in good condition

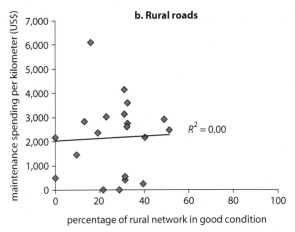

b. Rural roads

$R^2 = 0.00$

percentage of rural network in good condition

Source: Gwilliam and others 2009.

three or four times as high as that typically found in developed countries (MacKellar, Wörz, and Wörgötter 2000).

There is also substantial variation within Africa. While variable transport costs per vehicle-km generally fall in the range of $1.23 to $1.83, fixed costs, transport quality, and transport journey speeds vary. Transport time for long journeys is itself a good indicator of quality of service. As table 2.10 shows, transport quality in South Africa, where larger trucks are used, is higher than in Central or West Africa, but, on average, prices

Table 2.10   Performance of the International Gateway Corridors

Region	Gateway	Destination	Distance (km)	Transit time (days)	Price per tonne (US$)	Price per tonne-km (US$)
East	Mombasa	Kampala	1,100	5–6	90	.081
	Mombasa	Kigali	1,700	8–10	100–110	.059–.065
West	Lomé	Ouagadougou	1,050	6–8	60–70	.057–.067
	Cotonou	Niamey	1,000	6–8	65–95	.065–.095
Central	Douala	Ndjamena	1,850	12–15	200–210	.108–.113
	Douala	Bangui	1,450	8–10	200–210	.138–.145
South	Durban	Lusaka	2,300	8–9	90–130	.039–.057
	Durban	Ndola	2,700	9–10	130–170	.048–.063

Source: Teravaninthorn and Raballand 2008.

are lower. A recent study (Teravaninthorn and Raballand 2008) showed that, on average, transport prices in Central Africa are between two and three times as high as those in southern Africa.

High freight charges in Africa were initially attributed to the effects of infrastructure constraints on vehicle operating costs (Limão and Venables 2001). Certainly the structure of trucking costs in Africa differs considerably from that in most regions of the world. Compared to European operators, African truckers tend to have low fixed costs (resulting from low salaries and the use of cheap, old trucks) and high variable costs (mainly attributable to the high fuel consumption of these old and poorly maintained trucks). Poor road conditions reduce the life of trucks and tires, increase vehicle maintenance costs, and increase fuel consumption. In fact, fuel and lubricants account for between 40 and 70 percent of the total variable costs. In general, variable costs account for an unusually large proportion of total costs (over 70 percent in Central and West Africa); as a consequence, the incentive to make intensive use of the vehicles is weakened. The age of the truck fleet and the low utilization of vehicles seem to be even more critical than the unit cost of inputs. Annual truck mileage is lower in many Central, East, and West African countries than in developed countries and many other developing countries. For example, average truck mileage is less than 70,000 km per year in Cameroon, Ethiopia, Malawi, and Niger, compared with about 110,000 km in Pakistan and South Africa.

More recent studies have tended to emphasize the institutional and regulatory influences on freight charges. Teravaninthorn and Raballand (2008) have shown that the range of transport costs is less than the range in prices, with variable operating costs varying by a factor of 0.5 but prices varying by as much as a factor of 4. For example, the average transport price per tonne-km ranges from 4 to 5 cents in southern Africa, from 6 to 8 cents in West and East African corridors, and from 10 to 25 cents in the Central African corridor. This finding suggests that there might be significant degrees of monopoly in the higher price markets.

At first glance, that explanation would appear unlikely, as the freight transport industry is generally fragmented in West and Central Africa, with virtually no large trucking companies in the business. But the small operators are typically tightly regulated by freight bureaus, shippers' councils, and trade unions. And the devices used to ensure an equitable distribution of income among operators—most notably "tour de role" dispatching—increase costs.[4] This increase is accentuated by the degree to which restricted competition between haulers allows monopoly profits to be taken.

East Africa has a more competitive and mature market. There are about 20 large companies with more than 100 trucks each on the main East African corridors, and the largest Kenyan company has a fleet of over 600 vehicles. The large companies account for about 20 percent of the total market—a figure comparable to that found in Europe and North America. Southern Africa also has a more mature structure, particularly in the regulatory and logistical arenas. Differences in market power thus account at least in part for the high prices in some regions.

That is not all, however. A peculiarity of African transport is that, contrary to experiences in the rest of the world, the price per tonne-km for long-distance freight destined for international markets is higher than that for domestic traffic within a country. Procedures used by customs and border-crossing officials contribute to the low annual vehicle usage figures: there seems to be a strong positive correlation between transport prices and the number of border crossings. This suggests that there are serious deficiencies in the regulatory regime relating to transit traffic, substantiated to some extent by the existence of high profit margins in international movements. These high profits are achieved despite low annual utilization of vehicles and many nontariff barriers in Central and West Africa. The most plausible reason for this peculiarity lies in the role of the official and nonofficial regulation of the sector.

Government-imposed procedures also contribute to high freight charges. International traffic is strictly governed in both West and Central Africa by bilateral transit agreements, implemented by national freight bureaus. Quotas are set on the proportion of each trade that can be carried by the party countries, and cabotage is banned. The freight bureaus are able to use their formal powers to manage the issuance of cargo- and transit-related documents to act as monopolist freight allocation bureaus and are instrumental in maintaining high freight rates in collaboration with the truckers' unions. This finding is supported by customer research. The perception of international freight forwarders, expressed in the World Bank's Logistics Performance Index, place the four African subregions below all other regions of the world, with southern Africa the best of the four and West Africa the worst (World Bank 2010).

Operations to and from South Africa are governed by bilateral agreements, which provide for a sharing of information on traffic development and define the types of permits that can be issued. This system restricts the carriage of bilateral trade to operators from the two countries concerned and prohibits cabotage. But it does not establish quotas, and it allows rates to be determined by the market to enable direct contracting between shippers and transporters and to give incentives to efficient operators. The southern African international transport market is a good model for the rest of the continent because it combines liberalization of entry with enforcement of quality and with load control rules applicable to all operators.

Currently, around 70 percent of the main trade corridors are in good condition, and donors are increasingly channeling resources to infrastructure improvements along these strategic routes. But there is also recognition that it will take more than good infrastructure to make these corridors function effectively. Neighboring countries have increasingly organized themselves into corridor associations to address the nonphysical barriers to transit, with a particular focus on cutting lengthy delays (between 10 and 30 hours at border crossings and ports) by creating one-stop integrated frontier posts and improving ports and customs administration.

The southern African corridor performs significantly better than those in Central and West Africa, approaching developing-country norms in terms of freight tariffs; but even here, the duration of transit leaves much to be desired. Notwithstanding the emphasis on trade facilitation, the AICD analysis indicates that the high cost and low quality of road freight service in Central and West Africa is primarily attributable to a highly regulated and cartelized trucking industry, making liberalization the number one priority to improve road transport in that region.

The Way Forward

Africa's road network, though physically sparse, is relatively large compared to the size of its population, and even larger when seen in the context of national income. Countries, on average, spend around 2 percent of their GDP on roads. Within this envelope, there is a significant bias toward capital expenditure. This bias is further exacerbated when one considers that countries are typically able to execute only around 60 percent of budgeted capital spending. As a result, countries are budgeting, on average, only 30 percent of road expenditure to maintenance, versus a norm of more than 50 percent in more mature road systems. Nevertheless, even with this degree of capital bias, only about half of the countries surveyed have capital expenditures large enough to clear current network rehabilitation backlogs within a reasonable time period. At the same time, fewer than half of the countries are allocating enough resources to cover routine and periodic maintenance requirements. As a result, a significant number of countries are in a vicious cycle of low maintenance budgets leading to network deterioration leading to an escalating rehabilitation backlog—a backlog that they lack adequate capital resources to clear. Recent escalations of unit costs for road maintenance and reconstruction are likely to further dilute the adequacy of road budget allocations.

The policy response to this situation has been the widespread adoption of second-generation road funds, though not all have been well designed or well implemented. In many countries, the fuel levy is too low, and in some, collection of the levy has posed a serious problem. Nevertheless, countries with road funds—in particular those that also set fuel levies at a reasonably high level—have systematically better road financing, exhibit a lower degree of capital bias, and are much closer to covering road maintenance requirements. While income and geographical factors have a significant impact on the condition of networks, quasi-independent road funds and road agencies are also highly beneficial.

Lack of funding and institutional capacity shows up most strongly in the condition of the unpaved and lower tiers of the network. There is thus a need to spend as cost-effectively as possible, in particular by exploring the potential for cost savings through the adoption of more appropriate technological standards. Even within the current technology, there is evidence of substantial overengineering of the main road networks relative to traffic volumes. The rural networks, on the other hand, tend to be somewhat underengineered. Road transport operations, though private, are costly and relatively inefficient, with a lack of competition accentuated by poor administrative procedures for allocation of traffic, and inefficiency and corruption at ports and land borders. The priorities for the future all stem from this analysis.

Priority 1. Consolidate road-funding arrangements.

Countries with (well-financed) road funds have been shown to do significantly better at capturing resources for maintenance than those without them. But the quality of the administrative arrangements makes some road funds more successful than others. For consolidation of the gains already made in the region, the following suggestions should be heeded:

- Countries without second-generation road funds should establish them immediately.
- All road funds should be founded in law rather than by administrative decree, should provide for direct transfer of levy revenues to the fund, and should have majority user participation in managing the road fund board, with published auditing.
- Governments should require the road fund board to demonstrate what level of fuel levy or other revenue source is necessary to prevent deterioration of the network, and what is necessary to overcome backlogs in maintenance over a reasonable period.
- Road boards should be required to develop transparent formulas or procedures to govern the allocation of road fund revenues to differing road categories.

Priority 2. Commercialize maintenance implementation arrangements.

The development of commercially structured road authorities, independent of direct ministerial control, has improved performance and facilitated the introduction of new procedures in several countries. It is therefore recommended as a parallel approach to road maintenance and includes the following aspects:

- Establishment of quasi-autonomous road authorities with user representation on boards
- Introduction of performance-based road maintenance contracts
- Development of information and training programs for road maintenance contractors.

Priority 3. Make a concerted effort to improve road safety.
Africa has the worst road accident record ·in the world. Programs to reduce accidents have succeeded elsewhere. Recommendations include

- Establishing a high-level national safety council
- Conducting safety audits on all new road and road improvement designs
- Developing a comprehensive national road safety program.

Priority 4. Liberalize the road haulage sector.
Cartelization of operations and failures in market regulation (including the enforcement of a "tour de role" dispatching for import traffic) limit the competitiveness and hinder the efficiency of the trucking industry. To overcome these problems, countries should consider the following recommendations:

- Legislation should be introduced restricting entry to road haulage markets on qualitative conditions only (including operator, vehicle, and driver licensing).
- Road haulage associations should be excluded from the setting of prices or the allocation of traffic among members.
- Liberal approaches should be adopted toward foreign haulers involved in cabotage markets.

Notes

1. The main source document for this chapter is Gwilliam and others (2009). The Road Network Evaluation Tool (RONET) analysis was done by Alberto Nogales. Source materials from the Sub-Saharan Africa Transport Policy Program documentation include Stock (1996) and Stock and de Veen (1996). Heggie and Vickers (1998) and Malmberg Calvo (1998) provided important information on road management issues.
2. In chapters 7 and 8, the low-income, aid-dependent countries are further subdivided into "fragile" and "nonfragile." For more on this classification see World Bank (2007b).
3. Note that the totals vary from 100 percent because of rounding.
4. "Tour de role" dispatching involves vehicles queuing at the dispatch point, with work allocated to vehicles strictly in accordance with their position in the queue.

References

African Development Bank. 2003. "Review of the Implementation Status of the Trans-African Highways and the Missing Links." SWECO International AB and Nordic Consulting Group AB, Stockholm.

Benmaamar, M. 2006. "Financing of Road Maintenance in Sub-Saharan Africa: Reforms and Progress towards Second Generation Road Funds." Sub-Saharan Africa Transport Policy Program Discussion Paper 6, World Bank, Washington, DC.

Briceño-Garmendia, C., K. Smits, and V. Foster. 2009. "Financing Public Infrastructure in Sub-Saharan Africa: Patterns, Issues, and Options." Africa Infrastructure Country Diagnostic Background Paper 15, World Bank, Washington, DC.

Carruthers, R., R. R. Krishnamani, and S. Murray. 2009. "Improving Connectivity: Investing in Transport Infrastructure in Sub-Saharan Africa." Africa Infrastructure Country Diagnostic Background Paper 7, World Bank, Washington, DC.

Gwilliam, K., and A. Kumar. 2003. "How Effective Are Second-Generation Road Funds? A Preliminary Appraisal." *World Bank Research Observer* 18 (1): 113–28.

Gwilliam, K., V. Foster, R. Archondo-Callao, C. Briceño-Garmendia, A. Nogales, and K. Sethi. 2009. "The Burden of Maintenance: Roads in Sub-Saharan Africa." Africa Infrastructure Country Diagnostic Background Paper 14, World Bank, Washington, DC.

Heggie, I. G., and P. Vickers. 1998. "Commercial Management and Financing of Roads." World Bank Technical Paper 409, World Bank, Washington, DC.

Limão, N., and A. J. Venables. 2001. "Infrastructure, Geographical Disadvantage, and Transport Costs." *World Bank Economic Review* 15 (3): 451–79.

MacKellar, L., J. Wörz, and A. Wörgötter. 2000. "Economic Development Problems of Landlocked Countries." Transition Economics Series 14, Institute of Advanced Studies, Vienna.

Malmberg Calvo, C. 1998. "Options for Managing and Financing Rural Transport Infrastructure." World Bank Technical Paper 411, World Bank, Washington, DC.

Pinard, M. I. 2009. "Review of Progress on the Commercialization of Road Agencies in Sub-Saharan Africa." Sub-Saharan Africa Transport Policy Program, World Bank, Washington, DC.

Pinard, M. I., C. S. Gourlay, and P. A. K. Greening. 2003. "Rethinking Traditional Approaches to Low-Volume Road Provision in Developing Countries." Transportation Research Board Paper LVR8-1153, Transportation Research Board of the National Academies, Washington, DC.

Rizet, C., and R. Gwet. 1998. "An International Comparison of Road Haulage Prices in Africa, South-East Asia and Latin America." *Recherche Transports Sécurité* 60: 69–85.

Rizet, C., and J. Hine. 1993. "A Comparison of Costs and Productivity of Road Freight Transport in Africa and Pakistan." *Transport Reviews* 13 (2): 151–65.

Robinson, R., and D. Stiedl. 2001. "Decentralisation of Road Administration: Case Studies in Africa and Asia." *Public Administration and Development* 21 (1): 53–64.

SADC (Southern African Development Community). 2003. "Guideline on Low-Volume Sealed Roads." SADC, Gabarone, Botswana.

SSATP (Sub-Saharan Africa Transport Policy Program). 2004. "RMI Matrix for August 2004." World Bank, Washington, DC.

———. 2007. "RMI Matrix for September 2007." World Bank, Washington, DC.

Stankevich, N., N. Quereshi, and C. Queiroz. (2005). "Performance-Based Contracting for Preservation and Improvement of Road Assets." Transport Note TN-27, World Bank, Washington, DC.

Stock, E. A. 1996. "Problems Facing Labor-based Road Programs and What to Do About Them—Evidence from Ghana." Sub-Saharan Africa Transport Policy Program Working Paper 24, World Bank, Washington, DC.

Stock, E. A., and J. de Veen. 1996. "Expanding Labor-Based Methods for Road Works in Africa." Sub-Saharan Africa Transport Policy Program Working Paper 22, World Bank, Washington, DC.

Teravaninthorn, S., and G. Raballand. 2008. *Transport Prices and Costs in Africa: A Review of the Main International Corridors.* Washington, DC: World Bank.

Transpotek. 2001. *G2 Geometric Design Manual.* Pretoria: Council of Scientific and Industrial Research.

TRL (Transport Research Laboratory). 2001. "Management of Rural Road Networks." Overseas Road Note 20, TRL, Crowthorne, Berkshire, U.K.

World Bank. 1988. *Road Deterioration in Developing Countries: Causes and Remedies.* Washington, DC: World Bank.

———. 2007a. "Rural Accessibility Index: A Key Development Indicator." Transport Paper 10, World Bank, Washington, DC.

———. 2007b. "Index for Countries Eligible for World Bank Loans and IDA Credits." Internal Memo 10, World Bank, Washington, DC.

———. 2008a. Privatization Database. World Bank, Washington, DC. http://rru.worldbank.org/Privatization.

———. 2008b. ROCKS (Road Costs Knowledge System) (database). World Bank, Washington, DC. http://go.worldbank.org/ZF1I4CJNX0.

———. 2009. RONET (Road Network Evaluation Tool) (software). World Bank, Washington, DC. http://go.worldbank.org/A2QQYZNFM0.

———. 2010. Logistics Performance Index (software). World Bank, Washington, DC. http://go.worldbank.org/88X6PU5GV0.

CHAPTER 3

Railways: Not Pulling Their Weight

Railways transformed the face of Africa in the late 19th and early 20th centuries, creating strategic corridors that opened the interior for the exploitation of mineral and other resources. But most lines remain isolated, with little network interconnection. Built to modest technical standards, railways were left unprepared to compete for time-sensitive traffic (including passengers) as road systems developed. Revenues have been generally insufficient to finance the modernization of track and rolling stock. Conservative management under state ownership has not helped, and facilities have suffered disproportionately in postindependence civil wars. While concessioning to the private sector promises to improve operational efficiency, the railways still face serious financial problems. New forms of partnership between states and the private sector are needed if the rail sector is to be revitalized.

Africa's Rail History: Opening Up the Continent

The first railways south of the Sahara were built in South Africa in the 1860s and 1870s, with lines heading inland from the ports at Cape Town and Durban.[1] While railways continued to develop in Cape Province, Natal, and Transvaal, it was not until the turn of the 20th century that large-scale railway development began in other parts of the continent. In most cases, the development consisted of isolated lines heading inland from a port to a trading center or mine, with a few branch lines added later. Many lines were state owned, but some were managed as concessions or constructed by mining companies. In the past 80 years, few lines have been constructed outside South Africa and its immediate neighbors. The most significant is the Tazara line, built by the Chinese during the 1970s, which links Tanzania and Zambia. Other major projects include the Trans-Gabonais (opened in 1987 principally to transport minerals), the extension of the Cameroon network from Yaoundé to Ngaoundere, and the northeastern extension of the Nigerian network from Kuru to Maiduguri.

Although there have been grand network plans for over a century, most railways in Africa consist of disconnected lines, either within countries or linking ports to their regional hinterlands. The only true international networks are those centered on South Africa and stretching north to Zimbabwe, Zambia, and the Democratic Republic of Congo, and, to a lesser extent, the old East African railways network in Kenya, Tanzania, and Uganda. This pattern of railway development reflects the historically limited amount of intercountry trade in Africa. Even today, trade volumes between adjacent countries are remarkably small. African railways are therefore closely linked to ports (in fact, much of Africa once had integrated port and railway organizations). Where railways traverse more than one country, freight rarely originates or terminates in the intermediate country or countries—with the notable exceptions of traffic between Kenya and South Africa and their neighbors (map 3.1).

Most railways in the region were reasonably successful until the 1960s. But as the road system developed in Africa, new and larger trucks increasingly captured the higher-value general freight. Rail traffic became limited primarily to bulk mineral and agricultural freight and semibulk freight such as fuel. The resulting decrease in revenues delayed the maintenance and replacement of deteriorating track and rolling stock. Therefore, even when railways tried to reclaim higher-value traffic (such as containers), their low quality of service prevented them from taking a significant market share from road competition.

Other factors contributed to the decline of railways in Africa. For example, governments required railways to operate unprofitable passenger services without compensation. This practice not only drew cash away from infrastructure improvements, but also tied up locomotives that could have been used for revenue-generating freight services. The many

Map 3.1   The African Rail Network in 2009

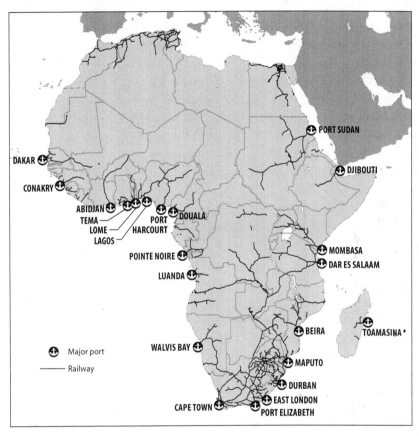

PORT SUDAN

DAKAR

DJIBOUTI

CONAKRY

ABIDJAN
TEMA
LOME
LAGOS
PORT
HARCOURT
DOUALA

POINTE NOIRE

MOMBASA
DAR ES SALAAM

LUANDA

BEIRA

TOAMASINA

WALVIS BAY

MAPUTO

DURBAN

EAST LONDON
CAPE TOWN
PORT ELIZABETH

Major port

Railway

Source: Bullock 2009.

wars and civil disturbances in Africa over the past 50 years have also hindered railway development—either directly, through the destruction of facilities (Angola, Eritrea, Ethiopia, and Mozambique), or indirectly, by cutting inland railways off from their ports (Burkina Faso and Malawi).

A Sparse and Disconnected Network

The rail system of Africa comprises various lines and small networks that, combined, offer low-density coverage and little interconnection between regions. At the end of 2008, there were 52 railways operating in 33 countries in Africa (appendix 3a). Most of these used one of two rail gauges[2]: Cape gauge (1,067 millimeters, or 3 feet 6 inches) or meter gauge.

The total African network size is around 70,000 kilometers (km), of which about 55,000 km is currently being used. The network is single track except for sections of the Spoornet network (recently renamed Transnet Freight Rail). Very little is electrified outside of South Africa (where 42 percent of the network—nearly 9,000 km—is electrified); the only other electrified sections are 858 km in the Democratic Republic of Congo and 313 km in Zimbabwe (not currently in use).

The spatial density of the rail network in Africa is low. The highest density is in South Africa (16 route-km per 1,000 square km [km²]), compared to a range of 1 to 6 route-km per 1,000 km² in most other African countries. Australia, Canada, China, and Russia, all of which have large undeveloped and sparsely populated areas, have densities between 5 and 7, while densities for most European countries range from 20 to 100. Thirteen countries in Africa do not have operating railways. Network density with respect to population, measured in route-km per million people, is highest in Gabon (520), Botswana (494), and South Africa (460). Most other African countries have densities ranging from 30 to 150 route-km per million people (see appendix 3a). In comparison, densities in European countries range from 200 to 1,000, and reach over 1,500 in Australia and Canada.

The main interconnected network in southern and Central Africa—which extends as far north as the Democratic Republic of Congo and southern Tanzania—uses Cape gauge. The same is true for railways in the ex-British possessions of Ghana, Nigeria, and Sudan. Meter gauge is used in all other former French possessions; in the disconnected Ethiopian line; and in the East African network that links Kenya, Uganda, and northern Tanzania. There are also a number of isolated standard gauge lines: those in Guinea and Mauritania are privately operated mineral lines; the standard gauge line in Gabon, although developed primarily for mineral traffic, is a public railway, which also carries general traffic and offers passenger services; and Eritrea has the only narrow gauge line in Africa.

Despite the variety of rail gauges, interoperability of railways is not a major problem. In only three places—two in Tanzania and one in Guinea—are there two different gauges in the same location. The Cape gauge network based in South Africa connects 11 countries, and the East African network connects 3. Two international meter gauge networks in West Africa connect landlocked Francophone countries to the coast: Ouagadougou-Abidjan (Sitarail), which links Burkina Faso to Côte d'Ivoire, and Bamako-Dakar (Transrail), which links Mali to Senegal. Another meter gauge network in East Africa links Ethiopia to Djibouti. Some other networks that do not cross international borders provide railheads from which traffic can continue by road. For example, in Benin the Organisation Commune Benin-Niger des Chemins de Fer et des Transports (OCBN) provides a link from Cotonou to Niamey through a railhead at Parakou; Camrail provides railheads for traffic between the port of Douala in Cameroon and the Central African Republic and Chad; and in East Africa, Tanzania Railways Corporation (TRC) carries traffic for Burundi and eastern Democratic Republic of Congo, and Kenya Railways Corporation (KRC) for Rwanda.

Over 50 companies operate in Africa. Many are small, although a single company, South Africa's Transnet Freight Rail, has about 40 percent of the operating network and carries 70 percent of the traffic. South Africa also dominates the rail passenger business. Mine-connected rail lines in both West and southern Africa constitute only 4 percent of the network but carry over half the freight (as measured by net tonne-km [ntkm]), most of which is carried on the Transnet Freight Rail coal and ore export lines. There are other mineral lines in Gabon, Guinea, Mauritania, and Nigeria, some of which also carry general traffic to and from mines.

Traffic Volume: Unprofitably Low

Traffic volumes on the region's railways are generally low by world standards. South Africa's rail system averages around 5 million traffic units (TUs) per route-km overall[3]—this figure is only 2.4 million when specialized coal and ore lines are excluded. The network with the next highest average is that of Gabon, with 2.7 million TUs per route-km. Cameroon's Camrail (1.1 million) is the only other railway with an average density of over 1 million TUs per route-km (see appendix 3b). Many railways average under 300,000. Even in South Africa, only 50 percent of the networks carry more than 2 million net tonnes per year. With such low traffic volumes, many networks in Africa struggle to maintain and renew their infrastructure.

Infrastructure Condition: Impeding Rail's Competitive Potential

Most networks in Africa, outside of South Africa, still operate at the standards to which they were constructed. They are small-scale, undercapitalized networks designed for relatively low axle loads and low speeds, ill-suited to modern requirements.

The rail track itself is often too light for even the moderate axle loads currently being operated. When the Dakar-Senegal railway was concessioned, the average age of track was reported as 37 years in Senegal and 51 years in Mali. Most track is even older. In addition, the strength of rail manufactured 60 or 70 years ago is often well below current standards, leading to fatigue failures and rail fractures. Additional difficulties arise in countries emerging from conflict. For example, in Angola and Mozambique, most infrastructure was destroyed in conflicts; mines had to be removed before rail lines could even be rehabilitated.

Control systems are also archaic. Many networks still rely on mechanical signals and train orders. While on most lines these systems are adequate from a capacity standpoint, human error often causes significant safety problems. Unfortunately, power signaling, where installed, often does not operate because of short circuits, lack of electrical power, and dilapidated cable networks. Rail telephone exchanges are similarly obsolete, having limited capacity and requiring spare parts that are virtually impossible to find. In addition, many structures, such as bridges and viaducts, are now over 100 years old. (See appendix 3a for more on railway assets.)

Because of chronic undermaintenance, many sections of the aging track have deteriorated, almost beyond repair. In most networks, considerable sections of track require repair or replacement. Major sections are inoperable in several countries, including Benin (23 percent), Angola (69 percent), and Uganda (91 percent). These networks will require rehabilitation before operations can recommence. In other countries, much of the network is not used on a regular basis (up to 60 percent in Ghana). Where services are operated, poor track conditions restrict train speeds on long sections, which reduces railway competitiveness and rolling-stock productivity.

The cost of repairs is beyond the financial capacity of most railways based on current traffic volumes. Conservative estimates put repair costs at $200,000 per kilometer in the most straightforward cases, and probably closer to $350,000 per kilometer on average. Funding repairs at these costs would absorb all operating surpluses for many years, by which time another backlog will have appeared. Rehabilitation is unlikely to be economically justified for many sections unless they show good prospects for bulk traffic or have no road competition. Lines carrying less than 1 million net tonnes per year are unlikely to warrant major rehabilitation, and lines carrying under 250,000 net tonnes per year probably cannot support anything more than routine maintenance.

Network Expansion Proposals: Often Lacking Economic Focus

There have been many proposals, some dating back a century, to create new routes for landlocked countries and to integrate the isolated networks. The most ambitious proposal came in 1976, when the African Railways Union prepared a master plan for a Pan-African rail network, which included 18 projects requiring 26,000 km of new construction. The plan was approved by the Organization of African Unity in 1979. In 2001, the African Railways Union published a revised master plan containing a sub-set of 10 corridors and, in 2005, further simplified the plan into three major transcontinental routes:

- Libya–Niger–Chad–Central African Republic–the Republic of Congo–the Democratic Republic of Congo–Angola–Namibia (6,500 km)
- Senegal–Mali–Chad–Djibouti (7,800 km)
- Kenya–Tanzania–Uganda–Rwanda–Burundi–the Democratic Republic of Congo, with possible extensions to Ethiopia and Sudan (5,600 km)

There have also been proposals for individual lines: a link from Isaka in Tanzania to Rwanda, with complementary links from Rwanda and Burundi to the Ugandan and Tanzanian network; a link through Kenya (or possibly Uganda) to southern Sudan; an extension of the Lilongwe line in Malawi; and a route from Walvis Bay in Namibia to Zambia and Angola. Company mineral lines have been proposed in Gabon, Mozambique, Namibia, and Sierra Leone. But few, if any, of the proposed links have moved beyond the drawing board.

In practice, some recent proposals have a clearer economic focus. For example, China is increasingly interested in oil and precious minerals in Angola, the Democratic Republic of Congo, and Zambia, and is investing in a new railway line to assist in the extraction and transportation of these resources to China. The core of the plan is the 1,860 km long Tanzania-Zambia Railway, which links the Indian Ocean port city of Dar es Salaam in Tanzania to Kapiri Mposhi, Zambia. This was built by the Chinese government in the 1970s, primarily to free Zambia from a politically based trade blockade by what was then Southern Rhodesia. But its traffic has diminished and it now has only about 20 percent of its original locomotive capacity. In 2001, China pledged to finance development of this rail line to create a railway crossing the continent from coast to coast. The Chinese plan would extend the line through the southern part of the Democratic Republic of Congo and link it with the current Chinese development in Angola.

Investment and Maintenance

With such low traffic volumes, African railways face a continuing problem in financing either new investment or maintenance of the existing system.

Infrastructure: Difficult to Finance on Low-Volume Lines

The capital cost of new rail infrastructure is high. The construction of a single-track, nonelectrified railway costs at least $1.5 million per kilometer in relatively flat terrain, and around $5 million in more rugged country requiring more extensive earthworks. The reconstruction of an existing line for which the right of way and earthworks already exist typically costs about $350,000 per kilometer using new materials; if secondhand materials such as cascaded rail can be used, the cost is lower—around $200,000 per kilometer. For lines that are to be upgraded, bridges may require strengthening to handle higher axle loads. Additional earthworks may also be required if alignments are to be improved. Hence, as a rule of thumb, the cost of upgrading can easily be twice the cost of simple track renewal. These costs exclude signaling, for which relatively cheap options are now available for the typical low-volume network.

Periodic replacement also imposes significant costs. Even if reconstructed infrastructure has a useful life of 40 to 50 years, the annual cost of maintenance is $5,000–$10,000 per kilometer, excluding any return on investment. If a low 5 percent return on investment is included, the annual cost increases to $20,000–$40,000 per kilometer. This means that a line that carries 1 million net tonnes per year would need to earn 0.5–0.8 cents per net tonne-km (c/ntkm) to fund periodic rehabilitation, while traffic with a density of 250,000 tonnes per year would need to earn 2–3 c/ntkm. If return on investment is included in the cost, the required returns quadruple to 2–3 c/ntkm for lines carrying 1 million net tonnes per year. Yields on most freight railways in Africa are around 4–5 c/ntkm and operating costs are 3–4 c/ntkm, leaving at most 1 c/ntkm for rehabilitation. Therefore, unless the investment creates a significant increase in traffic, full rehabilitation is commercially viable only for those lines with a density of 2 to 3 million net tonnes or more.

Investment Needs

A full analysis of the investment needs of railways in Africa would require detailed data on the conditions of infrastructure and rolling stock and traffic volumes for each railway. In the absence of such data, rough estimates have been made using aggregate statistics and broad assumptions.

The railway network in Africa north of South Africa and south of the Sahara consists of about 44,000 km of track, of which about 34,000 km is currently operational. Nearly all the lines are low volume and would thus justify only partial rehabilitation, possibly using cascaded materials.

Even assuming a relatively low unit cost—around $200,000 per km—probably no more than 15,000–20,000 km of the network can support this level of expenditure. Over a 40-year interval, the cost of infrastructure rehabilitation would therefore average around $100 million per year.

The cost of replacing rolling stock can be estimated in a similar manner. The railway network north of South Africa carries around 15 billion ntkm per year (excluding the mineral lines) and about 4 billion passenger-km (pkm). On average, 500 wagons, 20 passenger carriages, and about 20 locomotives will need to be replaced each year. Many of these will be secondhand from India or from South Africa. Based on these assumptions, the estimated cost of replacing rolling stock will average about $80 million per year, equivalent to about 0.4 c/ntkm or pkm. Allowing an estimated $20 million for facilities and maintenance equipment, the steady-state investment in the network north of South Africa should therefore be around $200 million per year.

The backlog investment is much larger. Assuming a 15-year backlog, an additional investment of about $3 billion would be required ($200 million per year over the 15 years). This expenditure could be spread over a 10-year period, equivalent to an annual cost of $300 million. The combined annual cost of rehabilitating and replacing rail infrastructure would therefore be $500 million over 10 years, after which investment would reduce to the steady-state level of $200 million per year.

Many proposed new routes would compete with existing road and rail routes. The rates that could be charged by lines running parallel with roads would be limited by the competing road freight rates, typically to 5 c/ntkm at most. For export mineral traffic, the rate that can be charged is also limited by the world-delivered market price, usually around 2–3 c/ntkm. As a consequence, it has been estimated that rail investment would be justified in purely commercial terms only if the forecasted traffic volumes were at least 2 to 4 million tonnes per year, though if they were only expected to cover their operating costs, they could probably be operated successfully at lower volumes of 0.5 to 1.0 million tonnes per year.

The Market

Railways in Africa are predominantly freight railways. Because of increasing competition with the road sector, they are experiencing slow—and sometimes negative—growth.

Some General Characteristics

Most railways in Africa carry far more freight than passengers—on average four times as much in traffic units. That ratio continues to increase: only on railways with limited competition from roads does passenger traffic constitute more than 20 percent of traffic units (as shown in figure 3.1 for TRC [Tanzania], Tazara, and Transrail prior to 2005). Figure 3.1 shows that the aggregate ratios for the concessioned and the unconcessioned railways do not differ widely and highlights the small scale of most railways in Africa. Excluding the South African railways, the busier railways typically carry 1 billion TUs per year; Transnet Freight Rail carries this volume in three days. (Other general traffic data can be found in appendix 3c.)

The average rail haul in the region is relatively long in the context of overall network size but not especially long compared to that of roads (figure 3.2). Some railways predominantly carry traffic from one end of the system to the other. For example, TRC, Tazara, and Transrail carry freight an average of 1,000 km. On the other hand, some smaller railways—such as the Mozambique and Uganda lines—feed freight to other railways, which subsequently carry traffic a few hundred kilometers farther.

South Africa at present accounts for over 70 percent of passenger-km in Africa, mainly because of its suburban commuter business. On most African railways, passenger trips primarily comprise travel between a country's capital city and major provincial centers. The average distances for passenger trips shown in figure 3.2 are therefore primarily based on these services. The Sitarail, Transrail, and Tazara networks have the only significant cross-border passenger flows. (Detailed passenger traffic data can be found in appendix 3c.)

Traffic Trends

Between 1995 and 2005, gross domestic product (GDP) growth in Africa averaged 4 percent per year. Trade and per capita GDP grew by about 1.5 percent per year. Countries that avoided political upheaval—such as Mali, Mozambique, and Tanzania—grew up to 50 percent faster than their neighbors. Despite the generally favorable economic background, however, only five railways saw an increase in both passenger and freight traffic. Two—in Namibia and South Africa—were parastatals. Three—Gabon, KRC, and Central East African Railways Company (CEAR)—were concessioned; the last of these grew despite cyclone damage. Outside of this group, only Botswana experienced an increase in passenger traffic. Railways have thus generally failed to capture traffic despite economic growth.

Figure 3.1   Passenger and Freight Traffic of Railways in Sub-Saharan Africa (Annual Average, 1995–2005, Excluding Spoornet)

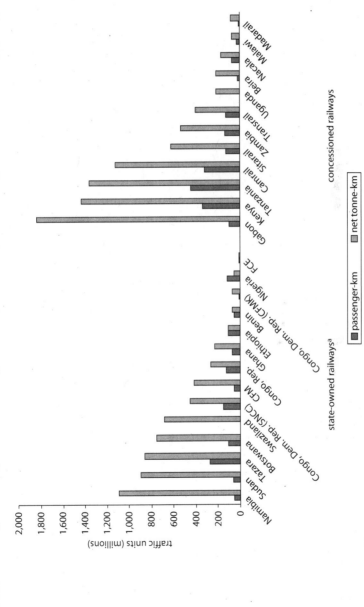

Source: Bullock 2009.

Note: CFM = Caminhos de Ferro de Moçambique; CFMK = Chemins de Fer Matadi Kinshasa; FCE = Fianarantsoa Côte Est Railway; SNCC = Société Nationale de Chemins de Fer Congolais.
a. Figures drawn from Bullock (2009) follow his distinction between systems that have been concessioned and those that remain in government ownership and operation.

Figure 3.2   Annual Average Distance Traveled on Railways in Sub-Saharan Africa, 1995–2005

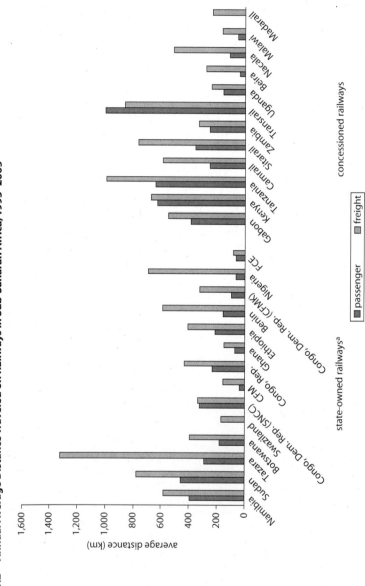

Source: Bullock 2009.

Note: CFM = Caminhos de Ferro de Moçambique; CFMK = Chemins de Fer Matadi Kinshasa; CFMK = Chemins de Fer Matadi Kinshasa; FCE = Fianarantsoa Côte Est Railway; SNCC = Société Nationale de Chemins de Fer Congolais.
a. Figures drawn from Bullock (2009) follow his distinction between systems that have been concessioned and those that remain in government ownership and operation.

In some cases, war and natural disasters significantly affected railway traffic. For example, Sitarail and the Democratic Republic of Congo's railways both experienced sharp reductions in traffic during periods of civil war. And CEAR suffered badly when a cyclone destroyed a major bridge; it took over two years to find funding for its repair. TRC (Tanzania) was badly hurt by a cyclone, too, in 1997. In other cases, traffic was limited by the availability of rolling stock, particularly locomotives across many railways.[4] When railways have improved this situation by obtaining new or secondhand locomotives or rehabilitating old locomotives, traffic has increased accordingly. Similarly, infrastructure rehabilitation on both Madarail and on the Sena line (part of the Companhia dos Caminhos de Ferro da Beira [CCFB] concession) has resulted in a sharp increase in traffic from a low base. Traffic trends over the decade (figure 3.3) were therefore determined more by supply factors than by underlying demand.[5]

Unfortunately, reducing traffic does not necessarily reduce the need for rehabilitation. Since the downturn in the world economy in late 2008, traffic for some commodities—such as transit cement and rice carried to Burkina Faso by Sitarail and wood exported through Camrail—has dropped 20 to 30 percent on a number of railways in the region, but the need for rehabilitation remains.

Passenger Traffic: Limited Prospects

Passenger rail services worldwide serve two distinct functions:

- Regional and long-distance intercity transport linking major centers to rural areas
- Transport of suburban passengers.

In many countries in Africa, railways have historically been the only practical mode of intercity passenger transport. In rare cases, rail is still faster than bus (for example, Yaoundé–Ngaoundere in Cameroon and Cuamba–Nampula in northern Mozambique), especially where unpaved roads present difficulties for road traffic in the rainy season. There are generally two passenger classes available, usually called first and third; the overwhelming majority of passengers travels third class (80 to 90 percent). Load factors on many trains are often quite high:[6] in Tanzania, the average third-class load factor was around 70 percent during the period 1995–2005. Passenger services also carry parcels and small freight, which can increase revenues by about 25 percent.

Figure 3.3 Traffic Growth on Railways in Sub-Saharan Africa

Annual average, 2001–05, compared with annual average 1995–2000

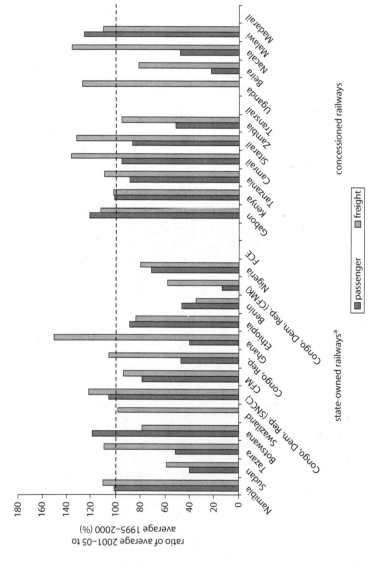

ratio of average 2001–05 to average 1995–2000 (%)

state-owned railways[a]   concessioned railways

passenger   freight

Namibia, Sudan, Tazara, Botswana, Swaziland, Congo, Dem. Rep. (SNCC), CFM, Congo, Rep., Ghana, Ethiopia, Benin, Congo, Dem. Rep. (CFMK), Nigeria, FCE, Gabon, Kenya, Tanzania, Camrail, Sitarail, Zambia, Transrail, Uganda, Beira, Nacala, Malawi, Madarail

Source: Bullock 2009.

Note: CFM = Caminhos de Ferro de Moçambique; CFMK = Chemins de Fer Matadi Kinshasa; FCE = Fianarantsoa Côte Est Railway; SNCC = Société Nationale de Chemins de Fer Congolais. No comparable data are available for FCE, Transrail, and Madarail. Some railways in the "concessioned" group were only concessioned close to or after 2005.

a. Figures drawn from Bullock (2009) follow his distinction between systems that have been concessioned and those that remain in government ownership and operation.

Figure 3.4   Comparison of Bus and Rail Fares and Travel Times

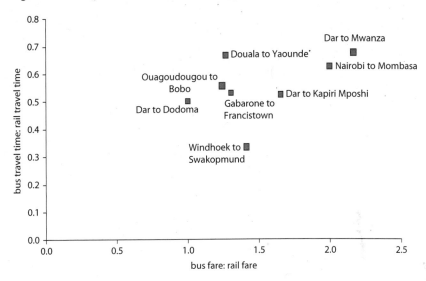

Source: Bullock 2009.

flows. International traffic tends to dominate railways that cross international borders. The main exception is the KRC, which transports much more traffic to and from Nairobi and other centers than to and from Uganda. Imports are primarily manufactured products such as cement, petroleum products, and general freight. Higher-value cash crops (such as coffee from Uganda) increasingly travel in containers, particularly on routes that cross a national border.

Severe directional imbalances in traffic are the norm. Even when the tonnage transported is nearly the same in both directions, many commodities require specialized wagons so that trains are rarely fully loaded in both directions. In some cases (such as export traffic from Zambia to connected ports), road vehicles delivering imports tend to backload freight at a marginal cost, leaving railways to transport the remaining freight without a compensating return load. Such practices accentuate the imbalance in rail traffic.

Rail traffic has decreased in many countries over the past years, coinciding with the abolition or restructuring of statutory agricultural marketing organizations. These organizations were often the only means for producers to market their crops, as they provided depots at key points on rail networks where producers could bring their products for storage and

Figure 3.5   Commodities Carried on Select Railways in Sub-Saharan Africa

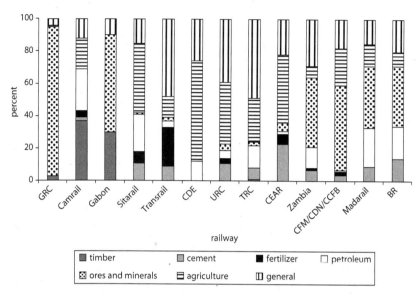

Source: Bullock 2009.
Note: CDE = Chemin de Fer Djibouti-Ethiopien; CDN = Corredor de Desenvolvimento do Norte; CFM = Caminhos de Ferro de Moçambique; GRC = Ghana Railway Company; URC = Uganda Railways Corporation. The data relate to specific years or averages of years around 2001. As the proportions do not change much from year to year, the broad picture shown is valid despite the fact that the data do not refer to the same year for each railway.

subsequent dispatch. Marketing channels for agricultural products are now more diversified, and, as a result, the railways have steadily lost market share. Abandoned rail-connected warehouses for export cash crops at ports such as Dar es Salaam are testimony to these changes.

Inland distribution networks for consumer and intermediate products have similarly changed. Although there are still inland depots for petroleum products, direct deliveries from main depots and refineries to end users are now more common, with small consignment sizes that are far better suited to road transport. General freight, whether containerized or not, is dispatched in relatively small consignments; mixed loads, with freight from two or three suppliers to the same destination, are common. Factor productivity is low (see appendix 3e). For traffic of this type, the costs of pickup and delivery can also make rail transport prohibitively expensive. In many cases, this small general freight and mixed-load traffic was lost to roads and has not been recovered even as railways were concessioned.

Freight Tariffs: Increasingly Competitive

Average freight tariffs between 1995 and 2005 were typically 3–5 c/ntkm (figure 3.6; appendix 3d).[7] Railways originally based tariffs on the value of the commodity being transported, charging low rates for low-value commodities such as fertilizers and high rates for manufactured goods.[8] Tariffs were sometimes affected by policy support for particular sectors, such as agriculture, often gained by special-interest lobbying.

Nowadays, tariffs are more determined by demand, being limited by competition either from roads or alternate routes, except in the occasional case of semi-monopolies—such as the Société Transgabonnaise (SETRAG) in Gabon. Railways with little competition, including the Democratic Republic of Congo railways (Société Nationale de Chemins de Fer Congolais [SNCC] and Chemins de Fer Matadi Kinshasa [CFMK]), Chemin de fer Congo-Océan (CFCO) in the Republic of Congo—for which road competition lacks security and is expensive (or impossible)—tend to have higher rates (see figure 3.6). But many railways do not fully understand their own cost structure, and their response to road competition has therefore been imperfect.

Other factors also affect tariff structures. For example, tariffs in Uganda's network are distorted by rail ferry operations, the short length of port-access lines, and a deliberate policy of equalizing tariffs across all three routes (direct rail, ferry via Kenya, and ferry via Tanzania) to promote competition.

Despite the pressure from road competition, tariffs still vary substantially both among commodities and among countries (figure 3.7). Tariffs for petroleum products and container traffic are generally high, while those for agricultural products and semibulk commodities such as cement and fertilizer are low. These differences reflect not only traditional, value-based tariff structures but also relative costs of carriage, volume (for example, many railways negotiate contract rates with high-volume users), and traffic direction. Thus, bulk commodities, which have higher net loads per wagon, are cheaper to carry than petroleum, which is normally carried in tank wagons that have a comparatively high ratio of gross to net tonnes and are almost always returned empty. Rates in the low-volume direction are generally around half to two-thirds of those in the high-volume direction, with rail rates similarly discounted under road rates.

The economic viability of transporting a specific commodity by rail is significantly affected by whether the origin and destination are rail connected—that is, whether a mine or a cement works has a rail siding

Figure 3.6 Average Tariffs for Passenger and Freight Traffic, 1995–2005

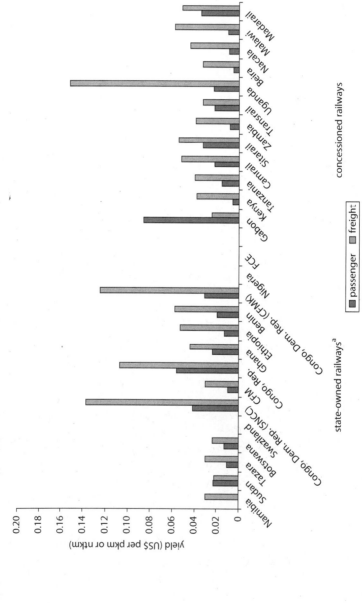

Source: Bullock 2009.

Note: CFM = Caminhos de Ferro de Moçambique; FCE = Fianarantsoa Côte Est Railway. No data are available for FCE, Nigeria, and Swaziland.

a. Figures drawn from Bullock (2009) follow his distinction between systems that have been concessioned and those that remain in government ownership and operation.

Figure 3.7 Average Tariffs by Commodity for Select Railways in Sub-Saharan Africa

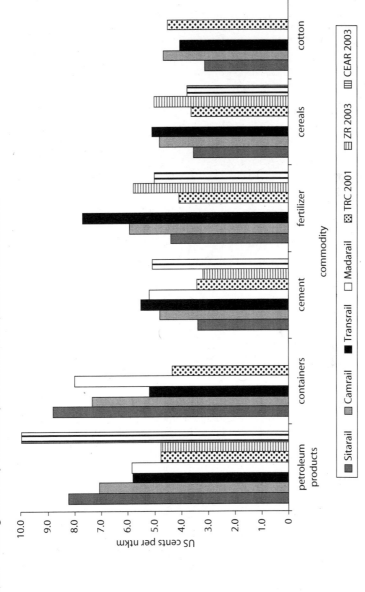

Source: Bullock 2009.
Note: ZR = Zambia Rail; Where not shown, average yields are for the period 1995–2005.

and ready access to a port or power station. If the origin and destination are not well connected, road shipment to and from the railway can cost up to the equivalent of 200 to 300 km of rail transport. Demand must be adequate for the construction of new rail siding to be economical. Traffic that comes from multiple origins and must be collected at a central depot before being dispatched by rail is therefore most vulnerable to road competition. On the other hand, mineral and other bulk loads from a single source tend to use rail as long as sufficient service capacity is available. Bulk loads are not immune to road competition, however; roads have been used for relatively short-distance intermine traffic in the Zambian Copper Belt, even though a rail network built for that purpose connects the mines and processing plants.

A cross-country comparison of freight rates and market shares needs to take into account not only physical factors such as infrastructure, vehicle type and quality, and freight, but also the direction of travel, overloading, and other institutional factors (figure 3.8). The wide variation in freight rates among geographical areas reflects regional variations in infrastructure and road vehicles, average length of haul, and institutional factors such as unofficial en route charges (bribes or forced extraction of illegal tolls), border-crossing procedures, and the impact of the freight associations common in Central and West Africa.

Some of the reasons for the regional variations are straightforward: the poor condition of roads in Central Africa and the Central Corridor in East Africa connecting Dar es Salaam, Burundi, and Rwanda; the very large trucks operating throughout southern Africa;[9] and the impact of the freight associations.

Why Are Railways Uncompetitive?

The inability to attract more traffic despite a large price advantage can be explained in several ways.

First, there is the extra cost of local road pickup and delivery for long-distance rail freight transport. Second, service quality (transit time, reliability, and security) is generally poor. Rail infrastructure is below par along most corridors. For a typical corridor, rail rates need to be about 15 percent less than road rates to cover the additional cost of road access to rails, and a further 15 percent less to compensate for inferior service quality.

The main obstacle to competitive rail service quality is institutional—a lack of trade facilitation and cross-border coordination. In the main

Figure 3.8   Indicative Freight Rates: 12-meter Container Inland from Port, 2003

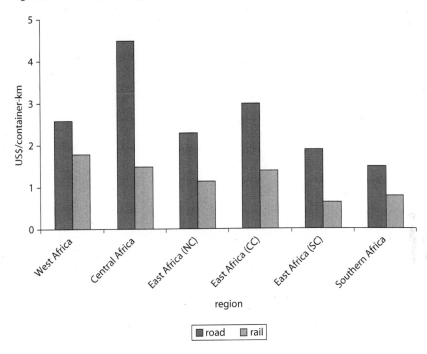

Source: UNCTAD 2003.
Note: CC = central corridor; NC = northern corridor; SC = southern corridor.

north-south corridor from South Africa to the Democratic Republic of Congo and Tanzania, rail transit times from the Democratic Republic of Congo to Durban have been quoted as 38 days—9 days for travel and 29 days for interchange and border crossing, despite the fact that the rail corridor is effectively under the control of a single operator from the border of the Democratic Republic of Congo to South Africa. By way of comparison, competing road transport by truck reportedly takes 8 days overall, only 4 of which are at border crossings.

Over and above these external disadvantages, many state-owned railways have difficulty competing against road operators because they do not have the freedom to set rates according to demand.

Competition from the road sector is strongest in southern Africa, which has the most liberal market structure, the largest trucks, and the best roads. Two other major factors influence road competitiveness: user charges and the prevalence of overloading. Few governments charge trucks adequate road use fees (see chapter 2 of this book), and overloading of trucks is commonplace, increasing necessary maintenance costs. Requiring railways to fund 100 percent of rail maintenance and improvements while tolerating inadequate road use fees and vehicle overloading on arterial routes creates a handicap almost impossible for most general freight railways to overcome.

Many individual African railways also face competition in the freight market from other corridors (Mbangala 2001). In West Africa, the inland countries (Burkina Faso, Mali, and Niger) have a choice of ports to and from which they can transport goods: Dakar (Senegal), Abidjan (Côte d'Ivoire), Conakry (Guinea), Takoradi and Tema (Ghana, by road), Lomé (Togo), and Cotonou (Benin). The Great Lakes region in East Africa has a similar range of competing outlets to the sea, only some of which are served by rail.

In sum, while most railways are able to carry bulk minerals with reasonable efficiency, they must offer a reasonable level of general freight service if they are to compete with roads. Conventional state-owned railways are poorly equipped to provide door-to-door service because of their fixed rates, low service levels, lack of commercial incentive to change, and the conservative management behavior that usually goes with these characteristics.

Concessioning can help. Concessionaires have already shown that they are prepared to use a range of initiatives to improve service quality and compete with roads. Some are physical, such as Sitarail's proposal to construct an intermodal terminal in Ouagadougou to service the surrounding region. Others are procedural, such as Zambia Rail's introduction of company customs bonds to reduce waiting times for import traffic at Victoria Falls.[10] Above all, however, private concessionaires have the commercial freedom, flexibility, and incentive to provide services that meet demand. Concessioned railways worldwide are increasingly integrated with transport chains either through participation in third-party logistics systems or by direct connection to primary production processes.

Institutional Arrangements

Until the 1980s, almost all African railway companies were publicly owned corporations, subject to general supervision by a ministry of transport mandated to develop and implement policy. Some had French-style contract plans that aimed to explicitly define the relationship between governments and railway companies. These arrangements were generally ineffective because governments rarely met their formal obligations to the public corporations' management.

A further step toward financial and managerial autonomy was the introduction of management contracts, under which an independent specialist agency agrees to manage publicly owned assets to achieve specified objectives. For example, the Indian RITES company supplied senior management to Zambia in the 1980s and Botswana Railways in the 1990s, and had a full management contract with Nigerian Railways in 1979–82. Togo Railways was managed by CANAC for some years but is now managed by RITES in association with a local cement company. The Democratic Republic of Congo has attempted two such contracts: the first, known as Sizarail, ceased with a change in government in 1997; the second is still in operation. The weakness of these arrangements was that so long as government was responsible for the provision and financing of all physical assets, the operational scope of the management contractor was severely limited.

For more effective commercial rail management, emphasis has been shifted to the creation of railway concessions since the early 1990s. In these concessions, the state remains the owner of some assets (typically infrastructure) but transfers the others (typically the rolling stock) to a concessionaire. The concessionaire assumes responsibility for operating and maintaining the railway. In some cases, such as the Sitarail concession, the government also purchases new rolling stock, which the concessionaire then finances with annual payments to the government.

The first concessioned railways were in West Africa: the Abidjan-Ouagadougou railway linking Côte d'Ivoire and Burkina Faso was concessioned in 1995, followed by railways in Cameroon, Gabon, and Malawi at the end of the 1990s. With the exception of southern Africa (Botswana, Namibia, South Africa, and Swaziland), which has not yet faced the financial crises that precipitated reform in most other countries, and countries suffering or recovering from civil disruption (Angola, Democratic Republic of Congo, and Zimbabwe), most countries in Africa are in the midst of some type of railway reform. Of the 30 countries with state-owned railways, 14 have opted for a concession arrangement, often under the pressure of multilateral and bilateral organizations that promise to finance asset rehabilitation and renewal. The railway in one country (Democratic Republic of Congo) operates under a management contract. Another four countries have begun the concession process, and others are planning to do so (map 3.2; appendix 3a).

Map 3.2   Railway Concessions Awarded in Africa since 1990

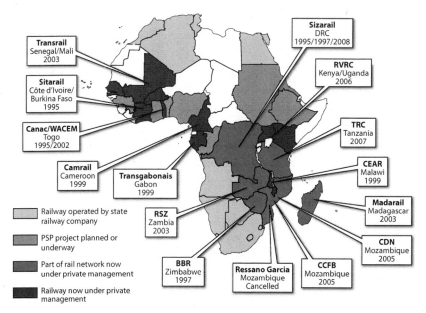

Transrail
Senegal/Mali
2003

Sitarail
Côte d'Ivoire/
Burkina Faso
1995

Canac/WACEM
Togo
1995/2002

Camrail
Cameroon
1999

Transgabonais
Gabon
1999

Sizarail
DRC
1995/1997/2008

RVRC
Kenya/Uganda
2006

TRC
Tanzania
2007

CEAR
Malawi
1999

Madarail
Madagascar
2003

CDN
Mozambique
2005

Railway operated by state
railway company

PSP project planned or
underway

Part of rail network now
under private management

Railway now under private
management

RSZ
Zambia
2003

BBR
Zimbabwe
1997

Ressano Garcia
Mozambique
Cancelled

CCFB
Mozambique
2005

Source: Bullock 2009.
Note: BBR = Belt Bridge Railway; CDN = Corredor de Desenvolvimento do Norte; RSZ = Railway Systems of
Zambia; RVRC = Rift Valley Railways Consortium; WACEM = West African Cement Company. Three different dates
are given for Sitarail because the concession was relet on three occasions.

Governance and Management of State-Owned Railways

Most of the remaining state-owned railways are subject to significant
political and governmental influence. Arrangements vary across countries, but typically the sector ministry (normally transport) exercises
political and administrative control, while the ministry of finance exercises financial control. Boards generally comprise a combination of
ministry and internal senior management officials—themselves often
appointed by the government—with occasional staff representation.
Parliaments provide nominal oversight. All too frequently, however,
this oversight is limited to an audit of company accounts presented in an
annual report, sometimes several years after the year in question.
Parliamentary sessions are often too short for the detailed review that
effective control would require.

The governing regulatory frameworks generally grant financial and
managerial autonomy to state-owned railways, and management methods
are supposed to be similar to those of private businesses. At the same

time, however, legal and regulatory frameworks provide greater opportunities for state intervention—at both the institutional and jurisdictional levels—than would be the case for privatized railways. Railway commercial initiatives are subject to frequent political interference, and government-authorized representatives in companies have decision-making capabilities. This latent conflict between the control and decision functions in state-owned railways discourages effective management.

Governments and politicians also have ulterior motives—often dictated by mutually exclusive social, electoral, and economic interests—which further complicate both the management of state-owned companies and the evaluation of their performance. Management often focuses on merely breaking even on a cash basis, which almost inevitably leads to financial difficulties when asset renewals are due.

Structure of Concessions

Railway concessions vary substantially in terms of contract length, the range of assets transferred to the concessionaire, the attribution of responsibility for investment during the concession, and the limitations on the commercial freedom of concessionaires, particularly in regard to passenger services.[11] The concession contracts in Africa to date are summarized in table 3.1.

Few governments have seriously considered the European model of full vertical separation in which track management and train operations are performed by different companies. There is thus little scope for extensive competition between different companies operating on the same track. But there are a number of cases of independent, noncompeting companies running trains on state-owned or concessioned railway lines. Magadi Soda Works ran its trains to Mombasa over the KRC line in Kenya and continues to do so over the concessioned Rift Valley Railways line. Senegal's concession to Transrail excluded the Dakar suburban service and traffic from the Société d'Exploitation Ferroviaire des Industries Chimiques du Sénégal (SEFICS), both of which now pay track charges to use Transrail track. In a rather more complex case, the concession offering in Zambia, which has extensive intermine operations in the Copper Belt, allowed bidders to choose to include any combination of Zambia's three railways: mainline operations, intermine operations, and passenger services. The winning bidder initially chose to include all three but subsequently decided to include substantially fewer intermine services in the concession. Those not included in the concession are still able to run trains over the concessioned tracks.

Table 3.1 Key Features of Concessions, 1993–2008

Country	Concessionaire	Date of contract	Initial duration of contract (years)	Initial capital of concession (US$ millions)	Planned 5-year investment (US$ millions)	Public service obligation
West Africa						
Burkina Faso	Sitarail	1995	15	8.8	63.3	Yes, but renegotiated
Côte d'Ivoire	n.a.	n.a.	n.a.	n.a.	n.a.	n.a.
Mali	Transrail	2003	25	17.2	55.4	No
Senegal	n.a.	n.a.	n.a.	n.a.	n.a.	n.a.
Togo	CANAC[a]	1995	n.a.	n.a.	n.a.	No
	WACEM[a]	2002	25	n.a.	n.a.	n.a.
Central Africa						
Cameroon	Camrail	1999	20	18.5	89.6	Yes
Democratic Republic of Congo	Sizarail[a]	1995	n.a.	n.a.	n.a.	n.a.
	Vecturis[a]	2008	2	n.a.	n.a.	n.a.
Gabon	Trans-Gabonais	1999	20	n.a.	n.a.	n.a.
	SETRAG	2005	30	n.a.	157	Yes

East Africa

Kenya	RVRC	2006	25	n.a.	About 100	Yes
Uganda	n.a.	n.a.	n.a.	n.a.	n.a.	n.a.
Tanzania	TRC	2007	25	n.a.	88	Yes

Southern Africa

Malawi	CEAR	1999[b]	20	n.a.	n.a.	Yes
Mozambique	CCFB	2004	25	19.7	152.5	Yes
Mozambique	CDN	2005	15	n.a.	n.a.	Yes
Madagascar	Madarail	2003	25	5.0	36.1	Yes
Zambia	RSZ	2002	20	6.1	14.8	Yes
Zimbabwe	NLPI	1998	30	n.a.	85[c]	No

Sources: Data collected from companies; Pozzo di Borgo 2006.

Note: CDN = Corredor de Desenvolvimento do Norte; RSZ = Railway Systems of Zambia; RVRC = Rift Valley Railways Consortium; SETRAG = Société Transgabonnaise; WACEM = West Africa Cement Company; n.a. = not applicable.

a. Management contract.

b. Transfer finally occurred in 2005.

c. Reported construction cost.

There is usually specific provision for the financing of system rehabilitation at the beginning of a concession.[12] In addition, concessionaires are normally responsible for financing track and rolling-stock maintenance and renewal during the period of the concession. In some cases, concessionaires have received loans to finance rolling stock, but many low-volume operators use secondhand equipment instead.

Railway concessions in Africa generally rely on either of two models for financing initial infrastructure investment:

- Governments finance the initial track rehabilitation and renewal costs, generally with specific-purpose loans from international financial institutions (IFIs), which offer grace periods, lengthy loan tenors, and below-market interest rates.
- Governments do not finance initial track renewal but commit to compensate concessionaires for their investment by the end of the concession agreement (as in the case of the KRC/Uganda Railways Corporation [URC], TRC, and Zambia railways). Special cases are the Beitbridge Railway, which relies on take-or-pay clauses (which give it a guaranteed revenue against which it can borrow); and Nacala, which is being funded at semicommercial rates.

In both models, the government usually agrees to purchase the unamortized portion of any infrastructure investment that the concessionaire will have financed by the end of its contract. When concessionaires fear that governments might not be willing or able to make such payments, they might limit their infrastructure investments as the contract period nears. Kenya and Uganda solved this problem in the KRC/URC concession by obtaining a partial risk guarantee from the World Bank to securitize their payment obligations to the concessionaire. In the most common arrangement, the state remains the owner of some or all of the railway's assets (normally the infrastructure) and transfers responsibility for operations, risks, and expenses to the concessionaire in the concession agreement.

Regulatory Framework for Concessions

The introduction of concessions has necessitated substantial changes in railways' legal and regulatory frameworks. Such changes were particularly important in Anglophone countries, where railways were state owned and the responsible ministry imposed wide-ranging economic regulations while leaving railways to self-regulate safety.[13] Concessions require more transparent economic and safety regulations. Tanzania passed a new railway law in 2003, and Zambia has drafted a new law that has not yet been implemented. Although Malawi plans to amend its railway act, it has still not done so.

Concessions agreements almost always have a predetermined duration. The concessionaire therefore generally leases the infrastructure (and sometimes the rolling stock) from the government. This arrangement requires that the ownership of the assets be transferred from the existing state railway operating company to a successor asset ownership authority. While the specific arrangements vary, such bodies generally are responsible for ensuring that the concessionaire maintains the railway assets properly and for funding capital expenditure that is not the concessionaire's responsibility. They often also effectively regulate safety, as they award operating licenses on the basis of technical competence. In Francophone Africa, these are the "patrimony organizations" (legacy organizations such as the Société Ivoirienne de Patrimoine Ferroviaire in Côte d'Ivoire and the Société de Gestion du Patrimoine Ferroviaire du Burkina in Burkina Faso). Agencies were also established with similar functions in some Anglophone countries (such as the Reli Assets Holding Company in Tanzania). The new bodies are often in theory funded from concession fees, but failure to make adequate provision for them is an ongoing problem in some countries and severely handicaps their ability to provide effective regulation.

Contracts normally distinguish between freight tariffs, which are generally deregulated, and passenger tariffs, which the state tends to control. Regulated passenger services are often managed using agreed-upon schemes under which operators are eligible for financial compensation (public service obligations payments) whenever the regulated tariffs do not cover their operating costs. These schemes have often failed to protect private operators, however, as governments have not honored their subsidy commitments. Passenger tariff indexation, when applied (such as for Sitarail, CEAR, and Transrail), is triggered by changes in conventional inflation indexes. Most concession contracts prevent rail operators from using promotional tariffs for more than a year if they do not cover their operating costs.

Economic regulation is frequently left to the general powers of a competent competition commission. In Zambia, for example, the Competition and Fair Trading Act, as administered by the Zambia Competition Commission, has broad powers of referral for the abuse of market power by dominant suppliers. In Tanzania, a regulatory body established specifically for the transport sector (Surface and Marine Transport Regulatory Authority, or SUMATRA) has authority over all land and marine transport. The separate railway regulatory agencies of Mali and Senegal have merged into a common railway monitoring agency serving both countries. Concession agreements generally delegate powers of referral for tariffs and control over third-party access to either the government or an independent authority.[14] In reality, however, many railway concessions in Africa lack formal regulatory structures with real power and are thus susceptible to market abuse.

Despite the lack of effective regulatory agencies, railways in the region are unlikely to require frequent protection from market abuse because the road transport sector, which generally offers services competitive with rail, limits the market power of concessions. Where freight rates have increased following concessioning, there has generally been a corresponding improvement in service quality. In most cases, rail freight rates are effectively determined by competition, either from roads or from rail routes serving an alternate port (such as the ports of Beira for the Nacala corridor and Abidjan, Lomé, and adjacent ports for Transrail). Relatively few railways have true monopolies over freight (Trans-gabonais's transport of bulk minerals such as manganese is a rare example).[15] A detailed study of four transport corridors involving a railway concession (and in some cases an associated port) confirmed the general absence of market abuse by monopolies (Pozzo di Borgo 2006).

If a concessionaire fails to comply with the terms of a concession, there are normally procedures for terminating the concession. To date, however, only three concessions (Ressano Garcia, which never became operational, Trans-Gabonais, and the RITES contract in Tanzania) have been terminated,[16] while two concessions (Transrail and Rift Valley) have changed operators.

Concessions have not been without difficulties. Concessionaires have faced delays and disputes regarding government compensation for unprofitable services. Other conflicts have centered on concession fees, time frames, and staff no longer required following concessioning. The failure of government ministries to coordinate their actions—which have included administratively imposed salary increases, restrictions on access to container facilities, and unfunded public service requirements—has also negatively affected the performance of several concessions.

Concessionaires: Motivated by Broader Self-Interest

Rail concessions in Africa have attracted a limited pool of private operators, mainly from southern Africa or from outside Africa completely.

These operators are of two types: those seeking to vertically integrate their distribution chains by acquiring dominant positions in specific production and transport sectors, and those specializing in a single transport activity (such as railways or ports). The first group appears willing to accept low rates of return from individual components of their distribution chains (especially railways) as long as the control that vertical integration provides yields sufficient benefits overall. The best example of this type of operator is the Bolloré group, which is the largest or second-largest shareholder in several railway and port concessions in Africa and also operates as a freight forwarder. Previously, the group also had agricultural production subsidiaries.

The most prominent of the second type of operators include Sheltam from South Africa (another South African operator, Comazar, is now defunct), NLPI from Mauritius, and RITES from India. They invest in transport operations, suggesting that concessions can be sufficiently profitable to attract private operators. The business cases for their rail investments often appear weak,[17] however, suggesting that these companies may be seeking the financial benefits of managing large investment plans (financed for the most part by governments) rather than long-term business cash flows.

Private companies are the majority shareholders of all concessions to date (table 3.2). State participation is highest in Mozambique, which has a 49 percent stake in both the CCFB and Corredor de Desenvolvimento do Norte (CDN) and is also a significant shareholder of the adjacent CEAR concession, and Tanzania, where the government has a 49 percent stake in the TRC. The government of Madagascar owns 25 percent of Madarail, and governments own 10 to 20 percent of Sitarail, Transrail, and Camrail. Local private ownership of any kind within competing consortia has been generally limited and in any case appears to make the process more vulnerable to political manipulation. Madarail has the highest level of local private ownership, at 24 percent, compared to 10 to 20 percent for Sitarail, Setrag, and Camrail. Employee shareholding remains under 5 percent where it exists at all. The boards of concessionaires generally reflect shareholding arrangements and thus include government-appointed members.

Operational Performance

The productivity of labor and rolling stock of railways in Africa is low compared to railways elsewhere. This is not surprising given most networks'

Table 3.2   Initial Concession Shareholdings

Concessionaire	Shareholder	Percentage ownership
Sitarail	SOFIB[a]	67
	Governments of Côte d'Ivoire and Burkina Faso	30
	Employees	3
Transrail	Canac-Getma (France and Canada)	78
	Governments of Mali and Senegal	22
Camrail	SCCF (Cameroon)[b]	85
	Government of Cameroon	10
	Employees	5
Setrag	Comilog (France)	84
	Local private operators	16
RVRC	Sheltam (South Africa)	61
	Other foreign investors	15
	Local private investors	25
TRC	RITES (India)	51
	Government of Tanzania	49
CEAR	Edlow Resources and Railroad Development Corporation (United States)	51
	Mozambican local investors (including CFM)	49
CCFB	Ircon[c]	25
	RITES (India)	26
	Government of Mozambique (through CFM)	49
CDN	Same as CEAR	
Madarail	Madarail[d]	51
	Government of Madagascar	25
	Manohisoa Financière	12.5
	Other private operators	11.5
RSZ	NLPI	Majority
	Transnet (South Africa)	Minority

Source: Bullock 2009.
Note: Ownership in a number of concessions has changed since these data were published. CDN = Corredor de Desenvolvimento do Norte; CFM = Caminhos de Ferro de Moçambique; RSZ = Railway Systems of Zambia; RVRC = Rift Valley Railways Consortium.
a. Société Ferroviaire Ivoiro-Burkinabé (SOFIB) was majority controlled by Bolloré (France). Sixteen percent of stock was intended for sale on the Abidjan Stock Exchange.
b. Société Camerounaise des Chemins de Fer (SCCF), a holding company controlled by Bolloré. Comazar, a privately operated and managed company that included South Africa's Spoornet and Transurb Consult (a subsidiary of the Belgian National Railways), also held substantial shares of SCCF, but has since sold its interests in Cameroon and elsewhere to Vecturis, a Belgian firm founded by two ex-Comazar employees.
c. Indian Railways Construction Corporation.
d. Madarail was majority owned by Comazar at the time of concession.

low traffic volumes and poor infrastructure conditions (Mbangala and Perelman 1997). Concessioned railroads have better productivity indicators, a result explained in part by increases in traffic but mostly by major cuts in employment.

Labor Productivity: Low but Improving

Most railway companies in the region have streamlined their workforce to some extent over the past 10 to 15 years. This is often a prelude to concessioning but in some cases also reflects a company's general effort to improve efficiency. Although the labor productivity of most African railways has improved, it remains low by world standards:[18] few railways in the region annually achieve over 500,000 TUs per employee (figure 3.9).

South Africa's Transnet Freight Rail has the highest labor productivity of any railway system in the region. Its average productivity was 2.5 million TUs per employee between 1995 and 2005, and it reached 3.3 million in 2005 (Thompson 2007). This figure reflects the intrinsically high productivity of mineral transport: the labor productivity of its dedicated iron ore and coal export lines (Orex and Coalex) were 9 million and 38 million, respectively, compared to only about 1.5 million for its residual general freight business (about 40 percent of Spoornet's traffic).

Gabon also had high average labor productivity over that period, reaching 1.8 million TUs per employee in 2005. Like Spoornet, Gabon has a high proportion of mineral traffic; a third party owns and operates the trains used for its mineral transport, which further increases labor productivity.

The labor productivity of most other railways in the region is low. In some cases, this deficiency reflects the railways' lack of outsourcing and continued reliance on labor-intensive methods, for example, in track maintenance and wagon loading. The very low productivity of other railways (for example, Benin, Democratic Republic of Congo, Ghana, and Nigeria all achieve less than 100,000 TUs per employee), however, is a result of their failure to cut staff despite declining traffic. When wages are low, redundant employment may not be financially catastrophic for a railway. Nevertheless, having too little work for too many employees erodes morale and is a strong disincentive for improving efficiency in the use of other assets. Railways that pay low wages also find it hard to recruit and retain the technically competent staff required by the technology that could improve service quality.

Rolling-Stock Productivity

The productivity of rolling stock is determined by several factors: the proportion of usable stock, the proportion of available stock, the usage of available stock (in hours per day), the commercial speed of operations, and the power of available locomotives. Railways in Africa are deficient in all of these respects. Better management can certainly improve rolling stock and locomotive productivity by disposing of surplus assets and

Figure 3.9 Labor Productivity of Railways in Sub-Saharan Africa

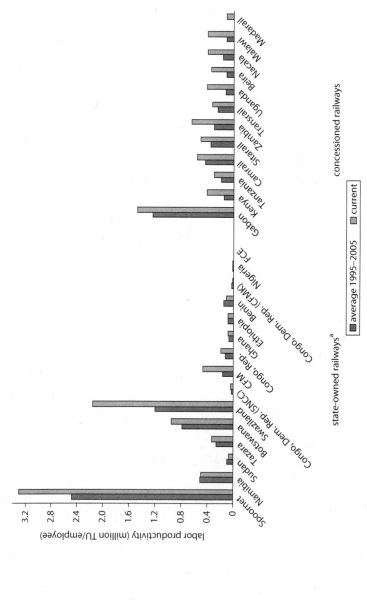

Source: Bullock 2009.
Note: CFM = Caminhos de Ferro de Moçambique. No data were available for FCE (Fianarantsoa Côte Est Railway). Some railways were concessioned close to or after 2005. This figure should therefore not be used to assess the effect of concessioning on productivity. Current figures are for the latest available year, typically 2005.
a. Figures drawn from Bullock (2009) follow his distinction between systems that have been concessioned and those that remain in government ownership and operation.

improving the supply chain for spare parts, but it cannot improve low axle loads and low commercial speeds.

Low fleet availability limits the locomotive productivity of railways in the region. On a given day, less than 40 percent of many railways' stock is available. In 2008, for example, the average availability of SNCC's fleet in the Democratic Republic of Congo was limited to only 10 of 22 main-line electric locomotives and 13 of 47 diesel locomotives, or 45 percent and 28 percent, respectively. At the other extreme, Swaziland, with a labor productivity reaching 2.159 million TUs per employee in 2005, also showed high locomotive productivity because, like Botswana, it carried a substantial proportion of transit traffic (75 percent), which is relatively simple to operate and for which third parties own and maintain the wagons. Gabon, which also has high locomotive productivity, and Swaziland are relatively new railways, while Botswana has benefited from substantial investment in the past 30 years.

Passenger carriage productivity varies widely among railways (figure 3.10). Between 1995 and 2005, for example, Camrail, Ethiopia, Nacala, and Tazara averaged around 5 million pkm per car annually, compared to under 500,000 pkm per car in the Democratic Republic of Congo and Sudan. Some railways with high productivities simply operate small fleets of overcrowded carriages. More typical are railways such as Camrail, which operates a regular service with reasonable load factors—say 40 to 50 passengers per vehicle (Murdoch 2005). For these railways, annual distance traveled per vehicle averages 100,000 to 130,000 km with an average load of 40 to 50 passengers; passenger carriage productivity therefore ranges from about 4.0 to 6.5 million pkm. As long as demand is sufficient to keep most of the fleet operating, availability is generally reasonable—often well over 80 percent.

Freight wagon productivity is around 1 million ntkm per wagon in Swaziland (largely due to the prevalence of transit traffic carried in "foreign" wagons, which do not appear in the base for the calculation, while the traffic that the foreign wagons carry in Swaziland is counted). Several other railways have a productivity rate of over 500,000 ntkm per wagon. Yet wagon productivity on many state-owned railways (including some concessioned to private operators at the end of the study period) is very low—less than 200,000 ntkm per wagon (figure 3.11). This is usually the result of demand for rail freight transport falling without corresponding reductions in the wagon fleet (wagons can have useful lives of 50 years or more). Wagon maintenance is straightforward, normally requiring only a limited range of

Figure 3.10 Passenger Car Productivity (Average, 1995–2005)

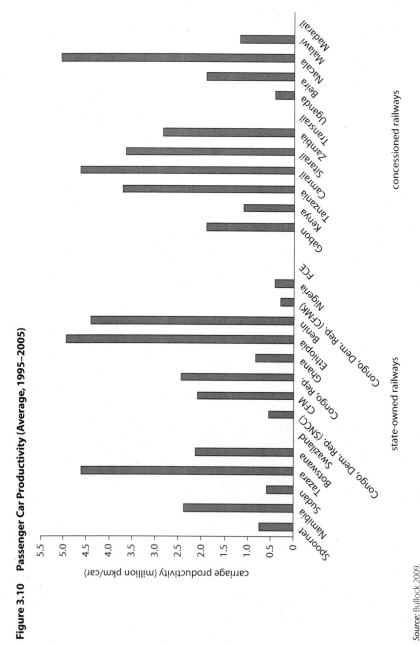

Source: Bullock 2009.
Note: CFM = Caminhos de Ferro de Moçambique; FCE = Fianarantsoa Côte Est Railway. No data are given for Swaziland and FCE because they are essentially transit railways operated by other companies' equipment.

Figure 3.11 Freight Wagon Productivity (Average, 1995–2005)

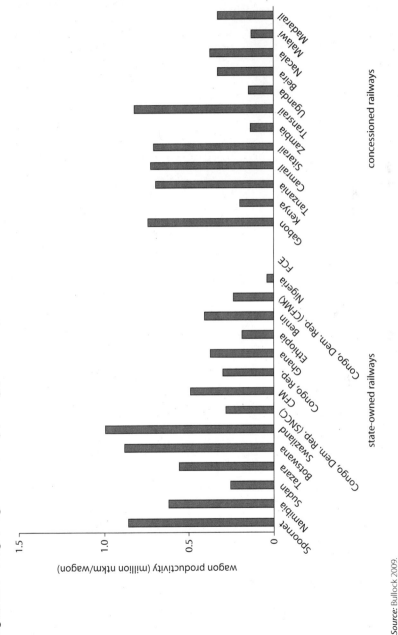

Source: Bullock 2009.
Note: CFM = Caminhos de Ferro de Moçambique; FCE = Fianarantsoa Côte Est Railway. No data were available for Madagascar-FCE. Some railways were only concessioned close to or after 2005. This figure should therefore not be used to assess the effect of concessioning on rolling-stock productivity.

spare parts. Wagon availability for a busy railway should therefore be well over 80 percent.

The average annual distance that a wagon travels depends on its cycle time (the interval between successive loadings), which in turn is a function of the efficiency with which both railway operators and customers load and unload the wagons. In general, a wagon on a well-run railway should be able to travel at least 50,000 km per year.[19] Given an average wagon load (excluding empty running) of about 20 tonnes on the region's 15-tonne-axle-load systems and about 30 tonnes on its 18 tonne systems, a well-run railway that is running 50,000 km per year per wagon should easily achieve annual productivity of 1 million ntkm per wagon. In practice, the low productivity of many of the region's railways for 1995–2005 reflects very low annual wagon usages of 10,000 km or less, the result of excessively large (and generally obsolete) wagon fleets. As can be seen from figure 3.11, 11 railways out of 26 (around 42 percent) achieve less than 300,000 ntkm per year (Sudan, Democratic Republic of Congo–SNCC, Republic of Congo, Ghana, Ethiopia, Democratic Republic of Congo–CFMK, Nigeria, Kenya, Zambia, Uganda, Malawi).

Impact of Concessioning on Productivity

Concessioned railway companies in Africa have higher labor and asset productivity than state-controlled companies. In fact, the labor productivity of concessionaires is on average twice that of their state-owned counterparts (Phipps 2008).

Changes in labor and asset productivity for four railways over the five years prior to concessioning and in the period since are illustrated in figure 3.12, using four key indicators: (i) labor productivity (traffic units per employee), (ii) locomotive productivity (traffic units per locomotive),[20] (iii) wagon productivity (net tonne-km per wagon), and (iv) carriage productivity (passenger-km per carriage).

Labor productivity increased in each concession. Camrail's labor productivity rose sharply upon concessioning as traffic grew, but it then stabilized after about three years. It now appears to be increasing once again. The civil war in Côte d'Ivoire caused service suspensions for Sitarail in 2003–04, which interrupted the operator's upward trend until the situation stabilized. After concessioning, CEAR retained only two-thirds of its staff, and at the same time, traffic grew by about 30 percent on an adjusted annual basis. Its productivity rose sharply as a result. The collapse of the Rivi Rivi Bridge left the northern half of CEAR's network and its associated staff with very little traffic, and consequently the operator's

Figure 3.12   Labor and Asset Productivity for Four Railways before and after Concessioning

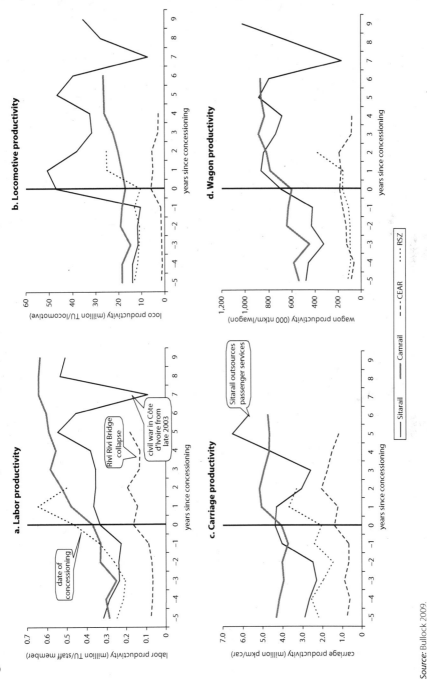

Source: Bullock 2009.

Note: Year of concessioning = year 0; index at year 0 = 100. Black vertical line represents year of concessioning. RSZ = Railway Systems of Zambia.

labor productivity fell in 2003–4.[21] With CEAR's takeover of the Nacala line in 2008 and the reopening of the Rivi Rivi Bridge, these figures should improve. Most of the other recent concessions are likely to experience similar increases in labor productivity, based on staff cuts: Madarail reduced its workforce by 50 percent, both the Mozambique concessions by about 60 percent, the Zambian concession by over 30 percent, and the Senegal concession by about 40 percent.

Sitarail and Zambia experienced sharp increases in locomotive productivity after concessioning, mostly due to the scrapping of their surplus equipment. Traffic growth in Cameroon resulted in steadily increasing productivity. The introduction of more powerful locomotives in 2007 approximately halved Camrail's fleet size, and productivity therefore doubled (not shown in figure 3.12). Locomotive productivity for CEAR has exhibited little change; in reality, however, the operator has not used much of its fleet and has bought some locomotives solely as sources of spare parts. Carriage and (especially) wagon fleets also showed improvements in productivity following concessioning, a result of traffic growth and scrapping of surplus stock.

The productivity increases stemming from staff cuts and the scrapping of rolling stock after concessioning make the managers of the former government-run railways look less effective than they actually were. In many cases, key managers remained after concessioning; the government railways' large surpluses of labor often reflected not managerial incompetence but political decisions to protect employees irrespective of railway efficiency.

Concessionaires, almost without exception, also operate their railways with better asset utilization. In some cases, this improvement reflects greater use of assets that were previously lying idle (this is particularly the case with wagons). In others, it reflects the fact that surplus assets that could not be written off by the state companies for bureaucratic reasons were not taken over by the concessionaire.

Service: Slow, Unreliable, and Unsafe

The key determinants of service quality for both passenger and freight services are adequate capacity and frequency, safety, security, cleanliness, speed, and reliability. Based on these criteria, the service quality of many railways in Africa is poor. While concessioned railways cannot necessarily reduce transit times, they generally try to improve other aspects of service quality.

Safety in particular is a cause for concern across the region. In the past 10 years, several major accidents have occurred, resulting in significant casualties. Some of these accidents were due to basic operating failures. Derailments, while a potential hazard on all railways, are extremely frequent in Africa. Although many occur at slow speeds in rail yards and pose a minimal safety threat, most African railways report over 100 derailments per year and some report 200, even 300. By comparison, the whole of the U.S. railway system typically has around 2,000 derailments each year, of which one-third occur on main lines, not in rail yards or on sidings; Canada has around 150 mainline derailments each year, and India less than 100. Relative to traffic volume, derailment rates in Africa are at an order of magnitude greater than most other regions, even allowing for track quality: U.S. Class 2 track (which has a 40 km/hr speed limit and is generally equivalent to the poorer segments of the mainline network in Africa) has one derailment for every 10 million wagon-km, while the rate for railways in Africa is some 30 times higher.

Financial Performance

Although almost all state-owned railways in Africa produce annual accounts, these are generally of little value other than as official records of revenue earned and expenditure made. Cash shortfalls are generally made good by grants from governments (often included as revenue). Most railways just about break even on a cash basis, after receipt of government support, but there is almost always a substantial deferral of necessary maintenance. Depreciation may be recorded on a historic or replacement cost basis, but, as a noncash item, it is of little practical consequence for most railways. When the maintenance backlog becomes too great, it is typically addressed using a loan from the government, with the expenditure listed in the books as an investment.

The profitability of commercial concessionaires can be assessed a little more realistically.[22] Sitarail and Camrail, which have been concessioned the longest, both make modest profits (Pozzo di Borgo 2006). CEAR in Malawi suffered long delays in finalizing the companion CDN concession in Mozambique and operated with working losses for several years around 2001. The performance of the Railway Systems of Zambia (RSZ) is unknown, and the Kenyan and Tanzanian concessions have not been in existence long enough to draw legitimate conclusions. Because of the lack of reliable information on the profits and losses of these concessionaires, a disaggregated approach to evaluating their financial performance, looking separately at the major elements of cost and revenue, is appropriate.

Costs per Traffic Unit

A railway's transportation costs per unit of traffic are determined by several factors: the unit costs of functional activities (track maintenance, train operations, and so on), traffic type, the efficiency of resource utilization, and the load factors achieved. The average cost per traffic unit across several railways in Africa between 2000 and 2005 is illustrated in figure 3.13.

Unit costs for most railways lie in the range of 2–5 cents per TU. Costs are lowest for Botswana—a relatively flat railway with modern equipment, good track conditions, and a base mineral traffic. They are highest for OCBN and Tazara.

Disaggregated Real Profitability Analysis

The following sections provide a more detailed analysis of costs, revenues, and overall financial performance for three railways—two from low-income countries (Tanzania and Zambia) and one from a middle-income

Figure 3.13   Cost per Traffic Unit for Railways in Sub-Saharan Africa (Average, 2000–05)

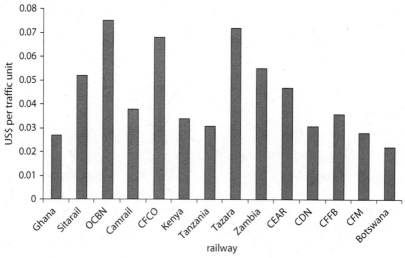

Source: Bullock 2009.
Note: CDN = Corredor de Desenvolvimento do Norte; CFM = Caminhos de Ferro de Moçambique.; OCBN = Organisation Commune Benin-Niger des Chemins de Fer et des Transports.

country (Botswana). All data are from the period 2000–02, before the concessioning in Tanzania and Zambia.

Costs for railways can be divided into four categories:

1. The avoidable costs of train operation. These are the costs that could be cut if some services ceased operation. They can conveniently be measured as the costs of train crew, rolling-stock maintenance, fuel (or power), and passenger handling (ticket selling/commission and some station staff).[23]
2. Rolling-stock capital renewal costs.[24] These can be derived by converting the original capital cost into an equivalent annual sum based on asset life (which differs according to the characteristics of individual assets) and, using a real discount rate, assuming a 4 percent real rate of return. These are effectively sunk costs.[25]
3. Infrastructure operation and maintenance costs. These are referred to as "access charges" in this report. There are many methods for determining what portion of these costs should be charged to each type of service; for simplicity, a straightforward full-cost allocation method is used here.
4. The capital cost of infrastructure renewal.

The first two of these categories are together referred to as the "above-rail costs." Estimates of revenues and costs will be used to assess the financial performance of the railways, disaggregated into passenger and freight services.

Passenger Service Profitability

None of the three railways studied can cover its above-rail costs for its passenger traffic. The only one to come close is Tanzania, which has the highest earnings per carriage-km; the other two cover only about 50 percent of their above-rail working expenses. Even Tanzania performs poorly when rolling-stock capital renewal is included in costs, based on current usage of rolling stock. When access charges are included (but not the capital cost of infrastructure renewal), the railways recover only between 20 and 40 percent of their costs. These figures might improve to between 30 and 65 percent with improved utilization of track and rolling stock (by halving the depreciation per unit of traffic).

Some railway tariffs (including those in Tanzania) are essentially administered within a government regulatory framework that considers only a subset of total costs. Nevertheless, many of the more poorly performing railways in the region would be unable to cover the above-rail costs of their existing set of passenger services even if they had the freedom to set their own tariffs. The cost recovery for passenger services on the three rail systems in 2002 is shown in figure 3.14.

In the early 2000s, long-distance passenger railways needed to earn around $1 per carriage-km to be financially viable in the long term. Earnings of $0.75 per carriage-km would have covered avoidable costs of operation and a reasonable amount of the periodic maintenance required for the rolling-stock capital renewal costs. Third-party grants would have been needed to fund renewal costs of rolling stock (such as new locomotives and new carriages). Most economy-class coaches in the region can carry about 80 passengers, and a dynamic load factor of 70 percent is a reasonable if somewhat ambitious assumption. Railways would thus require a minimum tariff for third-class travel of 1.5–2.0 c/pkm, below which they require government support.[26]

Freight Service Profitability

In contrast to passenger services, railways normally earn enough to cover the avoidable operating costs of freight services and sometimes enough

Figure 3.14   Passenger Service Cost Recovery, 2002

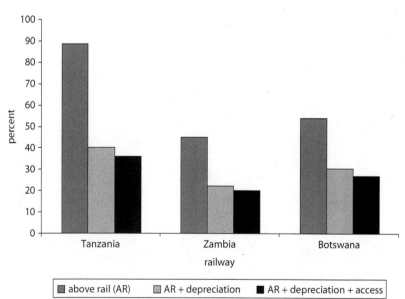

Source: Bullock 2009.

to cover rolling-stock capital costs and infrastructure cost. The cost recovery for freight services in 2002 is shown for the same three railways in figure 3.15. Each of the three railways earned enough in 2002 to easily cover their above-rail costs and most of their above-rail depreciation and access costs. Only Botswana had a cost recovery of over 100 percent, but even it did not earn enough to cover the cost of renewing infrastructure. In 2002, railways would need to earn $0.80–$1.00 per wagon-km on their freight services, with operating costs of $0.60–$0.80 to be fully self-sustaining.[27] (See Bullock 2009 for the calculations supporting this conclusion.)

Concession Financing: Toward a New Structure

The majority of concession financing is provided by governments, which in turn get such financing via low-interest sovereign loans from IFIs, usually on terms that are not commercially available.[28] Concessionaires provide a relatively low percentage of equity (see figure 3.16).

In most cases, the value of rolling stock transferred to the concessionaire outweighs the small amount of equity contributed by concessionaires (despite the poor condition of the rolling stock). As a result, the

Figure 3.15   Freight Cost Recovery, 2002

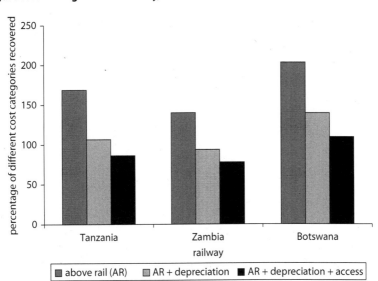

Source: Bullock 2009.

Figure 3.16   Financing Structure of Select Concessions

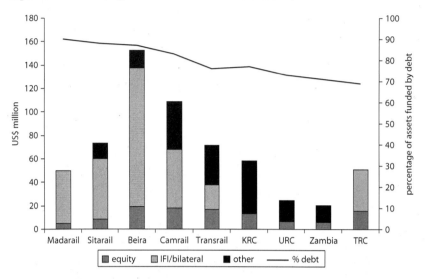

Source: Bullock 2009.
Note: The Madarail concession reflects the September 2005 restructuring of an IFI loan for €21 million on-lent by the government to Madarail via a grant, which is included in the IFI/bilateral funds listed in the figure. Since the Sitarail concession is an *affermage* leasing the assets from a state holding company, Sitarail does not carry the debt contracted by the state holding companies ($56.7 million out of $63.6 million in total debt). Nevertheless, because Sitarail services the debt, it has been included in the figure.

public sector assumes a significant portion of the financial risks associated with infrastructure investment. This situation reflects the weak financial basis of many of the concessions, which are prone to significant liquidity problems and which cannot support major investment on a commercial basis. Major-asset maintenance and reinvestment are therefore recurrent problems.

Concession fees often have two components: variable (generally a percentage of gross revenues) and fixed. In some cases, fees reflect the cost to government of providing assets to a concessionaire (as in a leasing agreement). More often, however, they are designed to ensure that private operators share their revenues with the government. Successful railway concessions also normally pay taxes (such as a value-added tax, personnel social taxes, and income tax), the sum of which exceeds concession fees when taken over the projected lifespan of many concessions. Over their projected operational life spans (typically 20 to 25 years), concession fees and income tax each range from 2 to 14 percent of gross revenues, while net profit margins range from zero for Madarail to 25 percent for Zambia (figure 3.17).[29]

Figure 3.17   Concession Fees

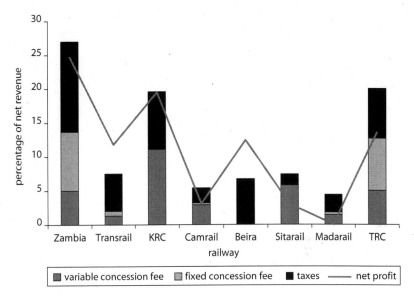

Source: Bullock 2009.

Bid projections must be interpreted with care. In the case of Zambia, the fixed component of the concession fee actually increased steadily throughout the concession period. The agreement stipulates that the concessionaire is responsible for paying the fee in full only if traffic levels are within 3 percent of the very ambitious traffic projections included in the reference financial model; otherwise, the fee will be adjusted downward. Based on these conditions, it is unlikely that the Zambian government has received any substantial payment from the concessionaire. Interestingly, the well-established Camrail and Sitarail concessions tend to project modest profit margins. These contrast starkly with the more optimistic forecasts of the newer concessions of Zambia, Kenya/Uganda, and Tanzania, whose projections of aggregate returns to government (through concession fees and taxes) and to concessionaires (in the form of profit) range from 35 to 50 percent of net revenue—equivalent to an operating ratio of 50 to 65 percent.[30] Very few railways worldwide achieve similar ratios, including larger systems with modern equipment and much denser traffic than is carried by African railways.

Governments should consider the combined impact of both taxes (primarily income tax) and concession fees when negotiating a concession, given the size of taxes and fees relative to the desired level of investment expenditure. A concession fee based on net revenue is undoubtedly easier to define,[31] but income tax provides more flexibility, as the tax liability would automatically decrease in years in which there are unforeseen difficulties.

Regardless of the terms of the concession agreement, governments and advisers must realize that concessionaires can support only a limited amount in financial outflows—whether in the form of concession fees, borrowing costs, or rolling-stock acquisition costs. Proposed concessions that include high levels of both debt and concession fees are more likely to require renegotiation in the future. In the case of Madarail, for example, debt obligations outlined in the initial investment plan would have reached 18 c/ntkm in the fifth year after concessioning (2008), which would have been impossible to service given the railway's average revenue of only 5 c/ntkm. As a result, the government of Madagascar agreed to assume two-thirds of Madarail's debt in June 2005, after less than two years of operations. Similarly, Camrail's debt obligations would have reached about 8 c/ntkm in its fifth year. In 2005, Camrail and the government agreed on a concession amendment that transferred the cost of future track financing to the government until 2015 and capped the concession fee at 4 percent of net revenue.

The Way Forward

Concessioning of railways in Africa has generally improved their performance. But sustaining that improvement will depend critically on addressing a range of observed defects in the way concessions are designed and managed, and in the relationship between rail and road pricing policies.

The Role of Concessions

Railways that have not been concessioned—except for those immediately adjacent to South Africa (Botswana, Namibia, and Swaziland)—have continued to deteriorate over the past decade. On the other hand, the asset and labor productivities of the concessioned railways have clearly improved. Better internal management has allowed concessionaires to streamline their cost and pricing structures, to seek new traffic, and to improve service quality. With two significant exceptions (Zambia and Transrail), the railways have fulfilled the passenger service requirements of their concession agreements without raising the cost of passenger travel. They have also taken more realistic views about the future role of rail in the passenger markets, recognizing the limitations of rail in markets where it is unable to compete with faster road transport. Although many governments in Africa consider concessions a last resort, they still appear to be the way of the future.

The Key Issues

Few, if any, concessions have generated the cash flow needed to invest in infrastructure, and concessionaires are especially averse to investing in infrastructure with a life significantly beyond that of the concession. Probably most disappointing to governments has been the lack of infrastructure investment not funded by IFIs.

Concessions in Africa are unlikely to be financially attractive to traditional operators and instead appeal to companies that can secure financial benefits not directly linked to the railway operations (such as controlling an entire distribution chain or supplying of rail equipment). Generating increased interest from private operators will require changes in the market environment and financial structure of concessions, especially in five priority areas:

Priority 1. Proper compensation arrangements for financially unviable passenger services

Governments should provide operators with timely compensation for unprofitable passenger services. Any arrangement should be simple, easily auditable, and subject to periodic review.

Priority 2. Improved capacity and willingness of private operators to finance track renewal

These improvements could be achieved in two ways:

- More realistic concession design and implementation, which would ensure that concessions (and therefore proposed track investments) were financially sound and that government's payment for the unamortized value of the assets owed to the concessionaire at the end of the concession period was reasonable (providing that the concession agreement allowed for a possible extension of the concession period)
- Independent finance of infrastructure renewal, perhaps through a land transport fund financed by both the road and rail sectors, into which concession payments could be made (instead of into the government general revenue fund)

Priority 3. Effective and efficient regulation of private rail operators
The main need here is to strengthen the regulatory bodies' capacity as
well as to impose annual independent financial and operational audits as
part of concession contracts. The regulatory bodies could be funded
through concession fees or a land transport fund.

*Priority 4. A consistent and professional government approach to
railway concessions*
Such an approach would require a properly staffed and funded oversight
body with sufficient authority to control government action toward private rail operators. It should have ready access to experts in railway technology and finance. Finally, the body should monitor the concession and
report to the country's ministers of transport and finance.

Priority 5. A consistent policy toward infrastructure use across modes
As shown in chapter 2, road users are often charged fees too small to
cover the costs of required maintenance. This allows road operators to
charge artificially low rates, which limits the rates that railways can charge
for freight transport. As a result, concessionaires have lower revenues and
thus fewer funds to maintain and upgrade rail infrastructure. A consistent
policy to address this problem should create a fairer and more competitive transport environment in Africa.

Notes

1. The main source document for this chapter is Bullock (2009). Other important sources are Pozzo di Borgo (2006) and Mbangala (2001).
2. Rail gauge is the distance between the inner sides of the heads of the two parallel rails that make up a single railway line.
3. The traffic units carried by a railway are defined as the sum of the passenger-km
   and the net tonne-km carried. This is a widely used standard measure, although
   it has some limitations as an indicator (for example, a first-class passenger-km in
   a French train à grande vitesse is treated the same as a passenger-km in a
   crowded suburban train). The relative weighting of passenger and freight is con-
   ventionally taken as 1:1, although alternative weightings have been used on
   some railways, usually in an attempt to reflect relative costs.
4. This situation also occurs at peak periods on much larger railways. For example, Spoornet endured heavy criticism in 2007 and 2008 for lacking sufficient
   capacity to carry coal and mineral exports to ports.
5. Years with abnormal events (such as wars and cyclones) were excluded from
   the averages. Hence the figure for Société Nationale de Chemins de Fer

Congolais (SNCC) covers only a very short period, as the railway was not in operation from 1995 to June 2004.

6. The dynamic load factor is the ratio of total passenger-km to total seat-km. Not all passengers travel to the end of a route, so occupancy is by definition much higher at the maximum load point.

7. Tariffs (in terms of 2008 U.S. dollars) were greater than these averages in many cases; the 2008 freight yield for Camrail was 9.7 c/ntkm, for Sitarail 6.4 c/ntkm, and for Transrail 8.0 c/ntkm. These may not be sustainable as fuel prices fall but it seems they will remain above the 10-year average.

8. This structure also reflects the relative densities of these traffics: a wagonload of coal will generally weigh more and cost more overall to haul—but less per net tonne—than a wagonload of textiles. Railways therefore normally charge a comparatively high rate per tonne for low-density freight.

9. Much of the long-distance freight in southern Africa is carried on large, double-trailer, seven-axle combination rigs, which have a nominal maximum gross vehicle mass of 56 tonnes. Typical payloads for dense loads such as cement or steel are 30 to 40 tonnes.

10. If the railway does not pay the bond, the wagons are detained while a message is dispatched to Lusaka, the consignee deals with the bank, and the documentation is returned. It could take some weeks before the traffic is cleared, tying up wagons in the interim.

11. Concessions do not always include the entire network. In some cases, branch lines were excluded, such as the Mulobezi and Njanji branches in Zambia, the Lumbo branch near Nacala in Mozambique, and the St. Louis branch in Senegal.

12. An exception is the Sitarail affermage, where the assets were leased to the concessionaire and responsibility for investment remained with the government.

13. Some countries had an independent government inspector of railways. The inspectors were frequently promoted from the railway, however, and desired to return after their government tenure. Such an arrangement discouraged an honest inspection of incidents for which the inspector's future superior would be ultimately responsible.

14. Many contracts (for example, those for Société d'Exploitation Ferroviaire des Industries Chimiques du Sénégal [SEFICS] in Senegal and Magadi in Kenya) include clauses that allow third parties to operate on the concessioned infrastructure. The Camrail and Sitarail concession contracts include usage exclusivity periods of five and seven years, respectively, during which third parties cannot operate trains on their networks. Others, such as Madarail and Transrail, allow access from the start.

15. And even here there is the long-term threat of the alternate rail route through the Republic of Congo.

16. This excludes the special case of Sizarail in the Democratic Republic of Congo, which was terminated following a military coup.

17. A Chinese consortium that bid for the Beira concession, which was awarded to RITES in 2004, had a calculated return on equity of only 2 percent in its financial proposals.

18. Comparisons of railway productivity should be made with care: the number of staff that a railway employs is a function of how much work (especially major-asset maintenance) the railway outsources and how much it keeps in house. Also, the almost universally used measure of work done by railways is traffic units (the sum of net tonne-km and passenger-km), which can be an unreliable indicator, as servicing one passenger-km generally requires more resources than one net tonne-km. Measures of productivity based on traffic units therefore favor railways that primarily transport freight, and particularly those transporting a high proportion of minerals, which are heavy and require only simple servicing. A rate of 1 million TUs per employee would be good in African circumstances. Transnet Freight Rail is helped by its heavy-haul lines and also because it has dropped most of its passenger services. Very few developed countries outside those having specialized long-haul freight railways have reached a rate of 3 million TUs per employee—most Western European countries are around 700,000 to 1 million TUs per employee, but this rate is affected by heavy passenger volumes.

19. It should be able to travel much more if the train carries a single commodity between only two locations. In the early 1980s, such a "block train" (a train run as a single unit and not at any time split up) ran on Zimbabwe's railways, carrying coal between Hwange and the Zisco steel plant at Kwekwe. The wagons on these trains traveled around 200,000 km per year.

20. The CEAR locomotive productivities ignore the scrap locomotives that were purchased for spare parts, which tend to inflate the productivity figure.

21. These statistics illustrate the difficulties with such broad measures of productivity. Because of the traffic shortages caused by the bridge collapse in 2004, CEAR locomotives did 25 percent of their work on hire to Caminhos de Ferro de Moçambique (CFM), which is not reflected in the traffic statistics.

22. Some suggest that although concessionaires publish low profits, they have charged significant fees for providing management services and the like. See Pozzo di Borgo (2006).

23. A proportion of infrastructure costs also depends on usage and should, strictly speaking, be included. But for many of the more basic low-density railways, the incremental impact of passenger services on infrastructure is relatively small unless the services are suspended, in which case significant changes in track and signaling standards can often be made.

24. These costs have been termed "above-rail depreciation," assuming that depreciation is based on the renewal cost of assets rather than the historic cost.

Costs calculated in this way are unlikely to appear in the accounts of railways in Africa.

25. Most rolling stock in use in Africa—except South Africa—is not in good enough condition to be resold.

26. This figure is obtained as follows: 80 seats per carriage at 70 percent dynamic load factor (that is, passenger-km: seat-km) is equal to 56 pkm per carriage-km (maximum). If the earnings needed were $1.00 per carriage-km (minimum) to include rolling-stock renewal, then the minimum tariff would be $1.00/56, or 1.8 c/pkm. This is rounded to 1.5–2.0 c/pkm. Lower load factors (which are a function of service frequency and train size) would increase the minimum, although in most cases it would still be comparable with bus fares. Service frequency and travel time remain the limiting factors for railways.

27. Excluding concession fees, typically around $0.05 per wagon-km.

28. Many other developing countries use the same practice to loan to publicly owned railways. In the mid-1990s, on-lending was usually made at a premium (for example, the International Development Association provided Côte d'Ivoire with a loan at 0.75 percent interest, which the government on-lent at 8 percent interest to Sitarail for its concession). To attract operators, subsequent concession loans featured sharply reduced premiums—as low as 0 percent in the case of Madarail. As a result, the average interest on the Madarail operator's debt is only 1.73 percent, with a 7-year grace period and a 25-year tenor.

29. Net profit margins equal total operating revenues minus total operating costs minus depreciation and interest on debt capital minus taxable income.

30. Operating ratio equals expenses divided by operating revenues.

31. Concessionaires can extract funds under the guise of costs in a number of ways, such as inflating "technical assistance" fees for providing management.

References

Bullock, R. 2009. "Railways in Sub-Saharan Africa." Africa Infrastructure Country Diagnostic Background Paper 17, World Bank, Washington, DC.

Mbangala, M. 2001. *Le transport ferroviaire en Afrique noire: Fonctionnement, performances, perspectives*. Liége, Belgium: Editions de l'Université de Liége.

Mbangala, M., and S. Perelman. 1997. "L'efficacité technique des chemins de fer en Afrique Sub-Saharienne: une comparaison internationale par la méthode de DEA." *Revue d'Economie de Développement* 3 (93): 91–115.

Murdoch, Jill. 2005. "Assessing the Impact of Privatization in Africa—Case Study of Camrail." World Bank, Washington, DC.

Phipps, L. 2008. "Review of the Effectiveness of Rail Concessions in the SADC Region." United States Agency for International Development, Gaborone, Botswana.

Pozzo di Borgo, P. 2006. "Review of Selected Railway Concessions in Sub-Saharan Africa." Africa Region Report, World Bank, Washington, DC.

Thompson, L. S. 2007. "Spoornet and Transnet Sectoral Reference Paper." Thompson, Galenson, and Associates, Washington, DC.

UNCTAD (United Nations Conference on Trade and Development). 2003. *Efficient Transport and Trade Facilitation to Improve Participation by Developing Countries in International Trade*. Geneva: UNCTAD.

CHAPTER 4

Airports and Air Transport: Policies for Growth

A viable, stable air transport industry is critical to Africa's integration into the global economy.[1] In an increasingly liberalized world air-transport market, however, many of Africa's indigenous air transport operators—state-owned flag carriers in particular—have failed. While the region's air traffic is growing, overall connectivity is not, and regional carriers have the worst safety record in the world. Furthermore, air traffic control (ATC) and airport infrastructure are inadequate. Fortunately, there are promising signs. New carriers are entering the intercontinental market and are beginning to realize the benefits of market liberalization. The challenge now is to build on these successes.

Airport Infrastructure

The discussion of air transport begins by looking at the capacity, condition, and utilization of airport infrastructure as well as the status of ATC and navigation aids for commercial air traffic in Africa.

Service and Connections: Falling Off
Africa has at least 2,900 airports.[2] Yet less than 10 percent of these receive scheduled services. Moreover, that number is falling. While 318 airports

received scheduled services in 2001, only 280 airports were estimated to be receiving services in November 2007, and for only 261 of these was service throughout the year. With the exception of airports in the Banjul Accord Group (BAG), between 20 and 40 percent fewer airports received scheduled services in 2007 than in 2001 (see appendix 4b).[3]

The level of international connectivity, measured in terms of the number of airports receiving direct international service, is also in decline (see map 4.1 and appendix 4c for shifts in overall connectivity).

Air Traffic Control and Navigation: Inadequate and Poorly Financed
Ground-based navigation installations are sparse in Africa (see appendix 4d). The main corridor in the east of the continent—stretching

Map 4.1   International Connectivity in Sub-Saharan Africa: Winners and Losers 2001–07

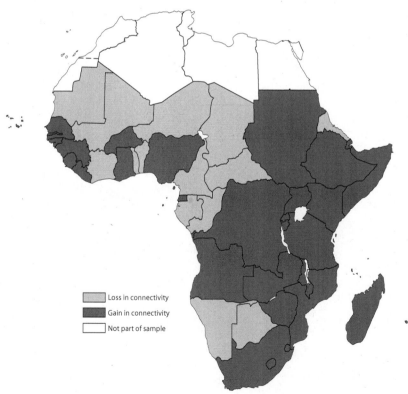

Source: Analysis by H. Bofinger.

from South Africa to the Arab Republic of Egypt—has the most ATC installations. Ghana, Nigeria, Tanzania, Uganda, and Zimbabwe have some. But the rest of Africa, including Ethiopia—one of the region's important hubs—lacks coverage. Malawi once had some installations, but the equipment became too expensive to maintain and fell into disrepair; it is no longer salvageable.

Even the existing ATC installations do not necessarily use radar separation, which is a technique for issuing directions and headings to aircrafts based on radar images. East Africa is typical. In Kenya, only Nairobi uses full-time radar vectoring,[4] while Mombasa switches to radar procedures only if weather conditions demand it. Tanzania has a good radar installation in Dar es Salaam, with a secondary radar range in excess of 300 kilometers (km), but lacks radar-certified controllers and therefore cannot use radar vectoring. The Ugandan military provided the country with radar services, using aged technology, until a new civilian system was installed in 2008. This unsatisfactory pattern is common throughout Africa. The safety risks that it entails will only grow as traffic increases.

The lack of radar coverage in the region is not an insurmountable challenge. Modern surveillance technology is moving away from radar installations toward the more advanced (and cheaper) automatic dependent surveillance-broadcast (ADS-B). In this system, the aircraft determines its position using a global navigation satellite system and transmits it to a ground station, which then relays it to the ATC center. Positions obtained using modern global positioning system (GPS) technology can be accurate within 30 meters, avoiding the challenges of using radar technology to locate aircraft accurately at long distances and to detect changes in their speed. ADS-B helps separate aircraft, which is not a problem in lightly trafficked areas, and provides important navigation information to pilots. Some ADS-B systems also allow nearby aircraft to broadcast their positions to one another, provided they have the proper equipment. ADS-B is being considered in a planned redesign of ATC in the Southern African Development Community (SADC) region. The air transport sector could clearly benefit from this new surveillance technology, which is only about a quarter of the cost of radar systems and has lower maintenance costs. In future, most aircraft will probably have their own GPS, and airports will learn to take advantage of the technology as it becomes more widespread.

Most airports in the region with an estimated capacity of 1 million passengers or more have an instrumented landing system (ILS).[5] They are far less frequent in smaller, older airports, however, where outdated nondirectional beacon systems are still prevalent. Today, satellite technology provides low-cost replacement options for many ground-based navigation systems. Nevertheless, it appears that in many cases either no plans have been made or no funding has been obtained by national civil aviation authorities (CAAs) for the replacement of increasingly obsolete technologies (Schlumberger 2007).

Airport Infrastructure Capacity

The effective overall capacity of an airport is determined by the facilities with the lowest capacity; such facilities may be airside (such as runways and airport parking space) or landside (such as terminals).

Airside capacity: Capable of economical expansion. A single-runway airport operating with a five-minute lag between flights could theoretically accommodate 144 flights in 12 hours—equivalent to over 1,000 flights a week. With an average passenger load of 120, such an airport could service over 17,000 passengers a day, or over 6 million passengers per year. Yet Johannesburg International Airport is the only airport in the region whose traffic volume exceeds this figure. Even assuming a 20-minute lag between flights, the theoretical capacity of a single-runway airport would be over 1.5 million passengers per year. Based on a comparison of theoretical runway capacity and actual air traffic (appendix 4e), Africa already has sufficient potential airport capacity. Existing airports should therefore focus on maximizing their effective capacity. When extra capacity is needed, rehabilitation is generally more economical than new construction (see appendix 4f).

Many African airports have a low-cost design that limits runway capacity. On landing, aircraft must use a turning bay at the end of the runway and taxi back up the main runway to the airport ramp, or apron, where they are parked, loaded and unloaded, refueled, and boarded. The access to the apron is usually in the center of the runway. This arrangement is fine if there is enough time between departing and arriving aircraft to complete the procedure, but high-volume airports require parallel taxiways with multiple turnoff ramps from the runway. A common, and economical, solution for airports with the turning bay configuration is to construct a parallel taxiway onto which aircraft move at the end of the runway. This makes a five-minute lag between flights quite manageable. An additional constraint is that airports often have narrow peak periods of aircraft arrivals, which puts pressure on both runways and terminals. In this case, flights should be rescheduled to avoid unmanageable traffic. Minor investment in taxiways and better management of capacity can thus obviate the need for major investments in new runways in most African airports in the near future.

Landside capacity: Careful management required. Inadequate passenger terminal capacity is more common. Data on passenger throughput of African airports are surprisingly sparse. Table 4.1 therefore gives firm figures only for years for which the data is thought to be most reliable, which explains the large number of empty cells in the table. A comparison of reported terminal capacity and passengers at African airports shows that several are operating at or above design capacity (table 4.1). Some airports have already begun to address the problem. For example, Nairobi's airport is upgrading its terminal to accommodate over 9 million passengers.

Decisions to upgrade airport terminals, however, must be made on a case-by-case basis. Airport planners usually assume the need for 20 square meters (m^2) of terminal per international traveler at any one time, or between 0.007 and 0.010 m^2 multiplied by the total number of annual passengers. But such formulae must be treated with caution, as space requirements depend on airport use patterns. In particular, the pressure on terminal capacity will be a function not only of the maximum number of flights per hour but also of the ratio of that maximum to the weekly average. For the three airports with the highest number of maximum flights per hour (Johannesburg, Nairobi, and Lagos), the ratio of maximum flights per hour to average flights per week was less than three to one, while many of the smaller airports have ratios of more than six to one (see appendix 4b). In such circumstances, rescheduling arrivals and departures may be a much more economical solution to overcrowding of smaller airports than investment in extra terminal capacity.

Infrastructure Conditions: Fraying at the Edges

Nearly all of the airports with services in November 2007 had at least one paved major runway. Only 12 of these airstrips were unpaved, most in countries with recent or ongoing military conflict. It appears, however, that 25 percent of the 173 African airports for which satellite images

Table 4.1   Airport Terminal Capacity vs. Reported Passengers and Estimated Seats

Country	City	Airport	Reported capacity (millions)	Reported passengers (millions)						2007 estimated seats (millions)
				2000	2003	2004	2005	2006	2007	
South Africa	Johannesburg	JNB	11.9	—	—	—	—	—	19	25.3
Kenya	Nairobi	NBO	2.5	—	—	—	4.3	—	—	6.3
Mauritius	Mauritius	MRU	1.5	—	—	—	—	2.2	—	3.0
Senegal	Dakar	DKR	1.0	—	—	—	—	—	—	2.5
Tanzania	Dar es Salaam	DAR	1.5	—	—	—	—	—	—	1.9
Zambia	Lusaka	LUN	0.4	—	—	—	—	—	—	1.3
Kenya	Mombasa	MBA	0.9	—	—	—	—	0.6	—	1.1
Zimbabwe	Harare	HRE	0.5	—	—	—	—	1.0	—	1.1
Mali	Bamako	BKO	0.4	—	—	—	—	—	—	0.7
Djibouti	Djibouti	JIB	0.5	—	—	—	0.1	0.5	—	0.6
Rwanda	Kigali	KGL	4.4	0.1	—	—	—	—	—	0.5
Nigeria	Kano	KAN	0.5	0.3	—	—	—	—	—	0.4
Malawi	Lilongwe	LLW	0.2	—	—	0.2	—	—	—	0.4

Source: Bofinger 2009.
Note: — = not available.

were available are in marginal or poor condition, and 21 percent are in poor condition. On the other hand, only about 4 percent of the region's air traffic passes through marginal or poor airports (see table 4.2).

There is limited reliable information on the quality of airside infrastructure. For example, the ILS at Maseru International Airport in Lesotho is so unreliable that the scheduling integrity of the only airline servicing the airport, South African Airlink Express, has been compromised.[6] In other cases, modern global navigation satellite systems may have been designed and financed, and are known by the financing agency to be complete and operational, but are not in the inventory of airside services and installations in the Aeronautical Information Manual or in databases such as that of Jeppesen.[7] Airside infrastructure is an area where more systematic collection and publication of data, either by the International Civil Aviation Organization (ICAO) or by the regional economic communities, could improve system performance.

Airports with higher traffic volumes generally have higher-quality airside infrastructure. Main hubs, such as Johannesburg and Nairobi, have adequate airside infrastructure, including standard runway length and ILS. Lower-quality infrastructure is much more prevalent among airports with low traffic volumes (below a million seats per year). For example, although relatively few airports in the region have unpaved runways, some countries have a high number of airports with poor runway conditions. Data from the International Air Transport Association (IATA) suggest that among African countries that have not recently undergone conflict, Tanzania stands out in having five airports using unpaved runways for advertised, regularly scheduled services. However, an informal domestic aviation sector in Africa, not recorded in the IATA data, may utilize even more unpaved runways.

Table 4.2   Overall Runway Quality in Africa

Rating	Airports	Percent	Seats	Percent
Excellent	31	17	69,666,792	63
Very good	51	28	26,574,283	24
Fair	52	29	9,285,100	8
Marginal	8	4	2,291,844	2
Poor	37	21	2,419,054	2
Total	179	100	110,237,072	100

Source: Author's analysis of data collected by the World Bank.

Airport Charges: High

Airport landing charges are high in Africa, although they vary considerably by airport and by aircraft. Comparison of charges for three aircraft types across 15 airports in Sub-Saharan Africa and 3 in North Africa with FraPort in Frankfurt, Germany (figure 4.1), shows that charges at Sub-Saharan African airports were on average 30 to 40 percent higher than at FraPort, while those in North Africa were comparable or lower. (Charges were particularly high in Cameroon, Côte d'Ivoire, and Ghana, but even adjusting for those outliers, they averaged 29 percent higher at African airports.)

That the discrepancy increases dramatically with aircraft size suggests that airports charge intercontinental travelers more, perhaps to generate foreign currency revenues. In some cases, passenger fees exceed $80 per passenger. On the other hand, airports in Sub-Saharan Africa rarely have other sources of revenue, such as shopping, car rentals, and duty-free concessions, which contribute a large proportion of overall airport revenues in industrialized countries. The higher charges in the region are therefore unsurprising.

Figure 4.1   Airport Charges Overall, by Aircraft Type across 19 Sample Airports

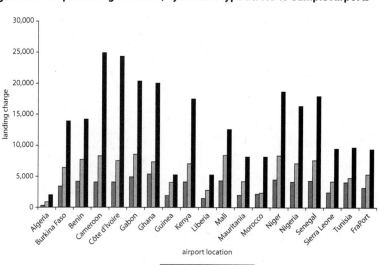

Source: ADPI 2008.

Ownership and Management: Scope for More Private Sector Participation

There are four ownership and operation schemes for airports: (i) public ownership and operation, (ii) regional ownership and operation, (iii) public ownership and private operation, and (iv) private ownership and operation.

The first model is still common in Africa. Like governments of poor countries in other regions, the governments of countries in Africa often consider airports to be public infrastructure that provides revenue and foreign currency. Even if the airport is corporatized (as in the case of the Airports Company South Africa), the state retains majority ownership. However, even airports with operational surpluses fail to undertake necessary maintenance and reinvestment (Button 2008). The success of this model is thus questionable.

Regional ownership is most common for secondary airports and is often used by central governments to remove less profitable airports from the national budget. It is also found in federal countries, especially those with strong airport markets, such as the United States. This form of ownership is unlikely to benefit regional airports in poorer countries with weak provincial government systems and is therefore generally inappropriate for Africa.

There are several models for public-private partnerships (PPPs): joint ventures, partial and majority divestitures, management contracts, and concession contracts. Table 4.3 shows the few recorded attempts at PPPs in African airports. They have occurred in markets of all sizes: Cameroon, a small market that serves below 1 million seats a year; Tanzania, which serves more than 1 million seats a year (an average size for the region); and South Africa, the largest market in Sub-Saharan Africa. Cameroon was the only country in the region with a management contract covering a system of seven airports owned by the Aéroports du Cameroun. Its major stakeholders were Aéroports de Paris, with 34 percent, and the government of Cameroon, with 24 percent (the remaining stakes were shared by other carriers and a bank). But when Aéroports de Paris failed to meet the agreed-upon requirements for funding the Douala International Airport rehabilitation in 2004, the government took over its share. This model has thus also proved less than perfect.

The majority of private participation in African airports is through concessions. Under a concession agreement, the government continues to fund infrastructure investment while the concessionaire assumes responsibility for service provision. This arrangement allows private firms to

Table 4.3 Public-Private Investments in African Airports

Country	Financial closure year	Project name	Type of PPP	Project status	Location	Contract period	Terminal year	Multiple systems	Number of transactions	Government granting contract	Investment year	% private
Cameroon	1993	Aéroports du Cameroon	Concession	Operational	7 airports	15	2008	Yes	7	Federal	1993	71
Côte d'Ivoire	1996	Abidjan International Airport	Concession	Operational	Abidjan	15	2011	No	1	Federal	1996	100
Djibouti	2002	Djibouti International Airport	Concession	Operational	Djibouti	n.a.	n.a.	No	1		2002	0
Kenya	1998	Jomo Kenyatta Airport Cargo Terminal	Greenfield project	Operational	Nairobi	—	—	No	n.a.	Federal	1998	100
Madagascar	1991	Aéroports de Madagascar	Concession	Concluded	12 airports	15	2006	Yes	12	Federal	1991	34
Mauritius	1999	Mauritius Airport	Management and lease contract	Concluded	Port Louie	5	2004	No	1	Federal	1999	100

Nigeria	2006	Murtala Muhammed Terminal One	Greenfield project	Construction	Lagos	25	2027	No	1	Federal	2006	100
South Africa	1998	Airports Company Ltd.	Divestiture	Canceled	Johannesburg, 11 airports	n.a.	2005	Yes	11	Federal	1998	20
South Africa	2000	Kruger Park Gateway Airport	Divestiture	Operational	Phalaborwa	n.a.	n.a.	No	1	Federal	2000	100
South Africa	2000	Rand Airport	Divestiture	Operational	Gauteng	n.a.	n.a.	No	1	Federal	2000	80
South Africa	2001	Mpumalanga Airport	Greenfield project	Operational	Nelspruit	—	—	No	1	State/ provincial	2001	90
Tanzania	1998	Kilimanjaro International Airport	Concession	Operational	Kilimanjaro	25	2023	No	1	Federal	1998	100

Source: Analysis by H. Bofinger of data from World Bank 2009.
Note: n.a. = not applicable; — = not available. There are more PPPs, such as the partial privatization of the airport holding company Aéroport de Libreville, Gabon, in 1996. But most others are more concentrated on management contracts and specified services, rather than full operations of and investments in airports.

offer specific services, such as SwissPort's passenger counter services in Johannesburg and Dar es Salaam and private contractors' cargo-handling functions in lesser-known airports, such as Mwanza in Tanzania. Contract bidding occurs in regular cycles, and terms vary from airport to airport. Concessioning of specific services is a well-developed model in airports throughout the world, and may be the most appropriate and sustainable form of PPP for Africa.

Full privatization is rare among airports and is generally attractive only for airports with substantial passenger traffic that is potentially profitable. One example is that of the British Airports Authority, which owns the three main London airports (Heathrow, Gatwick, and Stansted) as well as the three main Scottish airports (Edinburgh, Glasgow, and Aberdeen). However, it has been argued that because of the authority's monopolistic nature, airport charges have soared, service quality declined, and reinvestment in basic airport infrastructure has been insufficient (Osborne 2007). Following an inquiry by the UK Competition Commission, the authority was required to sell off Gatwick, Stansted, and either Glasgow or Edinburgh.

The Airports Company South Africa, which owns 10 airports in South Africa, appears to follow this model. In practice, however, the company is controlled by the government of South Africa. Meanwhile, the privatization of complete airports is slowing worldwide: noticeably fewer transactions occurred in 2007 than in the immediately preceding years (ACI 2008). This trend is likely to continue.

Regulatory Institutions: Struggling to Maintain Adequate Staff and Funding

In most countries worldwide, a general aviation law establishes and authorizes regulatory bodies, which then implement necessary regulations. Many countries use U.S. Federal Aviation Administration standards. Air transport regulatory bodies generally comprise both a civil aviation authority and an airport operations organization (or organizations). In most cases, the CAA is either an agency of the ministry of transport (as in South Africa) or a statutory body under the sponsorship of the ministry. The CAA typically provides ATC and navigation services and is responsible for safety oversight and certification of airports, aircraft, and personnel. In some countries, the CAA acts as a government adviser or government agent in international air service regulation. The airport organization typically provides or regulates all airport services, including instrumented landing facilities.

CAAs are often set up as quasi-commercial bodies and publish annual reports and financial accounts. For example, the South African Civil Aviation Authority is funded by a combination of direct and indirect fees and direct government funding of its accident investigation functions. It charges direct fees to airports for its services, which are passed on to airlines as a charge per passenger landed. It also levies a general aviation fuel tax. In some countries with large land areas located under major air routes, overflight fees charged to transiting airlines provide significant air navigation revenues and thus an important source of CAA funding. The allocation of such funding can be politically contentious. The revenues from services provided by a truly independent regulatory body would be received directly by that body and applied to the sector. In many cases, however, the government treasury receives the revenues, and the agency is forced to negotiate for its share.

Two factors limit the effectiveness of regulatory bodies in safety oversight. First, airlines can offer highly trained professional safety inspectors substantially higher salaries than the typical CAA in Africa, which cannot afford sufficiently capable staff. Second, regulation is subject to abuse by political influence. For example, a politically well-connected person may be allowed to operate an aircraft that does not meet safety standards and would not be allowed to fly in another country. Political autonomy and independent funding are therefore essential for effective regulatory bodies. The poor safety record of air transport in Africa can be attributed to a lack of both.

Regional Safety Oversight Bodies: Filling the Gaps

To address Africa's shortcomings in oversight, regions have begun to pool resources. With support from the U.S. Department of Transportation's Safe Skies for Africa Program,[8] a regional CAA was recently formed in East Africa to augment the capacity of national air safety systems with pooled funds and shared staff. The Agence pour la Sécurité de la Navigation Aérienne en Afrique et à Madagascar (ASECNA) pools air navigation services and other infrastructure and manages eight airports in its 15 member countries. Based in Dakar, ASECNA manages 16.1 square km of airspace (1.5 times the area of Europe), providing services that are the responsibility of a CAA in many other countries. Finally, projects under the Cooperative Development of Operational Safety and Continuing Airworthiness Programme (COSCAP) of the International Civil Aviation Organization are being planned for several of the regional organizations in Africa, including SADC, the Economic and Monetary

Community of Central Africa (CEMAC), the Common Market for Eastern and Southern Africa (COMESA), and BAG. The aim of these projects is to resolve regional safety oversight issues and to harmonize regulations on a regional basis.

Operations

Starting from relatively low levels by world standards, air transport service and patronage have been growing steadily in all sectors and in most regions. Intercontinental traffic is concentrated in three hubs. Liberalization of the international markets has increased market concentration, and there are an increasing number of low-density markets with a sole supplier. Protection of national flag carriers is a continuing impediment to growth in some countries. Equipment is getting younger and is adapting better to specific market demands.

Traffic Rates: Low but Growing

African air transport has experienced significant growth in the past decade, especially between 2001 and 2004 (table 4.4). Nevertheless, with just under 12 percent of the world's population, Africa still accounted for less than 3.7 percent of the global market in 2007. Market supply, which in 2007 consisted of roughly 72.3 million passenger seats, grew by an annual average of 6.2 percent between 2001

Table 4.4   Estimated Seats and Growth Rates in African Air Transport Markets

Market	Estimated seats, 2001 (millions)	Estimated seats, 2004 (millions)	Estimated seats, 2007 (millions)	Growth, 2001–04 (%)	Growth, 2004–07 (%)	Growth, 2001–07 (%)
All Sub-Saharan Africa	50.4	54.5	72.3	2.7	9.9	6.2
Sub-Saharan domestic	18.2	19.4	27.5	2.1	12.4	7.1
Sub-Saharan international	11.8	11.9	14.3	0.3	6.5	3.4
Sub-Saharan intercontinental	19.5	22.1	28.1	4.1	8.4	6.2
Between North Africa and Sub-Saharan Africa	0.9	1.3	2.5	11.1	24.8	17.8

Source: Analysis by H. Bofinger of data provided by ADG Seabury.

and 2007. Growth was lower between 2001 and 2004 but surged to 9.9 percent between 2004 and 2007. Although all types of traffic have experienced growth, intercontinental traffic, international traffic from certain hubs (Addis Ababa, Nairobi), and domestic traffic in certain countries, such as Nigeria, have grown most quickly. One of the least-connected regions lies between the countries in West and Central Africa and the better-developed network in the east. As liberalization spreads throughout Africa, however, major carriers from the east have begun to fill this gap.

Growth in passenger traffic, measured in revenue passenger-km (rpkm), has mirrored supply growth. It grew steadily between 1997 and 2001 but experienced a mild downturn after September 11, 2001, followed by two more years of growth. The collapse of several African airlines in 2004 resulted in a significant reduction in intra-African traffic. New supply capacity entered the marketplace between 2005 and 2006, however, and traffic surpassed what was seen at the beginning of 2004.

Passenger growth, like supply growth, has been highly uneven. East Africa and southern Africa have benefited from the growth and development of three key players: South African Airways (SAA), Ethiopian Airlines, and Kenya Airways. In contrast, passenger traffic in West and Central Africa declined significantly after the collapse of supply by several regional airlines (including Air Afrique) and has not yet fully recovered. (More information on capacity growth is contained in appendix 4e.)

Intercontinental traffic: Heavy reliance on three regional hubs. Intercontinental capacity in Africa grew by 43.6 percent between 2001 and 2007, at an annual growth rate of 6.2 percent. In total, 158 carriers provided intercontinental services in 2007, with an average of 3.45 airlines competing in each of the top 20 markets (map 4.2).

Between 2001 and 2007, 50 operators left the market, of which Air Afrique, Swissair, and Ghana Airways had the most capacity. At the same time, over 80 operators entered—with nearly double the capacity of those that left. Service between South Africa and Egypt and the United Arab Emirates had the highest growth rates in terms of capacity offered along major routes. The only routes on which the number of intercontinental operators declined between 2001 and 2004 were between the United States and South Africa. The top five airlines—SAA, Air France, British Airways, EgyptAir, and Emirates—hold over 30 percent

Map 4.2   Top 30 Intercontinental Routes for Sub-Saharan Africa as of November 2007

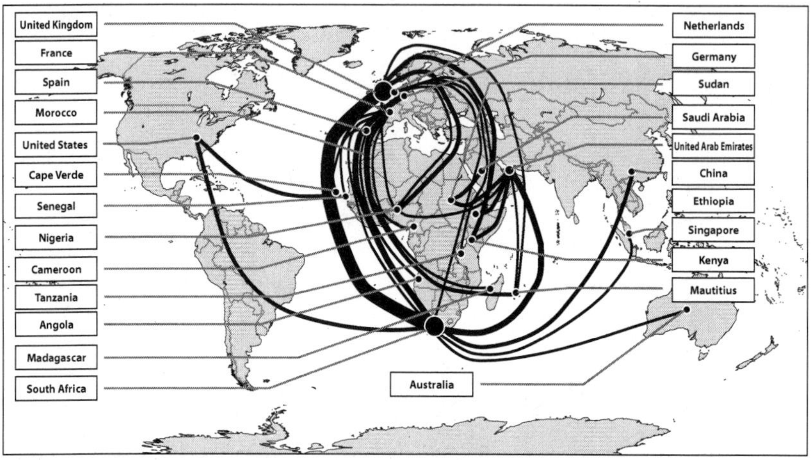

Source: Analysis by H. Bofinger.
Note: Johannesburg serves as the most important entry point, with the three largest partners (excluding North Africa) being the United Kingdom, Germany, and the United Arab Emirates (UAE).

of market share of all African intercontinental traffic. The top 20 airlines include 8 African carriers.

Most intercontinental traffic in the region passes through one of three major hubs: Johannesburg, Nairobi, and Addis Ababa. The route between the United Kingdom and Johannesburg is the most heavily traveled. Between 2001 and 2007, service from the Middle East to all three African hubs increased significantly. In 2001, for example, the United Arab Emirates had only 2 of the region's top 30 country pairs; by 2007 it had 5. Traffic from the Johannesburg hub to East Asia and the Pacific regions nearly doubled between 2004 and 2007 to 1.6 million seats.

International travel within Africa: Fewer connections, more passengers. International capacity within Africa grew by 3 percent per year between 2001 and 2004, and by 9 percent per year between 2004 and 2007 (figure 4.2). The acceleration from 2004 onward is accounted for by the entry of new carriers, as the industry recovered from the collapse of several African airlines that had caused a significant reduction in intra-African traffic in 2004.

Capacity growth was highest between Sub-Saharan Africa and North Africa, at 25 percent per year. International travel within Sub-Saharan

Figure 4.2   Estimated International Passenger Capacity between 2001 and 2007, as Measured in Seat-Kilometers

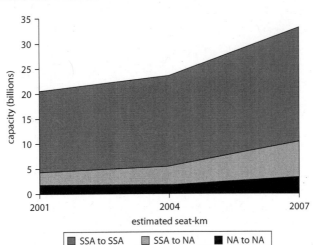

Source: Analysis by H. Bofinger.
Note: SSA = Sub-Saharan Africa; NA = North Africa.

Africa, which accounts for the bulk of intra-African international travel, grew at 6.5 percent. Over the same period, however, connectivity within Sub-Saharan Africa declined as the number of country pairs with connecting routes fell from 218 to 190. The loss of connectivity can be attributed largely to the collapse of airlines, including Air Afrique (see box 4.1), Nigeria Airways, Air Gabon, and the Ghana Airways Corporation. This type of collapse is somewhat anomalous, as it occurred during a period of overall capacity growth. Overall, 31 airlines left the market between 2001 and 2007, taking with them a combined capacity of nearly 8 million seats. At the same time, 34 new operators entered the market, bringing nearly double the lost capacity (15 million seats).

Connectivity is more developed in the eastern part of Africa, anchored by the major hubs in Johannesburg (South Africa), Nairobi (Kenya), and Addis Ababa (Ethiopia). These airports serve 36 percent of all international traffic within Africa (see table 4.5). Each has a dominant national airline: SAA, Kenya Airways, and Ethiopian Airlines account for 33 percent, 70 percent, and 83 percent of international traffic, respectively, at their hubs.

The highest growth in intra-African travel was exhibited by the countries of the BAG, including Nigeria, followed by the more developed regions of East and southern Africa, and North Africa. In contrast, because

Box 4.1

Air Afrique

Air Afrique was formed in 1961 as an African carrier headquartered in Abidjan, Côte d'Ivoire, and was owned by 12 West African countries, Air France, the Union Aéromaritime de Transport, and the Société pour le Développement du Transport Aérien en Afrique. The airline went from piston-engined propeller operations to jet-engined wide-bodies such as the Airbus 310 in the 1980s.

Just as with flag carriers, the airline became a regional symbol of pride and independence. But quality of service was sometimes compromised even in the best of times, for example, when reservation systems collapsed, making seat assignments impossible. In its last days, passengers were increasingly stranded. Some claimed that prioritized seating was given to nonpaying passengers of importance and that scheduling integrity had diminished. Efforts by the airline's president to restructure the airline in 2001 by cutting jobs were vehemently opposed by its employees, who at one point refused to fly an airplane with the president on board. The airline collapsed in 2001 after being sold to private investors and Air France for $69 million, with debts of $500 million (many of which accumulated when the CFA franc collapsed in the 1990s). Governance issues are also commonly cited as a cause for the fall. When the airline finally ceased operating, there were a reported 4,200 employees, with only seven aircraft flying.

Besides African destinations, the airline also flew to the Middle East, Europe, and the United States. Air Afrique's collapse removed a capacity of nearly 5 billion seat-km in 2001, similar in magnitude to the carrying capacity of Kenya Airways.

Source: Bofinger 2009.

of the collapse of Air Afrique and Air Nigeria, several nations surrounding the BAG countries have experienced negative growth (see map 4.3). The lack of development in these countries, all of which have air traffic of less than 1 million passengers per year, is cause for concern.

The North African market: Developing a hub. Two airlines, Royal Air Maroc and the slightly larger EgyptAir, carry 81 percent of the air traffic between Sub-Saharan Africa and North Africa. Three other North African airlines—Air Afrigiya, Air Algérie, and TunisAir—serve the remaining 19 percent. EgyptAir dominates along the east, and its route to and from Sudan accounts for nearly a fifth of all north-south travel. Royal Air Maroc predominantly serves the western side of the continent. The annual growth rate of traffic between North Africa and Sub-Saharan Africa

Table 4.5   Top 14 Airports in Africa Serving International Travel within Africa

Country	City/airport	Airport identification	Estimated seats, 2007 (thousands)	Overall percentage
South Africa	Johannesburg	JNB	5,742	20.0
Kenya	Nairobi	NBO	2,901	10.1
Ethiopia	Addis Ababa	ADD	1,706	6.0
Nigeria	Lagos	LOS	1,157	4.0
Senegal	Dakar	DKR	986	3.4
Zambia	Lusaka	LUN	959	3.4
Uganda	Entebbe	EBB	954	3.3
Zimbabwe	Harare	HRE	828	2.9
Ghana	Accra	ACC	813	2.8
Namibia	Windhoek	WDH	791	2.8
Tanzania	Dar es Salaam	DAR	749	2.6
Côte d'Ivoire	Abidjan	ABJ	717	2.5
Mauritius	Mauritius	MRU	544	1.9
Angola	Luanda	LAD	484	1.7

Source: Bofinger 2009 (based on data from Seabury ADG).

Map 4.3   Regional Growth Zones in Seats Offered, (all Travel)

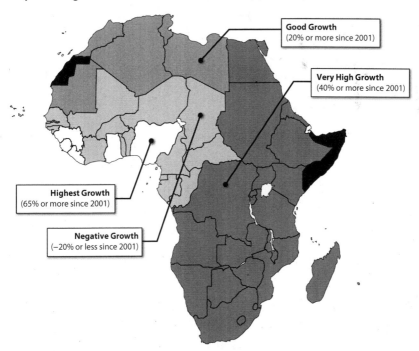

Source: Bofinger 2009 (based on data provided by Seabury ADG).

exceeded 18 percent from 2001 to 2007 and reached almost 26 percent between 2004 and 2007. There are new routes between 45 country pairs, 17 more than in 2001. Of these, 41 have a single-carrier monopoly, including all of the new ones. The new routes are primarily with Morocco and Libya.

Morocco is also an important hub for travel within Sub-Saharan Africa. The Libyan carrier Air Afrigiya, a relatively recent (2001) market entrant, offers a similar network to that of Royal Air Maroc. The developing hub system in North Africa is therefore remedying the lack of a strong Sub-Saharan carrier on the west side of the continent.

Domestic air transport: Growing despite national flag carrier protection.
The number of seats offered for domestic air travel within Africa grew by more than 12 percent annually between 2001 and 2004. Growth varies widely among countries, however, depending on topology, population density, per capita gross national income, and the size of the tourist market (see appendix 4g for detailed country figures).

South Africa (which accounts for 72.5 percent of all domestic services), Nigeria (accounting for another 10 percent), and Mozambique have experienced the majority of growth in domestic air transport in the region. In fact, excluding these countries, domestic air service in the region declined by nearly 1 percent between 2001 and 2004. Overall, the number of interconnected country pairs in Africa fell by 229 between 2001 and 2007, primarily a result of the collapse of major regional carriers (including Air Afrique and Ghana Airways).

In most cases, the state carrier is the only provider of domestic service in Africa. Of the 286 routes with service in 2007, only 54 were served by more than one provider (appendix 4h). Occasionally, however, flag carriers subcontract less heavily traveled routes to private operators. For example, Air Malawi, which has scheduled flights on the Lilongwe–Blantyre route, will sometimes hire a small operator with a single-engine aircraft for flights with low load factors. South Africa and Tanzania have the most competition for domestic air travel in the region. Only the most heavily trafficked routes in South Africa have more than one service provider. In contrast, each of Tanzania's 17 domestic routes was served by more than one carrier as of 2007. Their competitiveness may now be affected by the continued problems of the flag carrier, Air Tanzania.[9] The critical factor is not the actual number of airlines operating in any particular market but whether market entry is free enough to ensure efficient service.

Market Structure: Stable, but Changing in Composition

A small number of airlines dominate air travel in Sub-Saharan Africa. In 2007, 15 carriers provided 59.1 percent of the total seats in all markets (including the intercontinental market) in Sub-Saharan Africa, although that figure was down from 63.9 percent in 2001. In particular, SAA's market share fell from roughly 16 percent in 2001 to 14 percent in November 2007. British Airways also lost market share. On the other hand, Emirates, Ethiopian Airlines, and Qatar Airways are growing. Emirates has shown the greatest increase in capacity, from 960,000 seats in 2004 to over 3.6 million in 2004. It now has an almost 3 percent market share. Comair, an established South African airline with franchise agreements with British Airways, has also grown significantly. The market share of the top 15 carriers in an African market with a total seat capacity of 130 million seats and 319 billion seat-km as of 2007 is shown in table 4.6. The overall market is divided evenly between African and non-African carriers. (More information on market concentration can be found in appendix 4h.)

International transport within Africa: Liberalization increasing concentration. As of 2007, 15 airlines accounted for over 82 percent of all passenger seats offered for international travel within Africa. The top three

Table 4.6   Top 15 Airlines Overall in the African Passenger Market

Rank	Airline	Estimated total seat-km, 2007 (millions)	Market share, 2001 (%)	Market share, 2007 (%)
1	SAA	34,112	15.7	13.8
2	Air France	22,707	7.7	7.6
3	EgyptAir	21,636	7.0	5.4
4	British Airways PLC	17,150	9.7	4.4
5	Emirates	14,504	1.1	4.1
6	Royal Air Maroc	13,772	3.4	4.0
7	Ethiopian Airlines Enterprise	12,493	2.1	3.9
8	Kenya Airways	11,602	2.4	2.9
9	KLM	10,688	3.4	2.8
10	Air Mauritius	8,598	3.3	2.5
11	Deutsche Lufthansa AG	7,676	2.5	1.8
12	Air Algérie	5,851	2.1	1.7
13	Virgin Atlantic Airways Limited	5,171	1.4	1.5
14	Tunisair	5,035	1.9	1.4
15	Qatar Airways (WLL)	4,623	0.2	1.3

Source: Bofinger 2009 (based on data provided by Seabury ADG).

carriers—SAA, Ethiopian Airlines, and Kenya Airways—accounted for over 57 percent (see table 4.7). The number of carriers providing international service fluctuated between 67 and 78 between 2001 and 2007. In 2007, 76 carriers served 206 country pairs, down from 238 country pairs in 2001. The decline in the number of country pairs with service accompanied an increase in market concentration by dominant players: 16 of the top 60 routes were served by only one carrier in 2007, up from 10 in 2001. Market concentration increased even more in the rest of the market; 50 routes were complete monopolies, up from 24 in 2001. On the other hand, 25 of the routes served by a monopoly carrier did not exist in 2001, reflecting the willingness of airlines to risk serving a new country pair. Ethiopian Airlines and Kenya Airways were dominant in these new markets.

The 206 country pairs with service in 2007 accommodated an estimated capacity of 14.3 million passenger seats. SAA, Kenya Airways, and Ethiopian Airlines dominated 30 of the top 60 city pairs (as opposed to country pairs), which accounted for 80 percent of total capacity. Traffic among South Africa, Sudan, and Nigeria was among the

Table 4.7   Top 15 Airlines Providing International Service within Africa

Airline	Seat-km, 2001 (millions)	Seat-km, 2004 (millions)	Seat-km, 2007 (millions)	Annual growth, 2001–07 (%)	Annual growth, 2004–07 (%)
SAA	4,113	5,292	4,784	2.6	−1.7
Ethiopian Airlines Enterprise	1,335	2,119	4,235	21.2	12.2
Kenya Airways	1,780	2,366	4,163	15.2	9.9
Air Mauritius	488	545	730	6.9	5.0
Delta Air Lines Inc.	—	—	639	—	—
Virgin Nigeria	—	—	598	—	—
Air Namibia	336	523	564	9.0	1.3
Zambian Airways	63	14	559	44.0	85.3
Air Senegal International	131	417	442	22.5	1.0
Airlink (ex South African Airlink)	—	201	406	—	12.4
TAAG Angola Airlines	368	391	405	1.6	0.6
Bellview Airlines Ltd.	87	220	399	28.8	10.4
Air Zimbabwe (Pvt) Ltd.	402	175	383	−0.8	13.9
Comair Ltd.	—	291	366	—	3.9
Nationwide Airlines (Pty) Ltd.	31	117	263	43.1	14.4

Source: Bofinger 2009 (based on data provided by Seabury ADG).
Note: — = not available.

fastest growing in the region. (More information on city pairs can be found in appendix 4c.)

Monopoly: A hazard in low-density markets. The total number of passenger seats on routes served by one carrier (the monopoly market) grew by 6 percent annually from 2001 to 2007. Ethiopian Airlines is by far the largest monopoly carrier, serving 45 percent of the monopoly market, or nearly 1.2 million seats. Kenya Airways, at 22 percent, is a distant second. For comparison, SAA serves only about 1 percent of the monopoly market. It appears that Ethiopian Airlines has sought to expand into markets in which it can dominate. Its service in the monopoly market grew from a mere 327,400 seats in 2001 to its 2007 figure of 1.2 million, an annual growth rate of 27 percent. Furthermore, of the 21 country pairs for which Ethiopian Airlines is the sole carrier, only 6 did not exist in 2001, and 2 others were also served by a competitor that later abandoned the route. Kenya Airways seems to have followed a similar strategy at a smaller scale (though with higher growth rates), often driving out other operators by utilizing competitive advantages such as its well-developed hub system, newer fleet, greater ability to schedule capacity economically (with more types of aircraft available to meet demand), and the resources necessary to enter a price war if needed.

Conventional methods of measuring market concentration indicate that service between country pairs tends to be oligopolistic, which is common in low-density markets.

National flag carriers: Still protected. Of the 53 states in the whole African continent, 25 have a national flag carrier in which the state has at least a 51 percent share. There are two main groups of flag carriers: the three behemoths (Kenyan Airways, SAA, and Ethiopian Airlines); and the rest, most of which run large operating deficits. The high costs of fuel, maintenance, and insurance in Africa contribute to high operating costs for carriers. Many also serve very limited markets. Although the behemoths may run as separate corporate units, all three are primarily state owned. State ownership therefore cannot be solely responsible for the distressing financial condition of many flag carriers. The issue is rather that of small national market size and correspondingly low aircraft utilization levels. The outcome is also affected by the ambitiousness of the flag carrier in deciding how large a network to serve and also how well the fleet suits this size. The weaker flag carriers typically serve small domestic markets, which they try to subsidize from profits on international routes protected from competition by restricting the licensed air-service capacity of competitors. In fact, international routes could often be served more cheaply by larger international airlines, and smaller markets could be better served by small, private regional airlines. Attempting to privatize instead of liquidating flag carriers often leads to even larger sustained losses as countries pour good money after bad in support of essentially noncommercial operations.

Fleet Composition: Younger and Better Adapted to Market Size

Carriers in Africa operate a wide range of aircraft (300 different equipment codes are recorded). Table 4.8 lists the main types of aircraft in use, categorized by age group and origin ("Eastern" refers to the former Soviet Union) and by type (a combination of size and range). Two recent trends are apparent.

First, the fleet became much younger between 2001 and 2007, with aircraft built in the 1980s and later accounting for 75 percent of travel in 2007—up from only 50 percent in 2001 (see figure 4.3 and appendix 4i for details on aircraft age).

The second trend is in aircraft type, with a move away from wide-body and large jets toward smaller jets such as the Boeing 737 and Airbus 319 (see figure 4.4 and appendix 4j for country details).

Between 2001 and 2007, the share of city jets in large international markets stabilized at over 60 percent, but increased substantially in midsize markets, from 34 percent to 52 percent. In small markets, the share of commuter propeller aircraft increased from 33 percent to 40 percent. According to the declining use of wide-body aircraft, it appears that route lengths shortened, since wide-bodied aircraft are economically used only on longer flights (table 4.9).

Table 4.8   Breakdown of Aircraft Age for Analysis

Age rating	Aircraft type
Western, very old vintage	DC3 and similar; not in use in scheduled service
Western, very old	1960s–70s, includes 727s, 737-100s, and similar
Western, old	1970s–80s; 737 later series, early 747s
Western, somewhat recent	1980s–90s (for example, Boeing 757)
Western, recent	The newest aircraft, generally from the mid-1990s onward
Eastern	Former USSR vintage; not large role overall

Source: Bofinger 2009 (based on data provided by Seabury ADG).

Figure 4.3   Trends in Aircraft Age, 2001–07

a. Seat-kilometers flown by aircraft age, 2001

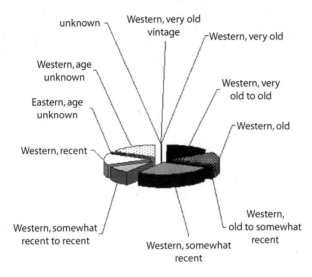

b. Seat-kilometers flown by aircraft age, 2007

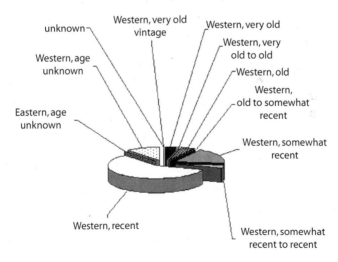

Source: Bofinger 2009.

Service Quality: The Regional Hub as a Counter to Diminished Direct Connectivity

It is still difficult to travel by air between African countries; often a connection in North Africa or Europe is required. Analysis of inter-African connectivity reveals a decline in international city-pair connections for

Figure 4.4   Trends in Aircraft Type, 2001–07

a. Seat-kilometers by aircraft size, 2001

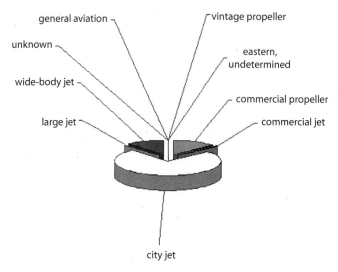

b. Seat-kilometers by aircraft size, 2007

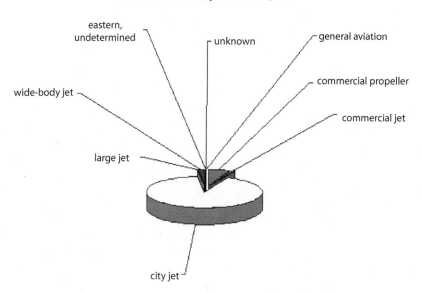

Source: Bofinger 2009.

Table 4.9   Breakdown of Aircraft Type by Market Size

Year	Overall national market size	International flights one week in November	General aviation (%)	Commuter prop (%)	Commuter jet (%)	City jet (%)	Large jet (%)	Wide-body jet (%)	Eastern built aircraft, unknown type (%)
2001	> 5 million	6,236	..	13	1	65	0	20	1
	> 1 million	2,169	..	27	1	34	5	34	1
	< 1 million	3,081	0.04	33	2	38	2	20	1
2007	> 5 million	10,638	..	14	7	61	1	17	0
	> 1 million	3,363	..	17	5	52	2	22	1
	< 1 million	3,167	..	40	3	39	3	11	4

Source: Bofinger 2009 (based on data provided by Seabury ADG).
Note: .. = negligible quantity.

almost half of the countries between 2001 and 2007. This decline accelerated between 2004 and 2007, affecting such diverse countries as the Central African Republic (only one international flight per week in November 2007), Chad, Eritrea, Mauritania, and the Seychelles.

Worst hit by declining connectivity has been a group of countries surrounding Nigeria in West and Central Africa, together with the smaller markets of Côte d'Ivoire and Ghana, both with fewer than 1 million passengers per year. This group includes the landlocked countries of Mali and Niger (along with the Central African Republic and Chad, which were already mentioned); it also includes coastal countries with smaller markets, such as Benin, Cameroon, the Republic of Congo, The Gambia, Gabon, and Togo. Air transport is financially unsustainable in these countries, especially as national flag carriers rely heavily on Boeing 737–type jets that are too large and too expensive to operate in limited markets.

The use of commuter propeller aircraft has increased slightly on international routes in these markets. While this increase is a step forward, service quality could be much improved by further reexamination of fleet composition, flight frequency, and routing. For example, West Africa lacks a regional hub of intercontinental travel (North Africa, East Africa, and southern Africa all have one). One suggestion, therefore, has been to explore the development of a hub in Lagos. Turboprop-type transport aircraft—such as the Fokker 50, the ATR 42-300, and the Bombardier Dash-8 Q400—could expand the range of the hub by serving surrounding countries (Bofinger 2009). This scenario is illustrated in map 4.4. The inner circle presents the range of an ATR 42-300, about 1,100 km. The middle range of roughly 2,000 km represents the range of a standard Fokker 50, while the outer ring, with a radius of 2,500 km, shows the range of a newer Bombardier Dash-8 Q400. Using the Fokker 50, the southern range of the hub would extend to Luanda, Angola. Even using the shorter-range ATR, the hub could service at least eight countries. Private operators such as Precision Air in Tanzania have been particularly successful in developing shorter routes with turboprop aircraft.

A central hub would have several other advantages. By a better match of aircraft type to market demand, it would make load factors more sustainable per aircraft and thus enhance regional travel. Concentration of traffic through a regional hub might provide service to several countries, including those with little other traffic. Permitting operators fifth- and sixth-freedom rights (under the so-called freedoms of the air) to carry passengers between two countries outside their own is a vital prerequisite

Map 4.4   African Countries Potentially Served by Commuter-Style Turboprop Aircraft Using a Hub in Lagos

Source: Bofinger 2009.

for the introduction of such a hub-and-spoke system.[10] Implementation of the Yamoussoukro Decision (see below) provides for this.

Airfares: Simply Structured but Expensive

Flying to and within Africa is generally considered more expensive than flying to or within Europe or the United States, although this is difficult to show statistically because of the complex fare structures of the more developed markets, where fares change from minute to minute, depending on load factors of individual flights. But there is little doubt that fares in general are higher per kilometer in Africa.

Pricing schemes in Africa are not complex. Airfares were examined for a representative sample of routes: 23 international routes within Africa, 29 intercontinental routes, and 21 domestic routes. Because many domestic routes are not well advertised, domestic airfares were most difficult to sample: only 13 price points were found. Standard booking Web sites were then used to determine the lowest-cost flights. Figure 4.5 shows the price of tickets per nautical mile for flights of various lengths, based on the samples. Air travel within Africa appears to be considerably more expensive per mile flown than intercontinental travel, especially on routes of less than 4,000 km. This result reflects the larger markets and higher competitiveness of the intercontinental routes.

Economic Regulation and the Yamoussoukro Process

Two common beliefs have limited entry into the air transport market of African countries. First is the belief that if services become too competitive after deregulation, then routes with low traffic volumes that are not economically viable will drop out of the system, isolating some parts of the country. Second is the belief that a national flag carrier, if owned and operated by the government and given sufficient market dominance, can support services on less viable—but socially necessary—routes with revenues from more profitable routes. As a result, each country protects its routes and allows airlines from other countries to enter its market only in exchange for a similar allowance.

Much of the world has relaxed or removed such strict regulations. In the United States, deregulation has had several positive effects: increased price competition, the disappearance of weaker carriers, the more efficient

Figure 4.5   Pricing of Flights within Africa versus Intercontinental Flights, Kilometers Flown

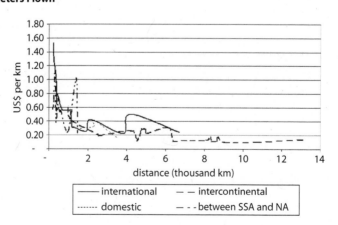

Source: Bofinger 2009 (based on data collected by the World Bank).

arrangement of routes, and the development of hub-and-spoke systems. In Europe, it has led to the rise of new low-cost carriers.

The Yamoussoukro process marked the beginning of Africa's march toward liberalization. On October 17, 1988, the ministers responsible for civil aviation in the African states met in Yamoussoukro, Côte d'Ivoire, to propose a new African air transport policy. The result of that meeting was the Yamoussoukro Declaration. Although it sought the gradual elimination of traffic restrictions, the declaration's primary goal was improved cooperation among African air carriers to allow them to better compete with non-African carriers. The declaration prompted the United Nations Economic Commission for Africa to initiate another conference of air transport ministers in Yamoussoukro, which resulted in the historic agreement on Pan-African liberalization of air services—the 1999 Yamoussoukro Decision (YD) (Schlumberger 2008).

The YD had several main objectives: the gradual liberalization of entry into the African market, including both scheduled and nonscheduled air services; the abolishment of limits on the capacity and frequency of international air services within Africa; the protection of universal traffic rights up to the fifth freedom; and freedom of operators to set fares. A monitoring body would supervise and implement the decision. Signatory states were obliged to ensure fair opportunity to compete in their air transport sectors, with plans for an African air transport executing agency to ensure fair competition. Special attention was given to improving air transport safety. Under the decision, all airlines were obliged to meet the standards defined by the ICAO, and states were asked to comply with established civil aviation safety and security standards and practices. Although most African states are bound to the YD,[11] in practice it is implemented by regional economic organizations, rather than the Pan-African body of the African Union.

The extent to which the YD has been implemented varies, as do the effects of implementation. The monitoring body has met only a few times, and competition rules and arbitration procedures are still pending. In 2007, at the Third African Union Conference of Ministers Responsible for Air Transport, the role of the executing agency was assigned to the African Civil Aviation Commission (an institution of the African Union). This agency has not yet proven effective in formulating and enforcing general rules and regulations governing competition. In contrast, operational implementation has been much more productive. Countries in all subregions now have greater freedom to negotiate bilateral agreements (table 4.10).

Table 4.10 Air Service Liberalization among Regional Groupings in Africa

Community	Members	General status of YD implementation	Status of air services liberalization	Pecentage of fifth- and seventh-freedom flights
Banjul Accord Group (BAG)	The Gambia, Ghana, Guinea, Mali, Nigeria, Sierra Leone, Togo	Principles of the YD agreed upon in a multilateral air service agreement	Up to the fifth freedom granted, tariffs free, and capacity and frequency open	43
Economic Community of Central African States (CEMAC)	Cameroon, Central African Republic, Gabon, Equatorial Guinea, Republic of Congo, Chad	Principles of the YD agreed upon in an air transport program; still some minor restrictions	Up to the fifth freedom granted, tariffs free, and capacity and frequency open; maximum two carriers per state permitted to participate	28
Common Market for Eastern and Southern Africa (COMESA)	Most states of East and southern Africa, except Tanzania, South Africa, Botswana, and Lesotho	Full liberalization agreed upon, but implementation pending until a joint competition authority established	Pending; once applied, operators permitted to serve any destination (all freedoms); tariffs and capacity/frequency to be free.	14

East African Community (EAC)	Tanzania, Uganda, Kenya	Directive issued by EAC Council with goal of amending bilateral accords among EAC states to conform to the YD	Air services not liberalized; amendment of bilateral accords still pending	16
Southern African Development Community (SADC)	Most countries south of Tanzania	No steps taken toward implementation, even though the civil aviation policy includes gradual liberalization of air services within SADC	No liberalization within SADC initiated	6
West African Economic and Monetary Union (WAEMU)	Benin, Burkina Faso, Côte d'Ivoire, Guinea-Bissau, Mali, Niger, Senegal, Togo	YD fully implemented within the WAEMU	All freedoms, including cabotage, granted; tariffs liberalized	44

Source: Bofinger 2009.

In West Africa, the West African Economic and Monetary Union (WAEMU) fully implemented the YD, and even went beyond it to guarantee cabotage rights. The BAG, also in West Africa, agreed to a multilateral air service agreement that was fully compatible with the decision.[12] In Central Africa, the CEMAC implemented all the necessary legislative and regulatory elements to comply with the provisions of the YD. In East Africa and in southern Africa, the COMESA achieved the most progress, but implementation is still pending, conditional on the establishment of a joint competition authority. The East African Community has chosen the effective strategy of directing countries to amend their bilateral agreements to conform to the decision, but the agreement has not yet been signed. The SADC, in the south, has progressed least; the dominant position of South Africa appears to be the main obstacle to the implementation of the decision. Overall, two-thirds of the air transport service in Africa is now liberalized.

An examination of the nationality of carriers flying international routes within a region clearly shows the effects of liberalization. Despite a net loss in the number of city pairs and country pairs served directly, there has been a significant increase in the percentage of routes served by carriers not based in either the country of origin or the country of destination (see table 4.11). The two main exceptions to this trend, the CEMAC and WAEMU regions, are explained by the failure of Air Afrique, which was not considered a national carrier in any country. Its failure therefore reduced the number of routes carried by a nonnational carrier.

In many cases, extraregional African carriers (such as an East African carrier traveling between two countries within WAEMU) are replacing the capacity of the lost carriers (Air Afrique, Air Gabon, Ghana Airways, and Nigeria Airways), while European carriers once flying similar routes (such as Air France) have almost completely disappeared in the region. This suggests that the larger and healthier carriers are consolidating services in these markets. While there is some anecdotal evidence that fares for flights from a carrier's home country to another country (third- and fourth-freedom operations) have declined because of the YD, there is no solid analysis using long-term fare data to support that proposition.

As with most efforts to liberalize air transport, countries wishing to protect unhealthy flag carriers have resisted implementing the YD (Schlumberger 2010). As in other regions, a few very large flag carriers dominate air transport in Africa (South African Airways, Ethiopian Airlines, and Kenya Airways). Smaller flag carriers, which sometimes consist of one or two aircraft in Africa, fly any profitable routes between their

Table 4.11 Percentage of Flights between Country Pairs Served by Airlines Not Based in Either Country

Regional community	Seats			Country pairs		City pairs	
	Total 2007	Annual growth 2001–7 (%)	Annual growth 2004–7 (%)	As of November 2007	Net change from February 2001	As of November 2007	Net change from February 2001
Arab Maghreb Union (AMU)	1,294,189	4.55	8.65	9	—	14	2
Banjul Accord Group (BAG)	568,306	0.32	13.87	13	—	15	1
Economic Community of Central African States (CEMAC)	152,984	–18.88	–35.58	6	–6	9	–9
Common Market for Eastern and Southern Africa (COMESA)	4,484,675	7.12	17.66	49	–4	71	–3
East African Community (EAC)	1,751,811	2.02	5.81	9	1	18	–2
Southern African Development Community (SADC)	5,663,632	4.27	10.00	34	–4	72	5
West African Economic and Monetary Union (WAEMU)	763,472	–5.42	–5.56	20	–2	21	–3

Source: Bofinger 2009 (based on data provided by Seabury ADG).

Note: — = not available. Flights are international flights within each region. Except for the Arab Maghreb Union, which is not part of the YD, all countries have shown an increased market proportion of these airlines between 2004 and 2007. The data for 2001 are skewed because several regional airlines with large market shares, such as Air Afrique, collapsed.

country and outside hubs, while attempting to sustain an otherwise unprofitable network. Liberalization allows the dominant carrier based in the regional hub to compete on profitable routes, and thus the small flag carrier becomes completely unsustainable. Efforts to protect a flag carrier deprive passengers of choices, which usually results in higher prices and lower service quality.

Safety: Achilles' Heel

African airlines, although they carried only 4.5 percent of total air traffic, were responsible for a quarter of all fatal air transport accidents world-wide in 2007. The African Airlines Association argues that this is a result of aging fleets: nearly a third of the region's 750 aircraft are over 20 years old. Soviet-built aircraft are still common in certain countries. But their danger relative to Western aircraft seems more a question of vintage rather than origin. While most accidents in 2006 involved old Soviet-built turboprop aircraft, more recent crashes have mainly involved Western-built aircraft. Data from around the world suggest that properly main-tained and operated Soviet aircraft are as safe as Western aircraft from the same vintage. Meanwhile, inquiries by the U.S. National Transportation Safety Board have highlighted several cases in which poor pilot training and assessment contributed to aircraft accidents in Africa.

The IATA identifies poor regulatory oversight as the top threat to air safety in Africa, followed by inadequate safety management systems. Only Cape Verde, Ethiopia, and South Africa meet international stan-dards for safety. Similarly, results from the ICAO's Universal Safety Oversight Program reveal that safety performance throughout Africa is very poor. For example, as figure 4.6 shows, West and Central Africa and East and southern Africa perform worse than the world average in every critical measure of safety implementation (in most cases by a factor of 2). A cross-sectional analysis of the region reveals that these deficiencies are highly correlated with accident rates, suggesting that institutional failings explain a large part of Africa's accident record. (More indicators of poor air safety can be found in appendix 4k.)

The high accident rate in the air sector in Africa has caught the atten-tion of donor countries, development institutions, and industry-related associations and organizations. The ICAO, the U.S. Department of Transportation, the Industry Safety Strategy Group (ISSG, formed by Boeing, Airbus, and several associations), AviAssist of the Netherlands, the French Civil Aviation Authority, and the World Bank have all imple-mented programs to improve air safety in the region. For example, the

Figure 4.6   ICAO Analysis of Safety Implementation

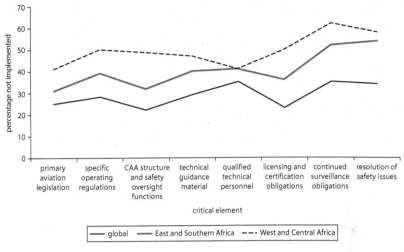

Source: ICAO 2007.

Department of Transportation's Safe Skies for Africa Program has helped East Africa establish a new regional safety oversight organization. The ICAO is helping to set up three projects under its Cooperative Development of Operational Safety and Continuing Airworthiness Program for the WAEMU, CEMAC, and BAG countries, which may eventually lead to additional regional flight-safety oversight agencies. Africa's regional associations are also pooling resources to address safety issues. For example, the African and Malgache Civil Aviation Authorities, an association of 15 civil aviation directors general from West and Central Africa, was established in 2001 to further cooperation in the supervision of aviation safety in the region.

The ISSG's program has established an overarching set of goals for the sector, which serves to coordinate donor and other aid activity. The ICAO, with assistance from the World Bank, is creating a central repository and database for projects related to air transport, which will be mapped to other metrics, such as the ISSG's program.

Progress in the region cannot yet be discerned if one looks only at accident statistics. Yet there have clearly been successes, such as the creation of a more independent CAA in Nigeria. The ongoing global recession and the potential for rising fuel costs are poised to limit growth in Africa's air transport sector. Continued improvement in the region's aviation safety is therefore more critical than ever to the success of the industry.

The Way Forward

Five policy objectives appear to be of the highest importance for meeting the challenges of growth in the African air transport sector.

Priority 1. Improve safety oversight

Three policy commitments are critical to improving the region's poor air safety record:

- Political commitment to the autonomy of the national safety oversight organizations, which may require both new laws and independent auditing
- Budgetary commitment of national governments to support regional safety oversight organizations and enable them to pay sufficiently competitive salaries to retain technically competent personnel, to be shared throughout the region
- Commitment to regional pooling of information and resources devoted to the supervision of aviation safety.

Priority 2. Invest in maintenance rather than construction of airport facilities

In general, Africa's runways are sufficient to meet demand. At the same time, some terminals are congested, and both airside and landside facilities are often outdated. Priorities for the region's investment strategy are therefore as follows:

- Discourage investment for replacing airports with new ones.
- Focus investment in maintaining and upgrading infrastructure, including runways, taxiways and aprons, terminals, and landside access to airports.
- Invest in smarter and less expensive ATC and navigational infrastructure.
- Encourage private sector participation in landside investments; in particular, landside service provisions (such as check-in, baggage-handling, and cargo terminal operations) could be outsourced to specialized firms.

Priority 3. Avoid spending to support unprofitable flag carriers

With only a few exceptions, flag carriers are highly unprofitable. But governments often continue to subsidize flag carriers for fear of losing unprofitable domestic routes. Countries should therefore pursue the following strategies:

- Liquidate perennially unprofitable flag carriers.
- Liberalize important routes, opening them to both foreign and domestic carriers.

- If necessary, supplement sustainable services with competitively tendered net cost contracts for economically unviable routes.

Priority 4. Reform the financing of air traffic infrastructure

In most countries, the two main agencies concerned with air traffic could be made more effective by adopting a more commercial attitude to the revenues yielded by the services they provide:

- CAAs, which rely on fees for funding, should be assured of at least a predictable share of revenues from overflying.
- Airport authorities, which are inherently profitable because of their monopoly position, should receive all revenues that they generate, but should also adequately maintain runways and terminals; surpluses could be taxed if necessary.

Priority 5. Further liberalize the air market

Implementation of the YD has improved international connectivity in countries that have lost carriers since 2004. The increase in fifth- and sixth-freedom operations conducted by Ethiopian Airlines, Kenya Airways, and SAA is particularly indicative of progress. Progress has been slower in countries that still protect their flag carriers. The following actions can hasten progress:

- Concentrate on developing regional agreements, which have been very successful when implemented.
- Immediately apply the liberalized policies to all domestic markets.

Notes

1. The main source document for this chapter is Bofinger (2009). The discussion of service liberalization is based on Schlumberger (2007, 2008).
2. http://www.aircraft-charter-world.com. A list of airports was composed by combining this Web site's list of airports for every country in Africa. Data sources for this chapter are described in appendix 4a.
3. The BAG comprises Cape Verde, The Gambia, Ghana, Liberia, Nigeria, and Sierra Leone.
4. Radar vectoring is the provision of navigational guidance to aircraft in the form of specific headings based on the use of radar. Radar separation is applied by a controller observing that the radar returns from the two aircraft are a certain minimum horizontal distance from each other, as observed on a suitably calibrated radar system. Secondary radar is a system that not only detects and

measures the position of aircraft, but also automatically asks for additional information such as identity and altitude.

5. ILS is a ground-based instrument system that provides precision guidance to an aircraft approaching and landing on a runway, using a combination of radio signals and, in many cases, high-intensity lighting arrays to enable safe landing in poor-visibility conditions.

6. This can occur where service networks with relatively short connections, as in modern hub-and-spoke arrangements, also have relatively low frequencies. If one airport cannot accept aircraft because of bad weather, the entire connection schedule is disturbed.

7. Jeppesen (also known as Jeppesen Sanderson) is a subsidiary of Boeing Commercial Airplanes that specializes in aeronautical charting and navigation services, flight planning, pilot supplies, and aviation training.

8. The Safe Skies for Africa Program was inaugurated by President Clinton on April 1, 1998. The goals of the program were to improve safety, security, and air navigation in Africa. The first eight countries selected to participate were Angola, Cameroon, Cape Verde, Côte d'Ivoire, Kenya, Mali, Tanzania, and Zimbabwe. Djibouti, Namibia, and Uganda were added in June 2003. Over the intervening years, Safe Skies assistance has been expanded to help regions share personnel and other resources to make up for a lack of qualified technical personnel in individual states.

9. Originally established as a state enterprise after the breakup of East African Airways in 1977, Air Tanzania has had a checkered history. In 2002, South African Airways signed an agreement with the government of Tanzania to be the strategic partner of the Air Tanzania Corporation, and purchased a 49 percent stake in the company. The new airline was launched in March 2003 with Dar es Salaam as a hub. After four loss-making years, the government bought out the SAA interest, terminated the agreement, and relaunched Air Tanzania in October 2007. In December 2008, the Tanzanian Civil Aviation Authority withdrew its air operator certificate and the company was banned by the IATA. The promised reestablishment of service seems unlikely to be sustainable.

10. The eight "freedoms of the air" are the focus of international regulation of air transport. The first and second freedoms allow aircraft to overfly a foreign country or to land for refueling. The third and fourth freedoms are commercial freedoms to carry passengers from a carrier's home country to another or vice versa. The fifth to seventh freedoms concern the rights to carry passengers between two foreign countries—as an extension of a flight from the home country (fifth), via a stop in the home country (sixth), or without ongoing service to the home base (seventh). The eighth freedom is the right to carry traffic between two points in a foreign country.

11. The Yamoussoukro Decision was agreed to on the basis of the Abuja Treaty, which set up the African Economic Community. Thus, only the 44 states that have signed and formally ratified the Abuja Treaty are parties to the YD. Nonsignatory states were Djibouti, Equatorial Guinea, Eritrea, Gabon, Madagascar, Mauritania, Somalia, South Africa, and Swaziland.

12. The regional associations overlap considerably. Both the WAEMU and the BAG countries are members of the larger Economic Community of West African States (ECOWAS). There is also considerable overlap of membership in the COMESA, East African Community (EAC), and SADC.

References

ACI (Airports Council International). 2008. *Airport Economics Survey, 2008.* Geneva: ACI.

ADPI. 2008. "Analyse Economique et Financière des Capacités de Développement des Aéroports du Mali: Projet d'amélioration de l'Aéroport International de Bamako Selnou." ADPI Designers and Planners, Mons, France.

Bofinger, H. 2009. "Air Transport: Challenges to Growth." Africa Infrastructure Country Diagnostic Background Paper 16, World Bank, Washington, DC.

Button, K. 2008. "Air Transportation Infrastructure in Developing Countries: Privatization and Deregulation." In *Aviation Infrastructure Performance: A Study in Comparative Political Economy*, ed. Clifford Winston and Gines de Rus, 193–221. Washington, DC: Brookings Institution Press.

ICAO (International Civil Aviation Organization). 2007. "Universal Safety Oversight Audit Program Report." ICAO, Montreal.

Osborne, A. 2007. "BAA Face Penalties If London Airports Cut Investment." *Telegraph Media*, October 5.

Schlumberger, C. 2007. "Emerging Issues for Air Navigation Services: A Challenge for Developing Countries." Paper presented at "Aviation Safety, Security and the Environment" conference, McGill University, Montreal, September 15–17.

———. 2008. "The Implementation of the Yamoussoukro Decision." McGill Institute of Aerospace Law, McGill University, Montreal.

———. 2010. *Open Skies for Africa: Implementing the Yamoussoukro Decision.* Washington, DC: World Bank.

World Bank. 2009. Public-Private Infrastructure Advisory Facility Database. World Bank, Washington, DC. http://ppi.worldbank.org/explore/ppi_explore Region.aspx?RegionID=1.

CHAPTER 5

Ports and Shipping: Moving toward Modern Management Structures

Africa has many ports, most of which are small by world standards.[1] Few can accommodate the largest ships. In general, African ports are poorly equipped, have low productivity, and are unprepared for the rapidly unfolding changes in global trade and shipping patterns. While they are moving slowly from public ownership and operation to the landlord port-management model, they still lag behind in the development of modern port-management structures compared to ports in other regions.

Coping with Rapidly Changing Trade Patterns

Transport demands are a function of trade patterns, which are changing rapidly. Africa's market share in the 30 most significant (in terms of traded value) non-oil exports fell from an average of 20.8 percent in the 1960s to less than 10.0 percent in the 1990s. In many countries, this decline was due to poor economic performance triggered by the upheavals of the post-colonial period, described in chapter 1. Over the past decade, Africa's market has recovered slightly in absolute terms, led by the growth of oil exports from West Africa, but not in terms of world market share. Changing trade patterns will alter the types of traffic transported.

Spatial traffic patterns are also changing. Trade has declined with Europe and has grown with East Asia. Trade with North America has risen as a consequence of the U.S. search for oil security. China, India, the Republic of Korea, and Malaysia are also quickly developing an interest in Africa's energy products.

Container Traffic: Fast Growth from a Low Base

Container traffic in Africa, with the exception of South Africa, is still at an early stage of system development. In 2005, African ports handled a combined 8.6 million twenty-foot equivalent units (TEUs),[2] of which Durban handled nearly 2.0 million. The three main South African ports together handled over 35 percent of this traffic—3 million TEUs. Although container traffic in Africa is growing rapidly, it started from a very low base (figure 5.1). Container traffic in West Africa, for example, has grown at an average annual rate of 14.7 percent—the highest of all African regions—but still accounts for less than 1 percent of container traffic worldwide. Traffic in East Africa, which is the second-fastest-growing subregion, is heavily concentrated in Mombasa (5 percent of the total for Africa). And in West Africa, five ports each handle more than 350,000 TEUs. In southern Africa, traffic rose from 1.35 million TEUs in 1995 to 3.09 million in

Figure 5.1   Container Trade Development Summary in the Study Ports, by Region, 1995 and 2005

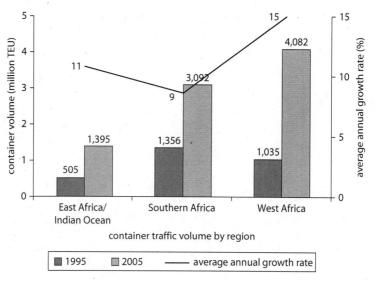

2005. As of 2005, all Africa accounted for little over 2 percent of container traffic worldwide.

Durban is by far the largest port in the region. Its container volume in 2005 was 1.9 million TEUs, more than twice the volume of any other port. Conakry and Cape Town are the next largest, handling 753,827 and 690,895 TEUs in 2005, respectively. Abidjan comes in fourth with a container volume of 500,119 TEUs (figure 5.2). Several ports—among them the larger ports of Abidjan and Luanda and the smaller ports of Cotonou, Nacala, and Walvis Bay—experienced dramatic growth of around 30 percent every year between 1995 and 2005, compared with the 10–15 percent typical among other fast-growing ports worldwide. In the future, these African ports are likely to see accelerated growth in container traffic.

Several important factors are influencing the growth of African container trade. First, increased stability and economic growth in the region has led to rising demand for manufactured goods mainly imported in containers. This is particularly true in countries that have benefited from surging petroleum revenues (Nigeria, for example). Second, the globalization of production has led to growing trade between Africa and Asia, including imports of Asian consumer goods. Third, global innovations have resulted in increased penetration of the container system into general cargo trade and have generated a cascade

Figure 5.2   Top 10 Sub-Saharan African Ports (TEUs per year)

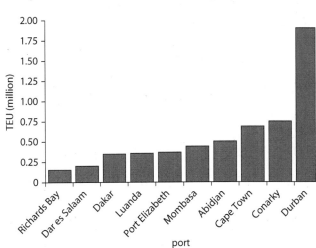

Source: Mundy and Penfold 2009.

effect, whereby major shipowners are gradually deploying larger and more modern container vessels in African trade. Finally, institutional reforms have allowed foreign expertise and investment to enter the port sector and have enabled public-private partnerships (PPPs) of various forms, such as concessions and management contracts for container-handling facilities.

But Africa is still at a relatively early stage in developing its container system. In 2006, the region had a population of 770.3 million and accounted for a total of 8.60 million TEUs in all its ports. For comparison, North America had a population of 528.0 million and accounted for a total traffic volume of 50.10 million TEUs. Clearly, considerable potential remains for container traffic volumes to increase in Africa.

Constraints on Growth: Transit Arrangements

Most landlocked countries have several outlets to the sea. For example, the five landlocked countries in West Africa have 15 transit corridors, while in southern Africa, Zambia alone has 5. In southern Africa, traffic often travels the longer route to the port of Durban as a result of the more liberal land transport and border arrangements on that route and the frequent sailings from the port. Table 5.1 identifies a number of regional ports and the markets from which they capture, or could capture, transit traffic. Container traffic development in Africa is presently constrained by transit arrangements in these corridors. More competition between corridors, as well as comprehensive corridor development programs (for example, the Maputo corridor), could reduce administrative blocks and allow goods to flow more freely. A revival of Africa's inland waterways could also play a constructive role (box 5.1).

Most road and rail systems serving the corridor ports are in poor condition and do not support container transport (Harding, Palsson, and Raballand 2007). With a few exceptions (such as in South Africa), containers are stuffed and stripped close to the port of entry or departure. As a result, the volume of containerized traffic moving to landlocked countries across land borders is very low. In a recent study, Mundy and Penfold (2009) did not find much evidence that national or regional transport authorities have prioritized port development, or that port management is generally involved in developing links to land transport.

Current practices impede development of both the ports and the economies they serve. Coordinated investments in ports, railways, and roads, along with other trade facilitation initiatives, could allow a number

Table 5.1 Regional Ports and Their Transit Traffic Markets—Actual and Potential

	Country	Port	Transit traffic markets	Volume, 2005	Comments
East Africa	Sudan	Port Sudan, Suakin	n.a.	—	Potential to reach Central African Republic, Sudan, Rwanda, Uganda, Burundi, Chad by rail
	Djibouti	Djibouti	Ethiopia	n.r.	Well established
	Kenya	Mombasa	Uganda	n.r.	Well established
	Tanzania	Dar es Salaam	Burundi, Rwanda, Uganda, Zambia	50,000 TEU	Established but constrained by capacity
	Mozambique	Maputo, Beira	Malawi, Zambia, Zimbabwe, South Africa, Swaziland	n.r.	Significant potential but volumes low
Southern Africa	Namibia	Walvis Bay	Botswana, Zimbabwe, South Africa	n.r.	Connections offered but volumes low
	South Africa	Durban, Cape Town, Port Elizabeth	Botswana, Namibia, Mozambique	n.r.	Significant capability by rail but volumes low
West Africa	Angola	Luanda	Congo, Dem. Rep.; Zambia; Zimbabwe	n.a.	No capability at present, but major rail refurbishment under way
	Congo, Dem. Rep.	Matadi	Central African Republic; Congo, Rep.	n.a.	No capability foreseen
	Congo, Rep.	Pointe Noire	Central African Republic	400 TEU	No capability at present
	Cameroon	Douala	Burkina Faso, Central African Republic, Chad, Mali, Niger	n.r.	Connections offered but volumes low
	Cameroon Development	Kribi	Kribi-Kissangandi Development Corridor is planned connecting Equatorial Guinea; north Gabon; Congo, Rep.; Congo, Dem. Rep.	n.r.	Under development
	Benin	Cotonou	Niger	n.k.	Established but constrained by capacity
	Togo	Lomé	Burkina Faso, Mali, Niger	n.r.	Connections offered but volumes low
	Ghana	Tema, Takoradi	Mali, Niger, Burkina Faso	n.r.	Ghana Gateway Program exists but faces capacity issues
	Côte d'Ivoire	Abidjan	Burkina Faso, Mali, Niger	n.r.	Resumes after the war; agreements with rebels to secure road access
	Senegal	Dakar	Mauritania, Mali	33,400 TEU	Established and with significant potential for further development

Source: Author's compilation of third-party industry sources and Mundy and Penfold 2009.

Note: — = not available; n.r. = not reported; n.a. = not applicable; n.k. = not known.

Box 5.1

Inland Waterways: A Neglected Asset

Inland waterway transport has historically been important for carrying primary product exports from landlocked countries but is now in decline. The three major lakes in East and Central Africa—Victoria, Tanganyika, and Malawi—once played an important role in transit and intraregional trade in the region. On Lake Victoria, in particular, waterway transport was linked to railheads at the inland ports of Kisumu (Kenya), Bell (Uganda), and Mwanza (Tanzania). The Ugandan and Kenyan lake operations were concessioned together with the railways in those countries, while in Tanzania, the lake services have been separated from the railways since the introduction of the Uganda and Kenya concessions. Only one service now operates on Lake Victoria, and some of the railway track leading to the ports is in poor state of repair, especially in Kenya.

A similar story applies in West and Central Africa, where the Congo basin has a navigable network of 12,000 kilometers and covers nearly 4 million square kilometers in nine countries. In principle, the Congo system could be a very valuable resource in a multimodal transport network serving the region. In practice, however, it suffers from outdated and insufficient infrastructure (as well as inadequate channel markings and maintenance, feeble regulation, and numerous nonphysical barriers to movement) and plays an ever more marginal role as a mode of transport. Recognizing this untapped potential, in October 2005, the executive secretary of the Economic and Monetary Community of Central Africa (CEMAC) encouraged the governments of Cameroon, the Republic of Congo, the Democratic Republic of Congo, and the Central African Republic to establish the Commission Internationale du Bassin Congo-Oubangui-Sangha to improve the physical and regulatory arrangements for inland navigation in the basin (CICOS 2007). A consultancy study has been undertaken to examine the current arrangements in the four participating countries, and to identify the steps that need to be taken to begin effective redevelopment.

Source: Author.

of the ports identified in table 5.2 to become more effective gateways for international trade, particularly containerized traffic. For example, the Maputo Corridor Development project comprises road, rail, border posts, port, and terminal facilities between Mozambique's port of Maputo and South Africa, Swaziland, and Zimbabwe, and it has significantly enhanced the attractiveness of the Maputo port.

Table 5.2 Major African Ports and Their Transshipment Potential

	Country	Port	Transshipment	Status as of 2010	Traffic, in TEUs (2005)
East Africa	Djibouti	Djibouti	Significant	Existing capacity constraints to be relieved by opening of new terminal in 2009–10	60,000
	Kenya	Mombasa	Substantial	Role declining because of pressing capacity constraints	54,576
	Tanzania	Dar es Salaam	Substantial	Initially took business from Mombasa, but now experiencing capacity constraints also	40,000
Southern Africa	South Africa	Durban	Substantial	Natural center for southern Africa, but now facing capacity constraints	212,000
West Africa	Nigeria	Apapa	Potential	Improvements in port efficiency helping to realize potential, but capacity constraints remain an issue	n.r.
	Cameroon	Douala	Potential	No capacity constraints at present, but may emerge on the basis of new facilities under development	n.k.
	Benin	Cotonou	Potential	No capacity constraints at present, but may emerge the basis of on nearby new port development (Seme-Kpodji)	n.k.
	Ghana	Tema	Significant	Currently constrained by capacity, but new development plans exist	50,000
	Côte d'Ivoire	Abidjan	Substantial	Business suffering as a result of recent conflict	300,000
	Senegal	Dakar	Substantial	Currently constrained by capacity and low efficiency; recent concession may improve situation	80,000

Source: Mundy and Penfold 2009.
Note: n.r. = not reported; n.k. = not known.

Transport investment is not necessarily the main component of a trade development program. For example, the Ghana Gateway Program has three main components—development of a free trade zone, trade facilitation, and investment promotion—and involves seven implementing agencies in an effort to approach development in a comprehensive way. The first phase of this project involved a comprehensive set of reforms focusing on frontline institutions such as the Ghana Free Zones Board, Customs Excise and Preventive Services, Ghana Immigration Service, Ghana Ports and Harbors Board, and Ghana Civil Aviation Authority. Such relatively inexpensive reforms may produce greater benefits than expensive investments in port capacity.

Container Trade: Exceptionally Imbalanced Flows

Most global container trade is imbalanced, with flows of loaded containers in one direction exceeding those in the opposite direction. This imbalance has only become more pronounced with the proliferation of large-scale manufacturing facilities in China. In East Africa, West Africa, and southern Africa, imports account for the majority of loaded container movement (see figure 5.3). Moreover, most containers are exported empty. In 2005, the ratio of empty exported TEUs to loaded exported TEUs was 90:10 in West Africa; 80:20 in East Africa; 65:35 in Southern Africa; and 80:20 in Africa as a whole. For comparison, on other arterial container trade routes, such as transpacific or Asia–Europe, the ratio ranged from 30:70 to 40:60. Thus, the imbalance is worse in Africa than in most regions of the world.

Container Transshipment

Transshipment is common for most African ports, as the national and regional markets do not generate sufficient demand to justify a place on the itinerary of the major intercontinental shipping lines. These markets are therefore dependent on calls from smaller container vessels carrying cargo that has been transshipped at a larger port. To play a role in transshipment, ports should have deepwater and good container-handling performance, and be unencumbered by excessive bureaucracy. Ports that can also generate gateway cargo are even more desirable. Based on these criteria, all three maritime zones in Africa must improve significantly to effectively handle container transshipment.

Regional transshipment ports on the East African coastline include Mombasa and Dar es Salaam. Both face capacity constraints likely to

Figure 5.3   The Imbalance of Sub-Saharan African Container Trade, 2005

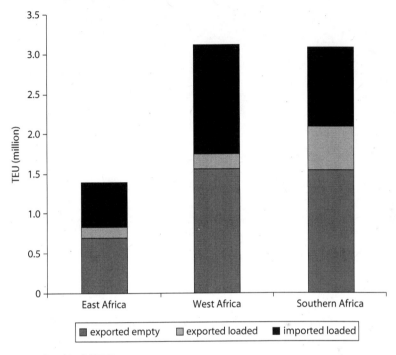

Source: Mundy and Penfold 2009.

curtail their transshipment activity, at least in the short term, although both are moving to install new capacity. In contrast, at the Port of Doraleh in Djibouti, a new terminal designed with transshipment in mind and developed by DP World, is now operational.[3] This terminal provides significant transshipment capacity for East Africa and the Indian Ocean and will compete with Aden and Jeddah (both also partly operated by DP World) for cargo from the main traffic lane through the Red Sea. The port may develop a large industrial area and could attract transshipment for Ethiopia and Sudan.

In southern Africa, Durban is well established as the major container transshipment center, but it too has been struggling to keep pace with demand. There are plans for new facilities (such as the new Pier 1), but demand may still outstrip the capacity of these additions. A number of carriers that use Durban for transshipment are seeking alternate ports in the Indian Ocean islands, notably Mauritius, despite the extra sailing time required to service the region from Mauritius rather than Durban. There are also doubts about whether the cost of expanding capacity in Mauritius to accommodate transshipment traffic can be met with transshipment revenues, which are usually lower than those generated by gateway traffic. Elsewhere in South Africa, Transnet has opened a new terminal in Coega, designed to play a major role in transshipment operations, and has announced plans to develop more facilities in Richards Bay, which could offer alternatives to Durban.

On the West African coast, Abidjan has enjoyed some success as a container transshipment port. In recent years, however, it has suffered because of internal strife in Côte d'Ivoire and disputes over the award of the concession of operating rights for the container terminal.[4] There are plans for a number of new major hubs, but none is likely to be developed in the immediate future. Transshipment traffic for West Africa, unlike that for the east and south, is fed primarily from outside the region, via Algeciras and the new Tangier terminals.

There is clearly potential to further develop container transshipment capacity in Africa. But prospects for expanded capacity may depend on initiative from a major line or consortia to drive hub development.

General Cargo Traffic: Growing by Default

General cargo traffic in Africa is growing more quickly than in other regions of the world, largely because the region is behind the rest of the world in the development of containerization. Figure 5.4 shows growth from 1995 to 2005, broken down by subregion.

Although exports of agricultural products and raw materials are considerable at a number of ports in the region, the balance of trade for general cargo traffic is heavily weighted toward imports (though not as heavily as the container sector). Transit traffic to landlocked countries is predominantly general cargo.

A positive economic outlook, even withstanding the global financial crisis, has increased revenues from oil production, and persistent constraints on the container traffic system bode well for continued growth in general cargo traffic in the near future. Capacity is sufficient to meet demand, though governments must ensure that this continues to be the case. Cargo-handling performance, measured in terms of tonnes handled per man-hour or per gang-hour, is below par by world standards, however, and calls for improvement.

Figure 5.4   Development of General Cargo Traffic, 1995–2005

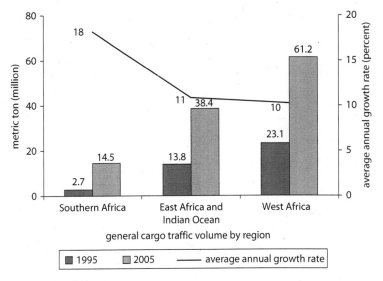

Source: Mundy and Penfold 2009.

Dry Bulk Traffic: Efficient Dedicated Terminals

The broad spectrum of dry bulk traffic in Africa (table 5.3) comprises two categories: major bulk, consisting of commodities such as coal, iron ore, and grain, which tend to be moved in substantial volumes; and minor bulk, consisting of cement, aggregates, clay, and other commodities that tend to be moved in smaller volumes. Dry bulk traffic is sometimes handled at common-user general cargo facilities. Major flows—both in terms of volume and value (such as grain at Mombasa and coal from Richards Bay)—use industrial-style terminals that are often privately owned and do not always publicly report traffic volumes. For example, Richards Bay has one of the largest coal-exporting facilities in the world; but while the general cargo port is publicly owned, the coal-exporting facility is entirely private. Since major global interests control the facility, port and shipping arrangements will likely conform to international standards.

Liquid Bulk Traffic: A Well-Oiled Commercial Chain

Liquid bulk traffic, predominantly oil, is a growing sector in Africa. The United States and the Asian countries have recently made significant

Table 5.3 Dry Bulk Operations in Africa

	Country	Port	Existing and planned dry bulk operations
East Africa	Kenya	Mombasa	The grain terminal in this port is under private sector operation. It was concessioned via an international tender and has operated very efficiently since the new consortia took over.
	Mozambique	Maputo	The port has recently set up a specialized ferrochrome terminal as a niche dry bulk operation, servicing exports of this commodity from South Africa. The port also operates coal export terminals.
	Madagascar	Talarno	A new port development is designed to facilitate exports from a new $350 million ilmenite mine being developed by Rio Tinto, by far the largest mine development undertaken in Madagascar for some time.
Southern Africa	South Africa	Richards Bay	The Richards Bay Coal Terminal is expanding its export capacity from 78 million to 92 million metric tonnes, at a cost of 1 billion rand, making it the biggest facility of its kind in the world.
West Africa	Cameroon	Douala	The master plan studies undertaken for the new port address how to exploit the country's natural resources, including dry bulk commodities such as bauxite, iron ore, cobalt, nickel, and rutile.
	Benin	Cotonou	The port is mainly used for the import of cereal and gypsum, but is currently operating beyond capacity. The new master plan incorporates an expansion at nearby Seme-Kpodji to accommodate growing volumes of these commodities.
	Togo	Kpeme	The privately operated port of Kpeme exports phosphate rock.
	Liberia	Harper	Carvalla Rubber Corporation plans to rehabilitate the port to provide required bulk export capacity.
		Buchanan	Arcelor Mittal has agreed to increase its investment in Liberian ore production from $1.0 billion to $1.5 billion. The ore will be exported from Buchanan, where significant upgrade works are planned to port facilities.
	Ghana	Takoradi	A new master plan has been commissioned for Ghana's two ports of Tema and Takoradi. For Takoradi, this will focus on the development and concessioning of new dry bulk terminals.
	Sierra Leone	Pepel	The government of Sierra Leone has granted African Minerals the exclusive right, under a memorandum of understanding, to rehabilitate the port of Pepel. The intention is to refine and expand the port to achieve a throughput of 40 million tonnes per year (mt/yr).
	Guinea	Kamsar	Kamsar is now the scene of some significant proposed development as part of the so-called Guinea Alumina Project. New port facilities will include a dedicated alumina export terminal.
	Guinea-Bissau		Angola has secured the right to develop a 3 mt/yr bauxite mine in Guinea-Bissau, and this will involve new port construction on the Buba River.

Source: Mundy and Penfold 2009.

investments in the region to establish the necessary export platforms, including pipeline and shipping jetty facilities. Figure 5.5 gives an overview of oil production in Africa. The region has 11 net oil exporters: Nigeria, Angola, Equatorial Guinea, Sudan, the Republic of Congo, Gabon, Chad, Cameroon, Mauritania, Côte d'Ivoire, and the Democratic Republic of Congo. Nigeria and Angola are the dominant oil states, in terms of both production rates and proven reserves. Recently, Ghana and Benin have begun to produce oil, although not enough to satisfy their domestic needs.

Africa is a significant supplier of oil to countries worldwide. It contributes more than 10.0 million barrels per day to the daily world output of 84.5 million barrels, accounting for almost 12 percent of the world oil supply and approximately 19 percent of U.S. net oil imports. The region's natural gas markets are also growing. Asian countries (including China, India, Korea, and Malaysia) are rapidly developing an interest in Africa's energy products. As a consequence, the energy sector accounted for a large part of the nearly fourfold increase in total trade between China and Africa in 2001–06.

The United States has invested substantially in Africa's energy sector, reflecting its desire to decrease reliance on the Middle East by seeking

Figure 5.5   Oil Production and Proven Reserves in Sub-Saharan Africa

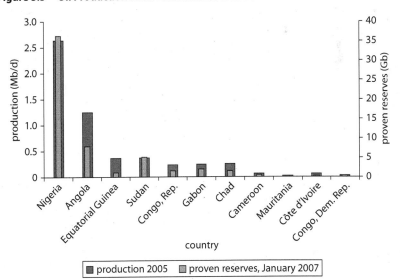

Source: U.S. Department of Energy 2006; *Oil and Gas Journal* 2006.
Note: Gb = 10^9 billion barrels; Mb/d = million barrels per day.

energy sources outside that region. The majority of U.S. energy investment in Africa—over $11 billion and growing—is in the oil and gas sectors of Equatorial Guinea, Nigeria, and Angola. Oil companies from the United States are also heavily involved in oil production in Chad and in the $4 billion investment in the Chad-Cameroon pipeline project. U.S. companies are producing and looking for oil and gas in South Africa, and are also exploring opportunities for energy investment in Benin, Guinea-Bissau, Madagascar, and São Tomé and Príncipe. Recently, there has been a large oil find at sea close to the Liberian–Sierra Leone border. There are few financial impediments to putting the right export platforms in place. In the past, state-owned organizations and private interests have usually tailored the development of new export capacity (ports and shipping) for the energy sector to meet the needs of producers outside the mainstream sphere of port operations. Future projects will probably adhere to this model, which has worked well in the past. (See appendix 5a for more information on the development of traffic types.)

Constraints on Economies of Scale

Countries in Africa have long since abandoned their efforts to enforce the United Nations Liner Code.[5] As a result, the African shipping market has been largely deregulated, allowing it to better integrate with the global market.

Shipping systems have evolved in a global context, the largest container vessels now possessing capacities in excess of 13,000 TEUs. The average size of container vessels serving African ports is relatively small, under 3,000 TEUs, but it is steadily creeping up in line with port system improvements. The acquisition of regional operators by global players and the replacement of direct service to or from ports of origin by transshipment through hubs have accelerated Africa's integration into the global liner network. For example, Maersk Line uses Salalah, Oman, as its hub for East African trade; for its West African trade it uses Tangier, Morocco, and Málaga and Algeciras, Spain.

The constraints on economies of scale imposed by size limitations on vessel access to African ports raise the costs of shipping to Africa. So do port inefficiencies and inadequate links between ports and hinterlands. As a result, feeder services (particularly in East Africa) and regional liner services (in West Africa) will continue to be important.

Costly delays are a problem in many ports. They are mostly a result of long processing times and poor handling in congested port areas rather than insufficient quay capacity. In 2006, a one-day delay cost a shipping line $35,000 for a 2,200-TEU vessel, with proportionally higher costs for larger ships. Shipping lines have responded by introducing congestion charges that range from the equivalent of $30 for a 20-foot container in Dakar to $360 in Tema in 2006. Where customs authorities allow the transport of boxes under bond (allowing customs clearance to be moved to an off-dock location), some ports have developed off-dock terminals to relieve container yard congestion.

The global financial crisis has temporarily relieved the pressure on prices and capacity, although not without adverse effects. A global decrease in maritime transport has left Africa with an oversupply of shipping capacity. Nearly 600 container vessels were without work in September 2009, and there was a significant increase in the number scrapped. The major shipping lines suffered large losses in the first six months of 2009, and more were expected to follow in the short term.

In sum, shipping to or from Africa remains expensive. This is not due to any inherent inefficiency or lack of competition in shipping operations (factors that explain high cost in other trade lanes). Rather it is due to the absence of the large and concentrated flows necessary to capitalize on economies of scale in deep-sea shipping. Also at fault are the high costs of land distribution, particularly to landlocked countries.

The Institutional and Regulatory Framework

The institutional and regulatory framework for the port sector has three components: port facility planning, customs arrangements, and regulation of port management (Bell and Bichou 2007). The treatment of each of these functions differs substantially among countries.

Planning and Reform: A Challenge for Government

New master plans for the port sector were either recently introduced or are under development in Namibia, South Africa, Tanzania, and 10 countries in West Africa. Although planning focuses on the development of facilities and physical capacity, a number of strategic issues must also be addressed.

Africa can support only a limited number of major regional hubs. Competition is already intense among ports in East Africa, and regional collaboration seems unlikely. A port must do more than invest in capacity to become a hub; it must also be able to offer low handling costs and have fairly high cargo potential in its local market. In addition, it should facilitate transit traffic by developing the main trade corridors from the port to the landlocked hinterland. The failure of governments and port authorities in Africa to speed international, intermodal transport by streamlining customs and other formalities at border crossings has stifled trade, slowed inland movement, and driven up prices. Although private operators are responsible for developing their logistics chains, they rely on governments to coordinate port, customs, and inland transport arrangements.

Governments have several responsibilities in strategic port planning: they must establish the respective roles of the public and private sectors, outline methods for attracting and selecting private partners, and identify the technologies and management arrangements needed to develop state-of-the-art ports. These responsibilities require the involvement of the international private sector, particularly in the container terminal business. Countries with congested city ports or limited water depth at quayside or in access channels will need to decide whether to rehabilitate existing ports or develop new ones.

Developments in the deep-sea shipping markets may also force countries to relocate their ports. For example, to be economical, a shipping route between Asia and Latin America requires vessels with capacities of 6,000 TEUs or more. Any such service would benefit greatly from a port of call in South Africa. But Durban has insufficient capacity, and the container terminal in development in Cape Town is too far from the industrial core of the country in Gauteng to be a strong hub port. Developing Richards Bay, which has deep water and ample space, might be a better option, and Transnet has reported plans to undertake development there.

Customs: Seeking Simplification and Automation

Customs and other procedures associated with the movement of goods across international borders increase the time and cost of transport and impede its flexibility (De Wulf and Sokol 2004). For example, in almost half the African countries surveyed in a recent study, it took more than one week to clear goods through the major port, compared with one day or less in many developing countries in other parts of the world. Several factors were identified as contributing to this poor performance (McTiernan 2006).

First, there is little mutual trust and understanding between customs authorities and the business community. The private sector sees customs administrators as primarily concerned with collecting revenue. In all countries but Togo, frontline customs officers are thought to be unaware

of, or unsympathetic to, the business headaches caused by their performance. This is particularly pronounced in countries where officers dress in
military-style uniform. In Kenya, Tanzania, Uganda, and Zambia, customs
officers are part of the national revenue authority and do not dress like
the military. Meanwhile, officers in Côte d'Ivoire, Ghana, and Nigeria display their respective rank on military uniforms and are perceived to be
more autocratic.

Second, many agencies are involved, making coordination difficult.
Some bodies—such as those certifying food, drugs, and agricultural
products—operate alongside but separate from customs. While port
authorities are separate, their processes and procedures are intrinsically
linked with those of customs. Ministries of trade and commerce sometimes slow customs processes by starting initiatives that, alongside
existing procedures, just add to the bureaucratic load.

Third, dissemination of information is poor. Some customs services
(for example, in Côte d'Ivoire and Senegal) make good use of the
Internet. Others have elaborate Web sites that have not been updated for
months, even years. Especially where the use of clearing agents is required
or commonplace, it can be difficult for businesses to identify the cause of
long residence times, whether related to customs procedures or those of
other agencies.

Fourth, there is little standardization of procedures and documentation.
Other than the Southern African Customs Union and the Trans-Kalahari
corridor of the Southern African Development Community, both of which
are adopting a single clearance document, trade blocs seem to have little
influence on customs practices. For example, the members of the East
African Community, all of which also belong to other blocs, have
adopted different practices in key areas. Kenya uses a version of the
Senegalese Trade-X system as the software for its clearance process,
while Tanzania and Uganda run ASYCUDA++.[6] Tanzania operates a full
inspection program subcontracted to a third party. Kenya relies on
importers to secure certificates of conformance with the Kenya Bureau
of Standards. Uganda has no inspection or certification program.

Fifth, corruption is a serious problem. In all the countries surveyed by
the Business Action for Improving Customs Administrations in Africa
(see McTiernan 2006), corruption was believed to be present at an individual level rather than systemwide or through organized syndicates. In a
commonplace scenario, individual customs officers are bribed to pass
undervalued goods. Customs and other officials require bribes to reward
them for using their discretion to speed the clearance process. The scope

for this type of bribery is reduced by automation. The more automation, the less opportunity there is for individual manipulation. The Democratic Republic of Congo, even with few systems and institutions, thus suffers from substantial low-level corruption. Nigeria, which has a large customs service and detailed processes, but no electronic system, is reported to experience much individual corruption on customs transactions. While the example of Rwanda demonstrates that it is possible to eliminate corruption even in a very poor country, the incentive for individual corruption is likely to remain substantial while incomes remain low.

For an approach to the problem, a number of changes have been already suggested (McTiernan 2006) and a handbook has been produced on reform options (De Wulf and Sokol 2005). With development of a consultative arrangement among stakeholders (including businesses), a basis might be found for rewarding a record of compliance with "fast track" systems; at virtually no risk to revenue, the burden of many procedures and costs could be lifted from those businesses that represent a low risk for compliance evasion. The different agency requirements could be integrated by the establishment of a "one-stop shop" for documentation and clearance. Acceptance of a common electronic documentation system such as ASYCUDA would be central to that goal, though customs officers should still be able to manually overrule a "green channel" designation automatically generated by the ASYCUDA++ system. But it is no coincidence that those countries that do not have electronic clearance in place are invariably seen as the most inefficient and corrupt. Simplification and automation are probably the most powerful practical weapons against corruption, alongside relevant training.

Some progress has already been made. Customs reform and modernization programs are currently under way in many countries in Africa, although in general, reform appears less advanced in West Africa than in East or southern Africa. In southern Africa, the Southern African Development Community is proceeding with the implementation of shared documentation and progressively reduced internal tariffs. It has not advanced as far as the Common Market for Eastern and Southern Africa, where internal tariffs have already been eliminated. A common authorized economic operator model is to be implemented as a top priority by five countries of the East African Community (Burundi, Kenya, Rwanda, Tanzania, and Uganda), with mutual recognition among them. When implemented, the model will be one of the first of its kind in the world and will likely benefit the business community.

Port Management Models

There are three main port management models (World Bank 2007).

Service port. In this model, the port authority offers the complete range of services required for the functioning of the port. The port owns, maintains, and operates every available asset (fixed and mobile), and cargo-handling activities are executed by labor employed directly by the port authority. Most service ports are government owned, though there also are some private service ports usually dedicated to a single major shipper or commodity (such as the Richards Bay Coal Terminal in South Africa).

Landlord port. This model is characterized by a mix of private and public sector functions. The public sector port authority acts as a regulatory body and a landlord, outsourcing port operations (especially cargo handling) and leasing infrastructure to private operating companies and industries. The private operators employ the dock labor, and provide and maintain their own on-quay equipment and buildings. Either the public or the private sector can be responsible for pilotage, towage, and line handling.

Whole port concession. Under this model, the public sector hands over complete responsibility for port management and operations to the private sector for a fixed number of years. Djibouti is the main example in Africa.

Africa lags far behind most of the world in introducing institutional reforms to the port sector. Ghana and Nigeria are the only countries in Africa that have comprehensively embraced the landlord port model, although others have arrangements that incorporate some of its elements. Container terminal activities are very attractive to the private sector and are therefore usually concessioned first. Lease contracts and build-operate-transfer concessions (where the concessionaire builds the facilities and operates them during the period of the concession but transfers them to the authority at the end of the concession) are the most common forms of concession (World Bank 2007). Such agreements have tapped the expertise of international terminal operators, and more African countries are now adopting some aspects of the landlord model (table 5.4).

The region has seen very little progress toward the establishment of independent port regulators, although experience shows good concession contracts can be self-regulating. (The institutional characteristics of the major ports are tabulated in appendix 5b.)

Table 5.4   Port Management Models by Region

| | Port management model | | | |
Region	Service port	Partial landlord	Landlord	Whole port concession
East Africa and Indian Ocean	Sudan Kenya	Tanzania Madagascar	n.a.	Djibouti Mozambique
Southern Africa	Namibia South Africa	n.a.	n.a.	n.a.
West Africa	Congo, Dem. Rep. Congo, Rep. Equatorial Guinea Benin Guinea-Bissau Cape Verde	Angola Gabon Togo Cameroon Côte d'Ivoire Liberia Sierra Leone Guinea Gambia Senegal	Nigeria Ghana	n.a.

Source: Mundy and Penfold 2009.
Note: n.a. = not applicable.

Private Sector Participation: Increasing Steadily

Changes in port management models have been associated with increased private sector participation in the funding of African port infrastructure (figure 5.6).

Twenty-six ports spread over 19 African countries reported 42 major private sector transactions in recent years (table 5.5). Most are concession contracts, and a large number of these are associated with the comprehensive port reforms in Nigeria. The management contract for the Mombasa container terminal and original concessions for the Gabon ports of Owendo and Gentil have been canceled.

The transactions listed in table 5.5 include private sector investment commitments of $1.3 billion. Of this total, about 62 percent relates to development of container terminals, 32 percent to multipurpose terminals, and very little to bulk facilities.

Ports in Nigeria attracted 55 percent of total private sector investment commitments in the sector; by far the largest commitment—over $300 million spread across six terminal concession contracts—involved the port of Apapa in Lagos (box 5.2). These transactions have generated substantial royalty payments from concessionaires to African governments—$1.7 billion in total, including over $1.0 billion from the Apapa concession.

Figure 5.6   Evolution of Private Sector Participation in African Ports

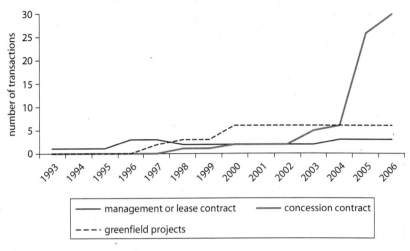

Source: World Bank 2008.

Private sector participation varies greatly among cargo sectors. Concessions have been most prevalent in the container terminal field (table 5.6). In some cases, the port authority or government agency has been reluctant to completely divest its assets, reportedly due to an inadequate rate of return on investment, and instead has chosen to remain as a part owner of the port or terminal operating company. This occurred in the Mozambique whole port concessions and the Tema container terminal concession in Ghana. Several of the global terminal operators—including APM Terminals, DP World, and International Container Terminal Services Inc. (ICTSI)—participate in many of the region's port concessions. Some are facing financial problems as a result of the global economic downturn and have announced that they will decrease the pursuit of new ventures (although companies such as ICTSI continue to expand). This general trend may not be the case in West Africa, however, where global terminal operators seem to be competing fiercely for new concessions. Private sector operation is standard in liquid bulk cargo facilities, but only one-third of the more than 50 dry bulk ports reviewed in Mundy and Penfold (2009) have concessioned any services to private operators, and none appears as a major concession initiative in table 5.6.

Some container terminal concessions have been controversial. For example, rival bidders brought legal challenges after the Dakar and Luanda container terminal concessions were awarded to APM Terminals

Table 5.5 Private Sector Transactions for All Port Sectors in Africa

	Countries	Ports	Number of transactions	Number of canceled transactions	Royalty payments to government (US$ millions)	Investment in facilities (US$ millions)
Management or lease contract	Cameroon, Kenya, Mozambique	Douala, Mombasa, Maputo	4	1	0	0
Concession contract	Angola, Comoros, Equatorial Guinea, Gabon, Ghana, Madagascar, Mozambique, Nigeria, Sudan, Tanzania	Luanda, Mutsamudu, Luba, Owendo, Tema, Toamasina, Beira, Maputo, Quelimane, Apapa, Calibar, Harcourt, Lilypond, Onne, Warri, Tin Can, Juba	32	0	1,366	1,052
Greenfield projects	Côte d'Ivoire, Equatorial Guinea, Ghana, Kenya, Mauritius	Abidjan, Luba, Tema, Mombasa, Freeport	6	0	316	236
Total			42	1	1,682	1,288

Source: World Bank 2008.

Box 5.2

The Nigeria Port Concessions

The Nigerian port system once comprised traditional service ports with inefficient central management. The government of Nigeria initiated major reforms
beginning in late 2004 to introduce the landlord model and concession over
20 terminals to the private sector. This was one of the most ambitious and far-
reaching port reforms undertaken in Africa or elsewhere. The reforms have already
benefited the ports.

Operational benefits include improved turnaround time for ships and cargo,
improved cargo-handling performance, and improved cargo and personnel
security measures. Prior to reform, the Nigerian Ports Authority was subsidized by
the government of Nigeria. Today, the reformed and downsized authority is largely
self-funding. Private operators are scheduled to invest in excess of $500 million in
port development, and will pay more than $5 billion to the government in
rental or royalty fees. Shipping lines also reduced their congestion surcharges
from $800 to $100 per container within a few months of concessioning, which
saved the Nigerian economy $310 million and reduced excessive charges and
corruption.

Source: Mundy and Penfold 2009.

and DP World, respectively. The concessioning process needs to be mod-
ified to minimize the effects of corruption and influence. One model for
reform is presented by Nigeria's Bureau of Public Enterprises, which
hired experienced independent consultants to design the concessioning
of the country's marine terminal facilities and oversee its implementation. The involvement of the bureau ensured that concessioning was
undertaken at arm's length from established port authority and government interests.

Regulatory Arrangements

In most countries, port regulation is undertaken either by a central ministry for transport or by a port authority (table 5.7).

These institutions fulfill a variety of economic and technical regulatory
functions. All are involved in either the day-to-day management and
operation of ports or, at the very least, formulating policy regarding port
activities. Only South Africa has an independent port regulator, which
monitors and enforces the compliance of the National Ports Authority

Table 5.6 Major Institutional Reform Initiatives Implemented or Planned for African Ports, as of 2009

Region	Country	Port	Year	Type	Duration	Contractor
East Africa	Djibouti	Djibouti	2000	Whole port concession, plus development of greenfield high-capacity container terminal	20 years	DP World
	Tanzania	Dar es Salaam	2000	Container terminal concession	n.k.	ICTSI, transferred to Hutchison
	Mozambique	Beira	1999	Whole port concession	25 years	Cornelder (67%), CFM (33%)
	Mozambique	Maputo and Matola	2003	Whole port concession	15 years with option of consortium including 10-year extension	MD and HC resold to DP World
	Mozambique	MIPS, Maputo	1996	Container terminal	15 years, extended to 2113	DP World
	Mozambique	Nacala	2005	Whole port concession	15 years	CDN
	Mozambique	Quelimane	2005	Whole port concession	25 years	—
	Madagascar	Toamasina	2005	Container terminal concession	20 years	ICTSI

Region	Country	Port	Year	Concession type	Duration	Operator
West Africa	Angola	Luanda	2007	Container terminal concession	20 years	APM Terminals
	Gabon	Owendo	2007	Multipurpose terminal concession	25 years	Gabon Port Management (Portek)
	Gabon	Gentil	2007	Multipurpose terminal concession	25 years	Gabon Port Management (Portek)
	Togo	Lomé	Planned	New container terminal concession	25 years	MSC (51%), Lomé (49%)
	Cameroon	Douala	2004	Container terminal concession	15 years	Consortium including APM Terminals
	Nigeria	Multiple	2007	Container terminal and other concessions	Various	Diverse investors at Apapa/Lagos container terminal APM Terminals
	Ghana	Tema	2003	Container terminal concession	25 years	Consortium including APM Terminals
	Côte d'Ivoire	Abidjan	2005	Container terminal concession	n.r.	Consortium including APM Terminals
	Liberia	Monrovia	Planned	Concession of multipurpose facilities	—	Subject to tender process
	Sierra Leone	Freetown	Planned	Concession of multipurpose facilities	—	Subject to tender process
	Guinea	Conakry	Recent	Concession of container terminal	25 years	GETMA International
	Guinea	Kamsar	Planned	Private sector concession in the Guinea Alumina Project	n.k.	n.r.
	Guinea-Bissau	Bissau	Planned	Concession of cargo-handling facilities	n.k	Not yet determined
	Senegal	Dakar	2006	Container terminal concession		DP World
	Cape Verde	Mindelo	Planned	Concession of cargo-handling facilities	n.k	Not yet determined

Source: Mundy and Penfold 2009.
Note: n.r. = not reported; n.k. = not known; n.a. = not applicable; — = not available. CDN = Corredor de Desenvolvimento do Norte; CFM = Caminhos de Ferro de Moçambique; ICTSI = International Container Terminal Services Inc; MD and HC = Mersey Docks and Harbour Company; MIPS = Maputo International Port Services; MSC = Mediterranean Shipping Company.

Table 5.7   National Institutions Responsible for Port Regulation in Africa, by Type

Region	Transport ministry	Port planning authority	Port operating authority	Independent agency
East Africa and Indian Ocean	Djibouti, Kenya	Mozambique, Madagascar	Sudan, Tanzania	n.a.
Southern Africa	n.a.	n.a.	Namibia	South Africa
West Africa	Angola; Benin; Congo, Dem. Rep.; Congo Rep.; Gabon; Equatorial Guinea; Togo; Ghana; Côte d'Ivoire; Liberia; Sierra Leone; Guinea; Guinea-Bissau; Senegal; Cape Verde	Cameroon	n.a.	Nigeria (planned)

Source: Mundy and Penfold 2009.
Note: n.a.= not applicable.

with the National Ports Authority Act and serves as the appeals body for complaints and grievances lodged against the National Ports Authority. Nigeria also plans to establish an independent regulator.

Infrastructure Development

The capacity of a port may be increased by increases in quay length or standing area (usually referred to as infrastructure) or by improvements in the amount or quality of loading and unloading equipment (referred to as superstructure).

Capacity and Demand: Some Ports Approaching Full Utilization

Estimates of port capacity and demand for a sample of ports (selected for their accuracy in reporting these figures) suggest that several ports have either reached or are close to reaching full capacity (table 5.8).

In East Africa, double-digit growth in the container sector has pushed the ports of Mombasa and Dar es Salaam to their capacity limits, and Sudan, Mombasa, and Dar es Salaam are reaching their limits in the dry bulk sector. In southern Africa, Durban has faced challenges in its efforts to expand container capacity to meet demand. And in West Africa, the ports of Luanda and Tema have insufficient container capacity, while Luanda, Douala, and Tema are struggling to handle overall cargo throughput.

By late 2006, African port capacity was estimated to be at 80 percent utilization overall and forecasted to remain at that level through 2010

Table 5.8 Annual Port Capacity and Current Demand, Selected Ports

Region	Port	Current capacity (as of 2006)	Demand (as of 2006 unless otherwise stated)
East Africa	Port Sudan	9 million (m) metric tonnes	7.5 m metric tonnes 400,000 TEU
	Mombasa	17 m metric tonnes 400,000+ TEU	15.87 m metric tonnes (2005) 358,762 TEU (2005)
	Dar es Salaam	4.1 m metric tonnes dry cargo 6.0 m metric tonnes liquid cargo 250,000 TEU	3.8 m metric tonnes dry cargo (2005) 2.0 m metric tonnes liquid cargo (2005) 350,000 TEU
Southern Africa	Cape Town	1.0–1.2 m metric tonnes general cargo 1.0 m TEU/yr containers Dry bulk and liquid capacity not reported	559,602 metric tonnes general cargo (2005) 690,895 TEU (2005)
	Durban	1.3+ m TEU (being expanded) General cargo, dry bulk, and liquid capacity not reported	1.9 m TEU (2005) 7.1 m metric tonnes general cargo 5.5 m metric tonnes dry bulk 7.1 m metric tonnes liquid cargo
West Africa	Luanda	400,000 TEU 4 m metric tonnes per year	377,208 TEU 3.2 m metric tonnes general cargo 2.2 m metric tonnes roll-on roll-off (ro-ro)
	Douala	270,000 TEU 6.5 m metric tonnes general cargo 1.0 m metric tonnes liquid cargo 200,000 TEU	190,700 TEU (2005) 5.8 m metric tonnes general cargo Liquid cargo demand not reported
	Cotonou	2.5 m metric tonnes general cargo 0.7 m metric tonnes liquid cargo	158,201 TEU (2005) 1.0 metric tonnes (2005) Liquid cargo demand not reported
	Tema	350,000–400,000 TEU 8–9 m metric tonnes	420,000 TEU 7.9 m metric tonnes, all noncontainerized cargo 500,000 TEU+ (2007)
	Abidjan	Not reported, but said to be approaching full capacity limits by 2010	21.4 m metric tonnes noncontainerized cargo (2007)

Source: Mundy and Penfold 2009.

(Drewry Shipping Consultants 2006, 2009). Port congestion in some parts of Africa (particularly in Nigeria and in Mombasa and Dar es Salaam) was close to reaching critical levels, although the pressure has been reduced because of the global financial crisis.

Cargo-handling rates are below international standards at all of the ports mentioned above. For example, Durban Container Terminal manages only about 17 container moves per hour, compared with the international norm of 25 to 30. To remedy the situation, Durban is upgrading cranes at existing facilities and has introduced new systems at Pier 1. Although superstructure and infrastructure are separated in South Africa, the fact that both are controlled by the publicly owned Transnet has clearly compromised their proper development. Improvements are required if South Africa's ports are to realize their potential as internationally important transshipment centers for southern Africa. Obstacles lie in the organization, provision, and management of equipment and handling space, as much as in basic quay capacity. Solutions include institutional reform and mobilization of private sector capabilities in port service management as well as public sector investment.

Port Development: Works in Progress

A number of countries in the region—including those still designing their master plans—have either proposed or already begun major port developments (table 5.9).

Smaller schemes span a diverse range of activities, such as dredging new channels and maintaining existing ones, improving navigation systems, rehabilitating berths, setting up new cargo-handling equipment, installing information technology (IT) systems, and purchasing security systems. The steadily increasing presence of the private sector in frontline cargo-handling operations provides added impetus for development.

Cargo-Handling Systems: A Very Mixed Bag

Cargo-handling systems in the ports vary widely, ranging from outdated to state of the art. (Available facilities for all ports are reported in appendix 5c.) A number of major ports—including Banjul, Dakar, Monrovia, Onne, Pointe Noire, and Port Harcourt—lack quay crane equipment and rely on ships' gear for cargo handling, while others have outmoded container gantry cranes.[7] The continued use of outdated equipment limits port productivity and contributes to the region's capacity shortage. New investment in cargo-handling equipment, rather than in quay capacity, is thus needed to allow African ports to fulfill their potential.

Table 5.9   Principal New Port Developments in Africa

Region	Country	Project
East Africa	Sudan	*Proposed:* introduction of new container and other cargo capacity at Suakin port
	Djibouti	*Actual:* new container terminal scheduled to commence operations in 2009, offering major new transshipment capacity
	Kenya	*Proposed:* second container terminal for Mombasa
Southern Africa	South Africa	*Actual:* development of new Pier 1 container terminal facility (Durban); opening of new port of Ngqura for container-handling operations; ongoing expansion of coal export capacity at Richards Bay; and major expansion of container terminal capacity at Cape Town through expansion of the terminal footprint, equipment, and other system developments
	Mozambique	*Proposed:* upgrade of container capacity in Maputo, deepening and further improvement of port of Beira
	Madagascar	*Proposed:* new port development at Talanaro to facilitate ilmenite exports
West Africa	Congo, Rep.	*In progress:* Extension of Point Noire breakwater and container terminal plus the deepening of Terminal G
	Gabon	*Proposed:* Expansion of Owendo quay and improvement of connecting road system
	Cameroon	*Actual:* dredging of Douala port *Proposed:* new container terminal development
	Benin	*Proposed:* new port development at Seme-Kpodji
	Togo	*Proposed:* new container terminal development
	Ghana	*Proposed:* extensive new port development at Takoradi
	Côte d'Ivoire	*Proposed:* major capacity expansion at the Port of Abidjan
	Liberia	*Proposed:* multipurpose terminal development
	Guinea	*Proposed:* extension of the container terminal
	Senegal	*Proposed:* addition of major new container port capacity

Source: Mundy and Penfold 2009.

Several ports have already benefited from public sector investment in new quayside container gantry cranes and landside-handling systems (notably by the Kenya Ports Authority in Mombasa and the National Ports Authority in South Africa). But the private sector, which has a growing presence in container handling, continues to account for the most investment in quayside and landside container-handling and IT systems. The gradual transfer of the financial burden of such investments from governments to the private sector has had positive results. This trend is also evident in the dry bulk sector, where the industrial character of many terminals is particularly conducive to private sector investment.

New equipment must be introduced in the proper context to realize its full benefit. For example, modern container gantries demand quay structures that can accept high loadings, and container terminal stacking areas must have sufficient structural strength to support multiple stacked containers. Modern container-handling systems demand not only the requisite equipment but also a high degree of organization by port management, proper IT support, and an increased emphasis on reducing damage to both personnel and property. Finally, proper environmental protection will assume much greater importance with the installation of new systems for dry bulk handling, particularly in facilities that handle commodities where spillage and contamination can occur. The importance of effective equipment maintenance and support systems has become clear in some state-owned ports that continue to deliver unsatisfactory performance despite the addition of new equipment.

Deficient soft infrastructure also represents a significant operational bottleneck at many ports in the region. In particular, customs procedures are often outdated or subject to corruption, and frequently delay cargo clearance (and have even prompted temporary port closures). Other obstacles include lack of IT-supported management, information, and communication systems both within the port area and down the supply chain. While upgrading physical equipment has been the focus of many port development projects, improving soft infrastructure is equally important to the continued development of the sector in Africa.

Safety and Security Arrangements

Safety at sea, and particularly in congested port areas, requires commitment to discipline in navigation. Since, by its nature, the shipping business is global, the rules must also be global. The function of the International Maritime Organization (IMO) has historically been to set these rules. Where the IMO's rules relate to the conditions governing crew employment, the International Labour Organization (ILO) has also been involved.

In principle, responsibility for implementation of the IMO and ILO standards rests with the countries in which the vessels are registered. But since many vessels carry flags of convenience,[8] appropriate action by the country of registration cannot be relied on. For that reason many of the IMO's most important technical conventions contain provisions for ships to be inspected at their location of business. "Port state control" is the inspection of foreign ships in national ports to verify that the condition of the ship and its equipment comply with the requirements of international regulations and that the ship is manned and operated in compliance with these rules.

While the primary responsibility for ships' standards still formally rests with the flag state, port state control provides a safety net to catch substandard ships. A ship going to a port in one country will normally visit other countries in the region before embarking on its return voyage, and it is to everybody's advantage if inspections can be closely coordinated. The IMO has therefore encouraged the establishment of regional organizations and agreements to govern port state control. Regional memoranda of understanding have been signed, including one for West and Central Africa. The African Union has also begun to take a more active role in this area. African experts on maritime security and safety met in April 2010 under the auspices of the African Union to consider an African Integrated Maritime Strategy, a step toward a holistic policy on this matter.

Maritime security is also an integral part of the IMO's responsibilities. In recent years, Africa has witnessed a resurgence of the problems of piracy, human trafficking, and dumping of toxic waste in its coastal waters—in addition to illegal fishing, which has been going on for decades unnoticed by poorly equipped African states. In particular, the rapid escalation of piracy off the coast of Somalia and the Gulf of Guinea has alarmed African states as well as the international community.

A comprehensive security regime for international shipping entered into force on July 1, 2004. The mandatory security measures, adopted in December 2002, include a number of amendments to the 1974 Safety of Life at Sea Convention (SOLAS), the most far-reaching of which enshrines the new International Ship and Port Facility Security Code (ISPS Code),[9] which contains detailed security-related requirements for governments, port authorities, and shipping companies in a mandatory section (part A), together with a series of guidelines about how to meet these requirements in a second, nonmandatory section (part B).

Most ports in Africa now have approval under the ISPS Code, but information on additional measures is sparse. A number of ports have closed-circuit television and automated port processes using electronic means to collect, analyze, and distribute data to improve real-time understanding and control of the port situation. The frequency of container scanning has also increased as part of supply-chain security initiatives. Lax security is particularly evident among smaller secondary ports. On the other hand, oil export terminals and South Africa's seven commercial ports have particularly strong security.

Meeting new industry security requirements (particularly those of the ISPS Code) can be expensive, especially for ports in developing countries. A recent study (Kruk and Donner 2008) examined compliance costs for 12 ports in both developed and developing countries. The average cost per TEU of container traffic was found to be $4.95, and the average cost per tonne of general cargo $0.22. The United Nations Conference on Trade and Development performed a similar study that gave substantially lower estimates, with average costs of $3.60 and $0.08, respectively. But Kruk and Donner (2008) found average security costs to vary widely among ports, ranging from $1.00 to $14.00 per TEU of container traffic and from less than $0.05 to $0.50 per metric tonne of general cargo. The three African ports had costs at the lower end of both ranges—between $1.00 and $2.00 per TEU and less than $0.05 per tonne of general cargo. Based on the results, the total cost of ISPS Code compliance for the three African ports taken together is just over $5 million.

Performance, Cost, and Quality

Measuring and comparing cargo-handling performance is feasible in certain cargo sectors but not really practical in others. For example, both container handling and general cargo handling are uniform enough to permit performance comparisons among ports, regions, and even continents. In measuring container-handling performance, both quay-side and landside performance share enough common denominators to be relevant. (Performance measures for the region can be found in appendix 5d.) Bulk handling, on the other hand, tends to be a bespoke business ranging across a wide variety of different commodities that use diverse handling systems. Performance comparisons in the dry bulk sector are therefore generally uninformative.

Quayside Container Handling: Below International Standards

Quayside container-handling performance is measured by the average number of crane moves per hour. Figure 5.7 shows the performance of the major African ports.

African ports perform poorly in this respect compared to other regions. Container-handling performance in modern container terminals utilizing container gantry cranes falls mainly in the 20–30 moves per hour

Figure 5.7   Container-Handling Systems at Major Ports of the Region

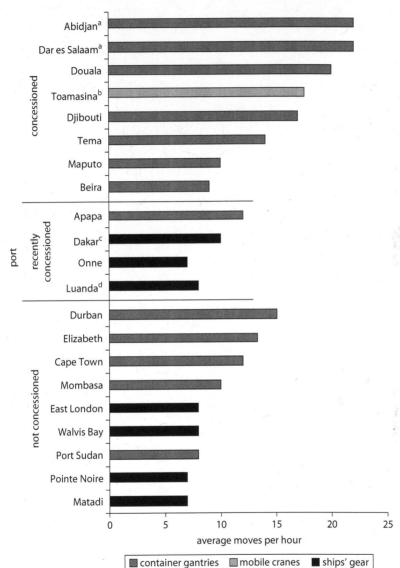

Source: Mundy and Penfold 2009.

Note: Handling rates reported are per hour, per item of equipment for container gantries and mobile cranes, and overall per hour for ships' cranes.

a. Abidjan and Dar es Salaam average more than 20 moves per hour.

b. Toamasina average moves for discharge (22.4) and moves for loading (12.8).

c. Dakar only concessioned in 2007.

d. Luanda only concessioned in 2007.

bracket, while the norm for ship-to-shore handling performance in the African ports considered is below 20 moves per hour (table 5.10).

Differences in handling volumes can explain part of the discrepancy in handling performance. Container terminals in Africa—particularly along the east and west coasts—handle much lower volumes than highly developed container terminals in other parts of the world, which translates into fewer exchanges per ship. Vessels in the region are also smaller, necessitating more complex vessel loading and unloading operations. Moreover, a significant number of ports in Africa do not as yet possess purpose-built container-handling cranes and rely on ships' gear for across-the-quay handling operations. Eight moves per hour is the norm for this latter type of operation.

Concessioning typically involves both investment in new equipment and improvement of management systems; the better management has also allowed ports to substantially enhance their handling performance without major upgrades of their quayside equipment. For example, within a few months of the concessioning of the Apapa container terminal in Lagos, delays for berthing space had dwindled, and leading shipping lines had reduced the congestion surcharge (charged to customers for moving traffic through the port) from $800 to $120 per container, saving the Nigerian economy an estimated $310 million per year. Similarly, the incoming operator in Dakar, DP World, has realized significant

Table 5.10   Gantry Crane Productivity, 2004 (Selected Terminals)

Port	Performance in net container moves per crane-hour
United States	
Virginia International Terminals	25.0–30.0
Ceres, Baltimore	24.0
Europe	
Antwerp (Scheldt)	28.0
Rotterdam Delta	27.0
Asia	
Port of Singapore	33.0
Port Klang (Northport)	22.6
Africa	
Durban	15.0
Cape Town	12.0
Mombassa	10.0
Abidjan	20.0+

Source: Mundy and Penfold 2009.

operational improvements and achieved better performance through new equipment provision and the introduction of modern container terminal operating practices. Figure 5.8 shows that concessioned ports tend to outperform nonconcessioned ports in Africa, handling an average of 16 container moves per hour on average, compared to only 10 for publicly managed ports. They also have a much lower probability of relying on ships' gear for loading and unloading.

Landside Container Handling: A Problem of Organization

There are two major indicators of landside container terminal performance: truck cycle time and the average dwell time of containers in the terminal (figure 5.9). The truck cycle time measures the time between when a truck joins the queue to enter the terminal (to drop off containers) and when it exits the terminal (loaded with other containers). Based on international experience, the benchmark for truck cycle time is one hour, though the growth in container traffic has made achieving that benchmark increasingly rare. The regional average for truck cycle times in Africa ranges from 4 hours in southern Africa to 10 hours in West Africa. Improving the unsatisfactory landside performance will require addressing basic terminal organization; using prebooking and IT systems; and

Figure 5.8   Container-Handling Performance by Equipment Type and Port Management Type

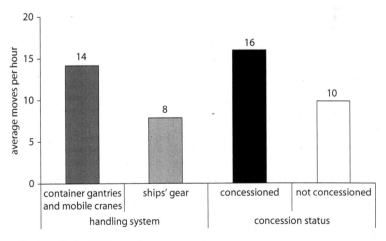

Source: Mundy and Penfold 2009.
Note: Handling rates reported are per hour, per item of equipment for container gantries and mobile cranes, and overall per hour for ships' cranes.

Figure 5.9   Typical Truck Cycle and Dwell Times by Region

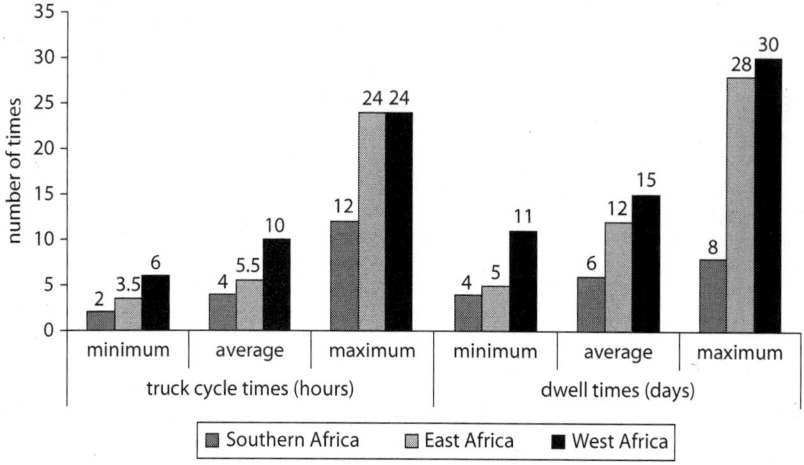

Source: Mundy and Penfold 2009.

introducing off-peak pickup times, modern gate systems, and other measures that alleviate congestion around the terminal (such as relocating
stuffing and stripping activities to satellite sites).

The accepted international target for container dwell time is less than
seven days. Dwell times in Sub-Saharan Africa range from an average of
6 days in southern Africa to 12 days in East Africa and more than 15 days
in West Africa (see figure 5.9). Southern Africa's superior performance can
be attributed to better container storage organization. Unlike terminals in
East and West Africa, most southern African terminals charge the consignee
a daily storage charge after five to seven days, and charges sometimes
increase the longer a container remains in storage. Furthermore, terminals
typically have rules to discourage the dumping of empty containers in a
terminal. (A range of access and landside quality indicators are shown for
all ports in Africa in appendix 5e.)

General Cargo Handling: Below International Performance Standards

In developed countries, handling rates for general cargo usually
exceed 30 metric tonnes per hour per crane. Only the South African
ports of Richards Bay and Durban approach this level of performance
(figure 5.10). More generally, ports in Africa fall far behind the developed

Figure 5.10   Performance in General Cargo Handling in Individual Ports of Sub-Saharan Africa

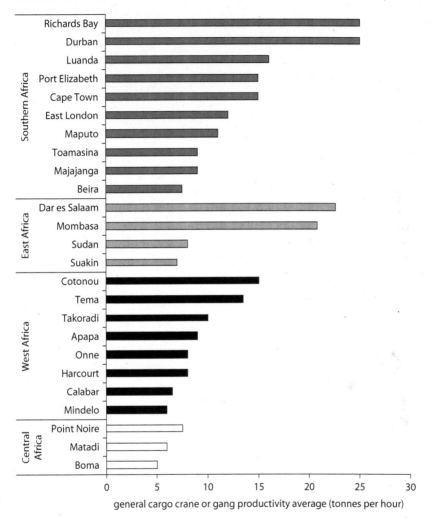

general cargo crane or gang productivity average (tonnes per hour)

Source: Ocean Shipping Consultants 2009.

country standard and will require modern systems and cargo-handling practices to bridge the gap.

While there is substantial variation in general cargo handling perform-ance within each subregion in Africa, there is also a clear difference in average performance between regions, with West Africa falling substan-tially behind East and southern Africa (table 5.11).

Table 5.11   Performance in General Cargo Handling across Regions of Africa

Region	Performance per hour per crane
East Africa	8–25 metric tonnes
Southern Africa	10–25 metric tonnes
West Africa	7–15 metric tonnes

Source: Mundy and Penfold 2009.

Dry and Liquid Bulk Cargo Handling: International Companies Meeting International Performance Standards

Both dry and liquid bulk cargo comprise a wide range of commodities, which makes measuring and comparing performance in this sector difficult. Moreover, privately owned industrial-style terminals that handle dry and liquid bulk cargo tend to keep their performance statistics confidential. Nevertheless, some conclusions about performance in the sector can be drawn.

The performance of private operators handling dry bulk and liquid bulk (particularly oil) cargo in Africa is likely to be comparable to that of similar terminals in mature markets because they are mostly global operators well versed in state-of-the-art techniques. On the other hand, general cargo quays handle a considerable proportion of dry bulk cargo in the region, which suggests that the low traffic volume of certain bulk cargo types does not justify dedicated facilities. There is therefore scope for the specialization of facilities as volumes increase.

Cargo-Handling Costs: High for All Cargo

Cargo-handling costs tend to be higher in Africa than in mature markets in most other parts of the world. This is a result of several factors. Technical deficiencies (including low operating efficiency, lack of maintenance, poor planning, and capacity constraints) and institutional deficiencies (including a lack of enterprise culture, outdated pricing structures, and weak regulation of the monopoly service provider) contribute to inflated costs. (Available data on costs and charges at African ports are given in appendix 5f.)

Container-handling charges at ports in Africa range from $100 to $300 per container, compared to between $80 and $150 per container elsewhere. Shipping lines are frequently involved in terminal operations in the region, particularly along the coast of West Africa. Shipping line involvement in terminal operations, either direct or indirect, has raised questions about possible abuse by shipping lines to gain market share in the ocean freight markets. Concessions should therefore include regulations to safeguard against this possibility. Such regulations might involve specifying that port installations are for common use and should not discriminate in the charges levied. Concession agreements did not place ceilings on container-handling charges until recently; ceilings were specified in the concessioning of container-handling facilities in Madagascar in 2005 and Nigeria since 2004.

Handling charges for general cargo are between $6 and $15 per tonne in the region, compared to between $6 and $9 per tonne elsewhere. A lack of proper facilities and equipment and ineffective management and operations generally contribute to higher charges. Furthermore, typical breakbulk cargo[10]—unlike general cargo such as palletized fruit or bagged agricultural products—is generally handled by publicly owned operators, which can reduce efficiency and increase costs.

Charges vary by trade lane and commodity. Figure 5.11 shows the range of basic handling charges from ship's hold to gate enforced by the port or terminal. These do not include the inevitably higher charges passed on by the shipping line to cargo shippers or supplemental charges such as for scanning or congestion. (More details on cargo-handling charges can be found in appendix 5f.)

Overall Quality of Port Services: Substantial Improvement Needed

With the possible exception of those in South Africa, ports in Africa are comparable to those in other emerging regions. If they are to catch up to ports in more developed areas of the world, they must make substantial improvements in port planning, infrastructure development, institutional reform, pricing structures, and interface with other transport systems. There are also external catalysts for improvement—for instance, the advance of global liner operators into the African region linking the continent with global liner networks. Africa is no longer served only by regional specialists. This has spurred port traffic growth and international investment interest in the ports sector. Finally, governments also must play a role in encouraging reform. Overall, the context is conducive for improving the quality of port services.

The Way Forward

Growth in maritime traffic in Africa promises to continue—as does pressure on the region's port system—once the effects of the financial crisis of 2008–09 have worn off. The liberalization of the international

Figure 5.11 Typical Gateway Container-Handling and General Cargo Charges Applied in Major African and World Ports

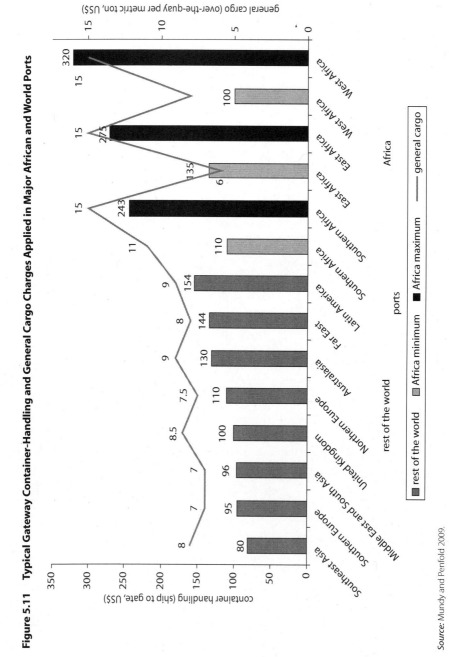

Source: Mundy and Penfold 2009.

shipping market will continue to have a positive and widespread influence; neither the quality nor quantity of international shipping is likely to be deficient.

The region's ports, however, have not kept up with the increase in traffic or changes in technology and regulation. Their performance lags behind that of most ports around the world. Several ports have exceeded their capacity limits, and others are approaching the limit. The presence of international container liner operators has stimulated port development in the region, but slow institutional and regulatory reform is a bottleneck to progress. Further concerns include corruption and unsatisfactory integration between maritime and land transport. The priorities for action therefore are primarily aimed at strategic elements and institutional reform.

Priority 1. Improving strategic planning for ports

Governments can improve strategic planning through the following:

- Establishing a strategic port development plan
- Coordinating planning for port facilities and local land use
- Seeking international agreements on port locations and developments, and on international transit corridor management.

Priority 2. Reforming port management structures

Most countries have replaced the traditional public sector service port structure, but many African countries have failed to do so. Reform should therefore include the following:

- A formal commitment to a modern landlord port structure or its equivalent
- Procedures for planning and implementing tenders for port concessions
- Transparent rules and procedures (including for international arbitration) to attract the best operators to concessions.

Priority 3. Reforming public administration

Customs administration is inherently susceptible to corruption and inefficiency. Public administration in the region requires reforms such as these to minimize opportunities for manipulation:

- Automating customs procedures and other procedures, such as health and safety inspection

- Developing portwide multiuser hardware and software systems to speed processing
- Establishing an independent port regulator.

Priority 4. Improving coordination with land transport

An efficient port minimizes the cost and time of transfers between land and sea transport. Improving this aspect of ports in the region will require taking these steps:

- Eliminating non-market-based allocation of inbound traffic to land transport operators (including both the protection of preferred carriers and noncompetitive procedures for the allocation of traffics)
- Providing adequate infrastructure for road and rail access to port areas.

Notes

1. The main source for this chapter is a report prepared for Africa Infrastructure Country Diagnostic in 2008 and 2009 by Ocean Shipping Consultants, Ltd. (2009). The report covers traffic development, infrastructure development and investment, performance cost and quality, institutional and regulatory frameworks, and security arrangements. Bert Kruk and Michel Donner of the World Bank also contributed extensively to this chapter through their examination of the performance of shipping markets in Africa.

2. Containers with a standard cross section of 8 feet by 8 feet may be 10, 20, or 40 feet in length. For statistical purposes, it is conventional to express container traffic in TEUs.

3. DP World, a subsidiary of the investment company Dubai World, is a major operator of marine ports, with 49 terminals in operation (and a further 12 under development) that handled 46.8 million TEUs in 2008.

4. In 2004, the president of Côte d'Ivoire announced the award of a concession to operate the Vridi container terminal to a company (SETV) largely owned by the French logistics company Bolloré. The award was made without any competitive tendering. It was challenged by the chamber of commerce, other potential concessionaires, and also by the minister of infrastructure, who declared the award was illegal as it was sanctioned by neither his ministry nor the government. The minister of infrastructure was subsequently suspended by the president. Following the refusal by the Ministry of Transport to renew Bolloré's stevedoring license, the company took the case to the highest court in Côte d'Ivoire, which overruled the Ministry of Transport's decision. The World Bank withdrew its support but the concession went ahead. A compromise eventually emerged, with APM Terminals invited to hold a 47 percent

stake in the container terminal concession. Container movements reached 544,000 TEUs in 2008, and SETV has pledged to invest $62 million to further expand the capacity of the terminal.

5. The United Nations Liner code, which aims to protect the interests of developing countries by reserving 40 percent of the trade of liner conferences for ships of the country of origin or traffic destination, was introduced in 1974. But the container revolution largely undermined its effectiveness by moving a large proportion of the international freight movement out of the conference system, and attempts to adapt it to the new world container system have been unsuccessful.

6. ASYCUDA is a computerized customs management system, developed by the United Nations Conference on Trade and Development in Geneva, that covers most foreign trade procedures. The system handles manifests and customs declarations, accounting procedures, and transit and suspense procedures, as well as generating trade data for statistical economic analysis. It provides for electronic data interchange between traders and customs using EDIFACT (Electronic Data Interchange for Administration, Commerce, and Transport) rules. ASYCUDA maintains permanent regional support centers in Ouagadougou, Burkina Faso, for West Africa, and in Lusaka, Zambia, for East and southern Africa.

7. A quay is a concrete, stone, or metal platform lying alongside or projecting into the water for loading and unloading ships. A container gantry crane is a track-mounted, shoreside crane used in the loading and unloading of break-bulk cargo, containers, and heavy-lift cargo.

8. A ship carrying a flag of convenience is a ship registered under the maritime laws of a country that is not the home country of the ship's owners and that offers low tax rates and leniency in crew and safety requirements.

9. The code is a comprehensive set of measures established in the wake of the 9/11 attacks in the United States. Compliance is mandatory for the 148 signatories of the SOLAS.

10. Breakbulk cargo covers a great variety of goods that must be loaded individually and not in intermodal containers or in bulk.

References

Bell, M. G. H., and K. Bichou. 2007. *The Port Sector in South Africa: Towards an Integrated Policy and Institutional Reform.* Washington, DC: World Bank.

CICOS (Commission Internationale du Bassin Congo-Oubangui-Sangha). 2007. "Plan d'action stratégique pour la promotion de la navigation dans le bassin Congo-Oubangui-Sangha." HPC Hamburg Port Consulting GmbH, Hamburg, Germany.

de Wulf, L., and J. B. Sokol, eds. 2004. *Customs Modernization Studies*. Washington, DC: World Bank.

———. 2005. *Customs Modernization Handbook*. Washington, DC: World Bank.

Drewry Shipping Consultants. 2006. *Annual Review of Global Container Terminal Operators*. London: Drewry Shipping Consultants.

———. 2009. *Annual Review of Global Container Terminal Operators*. London: Drewry Shipping Consultants.

Harding, A., G. Palsson, and G. Raballand. 2007. "Port and Maritime Transport Challenges in West and Central Africa." Sub-Saharan Africa Transport Policy Program Working Paper 84, World Bank, Washington, DC.

Kruk, C. B., and M. L. Donner. 2008. "Review of Cost of Compliance with the New International Freight Transport Security Requirements: Consolidated Report of the Investigations Carried Out in Ports in the Africa, Europe and Central Asia, and Latin America and Caribbean Regions." Transport Sector Board, World Bank, Washington, DC.

McTiernan, A. 2006. "Customs and Business in Africa: A Better Way Forward Together." Business Action for Improving Customs Administration in Africa, London.

Mundy, M., and A. Penfold. 2009. "Beyond the Bottlenecks: Ports in Sub-Saharan Africa." Africa Infrastructure Country Diagnostic Background Paper 13, World Bank, Washington, DC.

Ocean Shipping Consultants. 2009. "Beyond the Bottlenecks: Ports in Africa." Africa Infrastructure Country Diagnostic Background Paper 8, World Bank, Washington, DC.

U.S. Department of Energy. 2006. "Annual Energy Review." Energy Information Administration, U.S. Department of Energy, Washington, DC.

World Bank. 2007. *Port Reform Toolkit*. 2nd ed. Washington, DC: World Bank.

———. 2008. Private Participation in Infrastructure Database. World Bank, Washington, DC. http://ppi.worldbank.org/index.aspx.

CHAPTER 6

Urban Transport: Struggling with Growth

Urban transport is not a mode of transport, of course, but rather a collection of modal facilities and services found in a particular location.[1] It is the density and complexity of those facilities and services that differentiate one system of urban transport from another. This chapter, unlike those that precede it, focuses on services more than physical infrastructure. For the infrastructure facilities discussed, data are not comprehensive but are based on a sample of 14 cities.[2] The sample data are supplemented from other sources where they are clearly unrepresentative (as in the case of urban rail services).

All of the sample cities are in low-income countries (table 6.1). The sample includes medium cities (population around 1 million), large cities (population of 2–4 million), and the two megacities (population over 5 million) of Lagos and Kinshasa. Density also varies across the sample, from under 1,000 inhabitants per square kilometer (km^2) in Kigali and Kinshasa to over 13,000 in Conakry and Douala. For comparison, the density of New York City is around 10,000 inhabitants per km^2.

Africa's cities are experiencing rapid population growth—typically between 3 and 5 percent per year over the past decade. Douala and Lagos each have grown by at least 6 percent per year. In 2000, one in three Africans lived in a city, and this share is expected to rise to one in two by

Table 6.1 Size and Other Characteristics of 14 African Cities

City	Population (millions)	Growth rate (%)	City population as share of national population (%)	City population as share of national urban population (%)	Density (1,000 inhabitants per square km)	Private cars per 1,000 inhabitants
Abidjan	3.5	3.7	20	46	6.2	52
Accra	2.8	4.0	13	28	8.1	65
Addis Ababa	3.1	<4.0	5	28	5.7	32
Bamako	1.2	4.8	9	32	4.5	108
Conakry	1.5	4.1	16	65	13.3	61
Dakar	2.8	4.4	30	49	5.1	39
Dar es Salaam	3.7	6.4	10	29	2.1	13
Douala	2.5	6.5	17	34	13.2	40
Kampala	2.0	5.0	7	59	2.1	—
Kigali	0.7	3.1	8	100	1.0	40
Kinshasa	8.0	4.1	13	32	0.8	—
Lagos	15.0	6.0	12	25	4.2	80
Nairobi	4.0	>4.0	12	29	5.7	—
Ouagadougou	1.1	4.4	8	52	2.0	78
Average	n.a.	4.7	13	43	5.2	55

Source: Kumar and Barrett 2008.
Note: n.a. = not applicable; — = not available.

2030. The growth has been driven by anemic economic conditions in rural areas rather than by burgeoning wealth in the cities, with people fleeing rural areas to escape failing crops, natural disasters, and conflicts.

The challenge posed by rapid growth is accentuated by the absence of policies on land use and economic development. This has led to urban sprawl, as migrants from rural areas settle in outer areas where land is most cheaply available. The declining population density associated with this sprawl has increased travel distances and pushed up the price of public transport. In most cities, authorities have had difficulty meeting the service demands of the new urban residents, particularly the poor, who are most dependent on the public provision of water, electricity, transport, and other services. As a result, the poor are often effectively excluded from work and social services. Meanwhile, the rising use of private cars has choked roads, endangering the safety of pedestrians and the health of city residents who breathe in automobile emissions. The need to coordinate land use and transport planning is widely recognized but presents a very difficult challenge to urban governance.

Infrastructure: Roads

Urban transport in African cities is largely road based. Most roads were built when the cities had a single center and before the rapid growth of personal motorized transport. The characteristics of the road networks in the 14 study cities are summarized in table 6.2. The primary road network usually radiates from the center of the city to surrounding areas but lacks orbital links. As a consequence, the region's urban road infrastructure is deficient in several ways.

First, there is not enough of it. Many African cities have expanded more quickly than the capacity of governments to provide infrastructure. As a result, road networks are incomplete and unconnected. New housing construction has been largely unplanned, without adequate provision for transport and other services. Overall, the road network constitutes less than 7 percent of the land area in most of the 14 study cities—only about one-third that in most developed cities worldwide (World Bank 2002). Service lanes are absent, and street lighting is minimal. The majority of the roads have one lane in each direction; where the roads are wider, one lane is often taken up by pedestrians and parked vehicles. It is also difficult to organize public transport services to serve areas of low density, and many outlying neighborhoods can be reached only by two-wheeled vehicles.

Table 6.2   Characteristics of City Road Networks

City	Length of road network (km)	Length of paved road network (km)	Paved roads as share of all roads (%)	Paved road density m per 1,000 people	Paved road density km per km²
Abidjan	2,042	1,205	59	346	2.1
Accra	1,899	950	50	339	2.8
Addis Ababa	—	400	—	129	0.7
Bamako	836	201	24	167	0.8
Conakry	815	261	32	174	2.3
Dakar	—	1156	—	467	2.1
Dar es Salaam	1,140	445	39	122	0.2
Douala	1,800	450	25	237	2.4
Kampala	610	451	74	225	0.5
Kigali	984	118	12	170	0.2
Kinshasa	5,000	500	10	63	0.1
Lagos	—	6,000	—	400	1.7
Nairobi	—	—	—	—	—
Ouagadougou	1,827	201	11	185	0.4
Average	—	—	33	318	1.7

Source: Kumar and Barrett 2008.
Note: — = not available. km = kilometer; m = meter.

Second, the proportion of paved roads is too low. On average, only a third of the roads in the sample cities are paved (table 6.2) but the range is wide: from barely 10 percent in Kinshasa and Kigali to more than 70 percent in Kampala. Paved road density is typically in the order of 300 meters per 1,000 inhabitants (or close to 2 kilometers [km] per km²). These densities are at the extreme lower end of developing cities worldwide, for which the average is close to 1,000 meters per 1,000 inhabitants, according to the Millennium Cities database (UITP 2001). Again, the range is wide. Dakar has 467 meters of paved roads per 1,000 inhabitants; at the other extreme, Kinshasa has just 63 meters, barely half that of the city (Dar es Salaam) in second place for lowest paved road density. In low-income areas, gravel and earth roads are still the norm, and poor drainage contributes to serious flooding during the rainy season.

Third, road infrastructure is poorly maintained. Although figures on road conditions are not widely available, the proportion in a poor state of repair is probably greater for urban roads of any specified daily traffic level than for nonurban roads with the same traffic volume. Estimates of the urban road stock were made for 20 of the 24 Africa Infrastructure Country Diagnostic (AICD) countries. The total network length was 268,490 km including South Africa, but only 104,250 excluding it.

Outside South Africa, less than half of urban roads are paved, and only a little over 40 percent are in good condition (figure 6.1). The poor state of roads has also limited options for urban transport and contributed to the wear and tear of transit fleets. In their current state, many roads cannot handle a conventional bus service.

Most of the countries surveyed have established a second-generation road fund (as discussed in chapter 2 of this book) and have begun to fund road maintenance through road use charges. Yet although most road use occurs in urban areas, and most of the revenues are therefore collected

Figure 6.1   Condition of Urban Roads in 20 AICD Countries

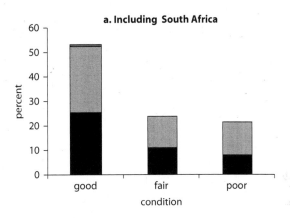

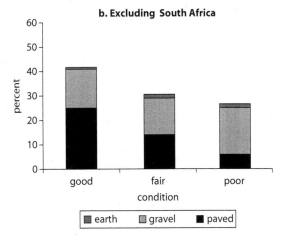

Source: Gwilliam and others 2009.
Note: Totals do not add up to 100 percent because of rounding.

from urban road users, the fiscal allocation usually does not reflect this situation. In Ghana and Ethiopia, between 20 and 30 percent of the road fund is allocated to the maintenance of urban roads. On average across all countries, however, urban roads receive only about 10 percent of road fund revenues—an amount inadequate for their maintenance needs. While the implication is that cities are expected to have other sources of income from taxes or trading revenue that they can devote to their roads, they often do not. A restructuring of road fund allocations to more closely reflect traffic patterns could help to alleviate this problem. In addition, new sources of revenue need to be developed. For example, cities could charge private cars for parking and tax new urban developments that impose a burden on existing transport networks.

Fourth, urban roads are poorly managed. Intersections are spaced close together and are poorly designed for turning. In all the cities under review, commercial activities (such as street vending) and parked vehicles force pedestrians off the sidewalks into the roadway, reducing road capacity and posing safety hazards. Competition between vehicles for space at bus stops often spills over into adjoining traffic lanes. Because traffic management is limited in scope and extent, accidents are frequent. Pedestrians account for two-thirds of traffic fatalities.

Fifth, local governments have paid little attention to facilitating the operation of public transport systems, which account for the majority of trips in all of the study cities. For example, dedicated bus lanes that speed the flow of public transport are rare; bus stops, bus shelters, and other facilities for passengers are scarce and in poor condition; bus bays are too narrow to accommodate multiple buses, so waiting buses often obstruct one lane of the road; and bus terminals, often in the heart of the city, are overcrowded and lack facilities for passengers. A few cities have introduced measures to improve bus travel, but they have not been properly enforced anywhere.

Finally, most cities have ignored the needs of pedestrians. Around 65 percent of the road network lacks sidewalks, and those that do exist are poorly maintained, have open drains, and are susceptible to takeover by the expansion of adjoining properties. Pedestrian crosswalks and bridges are not found outside of the city center, where they lack signals and are rarely respected by motorists or enforced by the police. Pedestrians often jump median strips and road dividers in high-traffic areas, triggering frequent serious accidents. Facilities for bicycles and other forms of nonmotorized transport are equally scarce, and the few bicycles in Kampala and Nairobi compete dangerously with motorized vehicles for road space.

Infrastructure: Rails

South Africa has by far the largest commuter rail networks in Africa. In Pretoria, Johannesburg, Cape Town, and Durban, Metrorail operates extensive EMU services,[3] each of which carry around half a million or more commuters each day, and it runs much smaller loco-hauled operations in Port Elisabeth and East London. In total, it carries over 500 million paying passengers each year. Metrorail operated as a distinct business unit within Transnet until it became part of the South African Rail Commuter Corporation in 2006. It has a fleet of 4,200 carriages (about 70 percent of which are operational) and runs services over more than 2,000 route-km, some of which it owns and some of which belong to Spoornet. Also in South Africa, a concession has been awarded for a standard-gauge rapid (160 km per hour) regional system between Johannesburg and Pretoria. Construction began in 2006 and the first stage is due for completion in 2010–11. This system differs from other urban railways in Africa because it is a "middle class" line, primarily aimed at diverting traffic from private cars in order to reduce road congestion.

Outside of South Africa, the Petit Train Bleu in Dakar has been for many years the only regular commuter service operating in the region. Since 1988, it has operated between Dakar and Rufisque on the main line of what is now the Transrail concession. Service is relatively frequent, with 19 pairs of trains reportedly carrying 25,000 passengers per working day. The Petit Train Bleu is operated by the Agence Nationale de Nouveaux Chemins de Fer, the agency responsible for the non-Transrail network in Senegal.

In other African cities, commuter services have been on a small scale, generally comprising one or two loco-hauled return services per day— one into the city in the morning and a return in the evening. Examples include Nairobi (on three routes), Lagos (one route), Accra (two routes), Harare (two routes), Bulawayo, Luanda (one route with six return services daily), and Maputo and Kinshasa (one route each). Annual passenger traffic is typically 1 or 2 million at most (Bullock 2009).

Sporadic attempts to develop commuter services in some other cities (such as the Njanji service in Lusaka) have generally failed. There are positive recent signs, however: a new service was inaugurated in Kaduna in 2008, and Accra has ordered new diesel multiple units for its suburban service. Several other cities also have plans to introduce modern commuter networks. Lagos is planning to complete a network of seven lines, totaling 246 km, by 2025; work on the first two lines, totaling 64 km, is already under way (Mobereola 2008). These services, however, will almost certainly require substantial external funding to cover both capital investment and recurrent operating costs. To best stimulate commuter services, new transport authorities should be established separate from the existing railway authority, as in South Africa. Such an enabling framework is essential if urban rail systems are to meet the transport demand of Africa's megacities.

Institutions

Jurisdiction over urban transport in Africa typically is spread over multiple tiers of government, an arrangement that inhibits policy integration and administrative consistency. Central governments still dominate urban transport, although some functions have been devolved to local governments in several cities (see table 6.3). Unfortunately, local authorities often lack the institutional and financial capacity to execute these functions. Poor accountability and a lack of coordination among institutions have also hindered the development of effective transport strategies.

The institutional arrangements for urban roads are particularly complex. Typically, several national and local bodies share jurisdiction, and separate legislation governs roads and transport services. In Conakry, for example, several institutions have responsibility for different segments of the road network. And in Ghana, responsibility for urban transport has devolved from central to local governments, which have neither the resources nor the technical expertise to carry out the functions assigned to them. Therefore, the Ministry of Transportation (through the Department of Urban Roads) is effectively responsible for road maintenance and development.

Impediments to Integrated Policy
Patterns of urbanization and land use drive demand for transport services and shape the context for road construction and passenger service provision. Effective urban public transportation therefore requires integrated management of urban planning, infrastructure maintenance, and services. Yet in the 14 study cities, the same institution rarely houses all three of these functions. Even when responsibility is retained by the central government, it is usually spread among several ministries.

The authorities in most of the 14 cities under review lack institutional capacity in land use planning and transport, and there is no effective

Table 6.3   Institutions with Responsibility for Public Transport in Cities

City	Entity responsible for urban planning	Entity responsible for transport planning	Entity responsible for building and maintaining of urban roads	Independent transport authority
Abidjan	Central government	AGETU (central)	Agence des Routes (for central services) and municipalities (for feeders)	AGETU
Accra	Town and Country Planning Department; Ministry of Local Government, Rural Development and Environment	Ministry of Transportation (central)	Ministry of Transportation	None
Addis Ababa	Ministry of Works and Urban Development (central)	Ministry of Transport and Communications (central)	Addis Ababa City Roads Authority	None
Bamako	DRCTU (municipal)	Direction Nationale des Transports Terrestres et Fluviaux (national)	Direction Nationale des Routes (District of Bamako)	None
Conakry	National Land Transport Directorate	Ministry of Transportation	Central government (trunk); city government (feeders)	None
Dakar	n.a.	CETUD (central)	CETUD	CETUD
Dar es Salaam	Ministry of Land, Housing and Settlement Development (central)	Ministry of Infrastructure Development; urban councils; SUMATRA; Dar es Salaam Rapid Transit	Ministry of Infrastructure Development; Tanzania Roads; municipalities	SUMATRA
Douala	Urban Community of Douala	Ministry of Transportation	Ministry of Works; Urban Community of Douala; city governments	None

(continued)

233

Table 6.3 Institutions with Responsibility for Public Transport in Cities *(continued)*

City	Entity responsible for urban planning	Entity responsible for transport planning	Entity responsible for building and maintaining of urban roads	Independent transport authority
Kampala	n.a.	n.a.	UTODA	None
Kigali	Ministry of Infrastructure (city of Kigali); ONATRACOM (district)	Ibid.	Ministry of Infrastructure	None
Kinshasa	Ministry of Planning	Ministry of Transportation	Ministry of Public Works and Infrastructure (municipal)	None
Lagos	Ministry of Local Government	LAMATA	Ministry of Public Works	LAMATA
Nairobi	Local government	Ministry of Transport	Ministry of Public Works and local governments	None
Ouagadougou	Ministry of Transportation (central); commune of Ouagadougou	Ministry of Infrastructure	Ministry of Infrastructure	None

Source: Kumar and Barrett 2008.

Note: For details on each city, see appendix 6a. n.a. = not applicable; AGETU = Agence de Gestion des Transports Urbains; CETUD = Conseil Exécutif des Transports Urbains de Dakar; DRCTU = Direction de la Régulation et du Contrôle du Transport Urbain; LAMATA = Lagos Metropolitan Area Transport Authority; ONATRACOM = Office National de Transport en Commun; SUMATRA = Surface and Marine Transport Regulatory Authority; UTODA = Uganda Taxi Operators and Drivers Association.

forum for communication between those responsible for the two functions. Land use is generally ad hoc, driven by developers' interests and informal settlements, and the transport system is expected to respond accordingly. Poor planning and communication, coupled with a lack of funding to address capacity constraints, has resulted in high levels of congestion.

A consequence of the functional separation is that the development of road infrastructure has generally focused on improving the flow of (mostly private) vehicles rather than of people. Public transport represents a significant share of traffic, so its passengers have benefited from road development. But public transport priorities within the road network have received little attention. For example, there has been little effort toward creating dedicated infrastructure for bus transit (see box 6.1). Some measures favoring bus travel, such as bus priority lanes, have been introduced, but they have not been properly enforced.

Box 6.1

Introducing Dedicated Infrastructure for Bus Transit

Over the past few years, the World Bank has supported government initiatives in several cities (Accra, Dar es Salaam, Lagos) to implement bus rapid transit (BRT) systems. These systems deliver fast, comfortable, and affordable mass transit. Exclusive right-of-way lanes allow BRT to emulate the performance and amenities of a modern rail-based transit system at a fraction of the cost.

The BRT systems in Accra and Dar es Salaam are expected to begin operation by 2011. The BRT system in Lagos, which was launched in March 2008, adapted best practices in Bogota, Columbia, and Curitiba, Brazil, to the African context. The BRT buses operate on an exclusive lane along the curb, which runs through the city for a distance of 20 km. Route franchising, improved ticketing systems, improved bus quality, and infrastructure investment have also benefited the city's public transport.

Lagos has already seen the positive effects of the initiative. Preliminary studies suggest that over 200,000 commuters use the BRT system daily. Compared to previous bus systems in Lagos, average fares are 30 percent lower, travel times are cut in half, and average waiting times are 35 percent shorter.

Source: A. Kumar, private correspondence.

The Strategy Vacuum

International experience suggests that if urban transport development is to be successful, it must be guided by cohesive policy. Yet none of the 14 cities studied has clearly articulated an urban passenger-transport policy and made it available to the public. Instead, it appears that ad hoc policy decisions respond to political pressures as they arise. This approach reflects the lack of a capable authority to coordinate regulation, transport planning, and infrastructure development. Such an authority requires a sufficient budget to attract and retain qualified staff and cannot be subject to arbitrary changes when the authority in charge of transport comes under pressure. Reasonable user charges, such as fees for operating permits or franchises levied on operators, could provide needed funding.

In practice, only a few of the 14 African cities have established agencies with overarching responsibility for urban transport. Addis Ababa has a city transport authority, but it is not autonomous. The agencies in Abidjan (Agence de Gestion des Transports Urbains, AGETU), Bamako (Direction de la Régulation et du Contrôle du Transport Urbain, DRCTU), and Dakar (Conseil Exécutif des Transports Urbains de Dakar, CETUD) lack sufficient authority to implement their plans and must instead work through other agencies of government. In 2001, Dar es Salaam established the Surface and Marine Transport Regulatory Authority (SUMATRA), a multisector agency with regulatory authority over rail, road, and maritime transport services, but without broader responsibility for urban transport planning. Only the Lagos Metropolitan Area Transport Authority (LAMATA) has any responsibility for road infrastructure development beyond initial planning.

Services

A breakdown of modal shares for urban transportation services in the 14 cities is presented in table 6.4.[4] Not all of the cities have performed sufficiently detailed traffic sampling to produce reliable statistics, and others have limited their analyses to motorized transportation and excluded pedestrians. Nevertheless, some consistent transportation patterns can be found across the cities.

As noted, urban public transport is largely road based. Buses (including large buses and minibuses) are the most common mode of public transit in most cities, with a modal share ranging from more than 70 percent in Dakar and Kigali to just over 10 percent in Bamako and 8 percent in Ouagadougou. Except in Addis Ababa and Ouagadougou, minibuses of

Table 6.4   Modal Shares of Transport in Cities (% of Trips)

City	Large bus	Minibus	Taxi	Motorcycle	Private car	Walking	Other
Abidjan	11	19	29	0	18	22	1
Accra	10	52	9	0	13	12	4
Addis Ababa	35	20	5	0	7	30	3
Bamako	1	10	5	56	19	—	9
Conakry	1	14	6	0	1	78	0
Dakar	3	73	6	6	11	—	1
Dar es Salaam	0	61	1	1	10	26	1
Douala	10	0	13	12	2	60	3
Kampala	0	41	—	20	35	—	4
Kigali	1	75	10	0	10	5	0
Kinshasa	—	—	—	—	—	High	—
Lagos	10	75	5	5	5	High	0
Nairobi	7	29	15	2	—	47	0
Ouagadougou	8	0	—	58	14	—	20
Average	7	30	8	12	12	37	4

Source: Kumar and Barrett 2008.
Note: — = not available. Rows may not total 100 percent because of rounding. Percentages for Lagos exclude walking trips.

up to 30-seat capacity are much more prevalent than large buses. In many cities, they have colloquial names—such as "tro-tro" in Accra, "danfo" in Lagos, "gbaka" in Abidjan, "sotrama" in Bamako, "matatu" in Nairobi, and "dala-dala" in Dar es Salaam—often relating to their origin or characteristics.[5] Midibuses are larger than minibuses, with passenger capacities of between 30 and 50 (including standing room). The passenger capacity of a bus of a given size varies depending on the load limits and seating rules of each jurisdiction. Midibuses also have colloquial names such as "cars rapides" in Dakar and "molue" in Lagos. Of the 14 cities, only Douala and Ouagadougou do not offer a minibus service. The government of Cameroon outlawed minibuses to stimulate development of a new large-bus operator, which explains the absence of services in Douala. In both cities, however, shared taxis fill the transportation void left by the lack of minibuses.

Overall, minibuses have a modal share that is twice that of large buses. To a certain extent it appears that larger buses and minibuses serve different routes. Large buses are more common on longer suburban routes, where their size allows them to offer lower fares. By contrast, minibuses tend to dominate congested areas, where their relative maneuverability allows them to charge higher fares.

In recent years, the poor state of roads and the inability of bus companies to maintain supply has led to an increase in the use of motorcycles for commercial transport in Douala, Lagos, and Kampala. The superior maneuverability of motorcycles allows them to more easily avoid potholes and navigate broken surfaces. Initially, motorcycle services provided access from residential areas to main roads, where passengers would then take taxis or buses. Motorcycle services now serve main roads and even the city center. Most of the motorcycles used for urban public transport have small engines (less than 100 cc [cubic capacity]). Drivers are often young and inexperienced and are not required to have a license, which leads to frequent—and often fatal—accidents. Most drivers own their own motorcycles or buy them on lease, paying in installments until the vehicle is totally owned, a process that can normally be completed within a year. Despite their widespread presence, motorcycle taxis are not ubiquitous; for example, they are rare in Nairobi and almost unknown in Dakar.

In comparison with Asian cities, African cities have few nonmotorized vehicles such as bicycles and rickshaws, probably due to the state of the roads. Not all cities have measured the prevalence of walking as a mode of transport, but for those that have, the figure varies enormously. For example, walking has a modal share of 60 to 80 percent in cities such as Conakry, and Douala. By comparison, estimates for Abidjan, Accra, and Addis Ababa range from 10 to 30 percent.

Railways generally play an insignificant role in urban transport in Africa. Dakar, Kinshasa, Lagos, and Nairobi have small suburban rail networks, but none has a modal share of more than 2 percent. Suburban rail systems are an important part of urban transport in major cities only in South Africa, the main new prospect being Gautrain, a regional high-speed line between Johannesburg and Pretoria.

In the future, bus rapid transit (BRT) systems may offer a less expensive form of public transport on a track segregated from other road traffic. Lagos was the path breaker—it opened the first 22 km of a system in 2008. Compared with some of the well-known Latin American systems, it is cheap and simple. It cost only $1.7 million per kilometer to build, but is not yet integrated with other modes or served by park-and-ride or feeder routes. It does not have electronic ticketing, but it is cheaper and quicker than other public transport alternatives and already carries 10 percent of the traffic to Lagos Island, with 25 percent of the travelers on its corridor in only 4 percent of the vehicles.

Other countries are following suit. Johannesburg plans a 300-km system called Rea Vaya, with three integrated types of service (trunk, feeder, and complementary) that will be integrated with the high-speed rail link to Pretoria and to the airport. Smaller systems were developed for other South African cities that were 2010 World Cup venues. At the time of this writing, Dar es Salaam was planning a BRT system with a route length of 130 km, 18 terminals, and 228 stations, with the intention that construction would commence toward the end of 2010 and take about two years to complete. Dakar and Accra also had schemes in development.

Buses Large and Small

Since the early 1990s, the 14 cities have taken different approaches to large-bus services (table 6.5). Accra, Dar es Salaam, Kampala, Kigali, and Lagos abandoned large-bus services altogether and now rely on private—and largely informal—minibus services. Accra, Kampala, and Lagos have attempted to revive large-bus operations, so far without success.

The government of Addis Ababa, on the other hand, continues to subsidize the city's public large-bus company (Anbessa), which it has allowed to remain in operation even though fares have been frozen since the early 1990s. In recent years, however, even Anbessa has faced a financial squeeze, and smaller buses have taken over a large share of the market.

Other cities, primarily in the Francophone countries of West Africa, have adopted a range of private and public-private solutions, although some are too recent for their success to be measured. Abidjan and Ouagadougou established large-bus services that are run by private operators but rely on government funding to cover operating deficits. Dakar and Douala have concessioned their large-bus services to private operators, albeit with some government support. In Dakar, the large-bus company is subsidized by the state. In Douala, one bus company has been given monopoly rights to operate on specified routes; other bus operations are suppressed. Bamako, Conakry, and Kinshasa have fully privatized large-bus services that receive no government subsidies.

Nairobi is the only city to have retained the private operation of its large-bus service since independence, although ownership has changed hands several times. The service was sold to the British operator Stagecoach in the early 1990s but was restructured as the Kenya Bus Service (KBS) in the late 1990s. It is owned and operated by the private sector.

The minibus sector has flourished since the early 1990s, with fleet size growing at a rate of up to 11 percent per year in some cities. This growth increased imports of mainly secondhand vehicles accommodating from 15 to 30 passengers. Ownership of services is almost invariably informal; most individual owners have one or two vehicles that they rent out to

Table 6.5   Large-Bus Operations in Cities

City	Large-bus operator	Ownership	Public support
Abidjan	SOTRA	60% public, 40% private	Government covers deficits (subsidy per passenger for some categories).
Accra	MMT Ltd.	45% public, 55% private (including state-owned enterprises)	Government provides vehicle financing and covers operating loss.
Addis Ababa	Anbessa	100% public (federal)	City government provides subsidy per passenger.
Bamako	8 different operators	All private	None
Conakry	Futur Transport[a]	100% private	None
Dakar	DDD	Private concessionaire	Government provides operating subsidy, and donors help finance vehicles.
Dar es Salaam	None	n.a.	n.a.
Douala	SOCATUR	Private concessionaire	Service exclusivity exists for five years.
Kampala	None	n.a.	n.a.
Kigali	ONATRACOM[b]	100% public	n.a.
Kinshasa	STUC	100% private	None, but India helps finance vehicles.
Lagos	None	n.a.	n.a.
Nairobi	KBS City Hoppa	100% private	None
Ouagadougou	SOTRACO	15% public (Ouagadougou commune), 85% private	Government provides subsidy in the form of exemptions from taxes and duties.

Source: Kumar and Barrett 2008.
Note: n.a. = not applicable; DDD = Dakar Dem Dikk; KBS = Kenya Bus Service; MMT = Metro Mass Transit; ONATRACOM = Office National de Transport en Commun; SOCATUR = Société Camerounaise de Transports Urbains; SOTRA = Société de Transport Abidjanais; SOTRACO = Société de Transport en Commun; STUC = Société des Transports Urbains du Congo.
a. Very few buses.
b. Buses used mainly for intercity transportation.

drivers. Drivers keep the fares they collect but are responsible for paying fuel costs, conductors' wages, terminal fees, and other incidental expenses. They therefore have a strong incentive to carry full passenger loads to maximize revenues and minimize variable costs (particularly fuel). Most minibus owners are government officials, businessmen, or professionals who seek to supplement their income while incurring minimal tax liability. Some owners, such as police and army officers and members of transport unions, can exploit their position to protect and enhance their businesses.

An owner of a reasonably maintained vehicle with a reliable driver can generate sufficient revenues to pay for capital and operating costs, including adequate maintenance. On the other hand, owners often choose not to reinvest in the business when vehicles require major repairs. The sector is therefore characterized by short ownership periods, few barriers to market entry or exit, and high turnover.

In a few cities, formal minibus operators compete with informal operators. Dakar, for example, has an estimated fleet of 3,000 cars rapides, 400 of which belong to one formal operator and 200 to another. In Dar es Salaam, a public bus company operates a fleet of 30 minibuses, which is a tiny share of the estimated 10,000 minibuses on the city's streets. And in Kinshasa, the private large-bus operator maintains 30 minibuses, a negligible share of the estimated 1,200 minibuses that circulate the city. Across the study cities, minibus ownership is dispersed across many people, most of whom operate informally (table 6.6).

Bus Fleets

Large buses carry 50 to 100 passengers, although the upper end of that range includes standing passengers. Most large buses have a single deck and two axles, although a few double-decker buses are used in Accra. Articulated (three-axle) buses are found in only 1 of the 14 cities (Abidjan), and semiarticulated (four-axle) trailer buses have been used in Kinshasa.

Most minibuses are light commercial vehicles converted to accommodate passengers. Some were originally crew buses (buses operated by a driver and conductor). Almost all are integral-construction vehicles,[6] although a few pickup conversions can still be found in Addis Ababa, where imports of integral small commercial passenger vehicles were for a time suppressed to protect the publicly owned operator (that policy has now been abandoned).

In East Africa, the most popular vehicles are Japanese and are imported secondhand through traders in the Persian Gulf. Most minibuses in Nairobi and Kampala are diesel powered to economize on fuel costs, but the altitude and terrain of Addis Ababa make gasoline engines preferable. European vehicles are more popular in West Africa, although the region, particularly Abidjan, also has a significant number of Japanese

Table 6.6   Characteristics of Minibus Services in Cities

City	Service designation (vehicle capacity in number of passengers)	Union or association for informal minibus operators	Degree of formality of sector	Ownership structure
Abidjan	Gbaka (22)	UPETCA, SNTMVCI	Mainly informal	Highly fragmented, 1–2 vehicles per owner
Accra	Tro-tro	GPRTU, PROTOA	Mainly informal	80% of owners with 1 vehicle each
Addis Ababa	Minibus (8), midibus (22)	Various	Mostly informal	80% of owners with 1 vehicle each
Bamako	Sotrama, dourouni	Yes	Mainly informal	Highly fragmented, 1–3 vehicles per owner
Conakry	Magbana (15–18)	None	Mainly informal	Highly fragmented, 1–2 vehicles per owner
Dakar	Car rapide (23–32)	Yes	Two formal private companies, plus informal	Two operators with large fleets, remainder highly fragmented
Dar es Salaam	Dala-dala (18–35)	DARCOBOA	Formal public company, plus informal	Public operator with modest fleet, remainder highly fragmented
Douala	None (outlawed), shared taxis used instead	None	Mainly informal	Highly fragmented, 1–3 vehicles per owner

Kampala	Known as taxis	UTODA	Mainly informal	80% of owners with 1 vehicle each
Kigali	Twegerane or shared taxi (14–20)	ATRACO, ONATRACOM	Mainly informal	Highly fragmented
Kinshasa	Minibus (5–26)	ACCO	Formal private company, plus informal	Formal operator with modest fleet, remainder highly fragmented
Lagos	Danfo (mini), molue (midi)	Several affiliated with NURTW	Mainly informal	80% of owners with 1 vehicle each
Nairobi	Matatu	MVOA	Mainly informal	80% of owners with 1 vehicle each
Ouagadougou	None, shared taxis used instead	No	Mainly informal	Highly fragmented

Source: Kumar and Barrett 2008.

Note: ACCO = Association of Congo Chauffeurs; ATRACO = Association pour le Developpement de l'Artisanat du Rwanda; DARCOBOA = Dar es Salaam Commuter Bus Owners Association; GPRTU = Ghana Private Road Transport Union; MVOA = Matatu Vehicle Owners Association; NURTW = National Union of Road Transport Workers; ONATRACOM = Office National de Transport en Commun; PROTOA = Progressive Transport Owners Association; SNTMVCI = Syndicat National des Transporteurs et Voyageurs de Cote d'Ivoire; UPETCA = Union Patronale des Exploitants de Taxi-compteurs d'Abidjan; UTODA = Uganda Taxi Operators and Drivers Association.

vehicles. In Lagos, the market came to be dominated by Volkswagen, whose vehicles have a flat area over the rear-mounted engine that provides space for market goods. Many of the larger minibuses in Accra are Mercedes, and French vehicles are most common in Dakar.

Most midibuses consist of a locally made body mounted on a light or medium truck chassis. Similar to the trend for minibuses, some Mercedes vans can be found in Accra, and Renault and Peugeot models are common in Dakar. Strong local assembly operations and dealer networks allowed Mercedes (specifically the 911 model) and Isuzu to dominate the markets in Lagos and Nairobi, respectively. Nairobi has also developed a niche market for luxury models in the more affluent suburbs.

Many of the large buses operated in Africa were supplied new by donors and have an average age of 9 years. Unlike large buses, minibuses are typically purchased secondhand and therefore tend to be somewhat older, with an average age of 14 years. In East Africa, minibuses are typically between 10 and 15 years old, although age varies widely throughout the region. Vehicles tend to be somewhat older in West Africa, and some larger minibuses are up to 20 years old (table 6.7). This partly reflects the

Table 6.7   Average Bus Age and Fleet Size

	Large bus		Minibus	
City	Average age (years)	Fleet size	Average age (years)	Fleet size
Abidjan	7	650	15	5,000
Accra	1–2	600	15–20	6,000
Addis Ababa	—	350	—	10,000
Bamako	17	168	15	1,800
Conakry	20	50	10–15	1,500
Dakar	—	410	15–20	3,000
Dar es Salaam	n.a.	0	15	10,000
Douala	15	100	15–20	2,000
Kampala	n.a.	0	10–15	7,000
Kigali	4	20	15	2000
Kinshasa	2 (STUC)	180	2 (STUC)	54 (STUC)
			15–20 (informal)	1,200 (informal)
Lagos	—	< 100	> 15	75–120,000
Nairobi	—	250	> 15	10,000
Ouagadougou	5	55	n.a.	0
Average	9	218	14	11,400

Source: Kumar and Barrett 2008.
Note: — = not available; n.a. = not applicable; STUC = Société des Transports Urbains du Congo.

region's less stringent technical enforcement. Body corrosion is the main reason for scrapping. Among cities in which large buses are still common, average age varies widely depending on access to subsidies and the influence of public ownership.

Midibuses can be even older than minibuses—some of the vans in Accra are approaching 30 years of age and others in Lagos are approaching 40 years. The government in Dakar is encouraging the replacement of its cars rapides, whose age can exceed 25 years. Midibuses tend to be more productive in Nairobi than elsewhere. Their replacement is therefore more economical and they are generally not as old.

Reliable data on vehicle productivity are scarce. Few buses have working odometers, and drivers count the number of paying trips per day rather than the distance traveled. The limited evidence available indicates that both large buses and minibuses travel an average of 190 km per day (table 6.8). In some cities, however, the average distances traveled by large buses and minibuses differ widely. For example, minibuses in Abidjan, Addis Ababa, and Nairobi travel substantially farther each day than large buses. The opposite is true in Accra and Bamako. Where minibuses run low daily distances, it is usually because they are subject to the tour de role dispatching practices described in an earlier chapter.

Table 6.8   Average Distance Traveled by Large Buses and Minibuses (kilometers per day)

City	Large bus	Minibus
Abidjan	161	250
Accra	160	140
Addis Ababa	138	180
Bamako	225	180
Conakry	180	180
Dakar	192	—
Dar es Salaam	n.a.	180
Douala	180	n.a.
Kampala	n.a.	100
Kigali	210	210
Kinshasa	200	200
Lagos	180	100
Nairobi	200	240
Ouagadougou	250	n.a.
Average	191	186

Source: City authorities.
Note: — = not available; n.a. = rfot applicable.

Availability and Quality of Services

Access to urban public transportation, as measured by seat availability per 1,000 urban residents, is much lower in Africa than in other regions. Most of the sample cities have 30–60 bus seats per 1,000 residents, although Addis Ababa, Kinshasa, and Ouagadougou each have no more than 10 per 1,000 (table 6.9). Overall, the 14 cities have an average of only 6 large-bus seats per 1,000 residents. For comparison, according to the World Bank's Urban Transport Indicators database, the middle-income countries of Latin America, Asia, the Middle East, and Eastern Europe (where private car availability is much higher) have an average of 30–40 large-bus seats per 1,000 urban residents. Based on the low density of paved roads, unplanned growth, poor road surfaces, and narrow streets in the region, it may safely be assumed that the geographic reach of bus services is seriously circumscribed in the 14 sample cities. Passengers suffer long waiting times, uncomfortable vehicles, and—potentially—the continued operation of unsafe vehicles.

Formal and informal surveys of users undertaken in the 14 cities examined in Kumar and Barrett (2008) suggest widespread customer dissatisfaction with bus services. Frequent complaints include poor road quality, overcrowding of buses, unpredictable and irregular service, and

Table 6.9   Availability of Public Transportation in Cities

City	Minibus	Bus	Taxi	Total
	Seats per 1,000 population			
Abidjan	24	5	26	55
Accra	26	22	—	48
Addis Ababa	4	6	2	12
Bamako	33	14	—	47
Conakry	17	1	16	34
Dakar	27	7.5	15	48
Dar es Salaam	57	0	—	57
Douala	16	4	27	47
Kampala	48	0	—	48
Kigali	52	1	5	58
Kinshasa	4	2	—	6
Lagos	60	0	—	61
Nairobi	40	3	—	43
Ouagadougou	0	1	6	7
Average	31	6		

Source: Kumar and Barrett 2008.
Note: — = not available.

inadequate terminal facilities. On average, passengers report walking for 10 minutes to reach a bus stop and waiting 30 minutes before a bus arrives. Trip times range from 30 to 45 minutes. Poor driving is prevalent in all 14 cities, and almost 50 percent of the operators interviewed identified poor driver discipline to be a serious business problem. Bad behavior among drivers, especially in the vicinity of passenger pickup points and interchanges, contributes to low service quality. For example, competition on common routes encourages drivers to block stops, drive aggressively, and stop in the roadway to pick up passengers, all of which increase traffic congestion.

Governance of minibus operations does little to improve low service quality. Self-regulation by operators' unions, which is common, means that routes run between terminals are controlled by unions. This limits the ease with which routes can be adjusted to meet passenger demand, and many passengers must therefore change buses to reach their destination, increasing the duration and cost of their trip. As a means of equitably distributing revenues and ensuring some discipline in operation, unions frequently require drivers to wait at terminals until their bus is fully loaded. As a result, passengers must walk to the terminal to secure a seat, then sit in it under a blazing hot sun to retain it. Waiting times at terminals can exceed one hour during off-peak periods. Finally, unions insist that vehicles be loaded in a strict rotation, which prevents passengers from rejecting vehicles that fail to meet expected standards for cleanliness or operating conditions. Under these circumstances, owners have little incentive to improve their vehicles, and investment in higher-quality vehicles is impractical.

Three in four passengers interviewed in surveys for this study rated overloading as their primary concern. Overcrowding of minibuses at the start of their journey is limited by the terminal management practices described above, as vehicles are dispatched once they are full. On the other hand, once the vehicles leave the terminal, there is little to stop drivers from overloading, especially after dark. Overcrowding on large buses is more frequent and much worse. Performance data from Anbessa in Addis Ababa indicate that loads at peak times may be as high as 150 percent of rated capacity. During the morning peak time in Kinshasa and Dar es Salaam, load factors of large buses reach an average of 200 percent, and passengers are forced to hang out of the bus or sit on the roof. Nairobi attempted to mitigate overcrowding by outlawing standing passengers on KBS routes and restricting the number of passengers on matatu (minibuses). As a result, the comfort and safety of passengers improved, but fares also rose since operators had fewer customers to cover the same operating costs.

Vehicle Maintenance

Operators of large-bus fleets perform regular scheduled maintenance. Nevertheless, repairs are too frequent relative to maintenance, and even the younger fleets suffer from low levels of availability. For example, the availability of the core fleet in Addis Ababa was reported to be only 83 percent. Availability is also particularly low in Accra, although this is partly a result of a lack of technical support and spare parts for the fleet's new Chinese buses. Some small private operators in all 14 cities conduct basic preventive maintenance, but the intervals between oil and filter changes vary widely. More commonly, repairs are undertaken only when absolutely necessary to keep vehicles on the road.

A consequence of poor maintenance is that the environmental performance of the minibus fleet has emerged as an important issue. For Lagos's large minibus fleet, the emissions problem is acute; in 2007, there were a few days when the city effectively closed down because of high pollution. Government agencies interviewed in several cities expressed some awareness of the problems associated with vehicle emissions, but only Accra (and to a lesser extent Dakar) has initiated a formal program to inform policy by quantifying the impact of emissions. There are two especially troubling sources of emissions: lead-based octane improvers in gasoline-powered vehicles, which continue to be used because of a lack of investment in refinery technology, and oil leaks caused by poor engine conditions. In the case of diesel engines, high sulfur levels in the fuel—again resulting from lack of investment in refinery technology—increase particulate emissions, an effect compounded by poor maintenance of fuel-injection equipment. Most engines now in use predate the introduction of the first European standards in the early 1990s. Meeting the even higher standards of today would require new equipment and improved fuels.

Most repairs, particularly of minibuses, are performed on the side of the road or in low-technology workshops using hand tools and no specialized equipment. Lax and corrupt vehicle inspection regimes and low capital investment in vehicles have allowed careless maintenance practices to remain sustainable. In some cities, obtaining a forged certificate of roadworthiness is reportedly easier and cheaper than passing an inspection test with a well-maintained vehicle. Cities are gradually recognizing the severity of the situation, with reforms initiated in Addis Ababa and planned in Kampala, where vehicle inspections are being privatized.

But for the time being, many vehicle operators flout basic safety standards for lighting, tires, and brakes. Routine vehicle inspections are clearly inadequate, and petty corruption among police officers prevents them from enforcing standards on the road. Overloading of vehicles is also a safety concern, although recent improvements in construction have allowed for increases in the permitted capacity of some vehicles.

Costs: Fuel, Labor, and Taxes

In the industrialized world, labor is the largest recurrent cost of conventional bus operation. But in African cities, fuel takes first place, accounting for half of the total cost of operations. Fuel is also the largest cost for minibus operations. That cost has risen with international oil prices in recent years. While Accra and Lagos stand out for their relatively low fuel costs, diesel fuel and premium gasoline typically cost between $0.80 and $1.00 per liter—and even more in some cities (table 6.10). Because of the region's high unemployment and low wages, labor can account for less than 25 percent of total operating costs for large buses in Africa. The significance of this cost structure is that the viability of bus operations is even more sensitive to fuel costs in Africa than it is in industrialized countries.

In all of the study cities, minibus operators also face nonoperational charges, such as petty extortion from enforcement agencies and local

Table 6.10   Fuel Prices in Cities, July 2007
(US$ per liter)

City	Premium gasoline	Diesel fuel
Abidjan	1.25	1.09
Accra	0.49	0.43
Addis Ababa	0.60	0.42
Bamako	1.17	0.90
Conakry	1.50	0.69
Dakar	1.10	0.90
Dar es Salaam	0.93	0.87
Douala	0.95	0.83
Kampala	1.02	0.88
Kigali	1.15	0.99
Kinshasa	0.92	0.81
Lagos	0.71	0.83
Nairobi	0.92	0.76
Ouagadougou	1.18	0.94
Average	0.97	0.78

Source: City authorities; World Development Indicators (data assembled by Kumar and Barrett 2008).

gangs, and payments to associations. The scale of these charges is difficult to assess accurately, and the claims of the operators are often strongly challenged by the associations themselves. Nevertheless, typical daily charges per minibus appear to range from about $1.50 in Accra to $10.00 in Kampala. Official association charges in Lagos are about $2 per day, and unofficial charges may be equally large. The associations reportedly do not declare the revenues raised through these charges to the tax authorities, but use them to enrich association officials and support grass-roots political interests.

Taxing the minibus sector is made difficult by the fact that minibus drivers typically rent their vehicles from owners on a daily basis and do not formally record their fare revenues. Accra and Addis Ababa have both addressed this problem, at least in respect to vehicle owners. In those cities, authorities estimate the likely gross revenues and profit margins from owning various types of vehicles and assess income tax based on those figures. For example, in Addis Ababa the authorities estimate that the owner of a minibus taxi that is less than 15 years old will earn annual revenues of Br 25,000 ($2,900) and a profit of Br 6,620 ($770). The owner then must pay Br 482 ($56) in taxes on that profit. In Kenya, import duty on vehicles (135 percent of vehicle value, excluding value added tax) contributes to the high costs of matatu operation, and is also a cause of the high average age of the vehicles operated.

Large-bus operators, by contrast, are subject to a range of business taxes, but investment incentives, such as accelerated depreciation allowances, usually provide the companies with some tax relief. Indirect taxes, such as duties on fuel and imported spare parts, can be very signif-icant. The large-bus operator in Nairobi once calculated that 24 percent of its costs were payments to the government. Nevertheless, efforts to relieve any one sector of the burden of indirect taxes are usually poorly targeted, with direct implications for the wider economy. For example, the government-mandated lowering of duties on spare parts for agricultural equipment in Kenya led tractor distributors to market common compo-nents to the wider transport sector. Conversely, any attempt to lower the burden on inputs in the bus sector would almost certainly leak to other sectors and to individuals.

Fares

Fare structures are very simple in Africa. Typically, a single flat fare applies to each route, with higher fares on longer routes. In cities where a single flat fare applies, route lengths tend to be determined in such a way as to avoid losses on longer routes.

Setting and Controlling Fares

Throughout the region, authorities are usually responsible for setting fares for services (table 6.11). But attempts to control large-bus fares are often unrealistic and counterproductive. In Addis Ababa, for example, fares for large buses officially remain at 1992 levels, and in Abidjan they have not been adjusted since 1994. Such artificially low fares have led to a drastic decline in the quality and coverage of large-bus services throughout the region. Only in Addis Ababa are public subsidies nearly large or regular enough to consistently cover operating deficits.

Controlling fares in the informal sector has proved even more difficult. In West Africa, governments usually have formal control of fares for minibuses and shared taxis; this is the case in Bamako, Conakry, Dakar, and Douala, though in Ouagadougou an operating company, the Société de Transport en Commun (SOTRACO), determines all bus fares.[7] Usually a set fare applies to passengers boarding at the departure terminal and along much of the route length, but passengers boarding close to the arrival terminal may be charged a lower fare. Passengers do not usually receive a fare rebate for alighting before the arrival terminal, though this is not unheard of. In cities that also control minibus fares, authorities usually ensure that fares for large buses operated by public companies are set below minibus fares. In East Africa, in contrast, minibus operators have more flexibility to determine their own fares. In Dar es Salaam, the regulator SUMATRA allocates routes, and fares are subject to negotiations with the bus operators' association.

In practice, attempts to impose price controls on the informal minibus sector usually fail to control real fares, but rather have the unintended consequence of route proliferation. In all 14 cities, minibus operators have shortened route lengths in response to fare controls, allowing them to charge fares that satisfy price controls but that increase trip costs for at least some passengers. Ultimately, both the cost of travel and travel times have increased. For instance, the official fare for a typical trip from Dakar to Pikine in Senegal is CFAF 110. But to make the complete trip, passengers must change vehicles twice and pay three fares totaling more than CFAF 200. Similarly, the fare for a trip of 5 km in Addis Ababa is set at Br 1.0, yet passengers routinely pay more than Br 1.5. Economic reforms in many of the cities have led to official deregulation of minibus fares, but in practice, some cities have retained partial administrative control.

Table 6.11 Fare-Setting Procedures for Large Buses and Minibuses

City	Fares regulated for large buses and minibuses?	Entity responsible for regulating fares	Year of most recent fare adjustment	Operating subsidy for large-bus operators?
Abidjan	Yes	AGETU	1994	Yes
Accra	Yes	Ministry of Transportation	2004	Yes
Addis Ababa	Large buses only	City government	1992	Yes
Bamako	Large buses only	Operators/government	2006	No
Conakry	Yes	Direction Nationale des Transports Terrestres, operators' syndicates	2006	No
Dakar	Yes	Ministry of Finance	2000	Yes
Dar es Salaam	Yes	Dar Commuter Bus Owners Association, SUMATRA, operators	2006	n.a.
Douala	n.a.	Ministry of Finance	n.a.	Yes
Kampala	Yes	UTODA	n.a.	n.a.
Kigali	Yes	Rwanda Utilities Regulatory Agency	2004	n.a.
Kinshasa	Publicly owned buses only	Operators/government	2006	No
Lagos	Yes (informally)	Bus association	2005	n.a.
Nairobi	Yes	Private bus association	n.a.	n.a.
Ouagadougou	Yes	Direction Générale des Transports Terrestres et Maritimes	2006	Yes

Source: Kumar and Barrett 2008.
Note: n.a. = not applicable (because no large-bus operator exists); UTODA = Uganda Taxi Operators and Drivers Association.

Fare Levels

The average fare in the 14 cities is $0.31 for large buses and $0.25 for minibuses (table 6.12). The difference between the fares charged by large buses and minibuses is not consistent: in some cities (Addis Ababa, Bamako, Dakar), large buses appear more expensive than minibuses; in others, minibuses appear more expensive (Abidjan, Conakry); in Kigali, fares for the two services are equal. Unfortunately, the wide variation in fare structures, the difference between route structures of large and small buses, and the tendency of private companies to fragment their routes makes comparisons of real bus fares among cities very difficult. What can be safely deduced, however, is that because the operators are private and unsubsidized, the real fare for minibus services does cover costs, at least in the short term.

In 12 of the cities (Addis Ababa and Nairobi are the exceptions), passengers confirmed in the surveys reported by Kumar and Barrett (2008) that operators arbitrarily changed fares depending on circumstances such as bad weather and congestion. In Lagos, for example, an operator may increase the nominal fare of ₦40 to ₦70 (or even ₦90 on occasions). In Nairobi, on the other hand, drivers display fares on the inside of their windscreen, making opportunistic fair increases reportedly much less

Table 6.12   Average Bus Fare
(US$ per trip)

City	Large bus	Minibus
Abidjan	0.40	0.40–0.70
Accra	—	—
Addis Ababa	0.25	0.12
Bamako	0.25–0.30	0.20–0.25
Conakry	0.18	0.21
Dakar	0.30	0.18
Dar es Salaam	n.a.	0.16–0.24
Douala	0.30	n.a.
Kampala	n.a.	0.20–0.25
Kigali	0.28	0.28
Kinshasa	0.33	—
Lagos	0.40–0.56	0.38–0.39
Nairobi	0.25–0.40	—
Ouagadougou	0.30	n.a.
Average	0.31	0.25

Sources: Various documents published by city authorities (data assembled by Kumar and Barrett 2008).
Note: — = not available; n.a. = not applicable.

common. Being able to depend on consistent rates is important; when fares are variable, poor passengers often do not know whether they will be able to afford the bus fare home after work. Passengers also report other operating practices that increase uncertainty. For example, buses will sometimes shorten a trip to take advantage of a better commercial opportunity in the other direction. So-called short-turning strands passengers along the road, and operators rarely compensate the victims fully. The surveys suggest that fare uncertainty is a serious concern of many passengers.

Affordability: Fares in Relation to Incomes

Affordability of public transport obviously varies widely with passenger income and trip distance. For most people in Africa, and certainly for poorer people, transportation expenses are incurred primarily for the journey to work and a smaller number of equally essential purposes, such as trips for medical care. Transport is thus a necessity of life that must be provided for in the household budget, not a luxury. Anecdotal evidence from limited surveys shows that rising transport fares can isolate some people from employment opportunities, though this problem does not appear to be widespread. In most cases, budgets are tight in the region, and ridership drops sharply following fare increases, although it often rebounds after a few months.

Most households reported some expenditure on urban transport, but a significant minority reported none. This is because in several of the cities under review, including Accra and Nairobi, low-income pockets can be found close to the city center (instead of on the outskirts, as in most developing cities), and residents can meet their transport needs by walking.

A standardized affordability index allows for comparisons across sample nations of the burden of public transport on the household budget. The index is based on the cost of 60 public transport trips per month—roughly equivalent to a daily journey to and from work. Data were collected from the most recent budget surveys available for each country and were analyzed at the city level. The total cost is expressed as a percentage of the monthly budget of an average household and of a first-quintile household in the 14 cities (see table 6.13). The results indicate that, averaged across all cities, the cost of 60 trips would absorb 8 percent of the monthly budget of an average household, but nearly one-third of the budget of the lowest quintile of households.

Actual expenditures appear to be rather lower than the above analysis suggests, with transportation accounting for an average of 6.5 percent of

Table 6.13 Spending on Urban Transport as a Share of Household Income

	Percentage of households reporting positive expenditure on transport	Percentage of household budget spent on transport for households with positive expenditure	Absolute monthly expenditure on transport for households with positive expenditure (US$)	Percentage of average household budget needed to pay for 60 one-way trips per month	Percentage of first-quintile household budget needed to pay for 60 one-way trips per month
Abidjan	77	10.1	31.47	10.5	42.9
Accra	95	6.0	16.36	—	—
Addis Ababa	87	3.3	3.83	6.3	18.6
Bamako	—	—	—	—	—
Conakry	—	—	—	—	—
Dakar	92	4.3	15.08	3.1	11.3
Dar es Salaam	92	11.6	12.04	11.6	53.2
Douala	77	4.0	6.94	10.4	23.5
Kampala	81	7.4	13.08	7.8	41.0
Kigali	80	4.4	14.55	5.1	46.0
Kinshasa	49	2.8	5.43	10.1	31.0
Lagos	58	13.8	14.44	27.5	105.2
Nairobi	61	10.1	25.97	7.5	33.6
Ouagadougou	3	5.5	0.30	8.9	35.8
Average	90	6.5	13.29	8.0	32.7

Source: Kumar and Barrett 2008.

Note: — = not available. All data are for capital cities, except for Douala and Ouagadougou, where spending at the urban level nationwide is taken as a proxy for spending in the capital city.

the budget of those households actually spending anything on transport in the 14 cities. There is very wide variation in this proportion: the share is just 3 percent in Addis Ababa but 14 percent in Lagos. When expressed in absolute terms, the amount that households spend on transport is much more consistent across cities, averaging $12–$16 per month. The exceptions are Addis Ababa and Kinshasa, where the expenditure is about one-third of that, and Abidjan and Nairobi, where it is about twice as much.

In some cities (Abidjan, Dakar, Dar es Salaam, Kampala, and Kigali), there is a close correspondence between the actual budget share and the budget share needed to purchase the 60 trips. Elsewhere the difference is quite large and can run in either direction, with households spending substantially more (Nairobi) or less (Addis Ababa, Douala, Kinshasa, and Lagos) than what is needed to purchase the 60 trips.

In all cases, however, first-quintile households are at a disadvantage. They would typically need to spend 33 percent of their budget to purchase the 60 trips and in many cases a lot more, indicating that this level of mobility is completely unaffordable for the poorest households. Calculations of the same index for a number of Indian cities indicate broadly comparable results, with the average household needing to spend 5–10 percent of its monthly budget on the 60 trips, and with that share rising to 15–25 percent for the poorest households.

The results presented here suggest that urban bus fares remain relatively high in relation to the purchasing power of the typical family, and very high in relation to incomes of the poorest. Nevertheless, even at low levels of expenditure, this translates into peak demand for around 200 seats per 1,000 residents, about five times higher than the supply available in any of the cities sampled.

Financing and Subsidies

Governments have tried to promote the use of larger buses, often with bilateral assistance from countries that manufacture them. The most successful experience seems to be in Addis Ababa, which has benefited from regular investment supported by bilateral assistance from the Netherlands and Belgium. In Kinshasa, the government-sponsored Société des Transports Urbains du Congo (STUC) has recently received a $33.5 million grant from the government of India to purchase new buses.[8] In Lagos, the state government has even recently set up a bus company (Lagbus Asset Management Ltd.). Originally conceived as a way to gain the advantage of purchasing buses in bulk for local operators using bilateral aid, the company has quickly converted itself into a government-subsidized operator.

But these attempts have faced numerous problems, including noncompetitive procurement of overpriced or inappropriate vehicles and insufficient local technical support. In Accra, the government has established a commercial operator to revive large-bus services. The government has already procured several hundred new buses from China's Yaxing company. The urban fleet in Douala received a similar upgrade in recent years, although in this case secondhand buses were imported from France. In both cases, a significant proportion is already out of service because of technical problems and difficulty obtaining spare parts. Meanwhile, artificial suppression of fares on large public buses has led operators to defer the maintenance and replacement of aging fleets. Despite the good intentions of a number of governments, it still remains to be seen whether public funding of new buses for a publicly owned operator is a sustainable strategy in the African context.

The private sector has done no better. Only in Nairobi does the private sector operate a significant number of large buses. The vehicles are composed of locally made bodies mounted on a truck-based passenger chassis. But a combination of government interventions in safety policy and competition from the matatus has made it more difficult to finance vehicle replacement; the average age of the fleet exceeded 12 years in 2005. Meanwhile, private financing of new larger vehicles is virtually nonexistent, partly because of the risk of losing capital investment to accident or theft—against which insurance costs would be prohibitive—and partly because of the longer payback periods for new and more expensive vehicles relative to secondhand, less expensive vehicles. In Dakar, the World Bank has supported an innovative scheme in which operators pool funds to commit to collectively finance bus investments. The scheme has yet to prove sustainable, though 505 buses were bought, as projections suggest that companies will need to charge higher fares to fully recoup their investments. In general, it would appear that the fragility of the regulatory environment will continue to discourage the private sector from investing in large buses.

Finding private financing for smaller vehicles has also proved difficult. The private sector has proved capable of raising funds through commercial borrowing only to purchase the most basic secondhand minibuses, for which payback periods are relatively short (box 6.2). Investors are often limited to using family savings for capital, often in the form of interest-free

> **Box 6.2**
>
> ## Financing Large vs. Small Buses in Nairobi
>
> The average price of a secondhand 14-seat matatu (five to seven years old) is approximately $11,800. This may be borrowed commercially, but it is more often assembled from family sources. The net return to the owner is about $21 per day after deductions for insurance, license, vehicle inspection, the cost of tires, and regular maintenance, all of which total about $6,200 per year. Based on these figures, the owner would recoup the capital cost in about two years, well within the average working life of the vehicle.
>
> By contrast, a new, locally bodied, 35-seat matatu built on a light truck chassis costs about $46,000. The purchaser normally would have to borrow from a commercial investor, who would insist on comprehensive insurance at a cost of about $9,200 a year, much more than the insurance normally used to cover smaller vehicles. The cost of insurance alone makes large new vehicles unprofitable. The Matatu Owners Association estimates that many who bought bigger matatus in 2006–08 are likely to go bankrupt.
>
> *Source:* Kumar and Barrett 2008.

loans from family and friends. Bank finance is rarely available because the banks are reluctant to accept the vehicles as collateral in the absence of a secure secondhand market, and because revenue streams in the informal sector are too unreliable to assure the banks of repayment.

Subsidies allow operators to charge fares that are low enough to be affordable for low-income passengers, while still providing sufficient capacity and quality of service to accommodate demand. In this respect, transport operations are a commercial enterprise, and the state reimburses the operator for providing discounts to certain customers (usually students or the aged). In many cases, however, governments have kept fares low but failed to pay the promised subsidies. This practice inevitably leads to deterioration in services—first in quality (because of reduced maintenance) and then quantity (because of an inability to finance fleet renewal) (Gwilliam 2000).

Large buses benefit from some form of public support in most of the 14 cities that have large-bus services. The only exception is Nairobi, where the operator KBS has full control over setting fares. In Accra, large-bus fares are too low for operators to fully recover their operating costs over the life of a bus. The government-sponsored operator Metro Mass Transit Ltd. (MMT) is facing severe cash-flow constraints and will soon require subsidies to remain solvent.[9] The government of Addis Ababa subsidizes bus fares in the city even though the operator Anbessa is federally owned. The government of Senegal has accepted that in Dakar, the private large-bus company Dakar Dem Dikk (DDD) will require a subsidy to operate at the regulated fare. Douala has a history of subsidizing fares on large buses or restructuring operators. In 2008, the Douala Urban Council bought 38 percent of the shares of the private company, Société Camerounaise de Transports Urbains (SOCATUR), which had previously taken over from the defunct state company, Société de Transports Urbains du Cameroun. The SOCATUR now operates under a contract with the government signed in December 2008. The Société de Transport Abidjanais (SOTRA), the large-bus operator in Abidjan, receives an annual subsidy that allows it to offer reduced fares to civil servants, the military, and students. Finally, in Ouagadougou, the government exempts the SOTRACO from tax and duty on fuel, tires, and other imports. Beyond direct operating subsidies, operating companies also benefit from soft loans on better-than-normal commercial terms to finance the acquisition of buses (Accra, Addis Ababa, Dakar, Douala, and Lagos).

Deficit financing of bus operators can also lead to inefficiency in the organization that receives the subsidy. Even with buses averaging five years in age, the large-bus operator in Addis Ababa can achieve only 83 percent fleet availability—well below what an efficient operator should be able to achieve (90–95 percent). The short-lived, publicly owned operator in Nairobi was unable to compete commercially despite its access to duty-free inputs and donated vehicles. The operator in Accra reported a 40 percent "leakage" of revenues, indicating that the main beneficiaries of subsidies in this case were the operator's employees. Subsidies through government capital grants for new vehicles can also undermine efficiency. Accra's buses have not been subjected to any formal specification or a transparent procurement process, without which they are unlikely to offer the lowest possible cost of operation over their life cycle. The latest public procurement in Lagos is reported to have increased the cost of the chosen vehicle by 60 percent over the price that private operators would expect to pay. In Addis Ababa, bilateral concessional aid has financed the importation of buses built in Europe, such that the main beneficiary is actually the European builder and not the local bus system (a situation not unlike colonial times).

In sum, the experience of financing bus operations differs widely, but there still appears to be no viable standard model for Africa comparable to the competitive tendering of franchises, which has worked well in many European countries.

Regulation

The regulatory framework for urban public transport typically comprises several elements, including service planning, controlling entry into the market by new operators, allocating routes to market participants, licensing vehicles and drivers, establishing procedures for vehicle inspection, and setting passenger fares and tariff structures. These functions are often dispersed among a number of agencies, both local and national (table 6.14).

The Gulf between Principles and Practice

In all 14 cities, commercial vehicles must be registered and licensed to carry passengers. Vehicles are inspected for roadworthiness at the time of registration and annually or semiannually thereafter. Inspection standards are often outdated, however, and fail to address environmental concerns, such as emissions and noise. Drivers of commercial passenger vehicles must also pass a test and obtain a special license. In most cities, the drivers of large vehicles must be more experienced and more highly qualified, while minibus drivers require no qualifications beyond those needed to operate a private car. Like vehicle inspections, driver training and testing are relatively weak, and most driving schools and testing stations do not have a full-size bus. Some of the 14 cities are taking measures to limit drivers' ability to bypass testing procedures by obtaining fraudulent documents or altering legitimately issued ones. For example, Addis Ababa is now introducing a more secure, counterfeit-proof system.

For the formal bus sector, many countries retain institutions and processes inherited from a colonial past, whether British or French. For example, in Francophone West Africa, the large-bus services in Abidjan, Dakar, and Douala are, in principle, tightly regulated, with a ministry of transport allocating routes to a monopoly supplier that charges specified, controlled fares. Large-bus services have well-defined route structures that are sometimes out of date but could in principle be revised to reflect population growth and movements.

Some of the old formal arrangements remain. In Douala, a transport-monitoring commission (Comité d'Organisation et de Suivi de Transports Urbains) operates in each municipality, with members representing

Table 6.14 Regulatory Framework for Urban Public Transport

City	System for allocation of routes to operators	Legal restrictions on entry of buses to the market	Entity responsible for licensing of vehicles	Entity responsible for vehicle inspection
Abidjan	Existing concessions for large-bus operations	Yes for large buses	AGETU	SICTA (private concessions)
Accra	None	None	Local authority	None
Addis Ababa	Transport authority	None	Department of Trade and Industry	Federal Transit Authority
Bamako	District and municipality	None	Direction Nationale des Transports Terrestres et Fluviaux	Yes
Conakry	None	None	Ministry of Transportation	None
Dakar	Ministry of Transportation	None	Ministry of Transportation	CETUD
Dar es Salaam	SUMATRA	None	SUMATRA	Ministry of Public Safety and Security (traffic police)
Douala	Comité d'Organisation et de Suivi des Transports Urbains	Yes	n.a.	None
Kampala	None	None	Licensing board	None
Kigali	None	None	Rwanda Utilities Regulatory Agency (regulator)	ONATRACOM
Kinshasa	None	None	n.a.	None
Lagos	None	None	Motor Vehicle Administration	LAMATA
Nairobi	Transport Licensing Board	None	Transport Licensing Board	None
Ouagadougou	None	None	Direction Générale des Transports Terrestres et Maritimes	None

Source: Kumar and Barrett 2008.

Note: n.a. = not applicable; LAMATA = Lagos Metropolitan Area Transport Authority; ONATRACOM = Office National de Transport en Commun; SICTA = Société Ivoirienne de Contrôle Techniques Automobiles et Industriels.

each of the relevant ministries and the operators. But decisions on the route structure, licensing, and fares are made by the ministries of transport and finance in Yaoundé. In Dakar, in principle, the Ministry of Transport controls route licensing, partly to protect the new bus company, DDD, from competition from cars rapides. In practice, however, government-granted route monopolies have not protected DDD. Effective allocation of routes to operators appears, in effect, to be controlled by the operators' syndicates. In Abidjan, the SOTRA operates under the technical supervision of the Ministry of Transport and the financial supervision of the Ministry of Economy and Finance, with a monopoly right to operate public transport service in a defined territory within the city.

But, as noted, most of the public companies covered by the traditional regulatory regimes have languished or failed, supplanted by minibus services operating outside the formal regulatory system. In most cases, rational public planning and administration of the route structure is non-existent, the replacement of formally operated large-bus services with informally operated minibuses having eliminated any vestige of strategic public control. Even where large-bus services still exist, they are a small part of the total supply of public transport, and not components in a well-planned integrated network.

Permits are routinely issued on request, without consideration of supply and demand in the city. Governments may also allocate vehicles to routes, as in the SUMATRA's allocation of the dala-dala routes in Dar es Salaam. But the allocation of vehicles to routes is rarely enforced, except in Nairobi. So, in practice, operating permits are valid throughout the jurisdiction of the issuing authority and are recognized by adjoining jurisdictions within metropolitan areas. This may not be a bad thing. Using permits to assign routes makes sense only if the issuing authority has a good understanding of the transport network and the changes needed to better accommodate passenger demand. In general, however, the 14 cities do not have sufficient understanding of the network to properly manage it. In Addis Ababa, while the transport authority at present issues route licenses, it intends to devolve licensing responsibility to the operators' associations.

The lack of formal regulation is offset by the existence of unions, associations, or syndicates that organize the activities of the sector and provide a degree of self-regulation. Almost all of the 14 cities have at least one syndicate that performs this function. In Kampala, membership in the Uganda Taxi Operators and Drivers Association (UTODA), the main industry union, is obligatory and may be violently enforced. The general practice is for the syndicates to collect dues from their members, who then have the right to use the terminal facilities managed by the syndicate. The syndicates also charge daily fees based on terminal use. A charge is normally paid on first use of the terminal each day, and this may then be supplemented by individual departure charges, sometimes based on the number of passengers carried, and also by further charges at the destination terminal and at major stops along the route. Some syndicates play a role in regulating routes and setting fares.

Self-regulation has created an orderly market and mitigated the worst consequences of unbridled competition on the road. Route terminals are well managed, and overloading and fare gouging are uncommon. Members who flout the rules are subject to disciplinary action. Nevertheless, union control has drawbacks: since the routes run between union-controlled terminals, the route network is overly rigid and generally fails to match transport supply to passenger demand. As a result, too many passenger trips involve one or more bus changes, which increase trip cost and length.

Inadequate Enforcement

All 14 cities lack sufficient institutional capacity and integrity to properly enforce vehicle standards. In Lagos, 37 percent of vehicles were operating without a valid certificate of roadworthiness, and 47 percent without a valid test certificate. In Accra and Addis Ababa, between 30 and 50 percent of vehicles were operated by unlicensed drivers. In both Abidjan (SOTRA) and Kinshasa (STUC), however, buses were required to undergo regular inspections by professional mechanics in dedicated garages, and bus drivers and conductors were professionally trained. Tata buses owned by the STUC benefited from technical assistance from Tata Motors Ltd. Until recently, Accra had only four vehicle inspectors, whose duties also included accident investigation. The city now has 14 inspectors, which is still not enough. The prevalence of unsafe vehicles is well known. In each of the cities surveyed, passengers had nicknames for unsafe vehicles, such as "DMC" for "dangerous mechanical condition."

To address the failure of the existing inspection regime, Lagos has introduced new tests for vehicles that are more than five years old.

The tests are carried out at licensed private testing stations, but so far, standards of integrity remain unsatisfactory. Both Addis Ababa and Kampala intend to privatize their vehicle inspection regimes.

In Accra, all vehicles intended for commercial passenger transport must be registered when they are first imported, converted for passenger carriage, or resold. At the time of registration, the vehicle must be tested for roadworthiness by the Driver and Vehicle Licensing Authority and then retested every six months thereafter, which is twice the frequency required for private vehicles. The institutional and technical capacity of the test centers, however, limits the effectiveness of the testing regime. The Driver and Vehicle Licensing Authority is also responsible for driver testing, the quality of which is dubious. Licensing requirements for owners of commercial passenger vehicles are either weak or nonexistent, which give transport operators little incentive to raise their standards. A stronger regime would require operators to maintain their vehicles in roadworthy condition and would enforce the requirement through inspections, tests, and sanctions. None of the 14 cities has such a system, and enforcement problems are common. In a survey in Lagos, 21 percent of drivers interviewed acknowledged that they did not hold a valid driver's license. Drivers commit many transgressions throughout the day, for which they pay petty bribes to police officers.

Drivers can work long hours—to a point that exceeds the safety threshold. In Kenya and Uganda, for example, driver shifts average more than 12 hours a day for 6 or 7 days a week, although driving hours are normally closer to 7 or 8 hours. But police interviewed for this study were generally unconcerned about drivers' hours of operation, since off-peak periods allow drivers to rest. Conditions appear to be less stressful in West Africa, where cars rapides normally have two drivers (who both work 8-hour shifts), a conductor, and a route assistant.

Safety

The highest road fatality rates (deaths per 10,000 motor vehicles) worldwide occur in African countries, in particular Ethiopia, Uganda, and Malawi, as shown in chapter 2 and appendix 2j. It is estimated that between 20 and 40 percent of fatalities, and a larger proportion of nonfatal injuries, occur in urban areas.[10] A high proportion of fatalities and injuries involve vulnerable pedestrians. For example, in urban areas of Zambia, pedestrians account for two-thirds of fatalities and over half of all road traffic injuries, compared with 30 percent of fatalities and 12 percent of injuries in rural areas. Similarly, in Ethiopia, pedestrians represented 85 percent of all injuries within Addis Ababa but only 40 percent nationwide (Downing and others 2000). Nevertheless, the interests of pedestrians continue to be neglected both in road infrastructure design and in traffic management and enforcement.

Proper institutional recognition of the problem is a good starting point. The establishment of a management unit at a high level of government has proved effective at the national level in Ghana, and at the municipal level in other parts of the world (for instance, in the Brazilian capital). Comprehensive programs have already had some success in KwaZulu-Natal, South Africa.

Because of its dominance in urban traffic, and in view of the conditions in which it operates, public transport plays a large part in urban traffic accidents. This has been specifically recognized in Kenya, where a 2003 law requires all public service vehicles to drive no more than 80 km per hour and to provide seat belts to all passengers. This law reduced passenger loadings and vehicle speed for both conventional large buses and matatus, which in turn reduced the financial viability of the services and put pressure on fares. The safety measures were reported to have reduced road fatalities by 40 percent and serious injuries by 50 percent in the first year of their operation (Chitere and Kibua 2005). This experience suggests that, perhaps with more careful design, safety measures can reduce road traffic injuries and fatalities in African cities.

The Way Forward

The picture of urban transport that emerges from the studies is one of inadequate and poorly managed infrastructure used by an insufficiently regulated vehicle fleet. As a result, formally operated modes of urban transport have given way to informally operated minibuses, which have worsened congestion and raised concerns about fare affordability for the poor, safety, and environmental standards. Regulation of public transport service has either failed or, worse, has bankrupted the large-vehicle operators. While minibus operators' associations often provide some degree of self-regulation, their primary goal is to maximize revenues, not to serve the interests of their customers. Improving urban public transport in Africa is crucial, with several priorities to be addressed.

Priority 1. Developing an appropriate metropolitan government structure

Many of the difficulties that the urban transport sector has faced can be attributed to a lack of strategic planning by a central authority. This can be addressed by a number of steps, including the following:

- Identifying and defining metropolitan areas within which spatial interactions (such as major commuting movements) are significant (this could relate to all public services or more narrowly to transport issues)
- Reassigning responsibility for all strategic transport issues (such as road and public transport network planning, traffic management, and public transport fare and service policy) to the metropolitan authorities
- Establishing financing arrangements for metropolitan services to ensure that all those who benefit from metropolitan-level services contribute to the costs of provision.

Priority 2. Establishing a sustainable financial basis for urban roads

The inadequate quantity and poor quality of urban roads is commonly attributed to the inadequacy of funding for roads at the urban level. Two steps can be taken to address this funding problem:

- Reserve an adequate share of road-fund revenues for urban roads. This can be done either by formula or by including urban road interests in the road board decision process.
- Identify new sources of funds for urban roads. This could be achieved either by earmarking existing road-based taxes, such as vehicle- and driver-licensing revenues and parking charges, or by developing new taxes, such as congestion charges.

Priority 3. Reducing road congestion

Congestion has commonly been attributed to a combination of financial and institutional weaknesses. Cities can take the following actions to address these weaknesses:

- Strengthen the technical competence of the metropolitan-level authority to enable it to manage effectively in a range of relevant areas such as road finance and traffic management.
- Establish strong traffic management agencies to ensure the adoption of strong traffic restraint rules and procedures.

Priority 4. Reestablishing a public transport regulatory framework
The proliferation of the minibus has occurred by accident rather than design, largely as a result of unrealistic fare and service obligations placed on the public sector and large-bus operators, unaccompanied by financial support. As large-bus companies fail, informal operators become responsible for the majority of urban public transport in the region. Cities must therefore do the following:

- Redefine or clarify public service vehicles to include all vehicles carrying passenger at separate fares, irrespective of size or type, so that the informal sector can be aligned with public service regulation.
- Establish public oversight of regulation enforced by operators' associations.
- Enforce the loss of operators' rights for public service providers that fail to meet the obligations included in their licenses or contracts.

Priority 5. Developing a comprehensive strategy to reduce road accidents
Despite the paucity of reliable statistics, there is little doubt that road accident rates in African cities are unacceptably high. Given what is known about the characteristics of the victims (largely pedestrians), the location of accidents (on links rather than at junctions), and the vehicles involved (often public transport vehicles), a range of potentially beneficial measures is known but frequently not implemented. A comprehensive strategy would thus need to include the following:

- Creation of a road safety unit at a high level of municipal or city government
- Better allocation of space for pedestrians in urban road design
- Better separation of commercial and traffic activities, if necessary by provision of attractive locations for hawkers off main roads
- Better enforcement of safety requirements for public transport and freight operators, including controls on speeding and overloading.

Notes

1. The main source document for this chapter is Kumar and Barrett 2008.
2. The data were collected between June 2004 and December 2006 for studies by the Public Private Infrastructure Advisory Facility (PPIAF), the Sub-Saharan Africa Transport Policy Program (Gleave and others 2005), and the World Bank.

3. An electric multiple unit, or EMU, is a multiple-unit train consisting of more than one passenger carriage; all carriages in the train carry passengers, using electric traction motors incorporated within one or several of the carriages.

4. The modal share describes the percentage of trips undertaken using a particular type of transportation.

5. The colloquial names sometimes refer to a fare. For example, in Ghana "trotro" means "three pence-three pence," and refers to the fare set in the early 1970s to undercut the government-set fares. Similarly, in Kenya the word "matatu" is derived from the local term "mang otore matatu," meaning "thirty cents," the standard fare once charged. In other cases, names refer to the vehicle type. In Nigeria "molue" means "molded," the vehicle being a molded body on a truck chassis. "Danfo" means "stands on its own" and refers to an integral-construction microbus.

6. Such vehicles are built with the body and underframe as an integral unit (instead of with the chassis and bodywork as separate constructions).

7. The SOTRACO is a limited liability company, created in 2003 to succeed the defunct Société de Transports Alpha Oméga, which wound up its operations in 2000 after encountering serious financial difficulties. Its objectives were to develop a public-private partnership involving experienced private operators in the transport sector in Ouagadougou, and to delegate management responsibilities to private shareholders. The commune of Ouagadougou owns 15 percent of the SOTRACO, and the private operator 85 percent. The government subsidizes the SOTRACO by exempting it from import duties and taxes on fuel and tires.

8. STUC is a French-style société d'économie mixte, created in 2004 with a mandate to find international partners to provide urban transport in Kinshasa and other cities of the Democratic Republic of Congo without any charge on the national budget. It started operation in February 2006 with 10 buses. In June 2006, it received 228 new Tata buses financed by the Indian government.

9. MMT was incorporated in 2003. The shareholders include State Insurance Company, National Investment Bank, Ghana Oil Company Ltd., Agriculture Development Bank, Prudential Bank, and the Social Security and National Insurance Trust. These together have 55 percent shareholding. The government of Ghana holds the remaining 45 percent of shares.

10. Based on discrepancies between hospital statistics and official police accident statistics, it is believed that there is significant underrecording of all accidents, in particular of nonfatal accidents and accidents involving women. In 2009, the United Nations Economic Commission for Africa (UNECA) undertook an extensive review of road accidents in Africa, which is due to be published late in 2010.

References

Bullock, R. 2009. "Railways in Sub-Saharan Africa." Africa Infrastructure Country Diagnostic Background Paper 17, World Bank, Washington, DC.

Chitere, P. O., and T. N. Kibua. 2005. "Efforts to Improve Road Safety in Kenya: Achievements and Limitations of Reforms in the Matatu Industry." Institute of Policy Analysis and Research, Nairobi, Kenya.

Downing, A., G. Jacobs, A. Aeron-Thomas, J. Sharples, D. Silcock, C. van Lottum, R. Walker, and A. Ross. 2000. *Review of Road Safety in Urban Areas.* Crowthorne, Berkshire, U.K.: TRL.

Gleave, G., A. Marsden, T. Powell, S. Coetze, G. Fletcher, I. Barrett, and D. Storer. 2005. "A Study of Institutional, Financial and Regulatory Frameworks of Urban Transport." Sub-Saharan Africa Transport Policy Program Working Paper 82, World Bank, Washington, DC.

Gwilliam, K. M. 2000. "Public Transport in the Developing World." Transport Series Discussion Paper, World Bank, Washington, DC.

Gwilliam, K., V. Foster, R. Archondo-Callao, C. Briceño-Garmendia, A. Nogales, and K. Sethi. 2009. "The Burden of Maintenance: Roads in Sub-Saharan Africa." Africa Infrastructure Country Diagnostic Background Paper 14, World Bank, Washington, DC.

Kumar, A. J., and F. Barrett. 2008. "Stuck in Traffic: Urban Transport in Africa." Africa Infrastructure Country Diagnostic Background Paper 1, World Bank, Washington, DC.

Mobereola, D. 2008. "Africa's Megacity Needs an Urban Rail Backbone." *Railway Gazette International*, November 14.

UITP (International Association of Public Transport). 2001. Millennium Cities Database for Sustainable Transport. UITP, Brussels.

World Bank. 2002. *Cities on the Move: World Bank Urban Transport Strategy Review.* Washington, DC: World Bank.

CHAPTER 7

Spending to Improve Connectivity

The foregoing chapters on the major transport modes and on urban transport identified deficiencies in infrastructure capacity, quality, and condition that call for investment if they are to be remedied. They also identified circumstances in which maintenance spending must be increased, in particular for roads. But they did not convert those requirements into specific spending requirements. That is the purpose of this chapter.[1]

In theory, investment requirements can be computed by summing the costs of all feasible investment projects—that is, the capital costs of all investments that show a positive net present value at a discount rate equal to the current cost of capital. But to make such an estimate would be an enormous, perhaps impossible, task. Even if it could be done, the result would, in its putative precision, be misleading. For one thing, the computation of the costs and benefits of regional projects would be vitiated by the political realities of present-day Africa.

In place of that approach, therefore, this chapter offers a model designed to estimate the cost of achieving specific connectivity targets considered appropriate to the African context without going through the exercise of appraising every project that might be found feasible based on a full economic analysis.

The Expenditure Model in Brief

The model presented here is based on the concept of *connectivity*, which presumes that the purpose of transport infrastructure is to facilitate transport services that connect people with one another, with markets, and with the social services that are available in urban centers. The extent and quality of transport infrastructure networks and facilities, and the standard to which they are maintained, are obviously critical to the notion of connectivity, as poor or inadequate infrastructure cannot provide a reliable base for reasonable access to people, places, markets, and services.

The connectivity model estimates the total cost of providing specified amounts of infrastructure at a specified standard to meet a specified degree of connectivity over a certain period of time. The cost estimates generated by the model are very sensitive to these specifications and thus, ultimately, to the targeted degree of connectivity that is to be achieved. In the model, each combination of specifications is called a scenario. The model, as it is described here, provides a reference set of parameters that make up what is called a base scenario. The estimated costs of this base scenario are the standard against which the costs of any other scenario may be compared.

The *base scenario* adopted here incorporates a level of connectivity in principle comparable to that of developed countries, with all facilities maintained in good condition.[2] Such a scenario would be out of reach for many countries—which is no doubt why the ambitious targets articulated in many national plans so often go unrealized. For that reason, the model permits the specification of less ambitious alternatives. The *pragmatic scenario* described in this chapter is one of many potential lower-cost alternatives to the base scenario. It aims for a somewhat lower level of connectivity, with infrastructure maintained in only fair condition. The scenarios are described in more detail in the section on the application of the model.

The model is presented in three stages. The first stage comprises inputs—that is, the scenario specifications and data needed to run the model. In the second stage, the costs of the base and alternative scenarios are calculated. The third stage comprises outputs, in the form of comparisons of the costs of the base and alternative scenarios. The relationships between the different components of the model are illustrated in figure 7.1.

Figure 7.1   A Model for Estimating the Costs of Transport Infrastructure Expenditure Needs

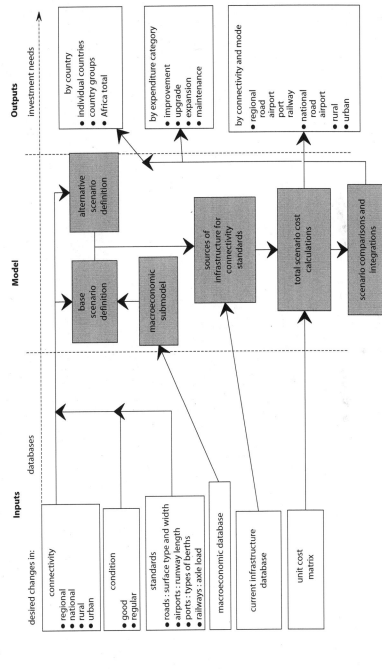

Source: Carruthers, Krishnamani, and Murray 2009.
Note: SSA = Sub-Saharan Africa.

The first stage begins with a specification of the three input components of each scenario for which costs are to be estimated:

- Connectivity targets for regions, countries, rural areas, and urban areas
- The initial capacity and construction of the infrastructure to be provided, referred to here as the infrastructure "category" (for example, a two-lane paved road or a one-lane gravel road)
- The condition in which the infrastructure will be maintained.

The inputs also include a macroeconomic database that provides economic and social projections needed to calculate scenario parameters. For example, information on international trade volumes is needed to estimate the number of port berths required for handling that trade. Other databases quantify existing transport infrastructure and the costs of improving, upgrading, and expanding that infrastructure to reach the specified levels of connectivity.

In the second stage, the model draws on various databases to calculate the links needed to achieve the connectivity targets articulated in the first stage. It then reviews the database of existing infrastructure to see how much of what is needed can be found there, irrespective of its current category or condition. The options are as follows:

- To use the existing infrastructure in its current category and condition
- To improve its condition (for example, from poor to good)
- To upgrade its category (for example, from a gravel road to a paved road)
- To build new infrastructure.

Each item of infrastructure, such as a link in a road network or a runway at an airport, is considered in light of these options. The model computes the costs of each option by applying a matrix of unit costs to each type of activity (for example, improving a road from poor to good quality and upgrading its category from gravel to paved). Although the model calculates the costs of these activities sequentially, in practice they are usually implemented simultaneously.

This second stage of the model yields the cost of meeting the standards specified in the base and alternative scenarios. That cost can be expressed as a total cost over a 10-year period, as an average annual cost, or as a percentage of the gross domestic product (GDP) per year.

The third stage of the model offers a disaggregated presentation of the costs of the base and alternative scenarios in three ways:

- By country, by groups of countries, and for the region as a whole
- By type of expenditure—differentiating among spending to upgrade and improve existing infrastructure, to provide new infrastructure, and to maintain all infrastructure
- By type of connectivity (regional, national, rural, and urban) and transport mode (road, rail, airport, and port)

The costs can be calculated for any combination of the three categories. For example, the model can estimate the cost of maintaining the roads used for regional connectivity in low-income, fragile countries.

A Detailed Look at the Model's Inputs

As noted in the previous section, the inputs to the model are (i) data from five databases described below and (ii) specified requirements, or targets, for connectivity, infrastructure standards, and infrastructure condition.

Five Databases

Five main databases were used in the study. For more detail on these databases, see Carruthers, Krishnamani, and Murray (2009).

Macroeconomic database. To estimate what has to be done to meet a connectivity target, the model requires projections of certain macroeconomic and social variables. Regional connectivity and national connectivity, for example, are defined in terms of air and road links between cities of various sizes.

The macroeconomic database included the following figures for each country:

- Current (as of 2008) and projected national population
- Current and projected urban population
- Current and projected total GDP
- National productive land area
- Urban land area
- Current and projected international trade, disaggregated by imports and exports and by containerized, general, and bulk freight.

The projections of city populations were taken from a widely used and readily available database of country and city populations (Demographia 2009) that is, in turn, based on United Nations estimates of the growth of urban populations. Because GDP projections are generally not available by country for periods of longer than three or four years, estimates were based on short-term projections for African countries done specifically for this analysis.

Geographic information system. The connectivity approach was underpinned by an extensive geographic information system (GIS) data platform assembled specifically for the Africa Infrastructure Country Diagnostic. The data platform included as much of the current transport infrastructure as possible, including interurban road and rail networks, airports, and ports. Used primarily to calculate the distance (in transport network kilometers [km]) between the geographic and demographic features of interest in each country, it includes geographical databases covering the spatial distribution of population, administrative boundaries, geographic and environmental features, and GIS references for all towns and cities of more than 25,000 people. To determine an appropriate standard for urban connectivity, the GIS platform was complemented by detailed databases on city population and population density, discussed above.

GIS-referenced locations for cities and towns were drawn from the Global Rural-Urban Mapping Project (GRUMP) of the Center for International Earth Science Information Network (CIESIN) at Columbia University's Earth Institute. The survey of road and rail infrastructure was based on references from the Digital Chart of the World. Road surface and width were determined manually from Michelin's regional map series of 2004 (1:4,000,000 scale). Locations for ports were based on the GIS data set available from the U.S. National Geospatial-Intelligence Agency (NGA), which publishes a World Port Index containing information on world ports and related facilities. GIS references for airports were shown on the same large-scale Michelin maps consulted for roads.[3]

Roads. The road network was assessed using a data set compiled for a previous World Bank study of road investment needs in Africa. That data set drew on spatially integrated data compiled by CIESIN. Other data for the roads database were drawn from Gwilliam and others (2009) and from national statistics on classified and unclassified road networks, as well as from various reports of the Sub-Saharan Africa Transport Policy Program (SSATP). The latter were particularly useful for data on urban roads. Various SSATP sources were also used for data on the condition of interurban and urban roads, and recourse was also made to many publications by national road agencies.

Other infrastructure data. Several additional sources were used for transport infrastructure data. Bofinger (2009) was the main source for information on airports and runways. Mundy and Penfold (2009) provided ports data, supplemented by data from Web sites maintained by national port agencies. The World Bank's railways database (World Bank 2010) was a main source for the length and gauge of national railway networks. Data on the length of operating routes that had long-term prospects for sustainable investment were based on Bullock (2009).

Unit costs. The database of unit costs covered all the construction and maintenance operations that might be needed to meet the specified connectivity targets. The source of the unit costs for road-related construction and maintenance was the same as that used in Gwilliam and others (2009). The unit costs for railway activities were based on those used in a selection of recent World Bank railway projects, checked against the cost data provided in Bullock (2009). Port unit costs and airport investment costs were provided by port and airport specialists at the World Bank.

The cost estimates for the connectivity targets are very sensitive to unit costs. As applied in this study, the model uses the same unit costs for all countries. In practice, however, the costs are known to vary substantially. For example, while the median estimated cost of rehabilitating a two-lane road in Africa in 2006 was $300,000 per kilometer, the upper quartile estimate was over $450,000. Moreover, the costs vary across countries, and are likely to be considerably above the median in landlocked countries. The implication is that the costs may be underestimated for some of the poorest countries—so that their needs are even greater than estimated in this chapter, and their shortfall greater than that estimated in the next chapter. This limitation can be overcome. The database design allows the costs to be scaled up or down for a specific country or group of countries, for all unit costs or just for those related to a particular transport mode or a construction or maintenance operation. For more detailed application to any individual country, it would be necessary to calibrate the cost model on local data.

The cost matrix is structured by type of operation (improving the condition of infrastructure, upgrading its category, building new infrastructure, or performing maintenance) and by mode (regional roads, regional ports, regional railways, regional airports, national roads, national airports, rural roads, and urban roads).

Standards of Regional, National, Rural, and Urban Connectivity

The connectivity approach consists of identifying the key geographic and demographic features of each country and then quantifying the transport infrastructure needed to connect those features. Features of international interest (such as capital cities, deepwater ports, and international borders) provide connectivity across the entire region, whereas features of purely national interest (mainly secondary cities and provincial capitals) provide national connectivity. In rural areas, the focus is on connecting agricultural land to markets, while in urban areas the focus is on connecting households to the activities that are necessary for their well-being. The model therefore considers four types of connectivity: regional, national, rural, and urban.

Regional connectivity. Regional connectivity is needed for the international movement of people and goods. The assumption is that connectivity requires a road network that links national capitals to one another, to all other cities with a population of more than 250,000,[4] to international land borders, and to deepwater ports. In the model, interurban road infrastructure is specified in terms of the actual road carriageway, without regard for bridges, tunnels, and other structures that would require a level of geographic specificity and knowledge that is beyond the scope and resources of the study. Because of this limitation, the estimates presented here are likely to underestimate the full cost of the reference standard of connectivity.

Another assumption is that larger cities and national capitals require airports with appropriate runways and terminals, and that current terminal capacity is sufficient to deal with current demand. Cost estimates therefore include only the additional area needed to satisfy projected increases in demand. To ensure regional connectivity, each country must have access to a deep-sea port of regional significance (not necessarily within the country) with appropriate container, general freight, and bulk freight berths of depths suitable for the current generation of ships.

Out of the current rail network of more than 62,000 km, only about 55,000 km are currently in operation. Low-volume lines—those with less than 1 million net tonnes of freight per year—are very unlikely to merit full rehabilitation, and lines carrying bulk traffic will normally generate greater (and more certain) benefits than those carrying general traffic. The result is that only about 29,500 km of line have a chance of justifying the investment needed to keep them in operation—and only in unusual circumstances could keeping them operational contribute to connectivity standards or provide cost-effective alternatives to road transport of freight. Nevertheless, because future demand for rail infrastructure is very difficult to assess, the rail connectivity standard keeps those 29,500 km of railway lines in operation and upgrades them to an 18 tonne or 25 tonne axle load depending on the volume of freight they handle.

National connectivity. National connectivity is provided by a transport network that links each country's provincial capitals to other medium-sized cities, defined as cities having a population of at least 25,000. The network is used for nationally traded goods, for access to services such as health and education, and for access to family members in other cities. A national connectivity network is generally limited to roads within a single country, except in a few cases where a lower-cost route between a medium-size city and the existing national network might overlap with a cross-border regional road or with the national network in a neighboring country. Medium-size cities with populations of more than 100,000 were assumed to require airports with shorter runways (1,524 meters) and terminals with slightly lower capacity standards (16 square meters [m²] per domestic passenger) than those needed for regional capitals. No additional railway or port facilities were assumed beyond those required for regional connectivity, the national requirements being fully satisfied by the regional infrastructure (provided that the infrastructure was up to standard).

Rural connectivity. Two approaches to estimating rural accessibility or connectivity were explored. The first is centered on a social criterion for connecting people, the second on a commercial criterion for connecting rural production to national and international markets. After consideration, the second approach was chosen.

The social measure of rural accessibility is based on the Rural Accessibility Index (RAI) discussed in chapter 2. Roberts, Shyam, and Rastogi (2006) have developed an index that measures the share of the rural population living within 2 km of a road that is passable in all weather. In the world's middle-income countries, 94 percent of rural people meet that criterion. But in African countries, the share is only 34 percent, with values ranging from 5 percent in Sudan to 67 percent in Lesotho. The estimates of the current RAI values are based on household survey results and extrapolations from respondents' perceptions of whether they live within 2 km of a paved road. It is impossible to know which roads they take into account when reporting their assessments to survey takers. But from the GIS data available on population distribution and existing roads, it was possible to estimate the road system necessary to satisfy different RAI targets. A target of 75 percent of the rural population living within 2 km of a single-lane road with a single surface treatment was taken as the base scenario, and a target of 50 percent living within 2 km of an improved gravel road with drainage was adopted for the pragmatic scenario.

The agricultural output measure of rural connectivity is the alternative approach; it, too, was introduced in chapter 2. The criterion used for both scenarios was that of connecting to a port or local market the areas producing 80 percent of current agricultural output. If the main product is for export, the link is to a port; if it is for local consumption, the link is to the nearest local market (defined as a town of at least 25,000 people). The difference between the scenarios is in the category of road provided: a single surface treatment road in the base scenario and an all-weather gravel road in the pragmatic scenario. The rural roads included in the assessment of rural connectivity were those needed for trucking consolidated agricultural output to the nearest market center or port. To connect areas that provide 80 percent of the value of current agricultural output would require a road network of just under 600,000 km.[5]

The market-access criterion of rural connectivity was ultimately chosen for the estimations reported in this study because it was more universally supported by specialists in transport and rural development. It is no more difficult to calculate the road needs for different standards of market access than it is for different standards of household proximity to roads. And except at very high levels of connectivity (connecting more than 95 percent of all production areas, for example), the length of the road network required to meet the target was generally less than for meeting comparable RAI standards. But the model retains the capacity to accommodate either method.

Urban connectivity. The basic standard of urban connectivity was taken to be a grid of all-weather roads suitable for buses. The grid had to be sufficiently dense that residents would not have to walk great distances to reach the nearest road. The Millennium Cities Database, compiled by the International Union of Public Transport in 1998, gives data for 100 cities around the world. It shows that, on average, there were about 300 meters of paved road per 1,000 people in the 15 cities ranked lowest on the basis of road density, and about 500 meters per 1,000 people, on average, for the 20 lowest-ranked cities.

Given that the connectivity associated with these figures varies with population density, a maximum walking distance condition was also included in the standard. Thus, for the base scenario, the urban connectivity standard was 300 meters of road per 1,000 people and a maximum walking distance of 500 meters, while in the pragmatic scenario, the standard was 200 meters of road per 1,000 people and a maximum walking distance of 1,000 meters. In both cases, the minimum paved road density could be no less than 150 meters per 1,000 people. The connectivity standards were then applied to the total projected urban population of each country in 2015.

The urban connectivity standards do not take into account the need for urban mass transit systems such as suburban railways, light-rail rapid transit, subways, or bus rapid transit. Although there is adequate information on existing systems, no criteria for provision of new systems were included in the standards. Nor do they take into account the additional road capacity that may be needed for private cars.[6] The exclusion of requirements for urban mass transit and added road capacity is another respect in which the model's estimates of spending needs may be understated.

Category of Infrastructure

The base scenario standard for the regional road network was a two-lane, asphalt-paved road, 7.3 meters in width, built with hard shoulders on either side and designed to withstand an 11 tonne single-axle load. National connectivity was provided in the model by interurban paved roads of at least one 3.65 meter lane, with shoulders 2.5 meters in width. In practice, politicians would probably argue for a two-lane, 7.3 meter road, as for the regional network. That would increase the costs estimated in this chapter and the financing shortfalls estimated in the next. A compromise that should be explored in further applications of the model would be a combination, determined by traffic volumes, of two-lane asphalt roads, two-lane roads with a slurry seal, and two-lane gravel roads. For rural roads, the base scenario called for a single surface treatment asphalt road. A single surface treatment road was taken as the standard for urban roads in the base scenario (table 7.1).

Regional airports were required to have a lighted, paved runway at least 3,000 meters in length, adequate for aircraft used on intercontinental flights, in both the base and pragmatic scenarios. They should have terminal space of 20 m² for each international passenger and 5 m² for every 1,000 tonnes of air freight. For national connectivity, the runway length

Table 7.1   Definition of the Base Scenario

Connectivity level	Connectivity target	Infrastructure standard	Condition of infrastructure
Regional			
Roads	Connection of all national capitals, cities with population of at least 250,000, deep-sea ports, and border crossings	Two-lane, paved	Good
Railway	Regional network of 39,000 km	20 tonne maximum axle load	Good
Ports	Access to a deep-sea port of regional significance with appropriate container, general freight, and bulk freight berths	One 300 meter berth for each 0.5 million TEUs container traffic	Good
Airports	Connection of national capitals and cities with population of at least 500,000	At least one runway of 3,000 meters. 20 m^2 terminal space per international passenger	Good
National			
Roads	Connection of provincial capitals and cities with population of at least 25,000	One-lane, paved	Good
Railways	Included in regional	Same as regional	Good
Ports	Included in regional	Same as regional	Good
Airports	Connection of cities with population between 100,000 and 500,000	At least one runway of 1,524 meters. 15 m^2 terminal space per domestic passenger	Good
Rural			
Roads	Market connectivity for 80 percent of current agricultural production by value	One-lane, single surface treatment	Good
Urban			
Roads	No more than 500 meters walking distance to paved road; 300 meters of paved road per 1,000 people	One-lane, single surface treatment	Good

Source: Carruthers, Krishnamani, and Murray 2009.
Note: TEU = twenty-foot equivalent unit.

was 1,524 meters and the passenger terminal requirement was 15 m^2 per domestic passenger.

For ports, both the base and the pragmatic standards were that each country should have at least one 300 meter berth for every 0.5 million TEUs (twenty-foot equivalent units) of container freight and for every 5 million tonnes of dry and liquid bulk freight.

For regional connectivity in rail transport, it was assumed (based on Bullock [2009]) that rail links should accommodate an axle load of at least 20 tonnes if they were expected to transport more than 5 million net tonnes per kilometer per year.

Because the road standards promised to be too expensive for many low-income countries, especially when maintenance was factored in, an improved gravel road with engineered drainage was chosen as the rural standard for the pragmatic scenario, while for urban roads, an improved gravel road with engineered drainage was adopted (table 7.2).

Condition of Infrastructure

The scenarios also differed in the condition assumed. For the base scenario it was assumed that all road and rail infrastructure should be in good condition. Maintenance cost models such as the Highway Development and Management Model (HDM4) attempt to identify the road condition standards and related maintenance expenditures that will keep the total costs of building, maintaining, and using roads to a minimum.[7] The base scenario reflects the levels of routine and periodic maintenance implicit in those standards.

The lower standards assumed in the pragmatic scenario would reduce overall costs in the 10-year period covered in this analysis but

Table 7.2   Definition of the Pragmatic Scenario

Connectivity level	Connectivity target	Infrastructure standard	Condition of infrastructure
Regional			
Roads	As for base scenario	One lane, paved	Fair
Railways	As for base scenario	18 tonne maximum axle load	Fair
Ports	As for base scenario	As for base scenario	Fair
Airports	As for base scenario	As for base scenario	Fair
National			
Roads	As for base scenario	One lane, single surface treatment	Fair
Railways	As for base scenario	As for base scenario	Fair
Ports	As for base scenario	As for base scenario	Fair
Airports	As for base scenario	As for base scenario	Fair
Rural			
Roads	As for base scenario	One-lane, single surface treatment	Fair
Urban			
Roads	No more than 1 km walking distance to road 300 meters of road per 1,000 people	One-lane, improved gravel	Fair

Source: Carruthers, Krishnamani, and Murray 2009.

not in the longer term taken into account in the full analyses of the cost-optimization model. While it is assumed in both scenarios that existing transport infrastructure will be initially improved to the level prescribed in the standard, it is also understood that when financial resources are severely constrained, the roads agency may be justified in deferring some periodic maintenance.

The ports database was used to gauge the extent to which the identified needs could be met by improvements in the condition of the existing facilities (as well as by extending their lengths or converting no-longer-needed general cargo berths into container berths). The 54 percent of airport runways not already in good condition were assumed to be brought into good condition for both the base and pragmatic scenarios.

Applying the Model

Applying the model involves three main activities: (i) specifying one or more connectivity scenarios for which spending requirements are to be calculated, (ii) calculating the infrastructure needed to satisfy those requirements in physical terms, and (iii) determining the cost of that infrastructure.

Specifying Scenarios

Scenarios and their relationship with connectivity targets, infrastructure categories, and condition standards were discussed in the previous section. Recall that two scenarios were defined: (i) a *base* scenario that reflects the situation in developed countries and the stated aspirations of many developing countries, and (ii) a *pragmatic* alternative that reflects the budgetary constraints of many low-income countries—and all low-income, fragile countries. The model is designed to accommodate any other scenario that might be useful.

Identifying the Physical Infrastructure Needed to Achieve Connectivity Targets

Estimating the network needs for regional and national connectivity was relatively straightforward once the population, GDP, and transport infrastructure databases were established. For urban connectivity, the standard was defined in such a way that estimating the roads needed to satisfy the standard in each country was also straightforward—depending only on the urban population and population density.

Rural connectivity presented a more complex challenge. As noted earlier, a standard based on connectivity of agricultural output was adopted. Connectivity needs were calculated using a GIS database of the value of the current agricultural production of each square kilometer of land, as well as the *potential value* of the same land if it were used to produce the most valuable crop feasible. Working from this database, the rural road network that would be needed to connect each agricultural zone to the already specified regional and national road networks was assessed, until cumulative values of 20 percent, 40 percent, 60 percent, and 80 percent of the total value of current national agricultural output were connected. Connectivity was assessed to the nearest significant town (25,000 population or more) or to the nearest port, depending on whether the most valuable crop currently planted in a given zone was destined for local markets or international markets.

The rural road network needed to connect zones that provided the same cumulative values of *potential* agricultural output to the regional and national road networks was similarly assessed. Determining the size of such a network was difficult, however, because in many zones the most valuable agricultural crop—coffee, for example—might have a high export value and a low local value. In other words, more zones would be connected to ports if the criterion of potential value were used. Therefore, the costs of trucking output from each zone to the nearest port was subtracted from the value of the highest export crop, and the costs of trucking output from the zone to the nearest significant town was subtracted from the value of the highest locally consumed crop. The connectivity requirement was based on the highest resulting value. In this way, many remote areas that would have been connected to a port using the unadjusted criterion of greatest potential output were connected to the nearest significant town instead.

In the next stage of the model, the macroeconomic and GIS databases were applied, together with the scenario definitions, to estimate how much infrastructure was needed to meet the connectivity targets. The resulting estimates were compared with the infrastructure now available in table 7.3, which lists infrastructure elements by total length and quantity as well as by category and condition.

The GIS data on city, road links, and airport runway locations were used in determining how much of the current infrastructure could be employed to meet specified targets. This exercise revealed that many existing infrastructure facilities were not located where they were most needed. So, although it might appear that more than enough infrastructure is available to meet connectivity needs, much of it is unusable.

Table 7.3   Transport Infrastructure: Current, Base Scenario, and Pragmatic Scenario

Transport infrastructure	Current	Base scenario	Pragmatic scenario
Regional roads	102,819 km	102,819 km	102,819 km
% two-lane	76	100	100
% one-lane	1	0	0
% other	23	0	0
% good condition	*32*	*100*	*50*
National roads	143,531 km	143,531 km	143,531 km
% two-lane	44	44	44
% one-lane	3	56	56
% other	54	0	0
% good condition	*28*	*100*	*50*
Rural social criterion	n.a.	1,187,050 km	850,450 km
Corresponding RAI	29%	75%	50%
Local access market criterion	n.a.	599,981 km	599,981 km
Corresponding RAI	n.a.	42%	42%
Urban paved roads	39,700 km	111,309 km	49,391
% good condition	*15*	*100*	*50*
Railways, km			
Length in operation	55,000 km	29,502 km	29,502 km
% good condition	*38*	*100*	*100*
Ports			
Container berths	80	255	255
General cargo berths	159	120	120
Bulk freight berths	105	75	75
% good condition	*45*	*100*	*100*
Airport runways			
1,524 to 3,000 meters, number	377	142	142
More than 3,000 meters, number	53	56	56
% good condition	*46*	*100*	*100*
Airport terminals			
Passenger space, m^2	296,500	405,700	405,700
Freight space, m^2	57,000	107,000	107,000

Sources: Carruthers, Krishnamani, and Murray 2009 (for base and pragmatic scenarios); CIA 2007; Bofinger 2009; Bullock 2009 (for current).
Note: n.a. = not applicable.

Meeting the regional connectivity requirements. Roads. Meeting the regional connectivity standard in both the base and pragmatic scenarios would require a network of approximately 103,000 km of two-lane paved roads. The current regional road network includes about 78,000 km of roads built to that standard, and less than 1,000 km of one-lane paved roads that could be upgraded to two lanes (table 7.3). To meet the targets, therefore, some 20,000 km of gravel roads that make up part of the current regional network would have to be upgraded, together with about 6,500 km of dirt roads and 3,500 km of dirt tracks. Only 32 percent of the network is in good condition, a reflection of the very poor condition of unpaved roads.

Because the proposed Trans-African Highway system is counted toward the regional connectivity standard, the model took into account all of the system's links, including segments planned but not yet built. The investment requirements presented here include the 52,450 km needed to complete and fully pave that system—and more. The Trans-African Highway was designed to connect capital cities to a common road network, whereas the standard proposed here for regional connectivity also calls for connecting large cities, ports, and airports. The length of road needed to meet this regional connectivity standard, therefore, is about double that of the Trans-African Highway. The construction specifications, however, are the same.

Airports. To achieve the regional airport connectivity standards would require a total of 56 runways of 3,000 meters and an additional 405,700 m^2 of passenger terminal space and 107,000 m^2 of freight terminal space (table 7.4). Although the number of total runways needed is only 3 more than the number currently available, 8 of the latter are in cities smaller than those specified in the connectivity standard, so 11 additional runways will be needed. Several of these can be provided by extending existing shorter runways.

Ports. A total of 255 container berths, 75 bulk freight berths, and 120 general freight berths would be required to service the international maritime trade of the African countries. The number of general freight berths needed will be substantially fewer than the current 159, as most general freight will be containerized within the next 10 years.

Table 7.4   Regional Airports: Current Characteristics vs. Characteristics Needed to Meet Connectivity Target

		Target	
Regional airports	Current	Base scenario	Pragmatic scenario
Airport runways			
Longer than 3,000 meters, number	53	56	56
% in good condition	46	100	100
Airport terminals			
Passenger space, m^2	296,500	405,700	405,700
Freight space, m^2	57,000	107,000	107,000

Source: Carruthers, Krishnamani, and Murray 2009.

The projected (solid) bulk freight berths do not include those in facilities for specific bulk products (such as grain terminals adjacent to ports for general cargo and containers).

Railways. Bullock (2009) estimates that there are about 65,000 km of railways in Africa, of which about 56,000 km are in operation; 31 percent of those in operation are in South Africa. Although Bullock does not specify their condition, he estimates the length of national networks that could be economically viable. Low-volume lines (those that carry less than 1 million net tonnes of freight per year) are unlikely to merit full rehabilitation, and lines carrying bulk traffic will normally generate greater (and more certain) benefits than those carrying general traffic. Applying these criteria to national rail networks, Bullock estimated that only about 29,500 km of line would have enough traffic to justify the expenditure needed to keep them in operation. This is the figure that was used here in computing the cost of upgrading to the standard of 20 tonne axle loads.

Meeting the national connectivity requirements. *Roads.* Only about 47 percent of the 143,500 km of roads needed to meet the national road connectivity standard are presently paved. Meeting the standard would require upgrading gravel roads and earth roads in approximately equal proportions. The share of national roads in good condition is just under 30 percent, significantly less than the share of regional roads in good condition. This is because more of the national roads are unpaved, and unpaved roads tend to be in worse condition than paved roads.

Airports. A total of 142 runways of between 1,524 and 3,000 meters are needed to meet the national airport standard. While this number is much smaller than the 377 runways already found in Africa, many of those are in cities smaller than the ones specified in the standard. Others appear to be for military use only, and a few will need to be extended. For technical reasons, all of the terminal space for domestic air passengers is included in the total required for regional connectivity. It is estimated that about 50 percent of the 400,000 m^2 of additional passenger terminal space needed to meet the regional connectivity targets would be for domestic passengers. No allowance was made for freight terminal space, which is likely to increase in the future.

The national connectivity targets for ports and railways are the same as the regional targets.

Meeting the rural connectivity requirements. A very long network of roads would be required to provide the degree of social accessibility corresponding to an RAI value of 100 percent (table 7.5). The network length required to meet the standard of market access for 80 percent of the value of agricultural output is a good deal lower.

For provision of market access for 80 percent of current agricultural output (by value), just under 600,000 km of road would be required—possibly 50 percent more than the current total, though exact figures for the current total of relevant roads are not available. But because many current roads are either poorly located or in bad condition, substantial upgrades and new construction are necessary. For connection of 80 percent of potential agricultural output, up to six times more new roads would be needed (table 7.6).

Meeting the urban connectivity requirements. In urban areas, about 111,000 km of paved roads are required to meet the connectivity target specified in the base scenario for the projected urban population (table 7.7). The pragmatic scenario would require almost 50,000 km. No African country now has a network of paved urban roads large enough to satisfy the base scenario; only two (Lesotho and Namibia) fulfill the requirements of the pragmatic scenario. Presently there are only about 40,000 km of paved roads at least one lane wide in the urban areas of Africa, so that about 71,000 km of additional urban paved roads would be required for the base scenario and about 9,000 km for the pragmatic scenario. The main source of these additional paved roads would be existing gravel and earth roads. But even making use of these, to reach the base scenario's urban connectivity standard would require more than 30,000 km of new

Table 7.5   Road Lengths Needed to Reach Rural Connectivity Standards

Road network	Road length (km)	Resulting RAI value (%)
Network needed to achieve 100% RAI	1,473,602	100
Network needed to achieve 75% RAI	1,187,050	75
Network needed to achieve 50% RAI	850,450	50
Network needed to connect 80% of current agricultural output	599,981	40
Network needed to connect 80% of potential agricultural output	912,487	55

Source: Carruthers, Krishnamani, and Murray 2009.

Table 7.6   Sources of Road Upgrades to Achieve Rural Connectivity Targets

Road network	To connect 80% of current agricultural output (km)	To connect 80% of potential agricultural output (km)
Total rural roads needed to satisfy connectivity criteria	599,981	912,487
From regional + national	243,356	242,309
From other classified paved roads	153,998	163,617
From classified unpaved roads	166,984	308,668
From unclassified paved roads	3,600	24,188
From unclassified unpaved roads	9,163	37,971
New roads or upgraded tracks	22,879	135,733
Rural Accessibility Index corresponding to this network (%)	40.0	55.2
Precentage of new roads or upgraded tracks in rural total	3.8	14.8

Source: Carruthers, Krishnamani, and Murray 2009.

Table 7.7   Types of Road Counted toward Urban Connectivity Targets

Road type	Target	
	Base scenario (km)	Pragmatic scenario (km)
Total paved roads needed to meet connectivity target	110,880	49,199
Existing paved roads	34,894	29,802
Existing gravel roads	30,941	9,238
Existing dirt roads	12,466	3,544
New paved roads	32,579	6,615

Sources: http://www.geohive.com/default1.aspx; Carruthers, Krishnamani, and Murray 2009.

roads, with fewer than 7,000 km needed for the pragmatic scenario. Because not all of the existing roads are in the right place, however, the actual need for new roads is likely to be somewhat greater than these figures suggest.

Estimating the Cost of Meeting the Connectivity Requirements under Both Scenarios

Once infrastructure needs and the means of meeting them are known, the cost matrix can be applied to estimate the cost of meeting connectivity targets.

Previous assessments of spending requirements in the transport sector (Fay and Yepes 2003; Estache and Yepes 2004; Chatterton and Puerto 2005) have focused on the costs of lengthening road and rail networks and then maintaining them. The target length of those networks usually has been derived from a simple econometric model or a benchmarking approach that uses industrial economies as comparators. The difference between the target and the existing network is then multiplied by the unit cost of new infrastructure to derive the cost necessary to bring the network up to the target level. Estimates of maintenance costs typically have been even more simplistic and are usually given as a percentage of the replacement value of the network.

These simplified approaches reflect the paucity of data on quantities and qualities of transport infrastructure. The model employed in this study makes use of many data sources not used by earlier investigators, several of which were compiled specifically for the purpose. These expanded and more reliable data allow better estimates of spending needs, despite some remaining gaps.

Four different types of infrastructure costs were estimated:

- The cost of *improving the condition* of current transport infrastructure to the standard defined in each scenario
- The cost of *upgrading the standard* of existing transport infrastructure to that defined in each scenario (for example, widening existing roads or upgrading their surface; extending existing airport runways, passenger terminals, and port berths; and increasing the permissible axle load of railways)
- The cost of *extending existing networks*—such as regional, national, rural, and urban roads—and increasing the number of infrastructure assets, such as port container berths, to supplement existing transport infrastructure and so reach the scenario targets
- And finally, the largest category, the cost of *maintaining networks and assets*—in their improved, upgraded, or expanded form—in the condition defined in each scenario

Each type of cost is dealt with in turn.

The cost of improving infrastructure conditions. Where available, data on current conditions (good, fair, or poor) were used; where such estimates could not be found, assumptions were made based on the proportion in each condition in comparable countries. To estimate the cost of bringing infrastructure in fair or poor condition up to good condition, the quantities of such infrastructure were multiplied by the unit cost of improvement—a one-time cost that can be incurred at any time. It was assumed that this cost could be spread equally over 10 years.

The cost of upgrading infrastructure standards. Infrastructure is categorized by its capacity. The essential question is whether a piece of infrastructure has the capacity to meet the connectivity demands made upon it. (For example, airports in many large cities have runways that are too short for the midsize aircraft—such as the Airbus A320 or Boeing 737—used on domestic trunk routes.) Hence, the infrastructure standards appropriate for each mode and market are specified. In some cases, these specifications were based on international standards, such as those of the International Civil Aviation Organization. In other cases, they were based on common engineering standards or on authors' judgment and experience. The costs of making the necessary upgrades were based generally on engineering estimates.

The costs of upgrading infrastructure in poor or fair condition were estimated in two stages: first, improving its condition to "good" at its present standard, and then upgrading it to the next standard. Where infrastructure was already of a higher standard than deemed necessary for its purpose, it was assumed that it would be maintained in good condition at its current standard.

The cost of extending network length and increasing facilities. A combination of methods was used to estimate the optimal or desired extent of transport infrastructure networks or assets. For each type of road, the network length needed to meet connectivity targets was compared against current length, estimated using GIS data. Optimum airport runway length was estimated for each city, also using GIS data. For port berths, the requirement was based on the port connectivity standard, applied to the output of a macroeconomic model that included, for each country, projections of GDP, imports and exports as a share of GDP, and the average value per tonne of freight (or per TEU for containerized trade). The resulting target quantities were compared with present levels, regardless of condition. The costs of extending networks or increasing the number of overall assets were then estimated. (The costs of bridges or tunnels were not included in either urban or interurban road-cost estimates.) For urban roads, neither the capacity needs of private cars (greater than those required for buses) nor the costs of urban mass transit systems were taken into account.

For interurban roads and railways, the methods used resemble those of previous studies. But for improving or maintaining other modes (rural and urban roads, airports, and ports), the cost estimates presented here are difficult to compare with those of other studies. To facilitate comparisons, however, this study disaggregates final cost estimates by transport mode and type of expenditure.

The cost of maintaining infrastructure. Most previous assessments of transport infrastructure costs made some attempt to include maintenance costs by adding a fixed amount (often 3 percent) of the replacement cost of the infrastructure. For most transport infrastructure, two types of maintenance were considered here—annual and periodic. In the model, both types are taken into account, but periodic costs are converted to annual sums. The resulting annual average costs of maintenance are specific to each country, although the unit costs are the same. This is because the better the current condition of an asset, the less needs to be spent on periodic maintenance. The annual cost of maintaining a facility in good condition is taken to be the same for any given type of infrastructure across all countries. While in some cases the estimates of maintenance costs were close to 3 percent of asset replacement costs, in general the estimates were higher than those of previous assessments, with a wide variation about the average.

Applying unit costs to the identified needs. Once all the necessary infrastructure operations are known (for example, the upgrading of earth roads or the construction of new facilities), the results are fed through a matrix of unit costs for building, upgrading, and maintaining each type of transport infrastructure at the levels defined in each scenario (Carruthers, Krishnamani, and Murray 2009). Data on unit costs used in the matrix were derived from fieldwork in a sample of southern African countries. The total expenditure for each scenario that results from these calculations is the final output of the model.

Outputs of the Model

The outputs of the model can be expressed in global terms, or disaggregated by country, mode, or type of expenditure. Costs are provided as totals for a 10-year period, as annual averages for each of the 10 years, and as a percentage of annual GDP. A Web-based version of the model is available at https://www.infrastructureafrica.org. Each output offers useful insights into the fundamental policy issues surrounding transport infrastructure provision.

Total Spending Needs in the Base Scenario

Considering the total expenditure needs under different scenarios highlights the connections between needs, affordability, and fundamental aspirations.

At about $12.7 billion, the annual cost of meeting the connectivity targets for transport in the base scenario would average slightly less than 2 percent of GDP each year for the 10 years between 2006 and 2015 (table 7.8). Maintenance of improved, upgraded, and expanded infrastructure would require almost 40 percent of the total expenditure, with upgrading requiring a further 30 percent, improvement about 20 percent, and expansion less than 15 percent. These allocations are substantially different from those made today, when construction and expansion take up the largest shares.

The total expenditure estimates listed in table 7.8 have been adjusted to reflect the impressive transport investments made by the South African government in preparation for the 2010 football World Cup. The 2010 World Cup transport projects included the massive expansion of public transport and road infrastructure, rail upgrades, development of intermodal facilities, bus rapid transit systems, inner-city mobility systems, call-center systems, airport-city links, freight services, and passenger safety and intelligent transport systems. The flagship projects—which by themselves totaled over $3 billion—included the Khulani corridor in the Eastern Cape (R 321 million), the N1 and N2 Toll Highway (R 5 billion), the Sani Pass road upgrade on the border between South Africa and Lesotho (R 200 million), and the Gauteng Freeway Improvement Scheme (R 23 billion). Another massive project is the expansion of airport facilities undertaken by the Airports Company South Africa, with an estimated cost of $1.5 billion.

Putting the Numbers into Perspective: Affordability

The 1.9 percent of GDP needed to achieve the connectivity standards of the base scenario is about the same as what the countries of the European Union invest in their transport infrastructure. But the European Union average is for countries that have been investing in their transport infrastructure for centuries, with few interruptions or periods of significant deferred maintenance. Perhaps a more realistic comparison is with the middle-income countries that a half-century ago were at a stage of development similar to that of Africa today. Brazil, Japan, and Republic of

Table 7.8 Average Annual Investment Needs: Base Scenario, 2006–15

| Infrastructure type | Expenditure purpose | | | | | As percentage of | |
	Improving condition	Upgrading standard	Expanding capacity	Maintaining infrastructure	Total	GDP	Total expenditure
	US$ (millions)						
Regional roads	519	1,083	172	905	2,678	0.4	21
National roads	451	1,237	174	1,015	2,877	0.5	23
Rural roads	812	397	63	1,205	2,477	0.4	19
Urban roads	275	566	684	622	2,147	0.3	17
Airports	40	23	84	710	856	0.1	7
Ports	203	70	449	153	876	0.1	7
Railways	128	265	100	282	776	0.1	6
Total for all types (without South Africa's World Cup investment needs)	2,429	3,642	1,726	4,891	12,689	1.9	100
As % of GDP	0.4	0.6	0.3	0.8	2.0		
As % of total	19	29	14	38	100		
Total for all types (with South Africa's World Cup investment needs)	2,429	3,642	3,569	9,553	19,193	2.9	100

Source: Carruthers, Krishnamani, and Murray 2009.

Korea—and even the Federal Republic of Germany in its post–World War II reconstruction phase—invested much higher proportions of GDP in their transport infrastructure. Some invested between 5 and 8 percent of GDP during the 1950s and into the 1960s—their period of highest economic growth (Korea's transport development was later than for the other countries). Since the 1990s, China has been investing more than 6 percent of its GDP in transport infrastructure, largely as part of its strategy to advance the relative economic growth of its inland provinces.

The amount that a country can afford to spend on transport depends on much more than sectoral needs alone. But in few instances have countries invested more than 5 percent of their GDP for a decade or more, while those countries that have invested less than 1 percent of their GDP have found such low levels to be unsustainable and have later increased investment. For example, China allowed its transport investment to fall to 1 percent of GDP for almost a decade before raising the rate to more than 6 percent in the 1990s (World Bank 1998). Since the per capita needs for transport investment tend to increase less quickly than GDP per capita, countries with a higher GDP per capita usually need to invest a smaller share than those with a lower GDP. On the other hand, countries that have invested less in the past need to invest more now to reach similar standards of connectivity. Other factors, such as prolonged conflicts, also influence required expenditures. During civil war, for example, not only are roads and bridges destroyed as strategic targets, but infrastructure maintenance becomes unsustainable. Civil war thus increases the cost of achieving connectivity standards even more than a history of sustained underinvestment.

Total Spending Needs in the Pragmatic Scenario

The objective of the pragmatic scenario is to reduce the spending requirements of the low-income countries (including the fragile countries) and to a lesser extent of the resource-rich countries. And the pragmatic scenario (table 7.9) does entail less spending: the average difference across Africa between the base and pragmatic scenarios is 40 percent (tables 7.8 and 7.9). The base scenario appears sustainable for the region's few middle-income countries—whether as an absolute amount or as a percentage of GDP. But for most other country groups, meeting the lower standards of the pragmatic scenario seems to be a feasible interim solution, with the base scenario remaining as a long-term objective. For a small number of countries, achieving even the pragmatic standards is not feasible in the short to medium term without massive external aid; such countries may need to consider reducing their connectivity objectives even further.

Table 7.9　Average Annual Investment Needs: Pragmatic Scenario

Infrastructure type	Investment purpose				Total	As percentage of	
	Improve condition	Upgrade standard	Expand capacity	Maintain infrastructure		GDP	Total expenditure
	US$ (millions)						
Regional roads	157	464	103	858	1,582	0.2	20.9
National roads	132	928	131	1,012	2,202	0.3	29.1
Rural roads	99	98	63	1,363	1,624	0.3	21.5
Urban roads	275	143	119	341	879	0.1	11.6
Airports	43	23	48	152	266	0.0	3.5
Ports	204	70	77	153	504	0.1	6.7
Railways	128	199	100	79	506	0.1	6.7
Total	1,039	1,925	641	3,958	7,563	1.2	100.0
As % of GDP	0.2	0.3	0.1	0.6	1.2		
As % of total	13.7	25.5	8.5	52.3	100.0		

Source: Carruthers, Krishnamani, and Murray 2009.

As noted, for Africa, excluding South Africa, the average annual cost of the pragmatic scenario is only 60 percent of the base scenario's cost ($7.6 billion vs. $12.7 billion). But the reduction is not equally distributed across expenditure types; for example, the difference between the scenarios is small for both maintenance and new construction but very large for infrastructure upgrades and improvements.

Of the 13 countries that would need to spend more than 5 percent of their GDP to achieve the base scenario standards, 9 are designated as low-income, fragile states; two, Madagascar and Mauritania, are nonfragile, low-income countries; and two, the Central African Republic and Chad, are designated as resource-rich states (figure 7.2). It is these 13 countries that would benefit most from reducing their transport sector expectations to standards lower than those of the base scenario.

By shifting from the base to the pragmatic scenario, the average expenditure need for this group would fall from an average of more than 11 percent of GDP to less than 7 percent. Guinea-Bissau would enjoy the largest

Figure 7.2   Scenario Costs in Countries Where the Base Scenario Would Cost More than 5 Percent of GDP

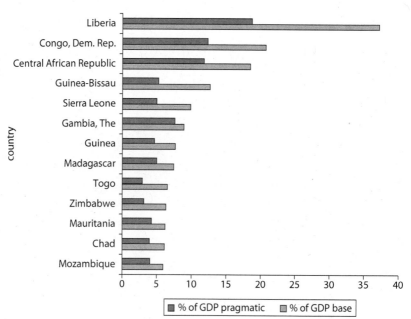

Source: Carruthers, Krishnamani, and Murray 2009.

percentage reduction in its needs (about 60 percent), while The Gambia would have the smallest gain (saving just 15 percent on its spending needs); the average reduction for these countries would be 42 percent. Liberia would have the largest reduction in absolute terms, from more than 37 percent of its GDP to less than 19 percent. Mixing the scenarios—applying different scenarios to different states—is another possibility (box 7.1).

Box 7.1

Mixing Scenarios

The variety of challenges facing the countries of Africa requires a variety of responses. Although for reasons of space this study does not explore a wide range of alternatives, the model is capable of doing so if required. As an example, the pragmatic scenario could be applied to the 13 countries that would have to spend more than 5 percent of their GDP to achieve the base scenario, while the base scenario could be applied to the others. Because 9 of those 13 countries are low-income, fragile states, it would also be possible to isolate them as candidates for the pragmatic scenario. The outcomes of these two options would be rather different in terms of the total spending requirements for all countries concerned. If the pragmatic scenario were applied to all the low-income, fragile states, but not to other low-income states, the total expenditure would be about $11.3 billion per year, about 10 percent less than the base scenario. If instead it were applied to all countries where the base scenario would require investment of more than 5 percent of GDP, the total spending requirement would be about $10.7 billion, or 15 percent less than that of the base scenario (see table B7.1).

There are advantages and disadvantages to either method of blending scenarios, and the choice between them will depend on the objective being sought.

Table B7.1   Comparing Blends of the Base and Pragmatic Scenarios

	Spending requirement		
Scenario	US$ (billions)	% of GDP	% of base scenario
Base	12.689	2.0	100
Pragmatic	7.563	1.2	60
Pragmatic for all low-income, fragile states	11.331	1.8	90
Pragmatic where spending requirement in base scenario is at least 5% of GDP	10.688	1.7	85

Source: Carruthers, Krishnamani, and Murray 2009.

Spending Needs by Country and Country Group

Low-income, fragile states would need to spend more than 8 percent of their GDP to achieve the connectivity standards of the base scenario, while the other low-income countries would need to spend just 3.4 percent of GDP—still a high percentage (table 7.10). Meanwhile, resource-rich countries would have to spend 1.7 percent of GDP, and the middle-income countries just 0.7 percent of their much higher GDP.

Spending needs as a share of GDP vary more widely when individual countries are considered, ranging from a high of more than 37.0 percent of GDP for Liberia to a low of 0.5 percent for South Africa. The pragmatic scenario, though aimed at countries for which the base scenario is unaffordable, would reduce costs across all groups of countries.

Considering the region as a whole, the resource-rich countries and other low-income countries would each require about 30 percent of all spending under the base scenario, with the low-income, fragile states taking 25 percent and the middle-income countries the remaining 15 percent. Those shares are not in proportion to their share of the region's total GDP or population. The low-income, fragile states have only 5 percent of the region's total GDP and 20 percent of the total population, but they would need 25 percent of the total expenditure to meet the connectivity standards of the base scenario. The other country groups would require a share of the spending envelope that falls between their share of GDP and of population.

The shares of total spending needs absorbed by the various country groups change when shifting from the base to the pragmatic scenario,

Table 7.10   Transport Infrastructure Expenditure as Percentage of GDP, by Country Group and Scenario

	Base scenario		Pragmatic scenario	
Country group	% of GDP	% of total investment	% of GDP	% of total investment
Low-income, fragile	8.2	30	4.8	24
Low-income, nonfragile	3.4	25	2.2	32
Resource-rich	1.7	30	1.0	31
Middle-income	0.7	15	0.4	13
Average of all African countries	2.0	n.a.	1.2	n.a.

Source: Carruthers, Krishnamani, and Murray 2009.
Note: n.a. = not applicable.

although the share required by the middle-income countries changes by just two percentage points and that required by the resource-rich countries by one point. For the low-income, fragile states, the share drops from 30 percent in the base scenario to 24 percent in the pragmatic, while the share of the other low-income countries increases from 25 percent to 32 percent. These fluctuations indicate that the reduced standards of the pragmatic scenario have the desired impact of reducing costs the most in the vulnerable low-income, fragile countries, and the least in the less-vulnerable countries.

There are at least three ways of normalizing expenditure: per dollar of GDP, per capita, and per unit of land area (table 7.11).

Of the 10 countries with the greatest spending needs per dollar of GDP, 9 are categorized as low-income, fragile states. By contrast, low-income, fragile countries do not figure prominently in the rankings of investment per capita or by land area. Liberia—with by far the highest expenditure needs per dollar of GDP—ranks only 29th in terms of expenditure needs per capita, but is 9th in relation to land area. Of the 10 highest-ranked countries by expenditure needs per dollar of GDP, 7 also appear in the top 10 using one of the other two criteria.

Understandably, sparsely populated countries tend to rank high in terms of spending needs per capita, and countries with a small land area rank high in terms of investment cost per square kilometer—but there are significant exceptions to these generalizations. Although all of the 10 highest ranked countries by expenditure needs per capita have populations of less than 5 million, the 12th-ranked country, South Africa, is ranked 4th in terms of total population. Of the 10 highest-ranked countries in terms of expenditure needs per square kilometer of land area, 9 have relatively small areas (being ranked in the last 10 in terms of size). The exception here is the Democratic Republic of Congo, which is ranked 5th in terms of expenditure needs per square kilometer and 21st in terms of total land area.

Spending Needs by Purpose of Spending
In both the base and the pragmatic scenarios, infrastructure maintenance requires the largest share of expenditure—about 39 percent in the base scenario (figure 7.3) and more than 53 percent in the pragmatic. Spending for maintenance also drops less than spending for other purposes in the shift from the base to the pragmatic scenario. While spending for maintenance falls from more than $4.9 billion per year in the base scenario to less than $4 billion in the pragmatic, a drop of 20 percent, spending to expand

Table 7.11 Highest Transport Infrastructure Spending Needs by Country, Relative to GDP, Population, and Land Area (base scenario)

	Ranked by percentage of GDP			Ranked by US$ per capita			Ranked by US$/km²	
Rank	Country	Percentage	Rank	Country	US$/pop	Rank	Country	US$/km²
1	Liberia	37.25	1	Equatorial Guinea	148.43	1	Mauritius	37,469
2	Congo, Dem. Rep.	20.72	2	Gabon	125.62	2	Guinea	8,940
3	Central African Republic	18.55	3	Mauritania	95.15	3	Cape Verde	4,621
4	Guinea-Bissau	12.72	4	Mali	78.83	4	Swaziland	4,472
5	Sierra Leone	9.92	5	Namibia	75.91	5	Congo, Dem. Rep.	4,309
6	Gambia, The	8.94	6	Central African Republic	59.62	6	Gambia, The	4,121
7	Guinea	7.69	7	Botswana	59.21	7	Equatorial Guinea	2,646
8	Madagascar	7.48	8	Congo, Rep.	44.17	8	Togo	2,494
9	Togo	6.58	9	Djibouti	41.84	9	Liberia	1,773
10	Zimbabwe	6.38	10	Cape Verde	37.65	10	Sierra Leone	1,682

Source: Carruthers, Krishnamani, and Murray 2009.

Figure 7.3   Comparison of Scenarios by Type of Spending

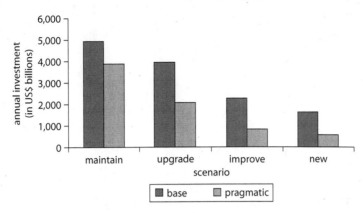

Source: Carruthers, Krishnamani, and Murray 2009.

capacity falls by more than 63 percent, to improve condition by 57 percent, and to upgrade category by 47 percent. The ratio of spending for maintenance to total spending is much greater in the model presented here than the actual ratio achieved in recent decades (most countries allocated to maintenance an average of between 25 percent and 33 percent of their total infrastructure spending). The higher figure here reflects the position taken by many lending institutions and sector professionals that it is often more productive and efficient to maintain existing infrastructure than to build new.

The balance of spending by purpose also varies by country groups. For example, middle-income countries have generally less need to upgrade their infrastructure and, hence, need to spend proportionately more on maintenance (table 7.12). Details of the spending needs by purpose for the pragmatic scenario are shown in appendix 6.

Spending Needs by Type of Connectivity

Regional, national, and rural roads each account for between 20 and 30 percent of overall spending needs in both scenarios (figure 7.4). Urban roads absorb a share of almost 17 percent of spending in the base scenario but less than 12 percent in the pragmatic. Airports, ports, and railways each receive between 6 and 7 percent of investment in the base scenario. These shares remain at more than 6 percent for ports and railways in the pragmatic scenario, while the airport share drops below 4 percent.

Table 7.12   Spending Needs by Purpose for Each Country Group (base scenario)

	Improve infrastructure (%)	Upgrade infrastructure (%)	Expand infrastructure (%)	Maintain infrastructure (%)
Low-income, fragile	20	36	14	30
Low-income, other	17	32	8	43
Middle-income	21	11	21	48
Resource-rich	19	28	15	37
All African countries	19	29	14	39

Source: Carruthers, Krishnamani, Murray, and Pushak 2009.
Note: Rows may not total 100 percent due to rounding.

Figure 7.4   Comparison of Scenarios by Mode of Transport

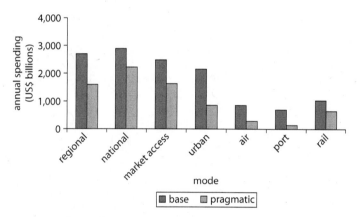

Source: Carruthers, Krishnamani, and Murray 2009.

Overall spending on airports is almost 70 percent less in the base than in the pragmatic scenario.

Within either of the scenarios, the allocation of investment needs by mode varies substantially between country groups. For example, the middle-income countries have proportionately less need for expenditure on regional, national, and rural roads, but greater needs for ports, airports, and railways (table 7.13).

As with the purpose of spending, the allocation of spending across modes of connectivity in both scenarios differs from actual experience in recent years. Spending for regional and national roads under the scenarios proposed here would be lower than at present, while spending for

Table 7.13   Percentage Allocation of Investment Needs by Country Group and Transport Mode (base scenario)

Connectivity/mode	Resource-rich	Low-income, fragile	Low-income, other	Middle-income	All African countries
Regional roads	23	24	20	14	21
National roads	22	23	26	17	23
Rural roads	20	26	22	2	20
Urban roads	18	17	15	19	17
Railways	6	4	6	12	6
Ports	7	2	4	20	7
Airports	4	3	8	16	7
Total	100	100	100	100	100
Share of total (%)	30	25	30	15	100

Source: Carruthers, Krishnamani, and Murray 2009.
Note: Columns may not total 100 percent due to rounding.

rural and urban roads would increase substantially, as rural roads have been neglected, except in the middle-income countries.

The greatest burden on the poorer countries is associated with improving rural connectivity. The costs (as a percentage of GDP) of connecting different shares of current and potential agricultural production by a paved road with a single surface treatment, as in the base scenario, are illustrated in figure 7.5. The dotted line shows that the average cost of connecting 80 percent of present output, by value, would be about 0.4 percent of GDP, while that of connecting 80 percent of potential output exceeds 0.5 percent.

The cost burden of this level of rural market connectivity varies greatly across countries. The solid line in figure 7.5 shows that the region's low-income, fragile states would need to spend more than 2 percent of their GDP to connect 80 percent of current output, by value, and 3.5 percent of GDP to connect the same share of *potential* output. The most significant differences in the cost of rural connectivity for African countries taken together and for the subset of low-income, fragile states arise when one attempts to achieve a high degree of connectivity for areas representing rising shares of the value of potential rather than current agricultural output. The emergence of the gap reflects the situation in the middle-income countries, where adding connectivity for 80 percent of the value of potential agricultural output using sealed roads would represent an investment of no more than 0.05 percent of GDP.

Figure 7.5   Rural Connectivity Costs for Different Percentages of Agricultural Production, by Value

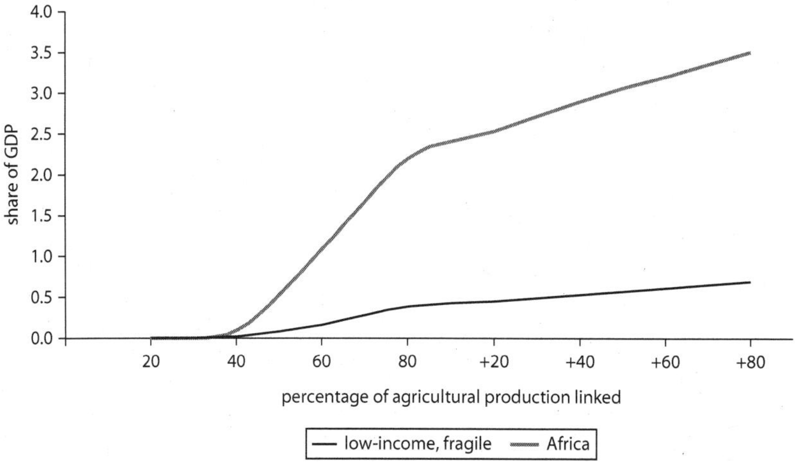

percentage of agricultural production linked

— low-income, fragile   —— Africa

Source: Carruthers, Krishnamani, and Murray 2009.
Note: Shares of GDP required have been calculated for the proportions of output connected marked, intermediate values have been interpreted to give a continuous line.

The cost of rural market connectivity for low-income, fragile states can be reduced to a cost of less than 1.5 percent of GDP by using all-weather gravel roads, as specified in the pragmatic scenario (figure 7.6).

Insights from the Connectivity Analysis

It should be remembered that this chapter describes a modeling exercise, the results of which are critically sensitive to the inputs. A number of elements that could lead to underestimating costs have been noted:

- Bridges and some other ancillary investments are excluded from the calculations.
- Urban roads that meet the connectivity targets in aggregate may not be suitably located for current development patterns.
- Standards may be set too low, particularly for national connectivity by road.
- Costs may be too low, particularly for landlocked countries or those with difficult terrain.

Figure 7.6   Rural Connectivity Costs for Low-Income, Fragile States with Different Categories of Roads

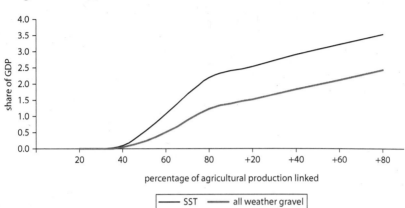

Source: Carruthers, Krishnamani, and Murray 2009.
Note: SST = single surface treatment. Shares of GDP required have been calculated for the proportions of output connected marked, intermediate values have been interpreted to give a continuous line.

The implication of this range of possible error in the cost estimations, which is also probably asymmetric, is that some countries are in a significantly worse situation than the financing shortfall estimations of the next chapter suggest.

Bearing that caveat in mind, the analysis still strongly suggests the need to reappraise the current allocation of public expenditure on transport infrastructure. For achievement of common connectivity targets—that is, to bring people closer to jobs, services, and markets—a much greater share of investment must be directed to local rural road access and urban roads, and, to a lesser extent, to railways, airports, and seaports. The recent wave of concessioning in the latter areas has helped redress the lack of investment, but many operations cannot earn sufficient revenue from their operations to attract private investment in infrastructure. Public-private partnering will be needed to close the investment gap.

Knowing how much infrastructure is needed to achieve any particular social or economic target is meaningless if, once obtained, the infrastructure cannot be maintained. The analysis shows that almost half of all spending on transport infrastructure will be needed to *maintain* the roads and other infrastructure that are improved, upgraded, and expanded under the base and pragmatic scenarios. (If the condition of infrastructure is not improved, even more will have to be spent on maintenance.) Because maintenance standards are lower under the pragmatic scenario, and because infrastructure networks and capacity are not expanded as far, spending for maintenance drops sharply in the pragmatic scenario but still dwarfs investment in improvements, upgrades, and extensions of infrastructure.

The proportion of transport expenditure allocated to maintenance has never come close to the 40 to 50 percent share shown here to be needed, despite the establishment of road maintenance funds in many of the countries included in this analysis. This persistent underspending on maintenance suggests that the road networks of many countries in the region may become unsustainable—unless a more judicious mix of investments can be found and followed.

The Asian Development Bank (ADB 2006) estimated the road network size that can be sustained by public sources. After reviewing current network size and quality, as well as actual maintenance spending, the ADB study found a negative relationship between network quality and network replacement value as a share of GDP. When the replacement value exceeds about 40 percent of current GDP, quality declines rapidly. Using this finding, the study concluded that the road network density and standards of several countries in the sample, particularly large countries with low GDP, were greater than their economies could sustain. The foregoing analysis supports that conclusion.

Notes

1. This chapter is based on Carruthers, Krishnamani, and Murray (2009).
2. However, the capacity of the facilities may be less than would normally be considered acceptable for main trunk routes in an industrialized country; see the section below on category of infrastructure.
3. The infrastructure elements included in the database are detailed in the individual country maps appearing in the country annex to Carruthers, Krishnamani, and Murray (2009).
4. In Uganda, no city but the capital has a population exceeding this threshold; in Ghana, there is only one other (Kumasi). Meanwhile, in Nigeria, there are 26 and in South Africa, over 30.
5. The alternative of extending the base scenario to provide connectivity to areas representing 80 percent of the *potential* value of output (that is, the value of output if the most lucrative possible crops were grown) was also considered but not adopted, as the cost would have been prohibitive for all countries involved.

6. This approach is defensible for low-income cities where the level of congestion is determined primarily by public transport, freight, and nonmotorized traffic.

7. The HDM4 is a computer software system for investigating choices of expenditure on road transport infrastructure. Originally developed by the World Bank, responsibility for management and further development of the suite of programs was taken over by the World Road Association (PIARC) in 1996. The current version was finalized in June 2005. It is now managed under a service concession contract with HDMGlobal, an international consortium led by the University of Birmingham, England.

References

ADB (Asian Development Bank). 2006. "Road Asset Management." Technical Assistance Report 5925, Asian Development Bank, Manila.

Bofinger, H. C. 2009. "Air Transport: Challenges to Growth." Africa Infrastructure Country Diagnostic Background Paper 16, World Bank, Washington, DC.

Bullock, R. 2009. "Railways in Sub-Saharan Africa." Africa Infrastructure Country Diagnostic Background Paper 11, World Bank, Washington, DC.

Carruthers, R., K. Krishnamani, and S. Murray. 2009. "Improving Connectivity: Investing in Transport Infrastructure in Sub-Saharan Africa." Africa Infrastructure Country Diagnostic Background Paper 7, World Bank, Washington, DC.

Chatterton, I., and O. S. Puerto. 2005. "Estimation of Infrastructure Investment Needs in the South Asia Region." Unpublished paper, World Bank, Washington, DC.

CIA (Central Intelligence Agency). 2007. *The World Factbook*. https://www.cia.gov/library/publications/the-world-factbook/.

Demographia. 2009. *Demographia World Urban Areas and Population Projections*. 5th ed. Belleville, IL: Wendell Cox Consultancy.

Estache, A., and T. Yepes. 2004. "Assessing Africa's Infrastructure Needs." Unpublished paper, World Bank, Washington, DC.

Fay, M., and T. Yepes. 2003. "Investing in Infrastructure: What Is Needed from 2000 to 2010?" Policy Research Working Paper 3102, World Bank, Washington, DC.

Gwilliam, K., V. Foster, R. Archondo-Callao, C. Briceño-Garmendia, A. Nogales, and K. Sethi. 2009. "The Burden of Maintenance: Roads in Sub-Saharan Africa." Africa Infrastructure Country Diagnostic Background Paper 14, World Bank, Washington, DC.

Mundy, M., and A. Penfold. 2009. "Beyond the Bottlenecks: Ports in Sub-Saharan Africa." Africa Infrastructure Country Diagnostic Background Paper 13, World Bank, Washington, DC.

Roberts, P., K. C. Shyam, and C. Rastogi. 2006. "Rural Access Index: A Key Development Indicator." Transport Paper 10, World Bank, Washington, DC.

World Bank. 1998. "China—Forward with One Spirit: A Strategy for the Transport Sector." Research Report 15959, World Bank, Washington, DC.

———. 2010. Railways Database. World Bank, Washington, DC. http:// data.worldbank.org/indicator/IS.RRS.TOTL.KM.

CHAPTER 8

Financing: Filling the Gaps

The cost of redressing Africa's transport infrastructure needs was estimated in chapter 7 as $19.2 billion a year (including the spending by South Africa associated with hosting the World Cup in 2010). Just over half of this amount is for capital investment ($9.64 billion a year), and the rest ($9.55 billion a year) is for operations and maintenance (O&M). The overall cost represents 3 percent of Africa's gross domestic product (GDP), with the burden varying greatly by country type. These estimates were based on the connectivity standards of the "base" scenario adopted in chapter 7. While the analysis does involve some bold assumptions, it is believed to be a reasonable basis for estimating needs.

This chapter presents a detailed analysis of the transport-related revenues and expenditures of the sample countries.[1] Public spending data are available for only 24 African countries, which collectively account for around 70 percent of African GDP. Therefore, wherever public spending is concerned, totals for country groups and various country types are extrapolated from the available sample based on country GDP. When this analysis is taken together with estimates of investment and maintenance needs from chapter 7, it becomes possible to estimate whether revenues are adequate to meet transport needs. The analysis is done both by individual country and by category, in all cases keeping investment and maintenance separate.

Expenditures

Expenditures considered include both on-budget and off-budget spending by countries (including state-owned enterprises and extrabudgetary funds), official development assistance (ODA) from the Organisation for Economic Co-operation and Development (OECD) countries, finance from non-OECD countries, and private participation in infrastructure (PPI).

Total Spending

Total spending on transport infrastructure, including O&M, amounts to about $16.3 billion per year, equivalent to 2.5 percent of GDP on average across all countries. If ODA and OECD finance is excluded, this falls to $13.5 billion, or 2.1 percent of GDP. Middle-income countries account for almost half of total spending, while low-income, fragile states account for less than 5 percent (about $600 million in total).

Spending as a percentage of GDP varies substantially by country, ranging from less than 1 percent in Chad, to almost 6 percent in Madagascar, to an extreme 13 percent in Cape Verde. Countries such as Chad, Côte d'Ivoire, Nigeria, and Senegal stand out for the very small share of total spending that is allocated to maintenance (appendix 7a contains country details). Country type is an important source of this variation. While transport spending in middle-income states and low-income, nonfragile states is around 3 percent of GDP, resource-rich countries and low-income, fragile states spend only half this proportion of GDP, although for very different reasons (table 8.1). Low-income, fragile states cannot afford to spend significantly on transport infrastructure. For resource-rich countries, transport simply does not seem to be a spending priority.

This level of effort by African governments to develop their infrastructure pales in comparison to what the East Asian countries have achieved in recent years. For example, in 2006, China's government invested around 5 percent of GDP in transport infrastructure, not including O&M (Lall, Anand, and Rastogi 2009). This compares with 0.74 percent of GDP directly financed by governments in Africa and 1.34 percent of total GDP invested in transport infrastructure.

Table 8.1 Annual Transport Spending by Finance Source and Country Type

Country type	Percentage of GDP							US$ (millions)						
	O&M	CAPEX					Total	O&M	CAPEX					Total
	Public sector	Public sector	ODA	Non-OECD financiers	PPI	Total CAPEX		Public sector	Public sector	ODA	Non-OECD financiers	PPI	Total CAPEX	
Middle-income	1.88	0.78	0.03	0.01	0.16	0.98	2.86	5,081	2,103	88	22	444	2,657	7,738
Resource-rich	0.32	0.74	0.11	0.34	0.21	1.39	1.72	720	1,646	234	745	469	3,095	3,815
Low-income, nonfragile	0.98	0.67	1.12	0.22	0.12	2.13	3.11	1,084	737	1,241	242	128	2,347	3,431
Low-income, fragile	0.16	0.56	0.61	0.13	0.04	1.33	1.49	60	214	234	9	14	511	571
Total	1.20	0.74	0.28	0.16	0.16	1.34	2.54	7,701	4,724	1,797	1,059	1,055	8,635	16,336

Source: Briceño-Garmendia, Smits, and Foster 2009 (for public spending); PPIAF 2008 (for private flows); Foster and others 2008 (for non-OECD financiers).
Note: CAPEX = capital expenditure. Aggregate public sector covers general government and nonfinancial enterprises. Figures are extrapolations based on the 24-country sample covered in phase 1 of the Africa Infrastructure Country Diagnostic (AICD). Totals may not be exact because of rounding errors.

Categories of Expenditure

Transport spending in Africa is divided almost evenly between investment (1.34 percent of GDP on average over all countries) and O&M
(1.20 percent of GDP on average). But the composition of spending
varies substantially among country groups. Middle-income countries
allocate two-thirds of transport spending to maintenance, which probably reflects the fact that they have already built much of the infrastructure they need. By contrast, all other country groups allocate at least
two-thirds of their transport spending to capital investment.

Sources of Funding

The public sector is by far the most important source of finance for transport spending in Africa. Overall, about three-quarters of transport infrastructure spending is provided by domestic public institutions. In the
middle-income countries, domestic public sector resources (comprising
tax revenues and user charges raised by state entities) account for
almost all finance for transport spending. In resource-rich countries,
about 60 percent comes from domestic public institutions, but this falls
to about half in the low-income countries. In the middle-income states
and low-income, nonfragile states, domestic public spending is focused on
maintenance, whereas in the resource-rich states and low-income, fragile
states, it is focused on capital spending. External finance is primarily for
investment—including asset rehabilitation and reconstruction—and in
most cases does not provide for O&M.

Overall, transport (roads in particular) is the most expensive type of
infrastructure in general government accounts. Expenditures range from
about half of all general government spending on infrastructure in middle-
income countries to 80 percent in low-income, fragile countries. From their
central government budgets alone, African countries allocate an average of
0.7 percent of GDP to spending on transport infrastructure (table 8.2). As
a percentage of GDP, budget spending on transport infrastructure is comparable across low- and middle-income countries. Given the much higher
GDP of the middle-income countries, however, absolute spending per
capita in these countries can be several times higher than in the low-income
countries. Table 8.2 looks only at on-budget transport spending (the sum of
on-budget operating expenditure [OPEX] and capital expenditure
[CAPEX]). In other words, these are annual budgetary flows. In contrast,
table 8.1 looks at total public spending (on-budget and off-budget).

For capital investment expenditures in transport infrastructure, the
domestic public sector also dominates in both middle-income and

Table 8.2   Transport Spending as a Share of Total Budget in Africa

	Percentage of GDP		US$ (millions)	
Country type	Transport	Total budget	Transport	Total budget
Middle-income	0.69	1.59	1,872	4,297
Resource-rich	0.83	1.67	1,836	3,711
Low-income, nonfragile	0.73	1.50	803	1,655
Low-income, fragile	0.58	0.71	224	271
Total	0.73	1.56	4,691	10,010

Source: Briceño-Garmendia, Smits, and Foster 2009.
Note: Based on annualized averages for 2001–6. Averages weighted by country GDP. Figures are extrapolations based on the 24-country sample covered in AICD phase 1. Totals may not be exact because of rounding errors.

resource-rich countries. But in total, external finance contributes roughly half of Africa's total capital spending on transport infrastructure. External sources include ODA from the OECD countries, official finance from non-OECD countries (such as China, India, and the Arab states), and PPI. ODA is by far the largest source of external finance for transport infrastructure in Africa, accounting for half the total. Non-OECD finance and PPI each account for a quarter of external finance (figure 8.1). Nearly one-quarter of the capital investment in resource-rich countries is financed from non-OECD sources (mostly China). ODA plays a substantial role everywhere except in the middle-income countries. Only a handful of countries (in particular, Mozambique, Nigeria, and Uganda) enjoy a significant contribution from the private sector. Although South Africa is by far the largest recipient of private transport investment in absolute terms, this total is only a small percentage of the country's public spending on transport infrastructure.

The sources of external finance exhibit clear patterns of specialization. For example, ODA is concentrated on road infrastructure. Much non-OECD finance has gone to the rail sector, due to the synergies with natural resource sectors that are an important focus of cooperation among developing countries. PPI has benefited only a small segment of high-volume toll roads but has contributed significantly to railways and ports.

ODA for capital investment in transport is particularly significant in the low-income states, with the nonfragile states receiving higher levels of support relative to their GDP (around 1.1 percent) than the fragile states (only 0.6 percent). PPI for transport has tended to go to middle-income and resource-rich countries, which have the greatest

Figure 8.1   Sources of Finance for Transport Spending in Africa by Country

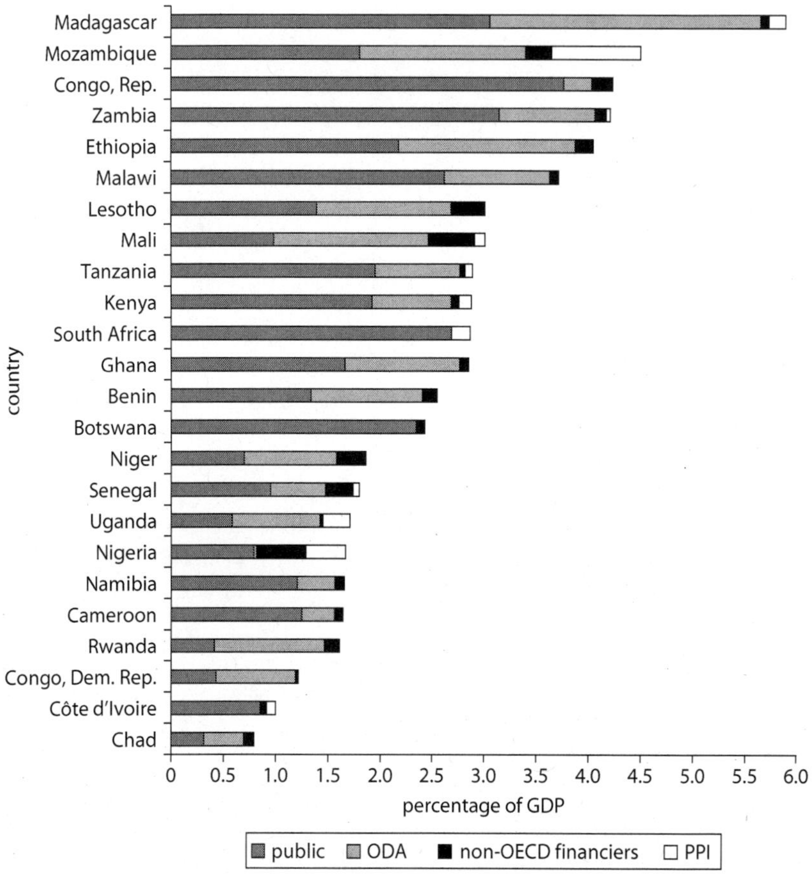

Source: Briceño-Garmendia, Smits, and Foster 2009.
Note: Based on annualized averages for 2001–06. Because numbers for Cape Verde are exceptionally high, at around 13 percent of GDP, the country is excluded from this figure to better represent the situation in the other countries.

ability to pay for services. Both groups have received around 0.2 percent of GDP annually in private capital for transport in recent years. Non-OECD finance for transport is more important than PPI everywhere but in the middle-income countries. This support is highest for the resource-rich countries (0.34 percent of GDP) but remains significant even for the fragile states (in excess of 0.10 percent of GDP) (figure 8.2).

The Balance between Investment and Maintenance

The balance of investment and maintenance expenditure varies significantly among countries (figure 8.3). Discounting the Democratic Republic

Figure 8.2   Sources of Funding for Transport Infrastructure Capital Investment

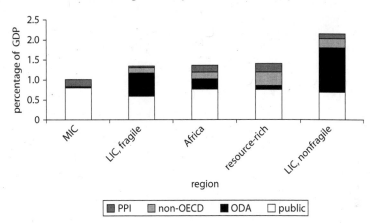

Source: Briceño-Garmendia, Smits, and Foster 2009 (for public spending and ODA); PPIAF 2008 (for private flows); Foster and others 2008 (for non-OECD financiers).
Note: MIC = middle-income country; LIC = low-income country.

of Congo, which spends little on either, and with the exception of Cameroon and Kenya, only the middle-income countries (South Africa and Namibia) spend more on maintenance than on investment.

The Balance between Finance Needs and Commitments

Sources of finance are not completely fungible (for instance, ODA funds for road rehabilitation may not be available for routine maintenance). Therefore, spending on maintenance (figure 8.4, panel a) and investment expenditures (figure 8.4, panel b) are examined separately. For purposes of comparison, the graphics are standardized based on the needs of each country as estimated in chapter 7. The sources of revenue to meet these needs are presented as cumulative bars in the graphs, grouped by country type.

A quarter of the countries (Benin, Botswana, Cameroon, the Republic of Congo, Kenya, Lesotho, and Malawi) appear to provide adequately for maintenance. Countries with good maintenance provisions are found in each of the four country types. Some of these look anomalous. For example, Kenya's maintenance expenditure appears to be adequate, and allowing for the inclusion of ODA, investment expenditure appears sufficient to meet assessed needs. Yet only 50 percent of its network is in good condition, and 34 percent is in poor condition (see appendix 2i). Similarly, Cameroon appears to be spending enough on maintenance (though not on investment), despite the fact that only 36 percent of its network is in good condition. These findings highlight the fact that countries may be currently committing enough to maintenance (which is good

Figure 8.3   Capital Investment and O&M Spending for Transport from All Sources by Country

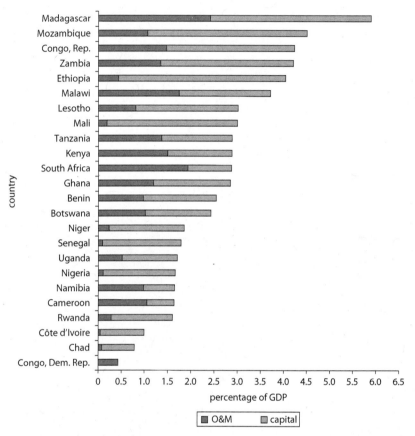

Source: Briceño-Garmendia, Smits, and Foster 2009.
Note: Based on annualized averages for 2001–06. Because numbers for Cape Verde are exceptionally high, at around 13 percent of GDP, the country is excluded from this figure, offering a better representation of the situation in the other countries.

news), but have road networks not in good condition because of large backlogs still to be overcome.

For many countries, however, the shortfalls are very significant. The worst overall deficiencies are found in the low-income, fragile countries. While a number of countries of each country type appear to be spending enough overall to meet the estimated capital investment requirements, Botswana, Cape Verde, the Republic of Congo, Nigeria, Senegal, and Zambia are the only countries able to cover their estimated investment needs without ODA. Even in these countries, investment expenditure

Figure 8.4   Transport Spending as Percentage of Needs

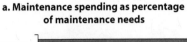

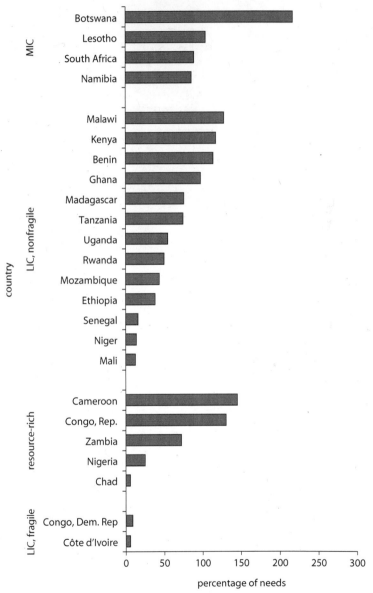

a. Maintenance spending as percentage
of maintenance needs

(continued)

Figure 8.4   *(continued)*

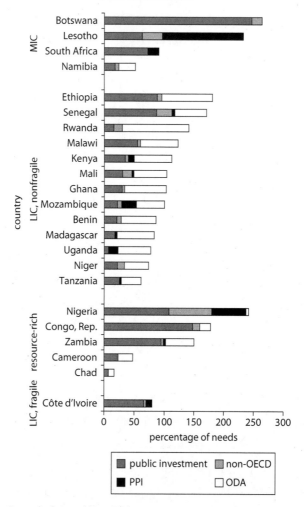

b. Investment spending as percentage
of investment needs

Source: Briceño-Garmendia, Smits, and Foster 2009.
Note: LIC = low-income country; MIC = middle-income country. Numbers for Cape Verde are exceptionally high, surpassing 600 percent in both cases. Accordingly, it is excluded from this figure and from figure 8.5 to offer a better representation of the situation in the other countries. The Democratic Republic of Congo is omitted because of the incompleteness of the public finance data for this country.

may not be excessive for two reasons. First, as explained in chapter 7, some types of investment needs (bridges, for example) were not included in the estimate, and there is a range of variability in unit costs not taken into account in the calculations. Second, these countries may simply be choosing to eliminate rehabilitation backlogs more quickly than assumed in the model. Overall, the inability of many countries to finance both maintenance and capital requirements on their own, or with commercial borrowings, has been disguised by heavy dependence on ODA for capital investment. For a better assessment of the burden of these shortfalls, the same basic data can be shown as percentages of GDP (figure 8.5a and figure 8.5b).

Figure 8.5   Needs and Spending as Percentage of GDP

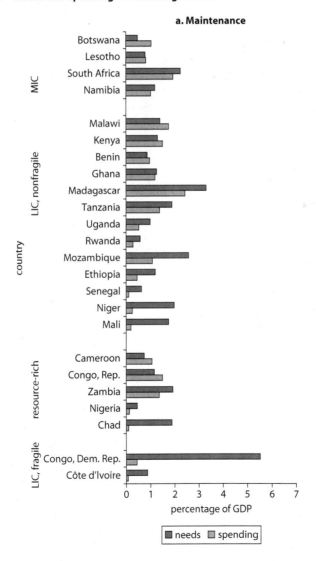

(continued)

Figure 8.5   *(continued)*

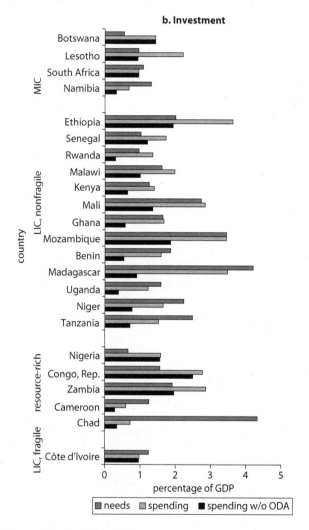

b. Investment

Source: Briceño-Garmendia, Smits, and Foster 2009.
Note: MIC = middle-income country; LIC = low-income country. Numbers for Cape Verde are exceptionally high; the country is excluded from this figure to better represent the situation in the other countries. The Democratic Republic of Congo is omitted because of the incompleteness of the public finance data for this country.

What Can Be Done about the Shortfalls?

Closing Africa's transport infrastructure funding gap will inevitably require both reforms to reduce inefficiencies and the creation of a more attractive investment climate for external finance.

Efficiency Improvements

Inefficiencies in transport spending are estimated to cost countries in Africa a total of about $4.1 billion a year. Addressing these inefficiencies would make an additional $2.4 billion of resources per year directly available to the sector institutions (as explained later in this chapter), as well as benefiting road users substantially. In some countries, these additional resources would completely eliminate spending shortfalls. In other countries (particularly the low-income, fragile states), however, a sizeable funding gap would remain. For the low-income, fragile states as a group, the funding gap would remain greater than $2.4 billion a year even if all spending inefficiencies were eliminated.

Three main opportunities for eliminating inefficiencies have been identified. First, raising user charges closer to maintenance cost-recovery levels would provide more efficient price signals and increase road agency revenues. Second, improving budget execution rates would more fully exploit resources allocated to public investment. Third, a higher allocation of resources to asset maintenance would substantially improve efficiency both by preventing costly rehabilitation (particularly for roads) and by yielding direct benefits to the users of infrastructure. In the first two cases, the efficiency gains directly benefit the government. The third reform would primarily benefit infrastructure users, although the government may also benefit (see appendix 7b for country-level calculations). In addition, there are other possibilities of reducing expenditures through reallocating sector funding, lowering the standards of provision, and reducing backlogs in maintenance spending.

Improved Collection of User Charges

In the road sector, lending institutions and governments are moving to employ indirect user charges such as fuel levies and taxes to cover road maintenance costs (see chapter 2). On that principle, fuel levies must be sufficiently high to cover the full maintenance costs imposed by the use of the road network. Currently, even if fuel levies were fully collected, only one-third of African countries could cover their maintenance costs. Undercollection of fuel levies for road sector maintenance is also an inefficiency, albeit a relatively small one. Underpricing for road use—that is, setting fuel levies too low to cover road network maintenance—is the more pressing issue, resulting in lost revenues estimated at $1.4 billion a year.

Improved Capital Fund Disbursement

Central governments are key players in infrastructure investment. Inefficiencies within the public expenditure management systems are therefore particularly significant. African countries, on average, fail to spend as much as one-fifth of their capital budgets for transport (table 8.3). The poor timing of project appraisals and late releases of budgeted funds because of procurement problems often prevent the use of resources within the budget cycle. Delays affecting fund releases within the budget year are also associated with poor project preparation, leading to changes in the initial terms agreed upon with contractors (such as deadlines, technical specifications, budgets, and costs). In other cases, funds are reallocated from transport to nondiscretionary spending driven by political or social pressures. Historically, the road sector has had the greatest difficulty spending the amounts allocated to it—sometimes as much as 60 percent of the budget goes unspent.

Only about 80 percent of the capital budget allocation for transport infrastructure is actually used. About $1.3 billion in public investment earmarked for the transport sector is therefore diverted elsewhere. If these inefficiencies were eliminated, countries could increase their capital spending on transport by an average of 25 percent without any increase in budget allocations. This assertion assumes that funds will reach their intended destinations, which is not always the case (Reinikka and Svensson 2002). It also assumes that budget estimates are realistic and aligned with resource availability. Nevertheless, the planning, budgeting, and procurement challenges associated with unused allocations should be central to the region's reform agenda.

Improving disbursement will not be easy. A principal cause of underexecution of capital budgets is overoptimistic budgeting resulting from inadequate absorptive capacity and weak sector policy. Improving budget

Table 8.3   Average Percentage of Capital Budget Actually Spent, by Country Type

Country type	All infrastructure	Transport infrastructure
Middle-income	78	100
Resource-rich	65	73
Low-income, nonfragile	76	72
Low-income, fragile	—	—
Africa	75	79

Source: Adapted from Briceño-Garmendia, Smits, and Foster 2009.
Note: — = not available. Based on annualized averages for 2001–06.

planning and expenditure forecasting in the road sector will thus require more discussion between the relevant transport ministry, ministries of finance and planning, and donors in the design of a national transport policy.

Better Allocation of Funds to Maintenance

On average, 30 percent of African infrastructure assets are in need of rehabilitation because of neglected maintenance in the past (figure 8.6).

The cost of operating a vehicle on an uncongested road depends on the type of vehicle, the physical layout of the road, and the condition of the road. All other factors constant, the cost per vehicle-kilometer increases as the condition of the road deteriorates, with the rate of cost increase dependent on the vehicle and the road. The rate of road deterioration depends on traffic volumes (particularly the volume of heavy vehicles), topography, and climate.

For paved roads, routine maintenance—including filling of potholes and patching—can slow deterioration. According to recent evidence concerning costs in the region, such maintenance should cost no more than $2,000 per kilometer per year for a two-lane road. Periodic maintenance in the form of surface overlays can return the road surface to its original condition if undertaken in a timely manner. This will probably cost about $20,000 per kilometer per treatment, and is likely to be required every five or six years. If routine and periodic maintenance are not performed, road deterioration will continue to the point of structural failure, which

Figure 8.6   Transport Infrastructure Assets in Need of Rehabilitation

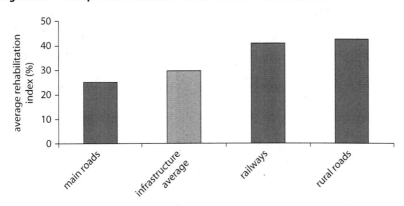

Source: Carruthers, Krishnamani, and Murray 2009.

can only be rectified by complete rehabilitation. This will probably cost at least $250,000 per kilometer. Timely routine and periodic maintenance defers—potentially indefinitely—the need for complete rehabilitation. Deterioration of gravel and earth roads has equivalent effects on vehicle operating costs, although they require different treatment strategies with distinct cost profiles. A wide range of treatments is possible, and the optimal strategy may vary substantially from case to case.

Underspending on routine and periodic maintenance is a major waste of resources for two reasons. First, there may be a cost to the road agency because the present value of completely rehabilitating roads is greater than the present value of sound preventive maintenance. The potential efficiency saving from adequate maintenance depends on the type of road, traffic volumes, and the discount rate. If the discount rate (that is, the opportunity cost of capital) is high, improved maintenance may not provide significant cost savings to the road agency.

Second, road users, however, certainly bear the higher operating costs of roads in a poor state of repair, which usually cancels any benefit to the road agency. Using the Highway Development and Management Model (HDM4), the costs of two maintenance and rehabilitation alternatives for road agencies were compared across several typical road classes in Africa. The alternatives were to (i) perform annual routine maintenance and rehabilitate the road when its condition became poor, and (ii) perform annual routine maintenance and proper periodic maintenance. Sixteen road classes were evaluated, based on two climate/terrain types, four traffic levels, and two road condition types. (The details of the analysis are presented more fully in appendix 7c.)

According to the analysis, performing timely periodic maintenance is likely to reduce agency costs if no discounting is applied, except where traffic volumes are very low (under 500 vehicles per day). At a 12 percent discount rate, whether timely routine maintenance reduces total agency costs depends on a combination of climate/terrain, traffic volumes, and initial surface condition. But when user costs are taken into account, the only situation in which timely periodic maintenance produces a net loss is when traffic volume is low and the initial condition is good. As surface condition deteriorates from good to fair, however, timely routine maintenance will once again produce a net benefit. Moreover, only a small proportion of road traffic meets the criteria that result in a net loss. While this analysis considers only a small set of the wide range of possible road scenarios, it can be safely concluded that timely periodic maintenance will yield high net social benefits regardless of whether the road agency benefits.

Accurately determining the respective benefit to the road agency and road users of more efficient maintenance would require a more detailed comparison of current and optimal maintenance strategies in each country. But as the benefit to road users outweighs the benefit to the road agency in most cases, the analysis that follows emphasizes the total benefit to society rather than just to the road agency.

The approach adopted uses the Road Network Evaluation Tool (RONET) analyses discussed in chapter 2 to compare the road-user cost savings achieved by better maintenance to the agency cost of the chosen maintenance strategy (figure 8.7).

The basic calculation assumes that countries attempt to secure the custom standard of maintenance. This involves applying a high standard of maintenance to the primary roads, a medium standard to the secondary roads, and a low standard to the tertiary roads (as discussed in chapter 2). This approximates the pragmatic scenario standards for roads discussed in chapter 7. The net benefit-cost ratios of applying a high standard of maintenance to the entire road network are very similar to those of the custom standard. This is because improving maintenance beyond the custom standard has further benefits on some links; meanwhile, on other routes with low traffic volume, the costs of a high standard of maintenance exceed the benefits of reduced vehicle-operating costs. Only where the maintenance programs are optimized (that is, where the optimal treatment is determined for each road on a link-by-link basis) is the ratio substantially higher. The custom standard calculation may therefore be viewed as a lower bound and the optimal standard calculation as an upper bound for the potential efficiency gains of an improved maintenance strategy.

The ratio of user cost savings to agency expenditures range between 1.1:1.0 (Nigeria) and 5.4:1.0 (Tanzania) for the custom standard and between 3.5:1.0 (Madagascar) and 8.8:1.0 (Cameroon) for the optimal standard (figure 8.7). The total agency and vehicle-operating cost savings per country for each scenario are estimated by multiplying the cost savings ratio by the estimated magnitude of current maintenance underspending (table 8.4). Given these ratios, priority must be given to maintenance expenditures whether that policy is immediately beneficial to the road agency or not.

Other Reallocations in the Transport Sector

Comparing actual expenditures with estimated needs suggests that some countries spend more than the amount that would ostensibly cover their needs. The sum of overspending in these countries is about

Figure 8.7   Efficiency Gains from Improved Maintenance

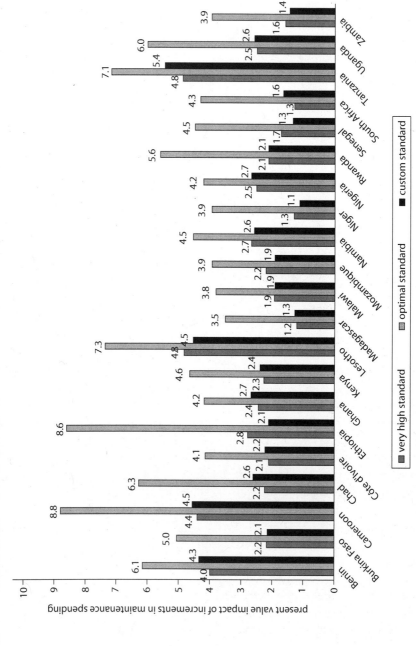

Source: Calculation by A. Nogales (based on data from Gwilliam and others 2009).

Note: The graph shows the present value impact in terms of the ratio of savings of user costs to unit increases of maintenance expenditures across three maintenance standards.

Table 8.4   Overall Value of Agency and Vehicle-Operating Cost Savings (US$ millions)

Country	Agency and user savings per dollar spent on maintenance, custom standard	Agency and user savings per dollar spent on maintenance, optimum standard	Potential savings, custom standard	Potential savings, optimum standard
Benin	3.3	6.1	0	0
Botswana	1.0	5.0	0	0
Cameroon	3.5	8.8	89	220
Chad	1.6	6.3	36	139
Côte d'Ivoire	1.2	4.1	50	172
Ethiopia	1.1	8.6	68	525
Ghana	1.7	4.2	119	315
Kenya	1.4	4.6	0	0
Lesotho	3.5	7.3	17	37
Madagascar	0.3	3.5	4	49
Malawi	0.9	3.8	7	27
Mozambique	0.9	3.9	37	160
Namibia	1.6	4.5	25	72
Niger	0.1	3.9	3	98
Nigeria	1.7	4.2	459	1,134
Rwanda	1.1	5.6	1	6
Senegal	0.3	4.5	4	59
South Africa	0.6	4.3	164	1,173
Tanzania	4.4	7.1	146	234
Uganda	1.6	6.0	111	420
Zambia	0.4	3.9	0	0

Source: Calculation by A. Nogales (based on data from Gwilliam and others 2009).

$1.9 billion a year. This spending—funded through public budgets—includes domestically raised funds and international aid (OECD and non-OECD sources). Most of it is driven by apparent overinvestment in some road networks, even as other roads in the same countries are undermaintained. In nine countries, the potential for reallocating this excess spending looks particularly substantial—in excess of 0.5 percent of GDP (figure 8.8).

The most dramatic example is Cape Verde, whose excess spending is equivalent to more than 10 percent of GDP; Ethiopia, the Republic of Congo, Botswana, and Lesotho all have excesses around 1 percent of GDP. It is possible that such overspending reflects a political decision to rapidly address a rehabilitation and investment backlog in the road sector, compressing a large spending program into a shorter time than is assumed in the model on which the estimates are based (see chapter 7). Nevertheless, in some cases this money might be better spent elsewhere.

Figure 8.8   Potential for Reallocation of Spending

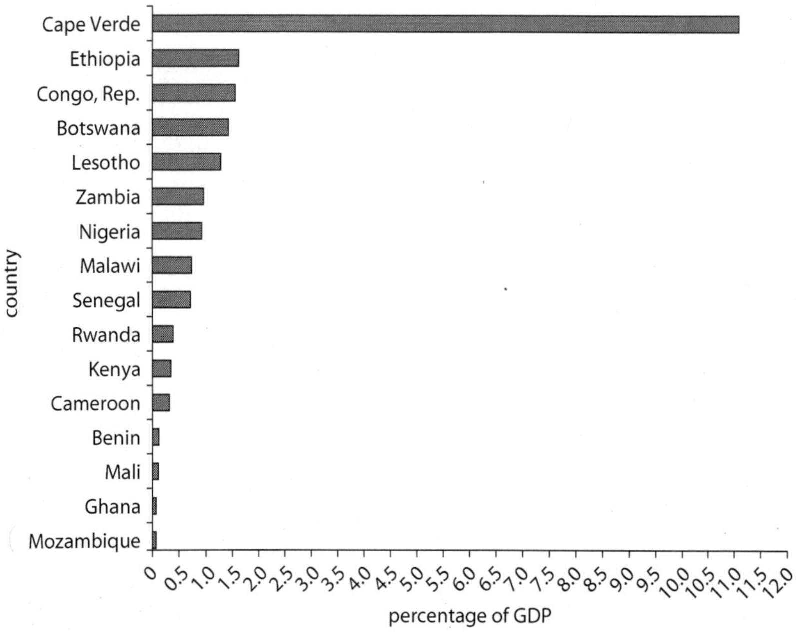

Source: Briceño-Garmendia, Smits, and Foster 2009.
Note: Based on annualized averages for 2001–06.

Estimates of the economic rates of return to key infrastructure projects are helpful in evaluating whether the apparent overspending on investment is beneficial. Across infrastructure interventions in Africa, the economic rates of return to road maintenance are the highest, averaging more than 100 percent—well above the typical rates of return for road rehabilitation and upgrading (table 8.5). Hence, countries that overspend on capital investment while underspending on maintenance do not appear to be allocating resources efficiently.

Lower Standards

To reach a given infrastructure connectivity target (as defined in chapter 7), a wide array of technical alternatives may be pursued, each with a distinct cost and quality of service. Where budgets are constrained, policy makers must choose between providing a high level of service to a relatively small cross-section of the population or a lower level of service to a larger cross-section. Thus, providing a high level of service may not be in a country's best interest.

Table 8.5   Economic Rates of Return for Key Infrastructure Interventions in Africa

Country type	Railway rehabilitation	Road rehabilitation	Road upgrades	Road maintenance	Irrigation	Power generation	Water
Middle-income	18.5	45.4	19.8	143.0	19.3	13.6	26.8
Resource-rich	10.8	16.2	17.4	114.5	24.2	20.2	37.0
Low-income, nonfragile	6.2	17.6	12.8	125.7	17.2	14.3	7.7
Low-income, fragile	2.5	9.2	12.0	67.6	—	24.7	36.9
Total	5.1	24.2	17.0	138.8	22.2	18.9	23.3

Source: Derived from Foster and Briceño-Garmendia 2009.
Note: — = not available.

The availability of cost-saving technologies varies considerably among transport sectors. In the case of roads, for example, the costs of reaching road connectivity targets vary depending on the chosen engineering standards. For the base scenario considered in this analysis, regional and national connectivity is achieved by a good-condition asphalt road network, with at least two lanes for regional connectivity and at least one lane for national connectivity. If a single-surface-treatment road in fair condition were substituted for an asphalt road in good condition, the cost of reaching the same connectivity targets could be reduced by 30 percent. Similarly, relaxing the standards for rural road construction allows a greater level of connectivity to be achieved with a given budget.

Addressing Rehabilitation Backlogs

The investment needs presented in this book are based on the objective of redressing Africa's infrastructure backlog within 10 years. Middle-income, resource-rich states and low-income, nonfragile states could meet this target within existing resource envelopes (including existing levels of ODA) if inefficiency was substantially reduced. The same cannot be said for the low-income, fragile states. For a few of these states, the infrastructure backlog is so great that policy makers should consider taking more time to attain targets, using lower-cost technologies, or both. Even the low-income, fragile states could attain their transport infrastructure targets without increasing their spending envelopes if they were willing to take 40 years instead of 10 to address their investment backlogs (assuming full elimination of inefficiencies).

Extending the time horizon for the achievement of these goals should make the targets more affordable. But how long would the extension need to be to make the infrastructure targets attainable without increasing existing spending envelopes? Figure 8.9 shows that by spreading the investment needs over 45 years rather than 10, low-income, fragile states could achieve their proposed targets within existing spending envelopes. Without efficiency gains, however, these countries would require much more than 45 years to meet their infrastructure targets or, alternatively, would need to double their spending to reach their target in 45 years.

Advocating that countries delay in making up backlogs, however, is not the same as advocating that they defer current and periodic maintenance. The latter would be a false economy, which would eventually increase the size and cost of the backlog.

Figure 8.9   Cost of Redressing Infrastructure Backlogs over Varying Time Frames

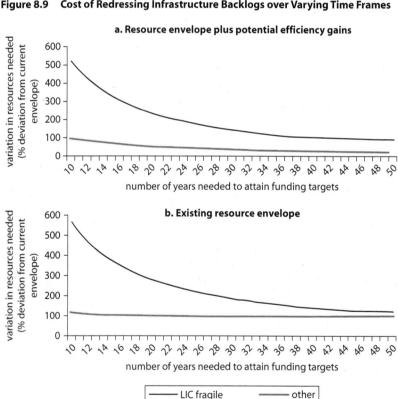

Source: Africa Infrastructure Country Diagnostic.
Note: LIC = low-income country. LIC nonfragile, MICs (middle-income countries), and resource-rich countries show almost identical patterns and, therefore, are taken as the single category "other."

In sum, governments could directly capture $2.4 billion by improving transport infrastructure management and institutions (table 8.6). Raising fuel levies to cost-recovery levels would secure $600 million per year. Potential savings from improved levy collection amount to $500 million, and $1.3 billion per year could be saved by raising capital budget execution rates through improvements to the preparation and procurement of projects. The greatest potential gain would come from reductions in vehicle-operating costs resulting from better road conditions. Road users would be the primary beneficiaries, saving an estimated $1.34 billion to $4.84 billion. These savings, however, would necessitate an increase in agency expenditures; therefore, they must be reduced by the additional maintenance expenditure required to realize them before being added to agency savings.

Looking across countries (see appendix 7d), about 10 countries could realize efficiency savings of 0.5 percent of GDP or more—and more than 1.0 percent in the case of Namibia and Malawi (figure 8.10). Nigeria has

Table 8.6   Potential Gains from Improved Efficiency in Transport Spending (US$ millions annually)

	Middle-income countries	Resource-rich countries	Low-income, nonfragile countries	Low-income, fragile countries	Total
Infrastructure spending needs	8,430	3,810	3,797	3,155	19,193
Spending directed to needs	7,738	3,113	3,266	571	16,336
Gain from eliminating inefficiencies	688	788	541	107	2,368
- Gain from raising capital budget execution	613	455	162	61	1,298
- Gain from cost recovery through fuel levy	38	163	211	46	574
- Gain from undercollection	36	170	169	—	497
(Financing gap) or surplus	(4)	91	10	(2,477)	(489)

Source: Briceño-Garmendia, Smits, and Foster 2009.
Note: — = not available. Totals may not be exact because of rounding errors.

Figure 8.10   Potential Efficiency Gains from Different Sources

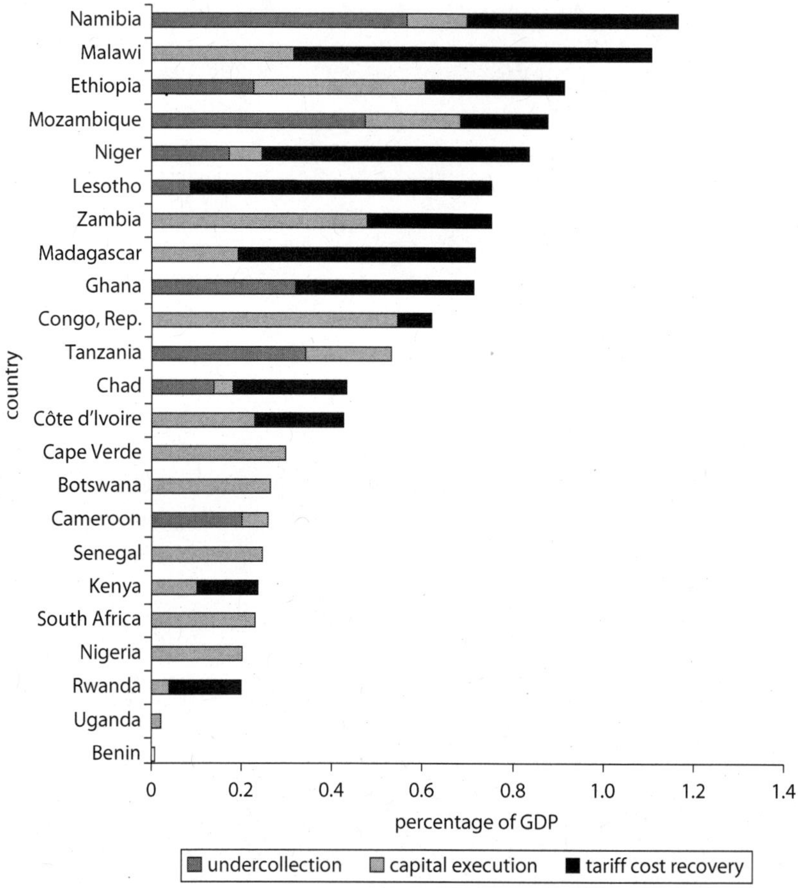

Source: Briceño-Garmendia, Smits, and Foster 2009.
Note: Based on annualized averages for 2001–06.

potential savings of around 0.2 percent of GDP, amounting to about $200 million a year. For most countries, insufficient expenditure on road maintenance and excessive user costs are the main sources of inefficiency. But in a few countries (such as Zambia, Ethiopia, and the Republic of Congo), low capital-budget execution is the most pressing issue.

Increasing Funding

Even if they can improve the efficiency with which current funding levels are employed, many countries will also require additional sources of

funds to meet their spending needs. But prospects for increased funding
for transport from all sources are limited (World Bank 2009). Domestic
public finance is the largest source of funding today, but it presents little
scope for an increase, except possibly in countries enjoying natural
resource windfalls. ODA to African transport infrastructure has grown
substantially in recent years, in line with political pledges, but this assistance could slow down because of fiscal pressures in donor countries
related to the 2008 economic downturn. Non-OECD finance has also
been rising steeply, but its future is now unclear. Private participation, also
very buoyant during Africa's recent growth upswing, will be particularly
vulnerable to the downturn in global markets. Finally, local capital markets have so far contributed little to infrastructure finance outside South
Africa, though they could eventually become more important in some of
the region's larger economies. These last two sources of funding are of limited relevance to the road sector in low-income, fragile states, where funding gaps are most significant, because of road users' limited ability to pay.

Raising More Domestic Public Finance

A key question is the extent to which countries may be willing to allocate
additional fiscal resources to infrastructure. Prior to the current financial
crisis, the fiscal situation in Africa was favorable. Rapid economic
growth—averaging 4 percent per year from 2001 to 2003 and 5 percent
a year from 2004 to 2008—translated into increased annual domestic fiscal revenues of just over 3 percent of GDP on average. In resource-rich
countries, burgeoning resource royalties added 7.7 percent of GDP to the
public budget. In the low-income countries, substantial debt relief increased
external grants by almost 2 percent of GDP.

Nevertheless, a surprisingly small portion of the additional resources
was allocated to infrastructure (table 8.7). This was especially true in
the resource-rich countries, particularly Nigeria. Huge debt repayments
absorbed the fiscal windfalls in these countries. As a result, budgetary
spending contracted by 3.7 percent of GDP, with infrastructure investment falling by almost 1.5 percent of GDP. In the middle-income countries, budgetary spending increased by almost 4.1 percent of GDP, but the
additional resources went primarily to social sector spending, and the
effect on infrastructure spending was almost negligible. Only in the low-
income countries did the overall increases in budgetary expenditure have
some effect on infrastructure spending. Even there, however, the effect
was fairly modest and confined to capital investment. The low-income,
nonfragile countries allocated 30 percent of their budgetary increase to

Table 8.7   Net Change in Central Government Budgets by Economic Use, 1995–2004

Use	Africa	Middle-income countries	Resource-rich countries	Low-income, nonfragile countries	Low-income, fragile countries
	Percentage of GDP				
Increase (decrease) in net expenditure budget	1.89	4.08	(3.73)	1.69	3.85
Increase in current infrastructure spending as a share of expenditures	0.00	0.02	0.03	0.00	0.09
Increase (decrease) in capital infrastructure spending as a share of expenditures	(0.14)	0.04	(1.46)	0.54	0.22

Source: Adapted from Briceño-Garmendia, Smits, and Foster 2009.
Note: Based on annualized averages for 2001–06. Averages weighted by country GDP. Totals are extrapolations based on the 24-country sample covered in AICD phase 1.

infrastructure investments. The fragile states, despite seeing their overall budgetary expenditures rise by about 3.9 percent of GDP, devoted only 6 percent of the gain to infrastructure.

Compared with other developing regions, Africa does a particularly poor job of collecting tax revenues, thus limiting its public financing capabilities. Domestic revenue generation is around 23 percent of GDP, trailing averages for other developing countries. That figure is lowest for the low-income countries (less than 15 percent of GDP per year). Despite strong growth in the past decade, domestically raised revenues increased by less than 1.2 percent of GDP. This suggests that challenging institutional reforms will be required to increase the effectiveness of revenue collection and broaden the tax base.

The capacity of African countries to borrow from domestic and external sources is also limited. Domestic borrowing is often very expensive, with interest rates far exceeding those on concessional external loans. Because of the scarcity of private domestic savings, public domestic borrowing tends to precipitate sharp increases in interest rates, particularly for the poorest countries. For many African countries, the ratio of debt service to GDP is more than 6 percent.

The ongoing financial crisis is expected to reduce fiscal receipts globally, and Africa will not be exempt. Growth projections for the coming years have been revised downward from 5.1 percent to 3.5 percent, which will reduce tax revenues and likely depress demand and willingness to pay for infrastructure services. Commodity prices have fallen to levels of the early 2000s. The effect on royalty revenues, however, will depend on the savings policies of each country. A number of oil producers have made a practice of saving royalty revenues collected from sales at prices above $60 a barrel, so the downturn will affect their savings accounts more than their budgets. In addition, many African countries are devaluing their currency, reducing the purchasing power of domestic resources. Overall, the global financial crisis will put substantial pressure on public sector budgets.

A further perverse influence should be noted. Based on recent global experience, fiscal adjustment episodes tend to disproportionately affect public investment—infrastructure in particular. During earlier crises in East Asia and Latin America, infrastructure spending—especially road maintenance—was vulnerable to budget cutbacks. Cuts in infrastructure investment in eight Latin American countries amounted to an average of 40 percent of the observed fiscal adjustment between the early 1980s and the late 1990s (Calderón and Servén 2004). This reduction was remarkable because public infrastructure investment already represented less than 25 percent of overall public expenditure in Latin American countries. These infrastructure investment cuts were later identified as the underlying problem holding back economic growth throughout the region during the 2000s. Similar patterns were observed in East Asia during the financial crisis of the mid-1990s. For example, Indonesia's total public investment in infrastructure dropped from between 6 and 7 percent of GDP in 1995–97 to 2 percent in 2000. Given recent spending patterns, changes in the overall budget envelope will likely affect infrastructure investment in Africa in a similar procyclical manner.

Official Development Assistance: Sustaining the Scale-Up
For most of the 1990s and early 2000s, ODA for transport infrastructure in Africa remained steady at around $1.3 billion a year. The launch of the Commission for Africa Report in 2004 was followed in July 2005 by the Group of Eight Gleneagles Summit, where the Infrastructure Consortium for Africa was created to focus on scaling up donor finance to meet Africa's infrastructure needs. Donors have so far kept their promises: ODA flows to African transport infrastructure increased by more than 50 percent between 2004 and 2007—from $2.0 billion to $3.2 billion.

More than 80 percent of this ODA comes from multilateral donors—the African Development Bank (AfDB), the European Commission, and the International Development Association (IDA) of the World Bank Group. Among bilaterals, France and Japan have made significant contributions. A significant lag occurs between ODA commitments and their disbursement, suggesting that disbursements should continue to increase in the coming years. The commitments reported above are significantly higher than the estimated ODA disbursements of $1.8 billion (see table 8.1). This gap reflects delays typically associated with project implementation. Because ODA is channeled through the government budget, the execution of funds faces some of the same problems affecting domestically financed public investment, including procurement delays and low administrative capacity. Differences between the financial systems of the donor country and the receiving country, as well as unpredictability in the release of funds, may further delay the disbursement of resources. Nevertheless, if all commitments up to 2007 are fully honored, ODA disbursements should rise significantly (IMF 2009).

ODA was set to increase further before the global economic crisis, but prospects are no longer as bright. The three multilateral agencies—the AfDB, the European Commission, and the IDA—secured record replenishments for their concessional funding windows for the three to four years beginning in 2008. In principle, the multilateral agencies could provide $5.2 billion per year for African infrastructure in the near future, with transport receiving a substantial share of that amount. In practice, however, the crisis may divert multilateral resources from infrastructure projects to emergency fiscal support. Historical trends suggest that ODA has tended to be procyclical rather than countercyclical (IMF 2009; ODI 2009). Bilateral support, based on annual budget determinations, may be more sensitive to the fiscal squeeze in OECD countries, and some decline can be anticipated.

Non-OECD Financing: Will Growth Continue?

Non-OECD countries financed about $1.1 billion of African transport infrastructure annually between 2001 and 2006 (see table 8.1). This is substantially less than what was provided by ODA over the same period, and it is directed toward very different targets. Non-OECD financiers have been active primarily in countries exporting oil (Angola, Nigeria, and Sudan) or other valuable minerals. Their involvement in African transport infrastructure has predominantly consisted of Chinese support for railway development and Arab support for roads.

Between 2001 and 2007, China provided financing commitments of around $4 billion to the African rail sector. The financing is for rehabilitation of more than 1,350 kilometers of existing railway lines and construction of more than 1,600 kilometers of new railroad. (For a perspective on these figures, the entire African railroad network amounts to around 50,000 kilometers.) The largest deals have been in Nigeria, Gabon, Mauritania, and Angola, although the Nigerian deal has been delayed.[2] Chinese financing in Gabon and Mauritania will facilitate export of iron and phosphate deposits, respectively. In Angola, part of a $2 billion credit is being invested in the refurbishment of the Benguela railway and the rehabilitation of the railway between the port of Namibe and city of Menogue.

By contrast, the cumulative value of Chinese financing for the road sector was only $600 million for the period 2001–07. Arab development institutions committed much more—about $1.8 billion over the same period—to financing African roads (Briceño-Garmendia, Smits, and Foster 2009).

China's official economic assistance quadrupled between 2001 and 2005, reaching more than 35 African countries. Most of the assistance has gone to resource-rich countries, some of it in the form of barter arrangements under the "Angola mode."[3] This south-south cooperation builds on economic complementarities: China has a strategic interest in Africa's natural resources, while Africa harnesses China's construction capabilities, thus helping African countries to develop their economic infrastructure.

The implementation processes for ODA and non-OECD finance are completely different. While ODA is channeled through the government budget, China tends to directly execute its own financing, often with associated imports of human resources. Although this approach raises significant challenges, such as ensuring that the recipient benefits from technical assistance in project implementation, it also circumvents some of the capital budget execution problems typically associated with public investment.

Non-OECD finance also raises questions about sustainability. Non-OECD financiers from China, India, and the Persian Gulf states put their resources behind sectors, countries, and circumstances aligned with their national business interests. They offer realistic financing options for power and transport particularly for postconflict countries with natural resources. But nongovernmental organizations are voicing concerns about the social and environmental impact of these projects. And because non-OECD financiers rarely offer operational, institutional, or policy assistance along with their funding, it is unclear whether the new assets are sustainable.

How the economic downturn will affect non-OECD finance is difficult to predict. Such aid, funded by domestic taxpayers in the donor countries, may be particularly vulnerable to budgetary cutbacks. The downturn in global commodity prices may also inhibit Chinese infrastructure finance linked to natural resource development.

Private Investors: Over the Hill?

All values reported in this section exclude royalty payments to governments for transport infrastructure, which—although valuable from a fiscal perspective—do not contribute to the creation of new transport assets. Since the late 1990s, private investment commitments in African transport infrastructure have surged, from $900 million in 1997 to $4.6 billion in 2006. Accounting for project implementation cycles, this translates into an average annual disbursement of $1.1 billion a year, or 0.16 percent of GDP (see table 8.1). These disbursements are very similar in magnitude to those received from non-OECD financiers.

For infrastructure as a whole, Africa's resource-rich countries have been receiving the largest volume of private participation. Low-income countries—including fragile states—are capturing annual average flows of well over 1 percent of GDP. Relative to their GDP, however, Africa's middle-income countries have done less well.

The picture for transport infrastructure is somewhat different. Private capital flows to the African transport sector have been volatile over time (figure 8.11, panel a). Occasional spikes have been driven by the financial closure of a handful of large projects, such as the N3 toll road project in South Africa in 1999 (worth a total of $600 million); the slew of container terminal concessions at Nigerian ports in 2005 (worth a total of $700 million); and the Gauteng light rail concession in South Africa in 2006 (worth a total of $3.8 billion). Aside from these megaprojects, the average annual private capital flow to African transport infrastructure during the 2000s has been no more than $300 million.

About 60 percent of private finance for African transport has gone to railways, accounting for around $5.2 billion of cumulative commitments. A further 24 percent has gone to toll road projects, amounting to cumulative commitments of $2.1 billion. The remaining 16 percent, or $1.3 billion, has been spent on seaports (figure 8.11, panel b). Private participation in African transport infrastructure is almost invariably through

Figure 8.11   Overview of Private Commitments to African Transport Infrastructure

a. Over time (US$ millions)

b. By subsector (US$ millions)

c. By country (US$ millions)

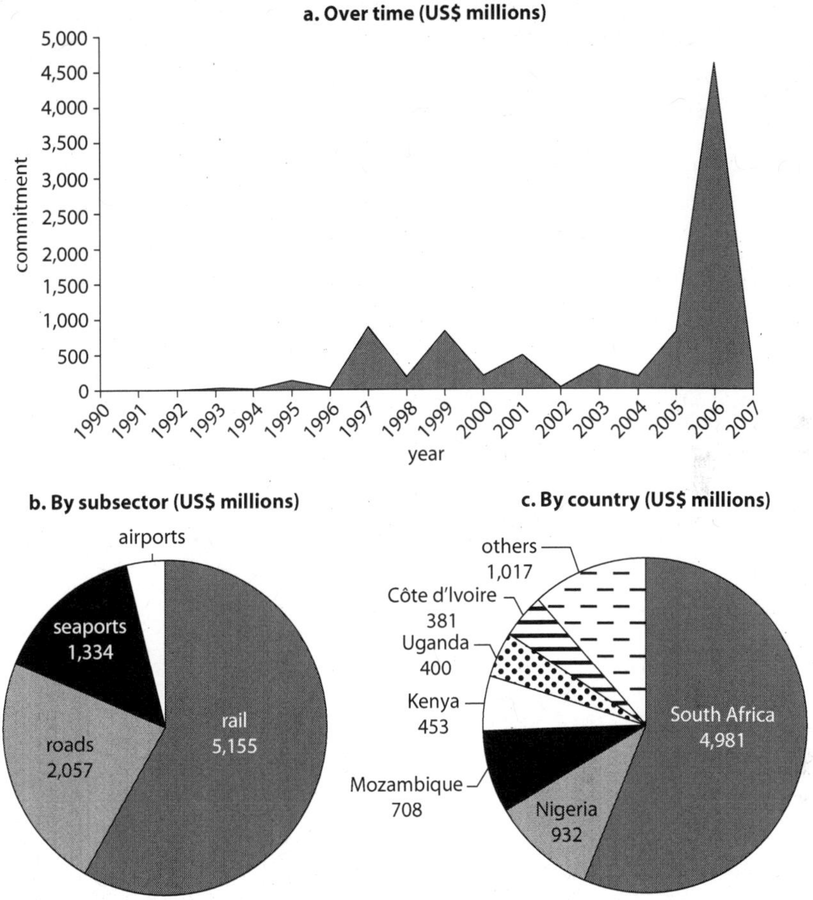

Source: PPIAF 2008.
Note: Cumulative investment commitments from 1990 to 2007, not disbursements. Chart is comprehensive; all countries excluded do not have any private investment in transport infrastructure.

concession contracts. As noted in previous chapters, a very limited portion of Africa's road network meets the minimum traffic thresholds required to support toll road concessions. Rail concessions are more numerous, but investment commitments—especially realized investments—have fallen well short of requirements and expectations because of the limited traffic volumes on the lines and the constraints on tariffs imposed by inter-modal competition. Seaport transactions have primarily taken the form of container terminal concessions, which are becoming increasingly common around the region.

More than half of the total private investment in African transport infrastructure has gone to South Africa, which captured cumulative commitments of almost $5 billion between 1990 and 2007 (figure 8.11, panel c). South Africa captured about 70 percent of private investment in African railways and roads but hardly any of the private investment in ports and airports. The next closest country is Nigeria, which captured $900 million of cumulative commitments over the same period, concentrated exclusively in ports and airports, with no private investment in roads or railroads. Eight countries have captured between $100 million and $700 million of cumulative commitments. In descending order, these countries are Mozambique, Kenya, Uganda, Côte d'Ivoire, Gabon, Tanzania, Cameroon, and Zimbabwe. In most cases, the bulk of these resources has gone to railroads, with the exception of one sizable toll road investment in Mozambique. Another 12 countries have captured modest amounts of private investment for transport, averaging around $40 million in cumulative commitments per country. There have been no toll road or airport investments in any of these countries—financing has been divided evenly between railroad and seaport projects. Countries such as Burkina Faso, Madagascar, Malawi, Mali, Senegal, and Zambia have also achieved significant railroad transactions, and Angola, Equatorial Guinea, Ghana, Madagascar, Mauritius, and Sudan have benefited from significant seaport transactions.

The global financial crisis is likely to affect private capital flows even more than official flows. In the aftermath of the 1997 Asian financial crisis, private participation in developing countries fell by about half over a period of five years. Meanwhile, existing arrangements in Africa are coming under stress as parties encounter difficulties refinancing short- and medium-term debt.

Local Sources of Finance: Possible in the Medium Term

Local capital markets are a major source of infrastructure finance in South Africa, but this is not yet true elsewhere. Local infrastructure finance consists primarily of commercial bank lending, some corporate bond and stock exchange issues, and, more recently, the participation of a small but growing number of institutional investors.

Along with information and communication technology, transport is reporting higher volumes of finance from local capital markets than are most other infrastructure sectors, although the absolute volumes remain small. The outstanding stock of finance for transport infrastructure on local capital markets was $17.1 million for South Africa and $6.2 million for the remainder of Africa. These volumes are low when compared with an annual investment requirement of $8.8 billion for the sector in Africa (note that the total financing requirement of $19.2 billion includes maintenance as well as new investment).

The stock of outstanding bank loans to the transport and communication sector was $8.5 billion at the end of 2006 (unfortunately, volumes for the two sectors cannot be disaggregated). South Africa accounted for about $5.0 billion of this total, with the rest of Africa making up the remaining $3.5 billion. This total represents only 2.9 percent of outstanding bank loans throughout Africa (Irving and Manroth 2009). As well as being limited in size, bank lending tends to be short in tenor for all but the most select bank clients, reflecting the predominantly short-term nature of banks' deposits and other liabilities. The longest maturities available—around 20 years—were found only in Ghana, Lesotho, Namibia, South Africa, Uganda, and Zambia. Eight other countries reported maximum loan maturities of 10 years or more. Even where 20-year terms are reportedly available, they may not be affordable for infrastructure. In Ghana and Zambia, for example, average lending rates exceed 20 percent. Very few infrastructure projects generate sufficient revenues to achieve that rate of return.

For most African countries, local banking systems are too small and too constrained by structural impediments, such as the lack of credits of adequate maturity, to assemble funds for infrastructural development. Syndicated lending to infrastructure projects with the participation of local banks, which has increased in recent years, may hold more potential. The volume of syndicated loans to infrastructure borrowers rose steeply from $600 million in 2000 to $6.3 billion in 2006, with 80 percent of this amount concentrated in South Africa (Irving and Manroth 2009). But there is so far only one example of a syndicated loan to the transport infrastructure sector in South Africa—the $475 million rand-denominated loan by three South African banks to Trans-African Concessions for construction of the N4 toll road. The second tranche of this loan had a maturity of 20 years.

In the past decade, governments in the region have extended the maturity profile of their securities issues in an effort to establish a benchmark against which corporate bonds can be priced. With the exception of South Africa, however, such corporate bond markets remain small and illiquid. At 13.0 percent of GDP, South Africa's corporate bond market is by far the largest in the region, with $33.8 billion in issues outstanding at the end of 2006, followed by Namibia's, with $457 million (7.1 percent of GDP). Outside South Africa, the few countries that had corporate bonds listed on their national or regional securities exchange at the end of 2006 had only a handful of such listings, and the amounts issued were small. Only $1.1 billion of corporate bonds issued by transport infrastructure providers was outstanding at the close of 2006 (table 8.8). The bulk of this—around $772 million—was issued by the South African National Roads Agency, and a further $298 million related to road financing in Namibia. Aside from the corporate bonds issued by these middle-income countries, the only other case found was a small issue of $62 million for the Port of Dakar in Senegal. The maturities reported on the transactions outside South Africa ranged from 6 to 10 years.

The region's stock exchanges have played a more significant role in the transport sector, raising a total of $13.6 billion of capital—more than 80 percent in South Africa and the remainder in a handful of countries including Côte d'Ivoire, Nigeria, and Sudan.

Institutional investors, including pension funds and insurance companies, could potentially become an important source of financing in the

Table 8.8   Outstanding Financing Stock for Transport Infrastructure as of 2006

	Bank loans	Corporate bonds	Equity issues	Total	Share of total stock (%)	Share of total infrastructure stock (%)
South Africa (US$ millions)	5,011	772	11,269	17,052	73	28
Middle-income countries (excluding South Africa) (US$ millions)	142	298	—	441	2	81
Resource-rich countries (US$ millions)	1,375	—	87	1,462	6	56
Low-income, nonfragile countries (US$ millions)	1,728	62	2,173	3,963	17	54
Low-income, fragile countries (US$ millions)	278	—	69	346	1	73
Total (US$ millions)	8,534	1,133	13,598	23,265	100	32
Share of total stock (%)	37	5	58	100		
Share of total infrastructure stock (%)	12	2	19	32		

Source: Adapted from Irving and Manroth 2009.
Note: — = not available. The stock includes bank loans, corporate bonds, and equity issues. The stock level reported under "transport" may be an overestimate because many countries report this category together with elements of communications and storage, and some countries together with electricity and water. Table is based on data from the following 22 countries: Cape Verde, Lesotho, and Namibia (middle-income); Nigeria, Sudan, and Zambia (resource-rich); and Côte d'Ivoire, Benin, Burkina Faso, the Democratic Republic of Congo, Ethiopia, Ghana, Kenya, Madagascar, Malawi, Mozambique, Niger, Rwanda, Senegal, Tanzania, and Uganda (low-income).

future, with more than $90 billion in assets accumulated in the former and more than $180 billion held by the latter. But as of today, less than 1 percent of those assets are invested in infrastructure, and even if that percentage were increased, it is likely that telecommunications would benefit much more than transport infrastructure.

Harnessing the significant potential of local capital markets, particularly local bond markets, to finance infrastructure is thus contingent on the development of these markets as well as on further reforms to deepen the local institutional investor base. Well-functioning and appropriately regulated local institutional investors (pension funds and insurance companies) would be natural sources of long-term financing for infrastructure because their liabilities are well matched to the longer terms of infrastructure projects. Private pension providers have begun to emerge as a possible source of infrastructure financing with the shift from defined-benefit to defined-contribution schemes, which are viewed as less costly, more transparent, and easier to manage.[4] Moreover, local institutional investors are also diversifying their portfolios, making infrastructure investments more attractive.

With regional integration, financial markets could achieve greater scale and liquidity. More cross-border intraregional listings—of both corporate bonds and equity issues—and more cross-border intraregional investment (particularly by local institutional investors) could help overcome national capital markets' impediments of small size, illiquidity, and inadequate market infrastructure. They could also facilitate the ability of companies and governments to raise financing for infrastructure. So far, this intraregional approach to raising infrastructure financing remains largely untested. One new initiative is the Pan-African Infrastructure Development Fund, a 15-year regional fund that in its first round in 2007 raised $625 million for commercially viable infrastructure projects in Africa, including funds from Ghanaian and South African institutional investors.

Costs of Capital and Sources of Finance

Each source of infrastructure financing has a different associated cost of capital (figure 8.12). For public funds, raising taxes is not a costless exercise. Each dollar raised and spent by an African government has a social value premium (or marginal cost of public funds) of almost 20 percent, reflecting the incidence of that tax on the society's welfare (caused by changes in consumption patterns and administrative costs, among other things). To allow ready comparisons across financing sources, this study

Figure 8.12   Costs of Capital by Funding Source

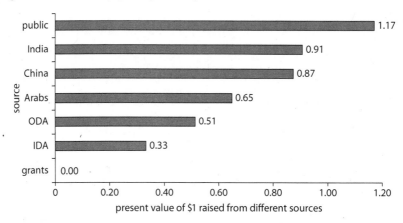

Source: Average marginal cost of public funds as estimated by Warlters and Auriol (2005); cost of equity for private sector as in Estache and Pinglo (2004) and Sirtaine and others (2005); authors' calculations.

standardized the financial terms as the present value of a dollar raised through each of the different sources. In doing so, it recognized that all loans must ultimately be repaid with tax dollars, each of which attracts the 20 percent cost premium.

Wide variation exists in lending terms. The most concessional IDA loans charge zero interest (0.75 percent service charge) with a 10-year grace period. India, China, and the Gulf states charge 4 percent, 3.6 percent, and 1.5 percent interest, respectively, with a 4-year grace period.

The cost of non-OECD financing is somewhere between that of public funds and ODA. The "subsidy element" for Indian and Chinese funds is about 25 percent and for the Arab funds about 50 percent.[5] ODA typically provides a subsidy element of 60 percent; this rises to 75 percent for IDA resources. In addition to differences in the cost of capital, sources of financing differ in their transaction costs, which may offset or accentuate some of the differences.

The Most Promising Ways to Increase Funds

What are the best ways of increasing the availability of funds for infrastructure development? The way to start is clearly to get the most from existing budget envelopes, which can provide up to $2.4 billion a year of additional resources internally. For many countries, this would be enough to close the funding gap. But for a number of others—particularly the fragile states—a significant gap would remain even if all inefficiencies were eliminated. Before the 2008 financial crisis, the prospects for reducing—if not closing—this gap appeared reasonably good. Resource royalties were at record highs, and resource-rich countries could use natural resource savings accounts to provide financing for infrastructure (if macroeconomic conditions allowed). All sources of external finance were buoyant and promising further growth.

As a consequence of the crisis, all sources of infrastructure financing in Africa may have less to offer rather than more, and the funding gap may widen further. It is worth noting, however, that the impact of the crisis has been less pronounced in Africa than elsewhere. In its *World Economic Outlook* issued early in 2010, the International Monetary Fund estimated that while economic growth in Africa had fallen from 5.2 percent in 2008 to 1.9 percent in 2009, it was expected to return to 4.3 percent in 2010 and rise further to 5.3 percent in 2011 (IMF 2010).

The Residual Funding Gap

The funding story is not entirely bleak. Assuming that current levels of ODA are unchanged and all efficiency gains are realized, 10 out of the 24 countries have more than enough funding to cover the estimated needs for the transport sector (figure 8.13). Even excluding ODA, four countries (Botswana, Malawi, Cape Verde, and the Republic of Congo) show small surpluses.

But when the efficiency improvements are not allowed for, the picture is far less encouraging, with no country in the sample showing a surplus of financing over estimated needs (figure 8.14).

Even when ODA is excluded and no allowance is made for potential efficiency gains, the funding gaps for some middle-income countries (South Africa and Cape Verde) and resource-rich states (Nigeria) amount to a very small proportion of GDP. Furthermore, addressing all the inefficiencies described above and capturing the user benefits for the public budget would be more than enough to close the overall funding gap for transport infrastructure at the aggregate regional level. This would also be the case in aggregate for the middle-income, resource-rich, and low-income, nonfragile states.

For several reasons, however, this is no grounds for complacency. First, the estimated funding gaps for the transport sector (see figure 8.13) are very significant for half a dozen countries. For the Democratic Republic of Congo, the gap is close to 20 percent of GDP (or $1.4 billion), while Chad has a transport funding gap of more than 4 percent of GDP. Mali,

Figure 8.13   Transport Infrastructure Financing Gap, Assuming All Efficiency Gains

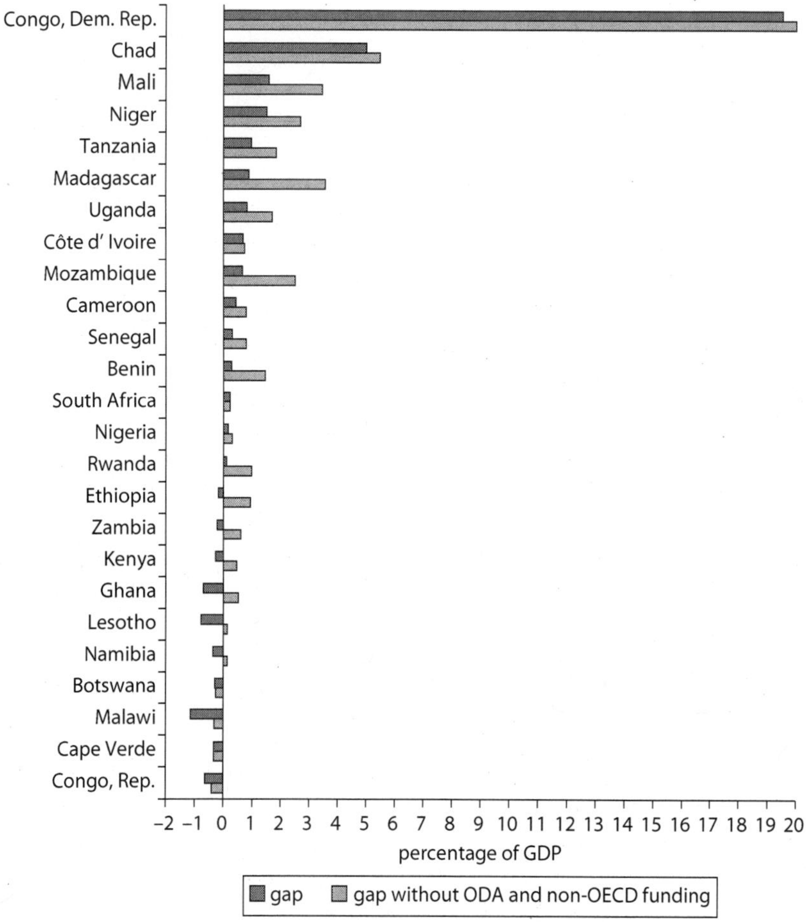

Source: Adapted from Briceño-Garmendia, Smits, and Foster 2009.

Niger, Tanzania, and Madagascar all have shortfalls of around 1 percent of GDP. As a group, the low-income, fragile states have a funding gap of $2.5 billion per year, representing more than 6 percent of aggregate GDP. About two-thirds of this funding gap relates to capital investment, with the remaining amount relating to maintenance spending.

In addition, the benefit from increased user charges is actually a transfer from users to government, not a real efficiency gain per se. The actual economic efficiency gain—the largest category of potential efficiency gains—arises in the form of operating cost savings to users, greater than,

Figure 8.14   Transport Infrastructure Financing Gap, Excluding Any Efficiency Gains

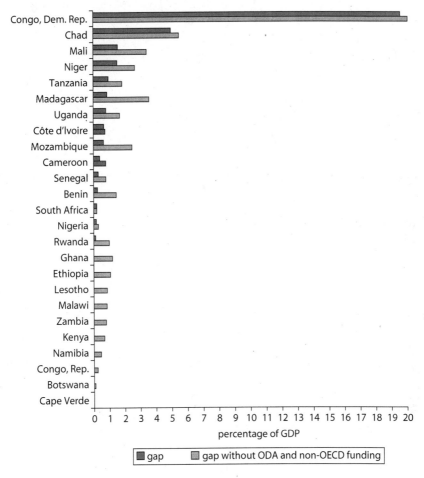

percentage of GDP

■ gap   □ gap without ODA and non-OECD funding

Source: Briceño-Garmendia, Smits, and Foster 2009.
Note: Based on annualized averages for 2001–06.

but resulting from, increased maintenance expenditures by the road agencies. Hence, converting the agency gain into real efficiency gains would be contingent on devising methods of recapturing some of the benefit to fund the investment. That puts the focus back on the need for strong and consistent policy making. While it may be unrealistic to expect that all the inefficiencies can be eliminated, even halving them would make a substantial contribution to the African transport sector.

The Way Forward

The estimated cost of meeting Africa's transport sector spending needs amounts to $19.2 billion a year. At first glance, this does not appear too far above current transport sector spending (including ODA) of $16.3 billion a year. Moreover, in aggregate, it would appear that 80 percent of the gap between spending needs and current spending could be eliminated by capturing an estimated $2.4 billion a year in efficiency gains, mainly in the road sector. The inefficiencies in question arise from underexecution of capital budgets ($1.3 billion a year), underrecovery of road user costs ($600 million a year), and undercollection of levies ($500 million a year).

Even this seemingly positive picture leaves no room for complacency, for three reasons.

First, the efficiency gains may not be easily achieved. The analysis underscores the importance of completing the reform agenda to ensure adequate funding for and spending on road maintenance, as well as to improve the effectiveness of project appraisal and procurement processes across the institutions responsible for implementing public investment programs (such as the road fund and road agency administrations discussed in chapter 2).

Second, the analysis depends on recent levels of ODA and other sources of external finance being maintained. Overall, these sources account for nearly one-quarter of transport infrastructure expenditures, and for the low-income, fragile states, they account for more than one-half. While statements of intent from the funding sources are quite promising, it still remains to be seen how well they survive the global financial crisis.

Finally, the analysis does not apply to all countries. The extreme cases are the low-income, fragile states, two of which would have a funding gap of $2.5 billion a year even if all efficiency gains were fully captured. Raising more funds for transport infrastructure—particularly road infrastructure—in low-income, fragile states will be challenging. Historically, the main sources of financing have been public budgets and ODA, both of which are likely to suffer as a result of the financial crisis. The potential of the private sector to contribute to road finance is relatively small, while non-OECD finance has tended to go preferentially to the railroad sector. Closing the gap for transport finance in low-income, fragile states will therefore likely entail delaying the achievement of targets or opting for lower-cost technologies and standards.

A number of priorities for action can be identified.

Priority 1. Consolidating commitment to adequate and efficient maintenance

Ensuring that maintenance is performed in an adequate and timely manner is the first priority. To this end, the following contributory actions are required:

- Further strengthening of road fund administrations and procedures to permit multiannual contracts
- Continuation of efforts to implement road works more effectively through quasi-independent road agencies.

Priority 2. Ensuring better budget execution ratios

Poor budget execution results in transport infrastructure expenditures falling below the budget allocations. A number of steps can be taken to improve this situation:

- Better consultation among sector ministries, finance ministries, and donors on the balance between needs and absorptive capacity
- Strict adherence to timetables for budget preparation
- Establishment of medium-term programs for each subsector, taking into account absorptive capacity as well as needs
- Maintenance of a pool of prepared projects so that any variations in budget availability can be accommodated.

Priority 3. Improving the accuracy of needs estimates on a country-by-country basis

The model used in this study is essentially a "broad brush" model. While it is available for further development and country application, it needs to be refined as follows:

- More comprehensive in its coverage of all of the component elements of expenditure
- Calibrated to local costs and conditions in each country.

Priority 4. Sustaining ODA

Many countries are heavily dependent on ODA for their investment expenditures on transport infrastructure. That support was likely to only increase before the ongoing world financial crisis. Now, if commitments are not maintained, there is a danger that some countries will divert even more of their domestic funding from maintenance to investment. The following steps may help to make sure that ODA is maintained:

- Further shifts of ODA to sector budget support, contingent on adequate allocations and execution of maintenance programs
- More commitment—on the part of both donors and recipients—to development policies and programs under the New Partnership for Africa's Development initiative.

Priority 5. Making infrastructure finance more attractive to the private sector

Concessioning has been used as a means of attracting private sector participation in infrastructure finance and management, particularly in the rail and ports sectors. But in the rail sector, this has not yet proved to be a sustainable source of capital funding. To make capital finance more attractive to the private sector, governments can commit to the following reforms of concessioning arrangements:

- Development of new railway concession models under which governments continue to participate in capital funding when major expansion of rehabilitation programs is required
- Firm contractual commitment to the adequate and timely compensation of public service obligations, particularly the maintenance of passenger services in rail concession contracts.

Notes

1. Cecilia Briceño-Garmendia and Nataliya Pushak are the authors of the main source document for this chapter. William Butterfield, Chuan Chen, Vivien Foster, Jacqueline Irving, Astrid Manroth, Afua Sarkodie, and Karlis Smits also contributed. Rodrigo Archondo-Callao and Alberto Nogales performed the calculations based on the Highway Design and Maintenance Model 4 (HDM4) and the Road Network Evaluation Tool (RONET).

2. Although first announced in late 2006, the deal had not been finalized by January 2010, when it was announced that the first drawdown of the $500 million loan for the Kano-Lagos railway rehabilitation was imminent.

3. The Angola mode was devised to enable African nations to pay for infrastructure with natural resources. In a single transaction, China bundles development-type assistance with commercial-type trade finance. A Chinese resource company makes repayments in exchange for oil or mineral rights. The China

Export-Import Bank acts as a broker, receiving money for the sale and paying the contractor for providing the infrastructure. This arrangement safeguards against currency inconvertibility, political instability, and expropriation.

4. For a defined-contribution pension scheme, under which pensions are based solely on the financial performance of saved contributions, infrastructure bonds may be a relatively attractive asset because of their long-term nature and the fact that they may give slightly better returns than other government bonds.

5. The subsidy element is the percentage difference between the present value of the loan and interest repayments of a loan that is made on standard market terms, and the present value of the loan and interest repayments of the loan in question.

References

Briceño-Garmendia, C., K. Smits, and V. Foster. 2009. "Financing Public Infrastructure in Sub-Saharan Africa: Patterns, Issues, and Options." Africa Infrastructure Country Diagnostic Background Paper 15, World Bank, Washington, DC.

Calderón, C., and L. Servén. 2004. "Trends in Infrastructure in Latin America, 1980–2001." Policy Research Working Paper 3401, World Bank, Washington, DC.

Carruthers, R., R. R. Krishnamani, and S. Murray. 2009. "Improving Connectivity: Investing in Transport Infrastructure in Sub-Saharan Africa." Africa Infrastructure Country Diagnostic Background Paper 7, World Bank, Washington, DC.

Estache, Antonio, and Maria Elena Pinglo. 2004. "Are Returns to Private Infrastructure in Developing Countries Consistent with Risks Since the Asian Crisis?" Policy Research Working Paper 3373, World Bank, Washington, DC.

Foster, V., and C. Briceño-Garmendia, eds. 2009. *Africa's Infrastructure: A Time for Transition.* Paris: Agence Française de Développement; Washington, DC: World Bank.

Foster, V., W. Butterfield, C. Chen, and N. Pushak. 2008. "Building Bridges: China's Growing Role as Infrastructure Financier for Sub-Saharan Africa." Trends and Policy Options 5, Public-Private Infrastructure Advisory Facility, World Bank, Washington, DC.

Gwilliam, K., V. Foster, R. Archondo-Callao, C. Briceño-Garmendia, A. Nogales, and K. Sethi. 2009. "The Burden of Maintenance: Roads in Sub-Saharan Africa." Africa Infrastructure Country Diagnostic Background Paper 14, World Bank, Washington, DC.

IMF (International Monetary Fund). 2009. *The State of Public Finances: Outlook and Medium-Term Policies After the 2008 Crisis.* Washington, DC: IMF.

———. 2010. *World Economic Outlook.* Washington, DC: IMF.

Irving, J., and A. Manroth. 2009. "Local Sources of Financing for Infrastructure in Africa: A Cross-Country Analysis." Policy Research Working Paper 4878, World Bank, Washington, DC.

Lall, R., R. Anand, and A. Rastogi. 2009. "Developing Physical Infrastructure: A Comparative Perspective on the Experience of China and India." Unpublished paper, India Development Finance Corporation, Mumbai.

ODI (Overseas Development Institute). 2009. *A Development Charter for the G-20*. London: ODI.

PPIAF (Public-Private Infrastructure Advisory Facility). 2008. Private Participation in Infrastructure Project Database. http://ppi.worldbank.org/.

Reinikka, R., and J. Svensson. 2002. "Explaining Leakage of Public Funds." Discussion Paper 3227, Centre for Economic Policy Research, London.

Sirtaine, S., M. E. Pinglo, J. L. Guasch, and V. Foster. 2005. "How Profitable Are Infrastructure Concessions in Latin America? Empirical Evidence and Regulatory Implications." Trends and Policy Options 2, Public-Private Infrastructure Advisory Facility, World Bank, Washington, DC.

Warlters, M., and E. Auriol. 2005. "The Marginal Cost of Public Funds in Africa." Policy Research Working Paper 3679, World Bank, Washington, DC.

World Bank. 2009. *Global Economic Prospects*. Washington, DC: World Bank.

CHAPTER 9

Governance: The Key to Progress

In each of the preceding chapters, the same message has emerged: inadequate infrastructure goes only part way toward explaining the poor performance of the transport sector in Africa. On the one hand, existing infrastructure has been used inefficiently, increasing investment needs and subsequent fiscal demands; on the other hand, institutional and policy deficiencies continue to mitigate the effectiveness of new investment. Given the history of clientelism and patronage-based decision making in Africa, it is recognized that effective governance is critical if sector development is to have a positive effect. Even Julius Nyerere, while rejecting what he considers the neocolonialist approach to the subject adopted by many aid agencies, accepts that many of Africa's problems arise from bad governance (Nyerere 1998). This chapter examines the impact of governance quality on transport infrastructure in Africa.[1]

The "Washington consensus" that emerged during the 1990s is based on a belief that good economic policy is essential to growth (Burnside and Dollar 1997). Some observers have gone so far as to equate good governance solely with good economic policy, and have tried to demonstrate, empirically, which economic policies are most conducive to growth (Osborne 2004).

Rather more broadly, governance has been defined as the means by which government is exercised (Kaufmann, Kraay, and Mastruzzi 2010). The Worldwide Governance Indicators (WGI) project of the World Bank defines governance as

> the traditions and institutions by which authority in a country is exercised. This considers the process by which governments are selected, monitored and replaced; the capacity of the government to effectively formulate and implement sound policies; and the respect of citizens and the state of the institutions that govern economic and social interactions among them. (World Bank 2010b)

This chapter uses this broad interpretation of the nature and role of governance.

The Context of National Governance

The most comprehensive attempt to assess the quality of governance worldwide is contained in the WGI report, produced annually by the World Bank. The WGI database uses the perceptions of multiple groups to develop an indicator set. The indicators relate to nations' overall economic levels and not to any specific sector. Each of the 212 countries in the database is given a mark between −2.5 and +2.5 on each of six criteria. Data for the estimation of the values are derived from a wide range of sources, details of which are set out in the database (World Bank 2010b).[2]

The following criteria for governance quality are adopted:

- Voice and accountability
- Political stability and absence of violence
- Government effectiveness
- Regulatory quality
- Rule of law
- Control of corruption.

The database shows governance in Africa in a poor light. While there are bad outliers in several regions (for example, Myanmar in East Asia and the Pacific, and Afghanistan in South Asia), and while Africa is not the worst region in the world (Central Asia, mainly comprised of the former Soviet Union countries, holds this place), the average score for Africa is the second worst, comparable with South Asia. Many African countries fall in the lowest quartile of rankings on all dimensions, and most fall in the lowest half. Only Namibia and Botswana appear in the top half of the rankings on all six dimensions, though South Africa and Ghana come close. Any discussion of the transport sector thus needs to be seen against the backdrop of what most agree is a generally poor level of governance across the region.

In turning more specifically to the transport sector, we concentrate on three issues relevant to the WGI definition of governance:

- The significance of national and regional traditions for sector operations
- The appropriateness and effectiveness of the institutions in the sector
- The human resource capacity of the country in question.

Traditions and Attitudes

The first aspect of governance emerging from the WGI definition concerns traditions and attitudes. Countries may have longstanding, entrenched attitudes that counter explicitly stated government objectives or that are unacceptable to the governed. This section considers some of the attitudes and traditions that have been particularly damaging in the context of transport infrastructure, including corruption, the unrealistic expectations of the private sector, state capture by elites, and the absence of a safety culture. Another harmful tradition, aid dependence, is discussed later in the chapter.

Corruption

The postcolonial history of Africa is an almost unrelieved story of corruption and the decay of governance, which has been well documented elsewhere (Meredith 2005). That is not the subject of this book, but it must be noted at the outset, as many of the failings in the transport sector are attributable to the attitudes toward power and governance that have affected all sectors. While there have been improvements in some countries, the recently released Corruption Perceptions Index (Transparency International 2009) finds 10 African countries in the bottom decile (with Somalia at the very bottom of the list). Of the 47 African countries reviewed, 31 scored less than 3 out of 10, "indicating that corruption is perceived as rampant." Without a more fundamental return to good governance, many of the reforms recommended for the transport sector will be either thwarted or perverted.

Various forms of corruption existed prior to decolonization. In West Africa, in particular, there was a long tradition of "dash"—gifts made in recognition of services rendered by public officials and others. What independence did was to enshrine this practice as an institutionalized element of everyday life. Because the new rulers were themselves effectively unconstrained, they were able to exploit their positions by routinely selling government contracts and positions to those willing to pay for them. As a consequence, the practice of bribery spread from top to bottom, particularly in systems for tax collection, customs administration, and policing (box 9.1).

The conditions conducive to corruption—the combination of a monopoly and administrative discretion—frequently arise in the transport sector. The artificial creation of queues for licenses, customs clearance, and so on provides a platform for the extraction of bribes. The poor performance of the African economies in the development of modern logistics systems, discussed below, is largely attributable to the widespread practice of bribery. Sequeira and Djankov (2008) find that bribe payments at ports in southern Africa, while varying by port and product, are generally high and frequent. Bribes can increase total shipping costs by up to 14 percent for a standard 20-foot container and the monthly salary of a port official by about 600 percent. Bribery thus produces a diversion effect as firms take the long way around to avoid the most corrupt port, and a congestion effect as this rerouting increases congestion and transport costs in the region. Further, though the cost of serving select corridors is the

---

Box 9.1

The Kenyan Government's Purchase of Luxury Vehicles for Official Use

A Transparency International (TI) report found that between January 2003 and September 2004, the government of Kenya spent at least $12.1 million on the purchase of luxury vehicles, largely for the personal use of senior government officials. The Ministry of Roads and Public Works ranked second among ministries in spending on luxury vehicles. The ministry spent close to $840,000 on the purchase of one Mercedes E240, four Land Cruiser Prados, two heavy-duty Land Cruisers, three Mitsubishi Pajeros V76 GLX, and a Land Rover Freelander. None of these expenditures fell within the cost estimate ceiling for government-fleet passenger vehicles stated in the Government Financial Management Act of 2004.

Source: Transparency International, Kenya and Kenya National Commission on Human Rights 2006.

same, overland transport rates for firms shipping to the most corrupt port are 71 percent higher than rates charged to the least corrupt port because of an imbalance in cargo flows.

Other important aspects of transport infrastructure and service development are similarly blighted by corruption. Major transport infrastructure projects typically require ministerial, or even government, approval, and are thus susceptible to influence at the highest level. "Gold-plated" schemes, such as newly constructed airports, are particularly remunerative to the government and thus distort investment priorities.

The creation of large parastatal transport-service providers has also been judged by international financial institutions as subject to malign influence. As a consequence, after a period of unsuccessful lending to support state-owned enterprises, the international financial institutions, led by the World Bank and the International Monetary Fund, began to emphasize funding tied to structural adjustment. Notable in this shift was an emphasis on the privatization of the inefficient parastatals to which two-thirds of the structural adjustment lending of the late 1980s was directed. Even this effort was thwarted in many cases, as strong governments took the opportunity to undertake secret, noncompetitive deals with friends and supporters (often in the military) to further bolster their own control of power. Eventually even the World Bank, which had been a strong supporter of privatization programs, concluded that economic reforms were likely to be unsuccessful without political reform to ensure good governance (World Bank 1989).

A number of the most notable transport infrastructure initiatives since the 1980s originated from this change of emphasis. Second-generation road funds were designed to depoliticize decision making on the allocation and administration of road maintenance funding (see chapter 2). The rail concessioning program in Africa, which followed from the successful experiences of Latin America, concentrated on ensuring a transparent process of competitive bidding as the basis for the transfer of management responsibility (see chapter 3). Similar emphasis on fair process is also to be found in the move toward airport service concessions (chapter 4) and landlord port structures (chapter 5). While some experience in these areas has been positive, the battle is not yet won; further suggestions for improving transport governance are contained in the final chapter of this book.

The Role of the State and the Private Sector

Many of the early postcolonial governments were heavily influenced by Marxist philosophy and saw socialism as the preferred political model. But, curiously, only President Sekou Touré in Guinea undertook the wholesale nationalization of existing enterprises. For example, in many countries, the former colonial expatriate bus companies were allowed to continue operating—but subject to new and more stringent regulations that ultimately destroyed most of them. As the state took a more directive role in the economy, whether in encouraging industrialization (as in Ghana under President Nkrumah) or developing the agricultural base (as in Tanzania under President Nyerere), the creation of new state enterprises was seen as a natural instrument of state-sponsored development. Moreover, as the "liberators" sought to increase their hold on power, the appointment of managers of newly created state enterprises became an important instrument of patronage. Business management skill was rarely a criterion for selection, and many of the new enterprises were doomed to failure from the start.

An analysis of the state's role in development has evolved over the past half century, and the debate over the state versus the market has shifted focus to the more fundamental crisis of state effectiveness. In some countries—for example, Sierra Leone—the crisis led to an outright collapse of the state. While state-dominated development has failed, it is now commonly accepted that development without an effective state is also impossible. The challenge for most developing countries is to build on the relative strengths of private markets while taking into account and improving the state's institutional capability. Building the requisite state capacity in Africa through institutional reform, sector reorganization, technical assistance, and policy advice has been supported widely by the development agencies over the last two decades.

Africa has seen some success in the reform of institutions overall. For example, most recently, Rwanda has moved from 143rd place to 67th place in the rankings developed by the Doing Business Indicators (World Bank 2010a). But the record in general is quite mixed. The most common problem lies in the poor understanding and unrealistic expectations that governments have of private sector concessionaires or franchisees. Excessively stringent fare controls, imposed without compensation, are largely responsible for the decline of formal bus companies, whether privately or publicly owned. Self-regulation by unsubsidized operators in both trucking (chapter 2) and informal minibus operations (chapter 6) has stabilized supply, but usually in the interests of operators rather than customers. Attempts to maintain loss-making rail passenger transport services through the terms of concession contracts (chapter 3) threaten to have a similarly disastrous effect in some cases. A better understanding of the impact of concession terms on the profitability of rail infrastructure will be necessary to attract significant private financing of new rail infrastructure. Ensuring that the costs and risks of rail infrastructure development are shared by the state and concessionaires may also be necessary.

Two conclusions can be made regarding this aspect of governance. On the one hand, cross-subsidization within protected state enterprises has not solved the problem of serving thin transport markets in Africa. On the other hand, the mechanisms for mobilizing private sector capital and initiative have been imperfect and require substantial improvement going forward.

The Role of Elites, or State Capture

Capture of the policy-making process is a subtle form of corruption. Private interests, working through or with politicians, influence the direction and content of policies to favor their own activities and investments. For example, the government concession of resources such as mineral deposits or hardwood forests in exchange for investment in a major transport asset, such as an airport or port, may be an effective way of mobilizing private finance. But it may also be a way for politicians to secure financial gain at the cost of public benefit.

State capture is also seen in the distribution of high-level appointments and the allocation of responsibilities and mandates related to the planning and funding of transport infrastructure, with current political party leadership often the most important agent. Other agents are the educated and wealthy who together make up the African power elite and present themselves as the legitimate representatives of the larger society. There is often substantial discretion in planning and funding decisions that are the mandate of top-level executives or elected officials. The lack of adequate consultation, and the absence of objective planning criteria or analysis, create opportunities for influencing the distribution of substantial public resources and incurring substantial social damage.

Since the 1980s, attempts have been made to separate operations from policy-making and regulatory functions in a number of transport sectors. It was expected that this decentralization of power would allow greater impartiality and transparency and, depending on legislative and contractual mandates, provide stronger incentives and controls for accountability. The resulting structures were considered less vulnerable to state capture than a vertically and functionally integrated public sector agency.

But the mixed performance of such unbundled structures in recent times offers important lessons. For an unbundled structure to perform successfully, there needs to be both adequate capacity in each of the new sector entities and effective market forces. Where the sector is small and professional capacity weak, or where corruption spans public and private sectors, unbundling may even increase the opportunities for corruption and governance failure. For example, under the early road fund models, corrupt officials were sometimes able to capture road boards that had been given additional autonomy over substantial funds. Under the more recent second-generation road funds, oversight has been made stronger and more transparent through the inclusion of road users on the boards; however, where appointments are subject to high-level political authorization, the process can still be compromised through the direct appointment of corrupt players. Similarly, corruption has flourished in semiautonomous port authorities and services where the appointments have been political or oversight weak. Thus, sector restructuring will reduce corruption only to the extent that the governance environment and institutional capacity are improved.

Absence of a Safety Culture

The African transport sector has the worst safety record of all world regions. This is most apparent in the air, road, and urban transport sectors, though there are also problems to be addressed in the port and rail sectors.

At first glance, the reasons for this poor safety record appear to differ substantially across sectors. In rail transport, the problems arise from low standards and poor maintenance of infrastructure. In road transport, there is a combination of poor infrastructure, inexperienced vehicle operation, and poor law enforcement. In air transport, the source of problems seems to be the lack of adequate training and supervision of flight crews, together with the inadequacy of the air traffic control systems. Urban transport suffers from inadequate separation of traffic from other activities as well as inexperienced operators and poor enforcement of regulations.

On further inspection, several factors can be found in common across sectors. First, when there are other serious threats to life and limb—including the perils of war, starvation, and pestilence—transport accidents become only one more source of danger and hence are not seen as a high-priority issue. Further, where governance is weak and enforcement corrupt, a comprehensive effort to come to grips with the problem is difficult in any sector. Few countries have established effective oversight; instead, there seems to be a pervasive resignation to transport accidents as an unavoidable peril of life. Ghana's National Transport Safety Council is an exception to the rule, and supports the general conclusion that it is possible to change the culture surrounding safety only by a major initiative sponsored by and supported at a high level of government.

Institutions

The institutional framework through which governance is achieved is taken to encompass the formal and informal institutions of a country—its bureaucracy, private sector, nongovernmental organizations, judiciary system, civil society, and so on—as well as its laws, the ways and means of enforcing these laws, the procedures in place for mediating conflict, and the sanctions enforced when laws are breached.

National Transport Institutions

Institutions play a central role in setting out a country's or sector's objectives and translating them into action. The existence of institutional capabilities for strategic thinking and long-term policy development and for actual implementation, evaluation, and control of policies is critical for growth. Implementing institutions determine how factors of production—land, capital, and labor—are obtained, how they are transferred, and how they are used. Legal and regulatory institutions are essential for efficient markets as they structure both the individual's and the firm's incentives for innovation, production, and exchange. Impartial contract-enforcement procedures also provide incentives for the development of complex commercial agreements. Defined and transparent procedures enhance predictability by restraining opportunism and reducing the arbitrary influence of elites. This greater predictability reduces the costs and increases the benefits of economic exchange.

Good institutions thus perform a number of functions: (i) they decrease information asymmetries as they channel information about goods, participants, and market conditions; (ii) they reduce risk as they define and enforce property rights and contracts determining who gets what and when; and (iii) they restrict the actions of politicians and interest groups by making them accountable to citizens.

National transport policy. Governments generally organize the transport sector in Africa through a ministry of transport mandated to develop and implement policy. Most African countries have a formal transport-policy statement, and many have a long-term investment program. Just over 60 percent have a long-term road investment program (SSATP 2007), and this tends to be newer than the sector policy statement. As more countries increase their dialogue with stakeholders on medium-term expenditure plans, particularly in the context of sector budget support, their investment programs are becoming more realistic. In some countries, however, such programs have little or no effect, mainly because of a lack of resources and (in some cases) lack of will to give expression to their goals and objectives.

Implementation of national transport policies is also typically weak and fragmented. In the case of roads, a ministry of construction as well as local governments may be involved in building, rehabilitation, and maintenance. Governments can choose to carry out these functions on their own or contract out some or all of these functions to the private sector. In some countries (though this is not common in Africa), there is a separate railways ministry, and it is quite common for ports and airports to be handled by a trade-related ministry.

The most common failing of this institutional structure is to leave sector strategies uncoordinated. In particular, rail administrations frequently complain that their own problems stem, at least in part, from road users being undercharged. A similar argument is often applied to the issue of road vehicle overloading. While the research is inconclusive, much evidence suggests that if road users were properly charged for the use of road infrastructure, more funds would be allocated to road maintenance, which would drastically reduce vehicle-operating costs. Similarly, a proper analysis of the costs of overloading might lead to decisions to spend more on initial road construction to handle higher axle loads, funded out of user charges, with a consequent reduction rather than increase in the costs per tonne-kilometer of road freight. The problem with this alternative approach is that the costs of upgrading the whole network could be very large, while raising axle-load limits without first having done the strengthening might cause additional counterproductive deterioration of the unimproved sections. This is an area where some further analytic work, using the data collected by RONET (Road Network Evaluation Tool) in the Africa Infrastructure Country Diagnostic (AICD) program, is called for.

Road transport. For road infrastructure, the main failure of governance has concerned the inadequacy of funding for maintenance. The reason for it was the failure of governments, and road agencies, to take into account the implications of their maintenance expenditure decisions on road transport operating costs. The institutional solution has been the establishment of second-generation road funds, with private sector representation on management boards. Road infrastructure conditions are generally better in countries with such funds than in those without them (see chapter 2). But current arrangements still do not meet the objectives of governments or the aspirations of users. Underfinancing of maintenance continues, to the tune of over $1 billion per year for the region as a whole, and users suffer losses of four or five times that amount as a consequence.

The reasons for continued underfunding of maintenance are largely institutional. Many of the funds remain based on administrative decree rather than on law. Funds are still frequently channeled through the national treasury rather than being paid directly, and fuel levies are set by ministers of finance with macro considerations in mind rather than by a road fund board operating as a commercial asset manager. There is thus much to do to improve the design of road funds and to convince governments to allow them to operate in a commercial manner. Moreover, allocation does not mean disbursement: one of the main problems in some countries has been that allocated funds were not disbursed. This applies to capital investment as well as to maintenance funding. Without continued commitment to a road fund's operation as a user-based agency to secure a more businesslike treatment of road maintenance, simply having a road fund does little to improve road conditions.

Commercialization has made even less progress at the implementation level than at the financial management level. Fewer than half of the initial 24 AICD countries have set up quasi-commercial road authorities. Even where quasi-autonomous agencies have been established, they often lack a commercial environment and continue to act like government departments without a clear understanding of their mission, functions, and work programs. Devices such as performance-based maintenance contracting, made possible by the existence of a fund not tied to the budgetary cycle, are employed less in Africa than in other regions.

Meanwhile, road transport operations are almost completely in private hands. Entry into the trucking industry, though formally requiring a license, is not very restrictive, and the industry is fragmented. But most countries in West and Central Africa have very strong truckers' unions, which, particularly at the major ports, control the allocation of traffic to members and effectively set rates. This cartelization of the road haulage industry, as well as that of urban bus systems, leads to inefficient operating practices. There is substantial evidence of severe overloading of vehicles, which not only is dangerous but also damages roads. In terms of the WGI criteria, the failures lie both in the appropriateness of the regulatory regime and in the efficacy of government implementation.

Rail transport. Nearly two-thirds of the countries in the AICD sample have concessioned their rail networks to private sector operators. In most cases this has improved their finances, but in very few has it generated any substantial amount of new investment financing. This result reflects both the fragile financial condition of many of the concessionaires and the continuing failure of many governments to recognize the realities of current conditions. In particular, the obligation to maintain some passenger services, whether formerly subsidized as a public service obligation or not, is commonly a drain on the concessions. Some concessions have already been renegotiated, and it is certain that a new form of public-private partnership, in which the government accepts more responsibility for infrastructure finance, will be necessary if further collapse is not to occur.

By far the largest rail system of all, in South Africa, remains in government hands, though in two separate organizations. The Passenger Rail Authority of South Africa is responsible for passenger services, while Transnet Freight Rail, formerly Spoornet (a subsidiary of the Transnet conglomerate, which also provides pipeline port infrastructure and port operations), is responsible for all freight services. Transnet Freight Rail benefits from having two very profitable freight lines—one carrying nearly 70 million tons of coal exports to Richards Bay and another carrying about half that quantity of ore exports to Saldanha—that cross-subsidize its general freight activities. It is also not burdened by generally less-profitable passenger services. It is doubtful whether the very opaque nature of cross-subsidization, inherent in this organizational structure, leads to the best decisions on resource allocation.

Air transport. Airports are generally operated by public corporations or by regional governments, though the larger ones increasingly concession specific services to the private sector. They are financed through charges to their customer airlines and service providers, which are ultimately passed on to individual passengers. In most cases, both types of charges are high by international standards. Some deficit financing is provided by their owners. Air traffic control and navigation services are usually the responsibility of a civil aviation authority. But revenue usually accrues to the government, with only a portion being retained by the authority.

Air transport services are provided in most countries by a mixture of national and foreign companies, some private and some public. Through their ultimate ownership of national landing rights, governments can exercise effective veto control of the services provided, but they are relatively powerless to generate service provision. Attempts to do this through state-owned national flag carriers, with an expectation that these carriers would be able to cross-subsidize loss-making routes, have not been successful. While about half of the countries in the AICD country sample have a national flag carrier, most of these are small and weak (with the exception of those of Ethiopia, Kenya, and South Africa). Most intercontinental services are provided at a lower cost by large foreign operators.

Port and maritime and inland waterway transport. In the port sector, many of the smaller countries have stuck to the traditional public service port-management model, though it is clear that the ports of the region that have moved either partly or completely to the landlord model perform better. This is not just because the concessionaires bring infrastructure finance but also because they bring best international practices to African port management.

The shipping system is rather better, largely as a consequence of the disappearance of the old measures protecting national shipping set by the former Liner Code of the United Nations Conference on Trade and Development. This liberalization has reduced costs, but the limitations of market size and port capacity—both in terms of channel depth and quay facilities—still discourage direct service on the main global itineraries.

Urban transport. Most cities have no transport authority to guide the development of their transport system; meanwhile, the few nascent authorities (for example, the Lagos Metropolitan Area Transport Authority) tend to be weak and poorly funded. The result is that there is usually little coordination between the policies governing public transport and roads and the necessary infrastructure.

Though about half a dozen countries have some form of public sector bus company, only Anbessa in Addis Ababa is the dominant operator in its area. For the rest, service is predominantly provided by informal operators subject to little or no public regulation, and hence managed by operators' associations. In many countries, there is no effective institution to exercise quality control over the operations of informal service suppliers. Such reliance on self-regulation is usually of benefit to suppliers rather than to passengers.

Regional and International Institutions
Several of the issues identified in this book have proved difficult for governments to handle because they were in one way or another supranational. Such issues include coordinating customs arrangements across land

transit corridors, choosing optimum locations for container transshipment facilities, licensing air transport services, implementing better air-safety and navigation systems, and developing international rail networks. Because many of the countries are small, or landlocked, or both, problems of governance in these areas are critical. As part of a review of transport governance in Africa, it is therefore necessary to look at the various international institutions of relevance to the sector.

Those institutions fall into four categories. Some are Pan-African and some are regional. And in each of these categories, some are multisector and some are sector or subsector specific. This brief review attempts to identify the role that each institution plays and its relation to other institutions, the factors that limit operational success, and the prospects for improved performance in the future.

Pan-African institutions. The Pan-African institutions bring together 53 African countries with a vision of regional integration across many sectors. Since the early 1960s, the United Nations Economic Commission for Africa has encouraged African states to combine their economies into subregional markets that would ultimately form one Africa-wide economic union. The Organization of African Unity, established in 1963, envisioned an African Economic Community from its outset. Progress in that direction has been slow. The Abuja Treaty of June 1991, which came into force in May 1994, provides for the African Economic Community to be set up over a 35-year period. A first step is strengthening existing regional economic communities (RECs) and creating new ones where needed. Tariffs and other barriers to regional trade would be harmonized within each REC to establish at the REC level a free trade area and a customs union. It was envisaged that eventually all RECs would be harmonized, and an African Central Bank and a single African currency established as part of an African Economic and Monetary Union. Efforts to achieve these Pan-African goals were revitalized by the Constitutive Act (2000) that created the African Union and confirmed the RECs as the building blocks of that union. The union also integrated the New Partnership for Africa's Development (in 2001), which included an Action Plan on Infrastructure (in 2002). Within this plan, the RECs have specific responsibilities for coordinating infrastructure development at a continental level and are backed by the financial and technical support of the African Development Bank. Thus the institutional framework of the key organizations is now in place for achieving the goals of the African Union.

Implementation of the wider political and economic agenda is progressing. The coverage of the RECs is comprehensive, and most have free trade areas and customs unions either fully in force or near completion, but there has been no progress yet toward their establishment at a continent-wide level. Still, the goal of free trade and deeper integration remains an overriding priority for the African Union.

The significance of Africa's efforts to increase regional integration in the transport sector is that free trade would eliminate many of the impediments to movement across national borders that have kept transport costs high. But a review of the state of regional transport integration painted a rather discouraging picture (UNECA 2004). The review shows there is a need to refocus policies, agree on and maintain appropriate networks, improve transit facilitation, increase the capacity of regional bodies, and mobilize much-needed investment. In the interim, the African Union has yet to exercise a strong influence on the transport sector, although coordination between the African Union Commission and the RECs is promoting the high-priority regional and cross-border projects of the New Partnership for Africa's Development.

Regional economic communities. The RECs are now well established. A protocol on relations between the African Union and the RECs was adopted in July 2007. Yet many operational difficulties still exist. In some instances, the activities of individual RECs overlap, as for example in the relationship between the Southern African Development Community and the Common Market for Eastern and Southern Africa (COMESA). Several countries are members of more than one REC. Cooperation at the regional level is further complicated by the fact that the RECs are not progressing toward an economic union at the same pace or by means of similar procedures and processes. It is not even clear that all existing RECs have the same long-term continental integration in view, or that there is the political will within all the RECs to submit regional concerns to the vision of the union.

The RECs have already had some significant impacts on the transport sector. The establishment of free trade areas and customs unions has facilitated coordinated development of transport corridors. Successes have rested on the mutual interest of neighboring countries, as in the Maputo corridor, where South Africa and Mozambique have coordinated plans for road and port development with border-crossing facilities.

Arguably the greatest influence of the RECs, however, has been in air transport. In particular, the West African Economic and Monetary Union and COMESA have been the focus for the liberalization of international air services provided for under the Yamoussoukro Decision of 1999. Though so far there has been little impact on the intercontinental or domestic markets, two-thirds of African air transport is now liberalized.

REC actions in other transport sectors have been less successful. There is a case for regional agreement on regional transshipment to a hub port in both East Africa and West Africa. But national competition for this trade continues, and several ports of suboptimal scale remain in business. Regional associations have little authority over member countries that fail to implement regulations agreed on at the regional level. Moreover, RECs suffer from insufficient staff, inadequate budgets, and dissimilar and often complex decision-making processes.

Pan-African Transport Associations. Pan-African transport associations exist in all subsectors. Many are offshoots of broader international federations. Rail systems are overseen by the African Union of Railways, which has produced plans for Pan-African trunk networks. But there has been little progress, largely because the individual links in such networks would require major investments by national authorities with more pressing infrastructure needs to consider. In the road sector, the initiative for the development of an African highway network has come primarily from the United Nations Economic Commission for Africa rather than from a Pan-African road infrastructure body. In air transport, the African Civil Aviation Commission (AFCAC)—a specialized institution of the African Union—has yielded the initiative to liberalize air service to the RECs. Similarly, in the troubled field of air transport safety, despite the existence of the AFCAC, most progress is likely to be achieved at a subregional level. In urban transport, the African Union of Public Transport (known also by its French acronym, UATP) has lobbied for more sustainable arrangements for urban public transport in the region. Despite their proliferation, few of these associations have great influence. Real influence comes only when an association has power to intervene, as in the case of the application of airport safety standards by the International Civil Aviation Organization.

Regional transport associations. Regional transport associations are also active in some sectors. The South African Railways Association, while initially established as a lobby group for equal treatment of road and rail infrastructure financing, has acted effectively in the planning of regional rail corridors. The parallel Association of Southern African National Road

Agencies attempts to improve coordination between countries in road development. Regional port management associations—the Port Management Association of Eastern and Southern Africa and the Port Management Association of West and Central Africa—attempt to coordinate and standardize port services in their regions, but have not been able to put together effective regional port development strategies. In air transport, the formation of the East African Civil Aviation Authority heralds an attempt to address the problem of staff recruitment, training, and retention through regional action.

Africa is thus not short of regional and international associations with a hand in transport. But few of these are secure or successful. It seems that international collaboration is most likely to occur either where an international supervisory body has some real leverage (as in air transport, with the International Air Transport Association and the International Civil Aviation Organization) or where there are a limited number of partners, all of whom can see the mutual benefits of combined action. This explains both the unsuccessful network plans and port concentration efforts and the essentially subregional nature of developments in the air transport and rail sectors. It is vital that Africa's relevant regional institutions improve their governance, coordination, and operations if transport infrastructure and services are to reduce the cost of doing business in Africa.

Capacity

The final requirement of good governance is the capacity to implement and oversee. There are two dimensions to this: financial and human resources.

Financial Capacity Constraints and Aid Dependence

The financial analysis outlined in chapter 8 showed that very few countries are in a position to maintain existing infrastructure or to undertake the investments necessary for even modest improvements. It will therefore be necessary for them either to settle for even lower standards or to continue for some years to depend on loan and grant funding to satisfy their aspirations.

Aid dependence is particularly high in countries that have suffered from economic crises, civil wars, and political instability. For example, in 2006, aid covered about 50 percent of road expenditures in Senegal and almost 90 percent in Rwanda. Many of the other low-income countries in

Africa also receive high levels of aid. Moss and Subramanian (2005) identify 16 low-income countries in Africa where inflows of official development assistance are equivalent to at least half of total government expenditure. Of the 12 poor countries where official aid accounted for 75 percent or more of government expenditure, 10 were in Africa. The concentration of aid is even higher when reviewed at the sectoral level. Such high levels of aid—when steered by clear development agendas—can be used to improve policy and planning capacity, establish strong institutions, and strengthen civil services, as the experiences of the Republic of Korea and Taiwan, China, make clear. Botswana shows that such processes can work in Africa. Yet for many African countries, while aid can release governments from binding revenue constraints and help strengthen domestic institutions in the short term, it may make it more difficult for good governance to develop if continued over the long term (Brautigam and Knack 2004).

There are several reasons for this weakness in governance. States that can raise a substantial proportion of their revenues from the donor community are less accountable to their citizens and have less incentive to invest in effective public institutions. Bureaucrats are rewarded for getting money from donors rather than focusing on core development functions and leading deep-rooted institutional changes. Most African countries have undertaken donor-recommended reforms in the transport sector, meeting requirements for continued aid. Such reforms are often legal measures that are easily accomplished on paper (such as the establishment of second-generation road funds). Regulatory reforms that require more fundamental institutional changes and challenge vested interests have been much slower to emerge.

Furthermore, large amounts of aid can also block governance improvements through institutional destruction and the creation of adverse incentives (Brautigam and Knack 2004). High numbers of donor-funded projects and reform agendas—each of which requires oversight, follow-up, and reporting—impose a high administrative burden on governments' often low and limited (absorptive) capacity. Senior officials spend much time facilitating or supporting donor supervision visits. The already low capacity is further weakened by donor competition for scarce staff skills and the provision of technical assistance that substitutes for the government's own capacity. Because governments cannot possibly manage the large number of projects donors want to fund, donors have set up units with off-budget funding. Technical-assistance staff members in these units seldom transfer skills but do the work themselves, thus limiting the government's ability to learn through doing (Gwilliam 2007). In addition to international staff, local staff are needed; in many countries, trained people are scarce. Donors consequently bid up the price of capable staff, poaching from both the private sector and the government. This poaching weakens institutions as it leaves them depleted, creates resentment, and lowers the morale of those left behind.

Within the road sector, the availability of donor funding for reconstruction leads to a neglect of routine maintenance—and so the conditions of existing roads start to deteriorate. Apart from the additional costs imposed by lack of maintenance, such funding allocation also undermines the development of maintenance planning and budgeting capacity in road agencies. Local technical capacity can also be undercut by the frequent and sustained presence of foreign technical assistance that is funded under project budgets. Far from helping develop effective state bureaucracies, certain aid practices reinforce the patrimonial elements within recipient governments. Projects provide all sorts of discretionary goods (such as vehicles, scholarships, international training, and so on) and are used to dispense favors by those in charge of the donor projects.

The conclusion seems clear. Continued aid will be necessary to help Africa raise the performance of its transport infrastructure to international standards. But increased attention needs to be given to the creation of aid mechanisms and processes that will avoid the perverse effects of aid dependence.

Human Resource Capacity

At the time when most African countries gained their independence, in the late 1950s, only 16 percent of the adult population was literate. The entire region, with a population of 200 million, had produced only 8,000 secondary school graduates, over half of whom came from Ghana and Nigeria (Ajayi, Goma, and Johnson 1996). Yet decolonized Africa entered independence with an impressive array of higher education institutions, set up by the colonial powers after World War II. The new governments saw these as primarily colonial remnants, irrelevant to their countries' immediate problems, and turned them into national universities under strict political control. How to balance the allocation of scarce resources among different types of educational institutions has been a controversial topic for years. For more than two decades, the World Bank and other international financial institutions have focused on primary over higher education; some critics see this as a major cause of the decline of Africa's higher education sector (Samoff and Carrol 2004).

By the late 1990s, the universities were in a state of crisis; it was argued that they could escape this crisis only through the restoration of academic freedom and institutional autonomy (Ajayi, Goma, and Johnson 1996). While the policies of the international financial institutions have moved back to favor higher education, and some improvements have occurred in recent years, the technical and managerial skills deficit is still substantial. More recently, attention has been focused on the inability of African countries to retain their high-skilled and tertiary-level-educated labor force (Marfouk 2008).

Inadequate skills and leadership impose a serious constraint on policy development and operational efficiency in the transport sector. They also prevent the full use of existing technical capacity. Road authorities often lack the skills needed to review the design, costs, and work schedules of various contracts. This deficit prolongs the contracting process and could even be a reason for the recent escalation in the unit costs of road construction. At the heart of the problem is the poor payment of public servants, which often encourages corruption and makes it difficult to retain critical skills in the public sector—as in air transport safety supervision.

Overcoming this problem is not easy. For example, the road construction industry in African countries has been dominated by large foreign-based firms, some of which operate in joint venture or in association with small local firms and a few medium-sized firms from the region. In recent years, the availability of staff from the downsizing of government departments' in-house "force account" units has generated a large number of small domestic firms. But such firms have a low survival rate (Brushett and Seth 2005). Few small contracting firms have been able to grow to medium size because of (i) limited access to construction equipment, (ii) limited access to capital and credit facilities, and (iii) lack of business training and technical and management skills. Concerted effort is thus still needed to develop an indigenous contracting industry.

The need has been recognized for some time. In 1993, a meeting of the Southern African Construction Industry Initiative reached consensus on the need to implement a national construction policy, to expand the role of domestic contractors and consultants through public-private partnerships, to study constraints on the development of the local road-construction industry, and to develop specific programs and measures to address these constraints. Subsequent regional initiatives through the Southern African Regional Construction Industry Council have proved ineffective relative to country-level initiatives such as the national construction councils established by Malawi and Zambia in the mid-1990s. That said, a national construction council can capture the ministry of construction, leading to fragmentation of contracts, collusion, and lower efficiency (as appears to be happening in Zambia). The usefulness of such entities thus depends on the existence of a suitable policy framework and a clear strategic vision and business plan. South Africa has the strongest program in the region, as construction industry development has become a critical element of the government's strategy for economic empowerment of the majority.

Training in road management and finance is also an urgent need for both the public and private sectors. With the assistance of the Sub-Saharan Africa Transport Policy Program, many senior executives have already received overseas training. But the involvement of regional associations is key to meeting a number of goals: strengthening program design; defining specific submarkets and developing relevant offerings to meet demand; promoting the wider involvement of training institutions, including those in Africa; and developing and disseminating materials for communicating innovations and advice (Brushett, Sampson, and Waithaka 2004).

Political instability also affects capacity—leaders whose hold on power is insecure seldom welcome the emergence of strong governing institutions that could serve as bases for the emergence of rival power. Such leaders would thus seek to undermine these institutions and put trusted individuals in control. In this context, the creation of road agencies has not always led to the expected improvement in sector performance, as agency leadership is frequently given to a politically connected candidate rather than one chosen competitively in an open international market.

Other constraints on effective governance include the absence of timely and reliable data and information. Data on the transport sector are hard to come by, and when available are inconsistent, incomplete, or plain incorrect. Traditional styles of decision making thus too often rely on considerations of status, experience, or skill and leave significant room for subjectivity and discretion. Where internal control processes are also weak, this situation can be manipulated by corrupt agents to their own advantage. Information and communications technology thus has a big role to play in managing and processing data and providing access to information, and thus in making transport operations more transparent.

The Way Forward

Poor governance is seen to be a critical factor in the inadequate performance of transport infrastructure in Africa. To a large extent, such governance reflects an economywide malaise that calls for reforms outside the transport sector. But there is also a range of sector-specific reforms in institutions, attitudes, and capacities now being implemented in some countries that may benefit the region as a whole.

Priority 1. Institutional reform

Given the failures of state enterprise and the dangers observed in relying on unregulated or self-regulated private sector supply, the suggested way forward is to concentrate on the establishment and strengthening of public sector planning and regulatory institutions to manage a predominantly private sector supply. While establishment of a general rule of law and some economy-wide antimonopoly powers may contribute to improved transport sector performance, most of these institutions will need to be sector specific. The most promising sources of sector improvements include the following:

- Further strengthening of road fund institutions and procedures
- Creation of commercially based highway implementation agencies
- Creation of metropolitan transport authorities
- Development of effective quality control procedures for trucking and urban bus systems
- Extension of air license liberalization to domestic markets
- Establishment of a direct financing mechanism for air traffic control services
- Conversion of service ports into landlord ports
- Creation of national transport safety councils.

Priority 2. Changing attitudes

Institutions are the organizational structures within which policy making and management take place. But if the prevailing attitudes of institutional managers and other actors are inappropriate, even the best-structured institutions can fail. The most important issue to address is the reduction of discretion in various administrative procedures as a defense against corruption. The following appear to be the most significant changes in relevant attitudes or cultures suggested to improve sector performance:

- Regular preparation and dissemination of reports (such as accounting and financial reports, asset inventories, annual reports) to aid institutional integrity

- Streamlining of customs procedures to reduce discretion in administration
- Development of formula-based procedures for the allocation of investment and maintenance funds
- Strengthening of concession award procedures
- Development of new "negative concession" structures to facilitate private sector supply of loss-making services deemed socially necessary
- Strengthening of supervision and monitoring mechanisms within the ministry of finance and parliament to enhance sector oversight.

Priority 3. Improving implementation capacity

The capacity to implement must also be improved. This priority fundamentally requires adequate human resource capability to oversee how resources are allocated and employed. The following appear to be the most critical improvements required:

- Reduced dependence on offline implementation units for aid projects
- Development of national transport sector training programs
- Establishment of national construction industry councils as nonexecutive agencies within a broader strategy for industry development
- Review of public sector staff recruitment and remuneration arrangements to improve effectiveness and reduce staff turnover.

Priority 4. Improving donor coordination

Donor agencies are closely involved with governments in many countries in supporting capacity building and in preparing and approving investment projects and programs. It is important that countries get the most that they can out of this involvement. The following steps are therefore suggested:

- Governments should, alongside donors, regularly review the effectiveness of their capacity building.
- Governments should encourage donors to accept common reporting systems, tender appraisal systems, and so on.

Notes

1. This chapter benefited from input by Kavita Sethi and Bruce Thompson.
2. The indicators have not been without criticism. Arndt and Oman (2006) point out the problems of correlated errors, sample biases, and a lack of

transparency, and they question the comparability of the indicators over time and across countries. While these indexes purportedly measure separate criteria, it has been argued that in practice they all tend to reflect a particular perception of good governance (Langbein and Knack 2008). Their "construct validity"—whether they actually measure what they purport to measure—has also been questioned (Thomas 2010). Iqbal and Shah (2008) highlight some anomalous conclusions and argue that the indicators primarily capture Western business perspectives on governance processes and completely neglect citizens' evaluations, and that they should not be used in making cross-country comparisons. For these reasons, the discussion here focuses on the indicators' general pattern rather than on specific values.

References

Ajayi, J. F. A., L. K. H. Goma, and G. A. Johnson. 1996. *The African Experience with Higher Education.* London: James Currey.

Arndt, C., and C. Oman. 2006. *Uses and Abuses of Governance Indicators.* Paris: Organisation for Economic Co-operation and Development.

Brautigam, D. A., and S. Knack. 2004. "Foreign Aid, Institutions, and Governance in Sub-Saharan Africa." *Economic Development and Cultural Change* 52 (2): 255–86.

Brushett, S., L. Sampson, and S. Waithaka. 2004. "Building Capacity in Management and Financing in the Road Sector: Meeting the Challenge." Sub-Saharan Africa Transport Policy Program Technical Note 37, World Bank, Washington, DC.

Brushett, S., and S. Seth. 2005. "Construction Industry Development and the Road Sector Effectiveness of National Construction Councils." Sub-Saharan Africa Transport Policy Program Technical Note 38, World Bank, Washington, DC.

Burnside, C., and D. Dollar. 1997. "Aid, Policies, and Growth." Policy Research Working Paper 569252, World Bank, Washington, DC.

Gwilliam, K. M. 2007. "Paving the Road for Better Capacity: Review of Capacity Development in the Lao PDR Transport Sector." World Bank, Vientiane, Lao People's Democratic Republic.

Iqbal, K., and A. Shah. 2008. "How Do Worldwide Governance Indicators Measure Up?" Paper presented at a World Bank seminar, Washington, DC, March 26.

Kaufmann, D., A. Kraay, and M. Mastruzzi. 2010. "The Worldwide Governance Indicators: Methodology and Analytical Issues." Policy Research Working Paper 5430, World Bank, Washington, DC.

Langbein, L., and S. Knack. 2008. "The Worldwide Governance Indicators and Tautology: Causally Related Separable Concepts, Indicators of a Common Cause, or Both?" Policy Research Working Paper Series 4669, World Bank, Washington, DC.

Marfouk, L. 2008. "The African Brain Drain: Scope and Determinants." Working Paper DULBEA 08-07RS, Department of Applied Economics, Free University of Brussels.

Meredith, M. 2005. *The State of Africa: A History of Fifty Years of Independence.* London: Free Press.

Moss, T., and A. Subramanian. 2005. "After the Big Push? Fiscal and Institutional Implications of Large Aid Increases." Working Paper 71, Center for Global Development, Washington, DC.

Nyerere, J. 1998. "Good Governance for Africa." *Southern African Political and Economic Monthly.* April. http://www.hartford-hwp.com/archives/30/083.html.

Osborne, E. 2004. "Measuring Bad Governance." *Cato Journal* 23 (3): 403–22.

Samoff, J., and B. Carrol. 2004. "Conditions, Coalitions, and Influence: The World Bank and Higher Education in Africa." Paper presented at the Annual Conference of the Comparative and International Education Society, Salt Lake City, March 8–12.

Sequeira, S., and S. Djankov. 2008. "On the Waterfront: An Empirical Study of Corruption in Ports." Unpublished paper, Harvard University, Cambridge, MA.

SSATP (Sub-Saharan Africa Transport Policy Program). 2007. "RMI Matrix for September 2007." World Bank, Washington, DC.

Thomas, M. A. 2010. "What Do the Worldwide Governance Indicators Measure?" *European Journal of Development Research* 22: 31–54.

Transparency International. 2009. *Corruption Perceptions Index.* Berlin: Transparency International.

Transparency International, Kenya and Kenya National Commission on Human Rights. 2006. "Living Large: Counting the Cost of Official Extravagance in Kenya." Transparency International, Nairobi, Kenya.

UNECA (United Nations Economic Commission for Africa). 2004. *Accelerating Regional Integration in Africa.* New York: UNECA.

World Bank. 1989. *Sub-Saharan Africa: From Crisis to Self-Sustainable Growth.* Washington, DC: World Bank.

———. 2010a. *Doing Business 2010.* Washington, DC: World Bank.

———. 2010b. *World Governance Indicators.* Washington, DC: World Bank.

CHAPTER 10

Conclusion: An Agenda for Action

Africa has been shown to have less transport infrastructure per square kilometer than any other world region. Moreover, much of the infrastructure that it does have was designed to low standards (as in the case of railways) or is poorly equipped (ports and air traffic control). Yet because national incomes are so low, transport infrastructure expenditures constitute a relatively high proportion of gross domestic product (GDP) for many countries. As a consequence, maintenance is often underfunded and the condition of infrastructure remains poorer than that in other regions.

Africa needs better transport infrastructure, which will inevitably require more spending. Yet inadequate infrastructure is only one factor behind the poor performance of the transport sector. As the chapters in this book have shown, the quality of the service that transport infrastructure provides is critically dependent on the efficiency with which the infrastructure is maintained, managed, and used. Inefficient use of existing infrastructure raises expenditure needs and fiscal demands, while institutional and policy deficiencies inhibit the effectiveness of new investment.

Improving transport quality thus depends not only on the level of expenditure but also on the appropriateness of the policies adopted and the quality of sector governance. This final chapter summarizes the main conclusions of the book on the issues relevant to policy, governance, and expenditure, with the first two of these areas presented as necessary conditions for properly identifying where infrastructure improvement is needed and for properly carrying out that improvement.

Critical Transport Policy Issues

This section sets the stage for a discussion of investment and fiscal needs by summarizing policy issues relevant to the more efficient use of transport infrastructure and services in the region.

Some Multimodal Issues

Some issues are multimodal because they apply either to all transport subsectors or to the relationships among sectors. Four such generic issues are discussed in the succeeding sections.

Mobilizing competition effectively. There is ample evidence, particularly in the road and air transport sectors, that competition among modes of transport improves service quality and reduces costs. Such competition may also improve infrastructure efficiency through the replacement of one mode by another. For example, road improvement in Mauritania has effectively eliminated the domestic air transport sector, while all African railways have found it difficult to retain passenger traffic on an economical basis when traveling by road is cheaper.

The relationships among modes are rarely simple. Where modes compete, traffic should in theory be allocated among them on the basis of their relative price, in turn reflecting their relative costs. But in practice this is rarely the case. Where traffic is heavily imbalanced, as in international trade, and cost structures differ across modes, both commercial pressure and economic efficiency may call for widely varying price-to-cost ratios. Taken to the extreme, however, such price discrimination may become predatory, giving one mode an advantage that is not justifiable from the point of view of the economy as a whole. Unfortunately, such predatory pricing is often difficult to distinguish from economically sensible price differentiation. This is complicated by the fact that modes may complement one another for some types of traffic while competing for others.

Despite these conceptual problems, it is important to pay attention to competitive conditions. Roads, as public goods, are typically provided to users at costs that do not even cover maintenance, while privately provided rail service is expected fully to cover its costs, including those of tracks. The viability of privately concessioned railways can be undermined by policies that undercharge road users and do not enforce truck load limits. National transport strategies that cover infrastructure costs of road and rail by charging users adequately for both would reduce states' budgetary burden while improving road conditions.

The net effect of modal competition on the distribution of traffic across modes is often difficult to predict because of the importance of security, reliability, and other noncost items in determining transport choices. For example, a comparison of road tariffs and tariffs on five concessioned railways showed road tariffs exceeding rail tariffs by between 44 and 213 percent (Bullock 2009). Given the cartelization and high profit margins of road haulage, increasing road user charges might reduce truckers' profit margins without diverting any traffic from truck to rail. But it would nevertheless improve the sustainability of rail systems by increasing their pricing power in market segments where the railways have a real comparative advantage. By the same token, substantial benefits could likely be obtained by promoting competition within the road haulage sector.

Revisiting attitudes toward private supply and profit. Private participation in supply is central to competition and can increase the efficiency of operations and the mobilization of private capital. But to tap the potential of private participation, governments need to understand the commercial realities that motivate private business. In the interest of consumers, monopolistic behavior should be constrained. But private firms will not participate if governments deny them a reasonable return on their investment—making a profit is not a crime; rather, it is a necessity for doing business and a proper incentive to allocate resources efficiently.

Plans to attract private sector finance and management should include an explicit determination of the objectives of private participation and the reasons for seeking it. Policy makers should recognize that private participation can bring efficiency benefits not only to transport modes with marginal commercial viability but also to those that are highly profitable (ports) or deemed desirable but highly unprofitable (some railway concessions). To attract private capital, policy makers should consider a wider range of scenarios for participation, including negative concessions and affermage arrangements. A national agency focused on privatization and its promotion could help in producing such policies and outlining areas of participation.

Public monopoly powers are exploited to generate government revenues from ports, airports, and air transport services in several countries. But it can be damaging for the government to exploit monopoly powers to generate excess revenues, even to support other unprofitable services. Internal cross-subsidies usually have adverse impacts. For example, South Africa's Transnet Freight Rail is organized to draw cross-subsidies for loss-making freight and passenger services both from the profitable ore and coal services and, through the Transnet group, from ports and pipelines. But the rail's core services and infrastructure have been weakened as a result. Locomotives are on average 25 years old and freight wagons are 25 to 30 years old—ages nearly double those recommended by international best practice. There is a capacity gap in the ore services, and the safety record of Transnet Freight Rail is low and appears to be deteriorating. The port system is also being denied investment. Despite the high technical competence of the South African system, the recent National Freight Logistics Study concluded, "restoring rail reliability is fundamental and is the single most important challenge facing the freight logistics sector in South Africa" (South African Department of Transport 2007).

Careful consideration thus needs to be given to establishing appropriate oversight and regulatory institutions. The creation and exploitation of monopoly powers by cartelization, particularly in the trucking sector, needs to be continually reviewed, with assessments covering both industrial structure and commercial behavior. Given the scope of this task, many countries could develop a small but skilled regulatory unit to advise governments, as well as regulators specific to particular modes.

One issue related to foreign private sector involvement in supply merits consideration. Concerns about reliance on foreign control of services critical to national security have been widely used as an argument for maintaining national air transport and shipping fleets and for limiting foreign capital in national infrastructure finance. In practice, uneconomical small airlines and shipping fleets protected by cargo reservations tend to push up costs and drain national resources (to the detriment of national security). And resistance to involving the global container-port terminal operators denies countries the efficiency and investment that such participation could bring.

Countries thus need mechanisms to reconcile private (and foreign) financing of transport infrastructure with economic, social, and national strategic objectives. Developing a range of contract designs appropriate to a range of objectives is an important part of this challenge.

Developing modern logistics systems. Logistics systems in Africa are viewed as poor by business users. In 2007, the Logistics Performance Index showed only South Africa in the top quartile of countries and only 5 of the 39 African countries in the top half; the situation in 2010 is virtually unchanged (World Bank 2007, 2010).[1] Africa would be the worst-performing region in the world if Afghanistan did not drag down South Asia's unweighted average of only six countries. The two dimensions in which Africa scores the lowest are infrastructure and customs.

Physical infrastructure needs are discussed below. As far as customs are concerned, the problem is largely an issue of corruption. In the Corruption Perceptions Index (Transparency International 2009), only Botswana appears in the top quartile of countries, while 17 African countries appear in the bottom quartile (more than one-third of the countries in that quartile). These statistics highlight the need to come to terms with the problems at border customs posts in the region. A shift toward regional free trade would help. But even without that, the successes achieved in southeast Europe—both through a comprehensive attack on the problems involving physical infrastructure, staffing, administrative procedures, and so on, and through regionwide agreements among countries—show that the problems are not insuperable.

Other factors in addition to infrastructure erode logistics system quality. Restrictions on the freedom to select haulers undermine the ability of third-party logistics service suppliers to operate a one-stop shop for international freight movements, of crucial importance to modern logistics systems. Weakness in information technology systems also makes monitoring and control of freight movements less effective. The lack of these supporting services severely impedes the growth of a third-party logistics sector, which could contribute to the development of global manufacturing and distribution chains.

Taking transport safety seriously. Inadequate safety provision is a problem across all modes, and the region has arguably the worst safety record in the world in the road, rail, and air transport sectors. The general lack of a culture of transport safety can be attributed to two factors common to all modes. First, necessary safety regulatory institutions are weak or nonexistent. Second, in the absence of adequate supervision, operator behavior is frequently dangerous. Other causes differ somewhat by mode. Rail accidents frequently result from the poor state of infrastructure. Road accidents are more typically associated with the poor separation of traffic movement from roadside activity and poor driving behavior compounded by lax enforcement. Air transport accidents appear to be associated more with poor crew training and lax supervision than with a lack of navigation aids or new aircraft. Whatever the sector, however, there is evidence to indicate that the problems are not insuperable if they are given adequate attention and priority.

The various sectorwide policy requirements, and the agenda for action that they suggest, are summarized in table 10.1.

Mode-Specific Policy Issues
In addition to the common issues discussed above, the various transport modes suffer from a range of modally specific problems.

Roads and road transport. The critical policy issues surrounding roads and the road transport sector concern financing maintenance, prioritizing

Table 10.1   Sectorwide Policy Requirements: An Action Program

Topic	Issue	Institutional requirement	Policy requirement
Competitive conditions	Unfair competition among modes	Give a single agency (a single ministry of transport or national transport council) responsibility for issues of modal coordination.	Subject issues of modal interaction to explicit policy review.
Attitudes toward private sector	Unrealistic expectations of private sector behavior	Establish competitively tendered concessions, and treat all obligations and payments as enforceable contractual conditions.	Focus government supervision on monitoring and enforcing contracts rather than on day-to-day intervention.
Logistics quality	Poor logistics systems development	Create a national logistics council to advise on trade requirements.	Reform customs administration. Liberalize entry to road haulage markets. Liberalize telecommunications markets.
Transport safety	Absence of a general safety culture	Create a national transport safety council and subsector-specific agencies.	Make safety an issue at the highest level. Develop subsector safety programs.

Source: Authors.

expenditures, increasing the efficiency of roadwork implementation, improving safety, and regulating haulage operations.

Road maintenance financing has been greatly improved in many countries by the establishment of road funds. But as shown in chapters 2 and 8, many countries still do not provide sufficient funding to maintain the road system in its current state of repair, much less to improve it and eliminate backlogs. While the road fund board may sometimes underestimate how much finance is needed, it is more likely that the board is constrained by the finance ministry, either formally or informally, to set the fuel levy at a level insufficient to meet maintenance needs.

Prioritizing road expenditures involves maintenance as well as investment decisions, and depends on complex judgments. In countries where the value of road assets is high in relation to GDP (as in Malawi and Namibia, discussed in chapter 2), the current road network may simply be too extensive to maintain. In these circumstances, rather than letting the whole network deteriorate, it may be better to deliberately abandon part of the network (perhaps encouraging communities to maintain it) to save the rest. Even in cases where such a drastic step is not necessary, it is sensible to relate the character and condition of the roads to traffic levels. Chapter 2 has shown that in most countries the most highly trafficked roads are designed to higher standards and maintained in better condition than the more lightly used roads. But the Road Network Evaluation Tool (RONET) analyses also show some evidence of overengineering on the main road networks and underengineering on the rural networks, suggesting the need for a change in priorities. Where to devote resources depends on the relative weights given to ensuring rural accessibility versus maximizing the short-term economic benefit of the (interurban) road system.

Roadwork implementation has been shown to be more efficient when done by a private sector contractor than when countries rely on force accounts. In turn, results-based maintenance contracts have been shown to be an effective way of mobilizing the private sector. There is now a move in some countries toward road asset management contracts that are even more comprehensive. Such countries must be able to enter into long-term contracts (facilitated by a road fund) and be unconstrained by a commitment to force accounts (facilitated by a quasi-autonomous roads agency). The establishment of such institutional arrangements is advisable.

Road safety, though a perennial problem, has only recently been recognized at the highest level of intergovernmental deliberations. At the 2007 Pan-African Road Safety Conference, participants resolved to set road safety as a national health and transport priority and elaborated a wide range of possible policy instruments to promote safety. But for these to be put into effect, most governments still need to establish an appropriate institutional framework (as attempted in Ghana) and to generate strong local impetus for a comprehensive road safety program (as attempted in KwaZulu-Natal, South Africa).

Cartelization and protection in the road freight sector have been shown to increase profits and prices, particularly in Central and West Africa. Governments condone, indeed encourage, such behavior by collaborating with truckers' associations in the administered, noncompetitive allocation of transit freight from ports, on the pretense that this is necessary to ensure a fair allocation of traffic between "home" and foreign carriers. These problems would be solved if entry into the industry were restricted only by quality licensing, and cartelization were subject to national antimonopoly legislation.

The main issues requiring action in the roads and road transport sector are summarized in table 10.2.

Table 10.2   Roads and Road Transport: An Action Program

Topic	Issue	Institutional requirement	Policy requirement
Maintenance finance	Insufficient fuel levy	Ensure a private sector majority on road boards.	Have road boards produce annual estimate of finance requirement.
Prioritization of road expenditures	Over- or underengineering	Establish a national "project preparation pool" subject to a common appraisal process.	Have road boards develop explicit policy on fund allocation.
Road work implementation	High cost Poor quality	Establish quasi-independent road agency. Abolish force accounts.	Increase private contracting. Move to performance-based maintenance contracting.
Road safety	Very high accident rates	Establish a national road safety council (NRSC).	Have NRSC launch intensive road-safety campaign.
Road freight transport regulation	Very high road freight rates	Restrict entry only by quality licensing. Make road haulage subject to competition law.	Abandon administered allocation of transit import traffics.

Source: Authors.

Rail transport. Most African railways were developed by colonial administrations to assist in the exploitation and export of agricultural and mineral resources. The most viable lines are still those specializing in the export of minerals from South Africa, Gabon, and to a lesser extent Zambia. With the exception of the South African (and more recently the Nigerian) urban commuter services, railways play only a small role in the passenger transport market. Given their limited social role, they have been seen as particularly suitable for concessioning to the private sector. Relevant policy issues mainly concern the suitability of the forms of concession adopted.

Public service obligations are frequently imposed on railways, whether they are state owned or concessioned to the private sector. In some cases, such obligations are imposed even though there are cheaper road services available. Some countries have agreed to pay rail operators to compensate for the imposition. But as discussed in chapter 3, these payments are rarely made in an adequate and timely manner. The policy response to this situation needs to involve not only a formal analysis of whether public rail service is a necessity but also a legal obligation for the state to compensate the private sector on a contractually predetermined basis.

Government capital contributions to concessions may be a way forward. As argued earlier, low-interest loans from international financial institutions to railway concessionaires have tended to disguise the real financial burdens of system maintenance in the long term. Chapter 3 showed that only lines with a density of 2 to 3 million net tonnes or more can fund full rehabilitation from a purely commercial viewpoint (including the costs of capital). But if governments were to bear the costs of capital, that break-even traffic volume would fall to below 1 million net tonnes per year. Hence, if governments wish to retain a public railway service, they will need to find some way of sharing the capital cost burden and set up contractual terms different from those employed to date.

Competition from the road sector has a significant effect on rail concession finances. Two linked elements of that competition are of particular concern. First, failure to enforce axle-load limits enables truck rates to compete "unfairly" with the railways. Second, overloading trucks increases road wear and maintenance costs. In many countries, the heavy trucks that cause such damage are not appropriately charged for it.

The main issues requiring action in the rail transport sector are summarized in table 10.3.

Table 10.3   Rail Transport: An Action Program

Topic	Issue	Institutional requirement	Policy requirement
Public service obligations	Unrealistic expectations of concessionaires' ability to cross-subsidize	Include any public service obligations in contracts, with compensation arrangements clearly specified.	Pay contract obligations on time.
Investment finance	Inadequate provision for investment	Develop "negative" concession or affermage models, with government participation in investment finance.	Clearly specify long-term investment requirements in invitations to tender.
Competitive environment	Unequal treatment of track costs for road and rail modes	Ensure that institutions or procedures for examining the consistency of modal policies exist at the central government level.	Have governments participate in finance of infrastructure investment and/or increase charges for road use.

Source: Authors.

Airports and air transport. Air transport is less well developed in Africa than in other regions and has typically been provided primarily by the flag carriers of the former colonial powers. Though new carriers are entering the market, and three major African airlines have a substantial share of it, some serious problems remain. The critical issues for the air transport sector relate to airport investment strategy, air traffic control (ATC), air service provision, and air transport safety.

Airport investment strategy requires careful reconsideration. Minor investments in taxiways and strategic rescheduling of flights to spread airport movements over a broader time period can in many cases overcome what are perceived as runway capacity limits. Such actions would free up resources for the improvement of landside facilities (which would also relieve the pressure at peak periods). If airlines were charged a modest premium for landing at peak periods, they would be more likely to alter their schedules.

Air traffic control services were shown in chapter 4 to be seriously deficient. This is because civil aviation authorities (CAAs) are expected to support themselves through fees, yet in many cases a percentage of these fees goes to the treasury. Not only are such authorities short of cash, but they find it very difficult to retain highly trained staff on public sector salaries. There are three possible steps toward solving this problem. First, it is likely that costs could be significantly reduced by replacing radar installations with more advanced, satellite-based technologies—careful attention needs to be given to what would be gained and lost by such a shift. Second, the development of commercial regional pooling arrangements for air traffic control might both reduce costs and better retain staff. And third, the CAAs could be guaranteed a more secure, predetermined share of revenue from air traffic control.

Air transport service regulation also needs reform. National flag carriers, historically protected by government negotiations of bilateral landing rights in the international and intercontinental markets, are no longer able to cross-subsidize domestic markets and should not be protected per se. Indeed, many of these carriers have failed, and air connectivity has suffered as a result. A new strategy needs to be based on extending the liberalization that has already occurred in the international market in Africa to all other sectors, together with developing hub-and-spoke networks based on major regional (not just national) airports. Employment of small turboprop aircraft could improve the economic viability of small airlines and thin routes, but only within an appropriate economic context.

Air transport in Africa has a very poor safety record, mostly confined to indigenous African air operators. The record of the major international operators is not significantly worse in Africa than elsewhere. While the average age of domestic operators' fleets is high compared with fleets in other regions, and there is a high proportion of old Eastern-bloc aircraft, the real source of the problem, according to a number of independent sources, is inadequate training and supervision. Skilled staff are difficult to hire and retain, and the supervision of both flight crew and maintenance staff appears to be below international standards. To some extent, these problems may be helped by greater liberalization, which would generate a more economically viable sector. But liberalization needs to be accompanied by much stricter enforcement of safety standards. To achieve this, civil aviation authorities will need to be strengthened and critical staff will need to be paid more.

The main issues requiring action in the air transport sector are summarized in table 10.4.

Ports and maritime transport. There is some disagreement over the status of current port capacity, with Drewry Shipping Consultants (2009) in

Table 10.4   Airports and Air Transport: An Action Program

Topic	Issue	Institutional requirement	Policy requirement
Airport investment strategy	Selection of investment program	Strengthen economic skills of CAAs.	Look for improvements in existing airports rather than entirely new locations.
ATC and navigation services	Adequacy of payments	Include provision for payments for ATC and air navigation services (ANS) in the CAA law.	Recognize need for a secure funding source for ATC and ANS.
Air transport service regulation	Failure of national flag carriers Loss of service on less profitable routes Poor network of regional services	Close small loss-making national flag carriers.	Liberalize entry to domestic markets. Subsidize unprofitable routes through competitive tenders. Encourage hub-and-spoke services through major regional airports.
Air transport safety	Poor safety record of some indigenous African carriers	Strengthen CAAs.	Increase commitment to enforcement of safety legislation.

Source: Authors.

particular arguing that quay capacity is for the most part adequate. The question turns on the efficiency with which goods are handled on quay. African ports in general have handling rates—both of containers and of dry bulk traffic—considerably below world standards. Investment in quay space and improvement in handling efficiency are not mutually exclusive, but one does not necessarily follow on the other. The question is how to get the best combination.

Improved port management can be obtained in many ports by moving from the traditional public service port model to the landlord model. The concessioning of facilities, in particular container terminals, has been shown in chapter 5 to be a common source of improvement. But concessioning is not always easy, and there have been several cases of litigation relating to poor concessioning procedures. Governments should therefore ensure that these procedures are clearly defined and transparent. Extended use of the major international container-terminal management companies or port managers is recommended. The development of port community systems has been shown to lead to better understanding, communication, and data exchange, and it is also important for security.[2] Customs and immigration reform can often contribute to the effective capacity of ports by reducing the standing time of goods in port and thus increasing warehouse or terminal standing-area throughputs.

Coordination with land transport is also poor in many ports. This is in part because the responsibility for coordination does not fall to any single party. Concessioning ports and railways to the same agency may help with coordination but risks creating excessive monopoly power.

The main issues requiring action in the ports and maritime transport sector are summarized in table 10.5.

Urban transport. Urban transport Africa is frequently chaotic. The urban road system suffers from inadequate funding (it usually gets only a small share of national road fund revenues), poor traffic discipline, high accident levels, and public transport provided primarily by an informal sector subject only to self-regulation, with adverse effects on users. Above all, it

Table 10.5   Ports and Maritime Transport: An Action Program

Topic	Issue	Institutional requirement	Policy requirement
Port management	Poor port performance	Engage in port reform and adopt the landlord port management model. Concession major terminals.	Develop new, transparent concessioning procedures.
Customs administration	High costs and long delays in customs clearance	Adopt customs systems and procedures of the World Customs Organization and United Nations Conference on Trade and Development.	Increase use of information technology and electronic data processing to reduce corruption.
Coordination with inland transport	No clear location of responsibility for modal coordination (access roads and so on)	Establish a port community system.	Encourage effective coordination through appropriate regulatory and pricing measures.

Source: Authors.

lacks any strategic vision or planning framework and requires a number of policy initiatives.

Low traffic speed and high accident rates have a number of roots. Road space is invaded by traders and pedestrians. Traffic composition tends to be very mixed. And there is usually very little attention given to enforcement of traffic discipline. Overcoming these problems requires appropriate institutions—particularly a strong strategic authority and a technically competent traffic management unit. But it also requires the involvement of the police and a wholehearted commitment to enforcement of traffic rules.

The regulation of passenger transport fares has in many countries had the perverse effects of bankrupting the large bus companies that have provided services in the past and of giving rise to informal sector operations that often charge higher rates. Attempts to rescue or restore the formal sector operators have usually failed because governments lack the funds to support them. What is needed instead is a competitive process for procuring bus services, one that makes the costs transparent from the outset. In most countries, this would require substantial institutional and policy reform.

Self-regulation of minibus transport is usually motivated by the desire to avoid predatory on-the-road behavior, such as racing and blocking, and to ensure an equitable distribution of income among members of operators' associations. But while it can reduce dangerous driving behavior, it usually does so through the imposition of tour de role dispatching procedures, which reduce vehicle utilization and hence increase fares. The introduction of tendering processes to eliminate both predatory road behavior and inefficient dispatching procedures could solve this problem.

The main issues requiring action in the urban transport sector are summarized in table 10.6.

Improving Governance

Many of the inefficiencies in transport infrastructure arise not because of failures to recognize appropriate policies but because of failures to implement them—in other words, failures of governance. Sometimes these failures occur because there is no appropriate instrument to implement policy (institutional failure) and sometimes because government serves its own narrow interests rather than the interests of the governed.

Table 10.6   Urban Transport: An Action Program

Topic	Issue	Institutional requirement	Policy requirement
Road maintenance	Increased operating costs and greater risk of accidents arising from badly maintained roads	Create a strong municipal or metropolitan transport agency.	Allocate adequate funding either from road fund allocations or from local or national tax sources.
Bus fare regulation	Decline of many companies because of unrealistically low fares	Establish an urban public transport authority to plan and procure services.	Use competitive tendering of services along with any fare controls.
Minibus service regulation	Undesirable operating practices of private associations	Establish a metropolitan or municipal regulator to oversee minibus operations.	Monitor behavior and enforce regulation effectively.
Road traffic management	High congestion and road accident levels	Establish a traffic management unit within the municipal or metropolitan transport agency.	Deal with invasion of road space and enforce traffic rules.

Source: Authors.

Institutional Weaknesses

Four main institutional weaknesses can be identified: the absence of any sectorwide strategic planning body, ineffective regulation of transport service providers, excessive aid dependency, and inadequate implementation capacity.

The strategic planning void. The inconsistency among subsector policies— particularly between road and rail infrastructure charging policies—has been noted earlier. The problem is that different modes are often handled by separate government ministries or by departments within a single ministry that are not well coordinated. One solution would be to establish either a national transport council (to coordinate the actions of several ministries) or a national transport policy committee (to overcome excessive departmental autonomy and encourage coordination within a single central ministry). In either case, the agency must be established at a high level.

The problem is particularly severe in urban areas, where the modes are at their most interdependent. Strategic metropolitan transport authorities are very rare, and where they do exist they may be dependent on other authorities for implementation. Although such agencies have been established in recent years in Dakar, Lagos, and other cities, they are typically still weak in both power and competence. The policy challenge is to establish a metropolitan authority with sufficient funds to perform its planning role effectively and sufficient leverage over the implementing authorities to ensure that their actions are in line with the metropolitan strategy.

Ineffective regulation. Effective regulation entails more than requiring that private service suppliers assume and carry out social obligations; regulators must devise mechanisms for getting the most out of private operators—within the constraints of resource availability. To do so requires understanding how commercial transport suppliers think and how to design regulatory systems that reconcile the search for profit with the achievement of socially desirable service structures. Competitively tendering franchises or concessions is a suitable way to achieve that reconciliation.

Faced by severe budget constraints, many African governments have turned to the private sector for both capital finance and management skills. This shift has brought its own problems. Where subsector control is highly centralized, as is common for railways, there is danger of developing a monopoly. Where the market structure is naturally fragmented, as in the trucking or urban minibus systems, there is danger of promoting predatory competitive practices. In both cases, the temptation is to arbitrarily impose fare or service requirements on private companies without regard to the realities of private business finance. Such heavy-handed regulation has often had very damaging effects on the quantity of service provided.

Aid dependence. The analysis of the transport sector's revenue sources provided in chapter 8 showed a high level of aid dependence in several countries. In the long term, the reduction of aid dependence will be both a consequence and a symbol of the growth of national economies and the maturity of transport sector policies. In the interim, aid dependence can have a number of adverse effects, some of which were set out in chapter 9. The tendency of international financial institutions to finance rehabilitation but not routine or periodic maintenance amounts to a disincentive to maintain. Cheap capital lent to finance rail concessions can disguise the long-term implications of concession finance. And in mounting large rehabilitation programs, both foreign technical assistance and highly skilled indigenous workers are too frequently absorbed in special project implementation units, a result that limits the dissemination of vital skills.

All of these tendencies need to be resisted as part of a policy to avoid the possible adverse consequences of aid dependence. There are signs of change. The World Bank's development policy loans, which are attached to the development of policy-based programs rather than specific investments, have the potential to support maintenance-oriented reforms.[3] Similarly, the European Union is experimenting with sector budget support in the road sector in Ethiopia, Madagascar, and Tanzania in which finance covers all activities, including maintenance, within a medium-term expenditure framework. In general, governments and aid agencies need to work together to ensure that aid does not inhibit the development of good, sustainable national policies and practices.

Implementation capacity. Finally, improving capacity at all levels will require a stronger formal education system and targeted improvements in both training and retraining sector workers with key technical and managerial skills. In several areas, such as air traffic safety inspections, retaining highly skilled labor will depend on making public sector salaries comparable to those in the private sector.

The main issues requiring action to overcome institutional weaknesses are summarized in table 10.7.

Behavioral Failures

In many cases, it is not the laws or even the institutions themselves that are inherently defective but the way in which the laws are interpreted and the institutions managed. A number of particularly egregious examples of behavioral failure exist in the transport sector.

Corruption. Corruption is rife. At the operational level, poorly paid officials create artificial delays in customs administration to extract bribes from operators for speedier service. This practice increases transport costs and adversely affects competitiveness. But it is very difficult to contain this petty corruption when much more elaborate corrupt practices remain at the higher levels of government. Decades of dictatorial rule

Table 10.7   Overcoming Institutional Weaknesses: An Action Program

Topic	Issue	Institutional requirement	Policy requirement
Strategic planning	Absence of mechanisms for the coordination of mode-specific policies at urban and national levels	Create a committee or council for coordinating central transport policy. Create a metropolitan transport agency.	Commit adequate resources and powers for the strategic planning body at the national or metropolitan level.
Regulation	Perverse effects of ill-informed or heavy-handed economic regulation	Separate regulatory and service supply functions. Establish professionally staffed procurement and regulatory agencies.	Set general government objectives and avoid political intervention by government in day-to-day administration.
Aid dependence	Institutionalization of perverse incentives	Establish strong institutions for sector regulation and administration.	Establish formal resource allocation procedures. Incorporate official development assistance in line-agency administration rather than in institutionally separate project management units (PMUs).
Implementation capacity	Weak skills and education Loss of skilled staff Failure to achieve effective skills transfer	Strengthen higher and technical education. Review salaries for high-skilled occupations. Phase out off-line PMUs.	Recruit based on merit. Avoid differential payment levels for PMU staff. Inject all technical support into line management.

Source: Authors.

buttressed by complex institutionalized systems of patronage have in many countries destroyed the integrity of public administration and the management capability of public enterprises. Even corporate private enterprise is driven by patronage and special interests rather than the goal of productive efficiency. Corruption is essentially a behavioral issue: addressing it has as much to do with applying existing anticorruption laws as it does with creating new ones.

Despite the unfavorable environment in which transport infrastructure institutions work, there is already some evidence that actions at the sector level can lead to improved behavior and performance.

- First, attempts can be made to eradicate situations that combine monopoly and administrative discretion—the institutional circumstances in which corruption thrives. Computerization of customs arrangements, vehicle inspections, driver's licenses, and other official documents can have this effect, and has been successful in reducing corruption in developing countries elsewhere.
- Second, liberalizing transport markets replaces incentives that protect corrupt operators with incentives that increase efficiency. Liberalization has already brought about significant improvements in the shipping and international air transport markets, but there remains considerable scope in domestic air transport and, in some countries, in trucking.
- Third, transparent management and regulatory institutions, working according to specified rules and subject to regular audits, tend to improve the efficiency of resource use, as exemplified by the development of road funding in road maintenance.

Failure to finance maintenance. Road networks throughout the region are inadequately maintained. Yet much higher rates of economic return can be obtained on maintenance investment than on most investment in new roads. Lack of maintenance is sometimes defended on the grounds that the internal rate of return to the road agency budget of increasing periodic maintenance expenditures may not exceed the rates of return in other sectors—especially when cheap funds can be obtained from the international financial institutions for rehabilitation (but not for maintenance). But this claim does not hold true from the viewpoint of the national economy, as explained in chapter 8, because the benefits of timely maintenance accrue primarily to road users and not to the agency itself. Failure to recognize the importance of maintenance is a major problem presently afflicting the sector.

Failure to compensate for the meeting of social obligations. Most African governments, wishing to keep public passenger transport costs down, have constrained both bus and rail passenger fares. But when fares are set at commercially unviable levels, they are likely to undermine the supply of public passenger services. Even when the rates are enforced only on publicly provided modes (notably rail or conventional large-bus services), they typically result in a shift of business to an informal sector with higher fares or lower service quality, thus failing to achieve their stated objective of assisting poorer citizens. The only way of avoiding this outcome is for governments to compensate transport suppliers for the social obligations that they impose on them.

Some governments already accept the need for such compensation. But only in rare cases are payments made at an adequate level and in a timely manner. Such payments are made in Addis Ababa, where the government successfully supports public bus service, but elsewhere sporadically paid subsidies merely postpone the eventual collapse of public bus services. The same appears to be true with the subsidization of rail passengers in some of the rail concessions. Where subsidized rail services have economically viable road alternatives, the subsidy drains resources from the economy. More-comprehensive and well-thought-out strategies for fare controls and subsidies are necessary to ensure the most effective use of transport infrastructure. The procurement of subsidized services by competitive tendering is one likely solution.

The absence of a safety culture. It is worth reiterating here that the scourge of transport accidents across the region can and should be the target of institutional action. Yet only changes in the behavior of individual transport users promise to significantly improve safety. The challenges of reeducation and safety enforcement may be among the most intractable facing the transport sector in Africa.

The main issues requiring action to overcome behavioral weaknesses in the transport sector are summarized in table 10.8.

Expenditure Requirements

The financial requirements of maintaining and improving transport infrastructure have been explored in two parts. First, in chapter 7, some estimates were made of the total expenditures necessary if the region is to achieve reasonable levels of infrastructure quality. Second, in chapter 8, these estimates were compared with recent expenditure

Table 10.8   Overcoming Behavioral Weaknesses: An Action Program

Topic	Issue	Institutional requirement	Policy requirement
Corruption	Corrupt practice at all levels of public administration	Establish anticorruption institutions at a national level. Establish independent auditing systems for public administrations.	Facilitate greater freedom of entry into the transport business. Formalize rules and computerize administration processes.
Maintenance finance	Underprovision of finance for asset maintenance	Strengthen road fund administrations.	Commit to full social cost-benefit appraisal of maintenance programs.
Public service obligation (PSO) compensation	Adverse effects of social service requirements on system viability	Enable competitive tendering of bus and air social service contracts. Establish formal procedures for review of PSO compensation in rail concessions.	Commit to making agreed-upon payments on time.
Transport safety	High accident and fatality rates, particularly on roads	Establish a national safety council.	Develop comprehensive programs in transport safety behavior.

Source: Authors.

levels to demonstrate the size and nature of the funding gap, and possible financing sources were discussed.

Estimating Financing Needs

Transport financing needs have been looked at in two different ways in this book. First, the mode-specific chapters discussed some of the main expenditure needs by subsector, though generally without attempting to identify and cost an optimum program. Those chapters also identified a number of investments that might seem politically attractive but are not likely to yield very good value for the money. In this category of potential white elephants were major new airports (when improving existing ones would be more economical) as well as some elements of the idealistic

Pan-African rail or road networks. But it was not possible within the scope of this book to undertake the systematic project-by-project economic evaluation that would be necessary to construct a set of prioritized investment projects. What was possible, however, was to see the obviously high economic returns promised by expenditures on improved maintenance, not only for roads but also for other modes.

Given the impossibility of providing a complete economic evaluation, chapter 7 estimated the needs for transport infrastructure expenditures on a different basis. Based initially on an examination of networks in more highly developed countries, a set of "connectivity targets" was postulated, covering regional, national, urban, and rural connectivity and including all the major modes. Networks based on these standards were compared with existing infrastructure networks to identify, by subtraction, a menu of expenditure needs. In some cases, this involved upgrading existing network capacity or conditions, while in others, it involved investing in new facilities. Observed costs of infrastructure works in Africa were applied to convert the program into a financial bill, and a 10-year program period was postulated for the achievement of the selected standards.

The "base" scenario specified this way was estimated to cost the region a total of $234 billion over 10 years, which would amount to 3.6 percent of GDP per year. For 13 countries, nearly all low income, the basic requirement would exceed 5.0 percent of yearly GDP over the period, with an average of 10.1 percent. Even including the relatively high levels of official development assistance (ODA) in the financing of transport infrastructure in low-income countries in recent years, this appears to be an unachievable objective.

For this reason, a more modest set of standards was postulated—the "pragmatic" scenario. In this scenario, the investment needed for the 13 countries with the highest requirements was reduced from 10.1 percent of GDP to 6.1 percent on average. This regional target seems more achievable, and so it was treated as the basic need in the subsequent analysis.

In total, in both the basic and the pragmatic scenarios, about 90 percent of the estimated expenditure needs are in the road sector, with that total fairly evenly divided among regional, national, local access, and urban roads (with the urban share falling a little in the pragmatic scenario). Most significant, the expenditure needs assessment concluded that 40 to 50 percent of the expenditure required should be spent on maintenance—a proportion that the region overall is not even close to achieving.

Securing Finance

The detailed analysis of the revenues and expenditures of 24 countries, described in chapter 8, showed average total annual expenditures on transport infrastructure in recent years contributing $16.2 billion toward the estimated needs (in the scaled-down pragmatic scenario) of $18.2 billion. This is 2.5 percent of national GDP on average. At first glance, it appears that a surprisingly high proportion of needs are being met.

The analysis also identifies three important inefficiencies in the financing arrangements, which, if addressed, could reduce the funding deficit even further. These are the undercollection of fees from users, the underexecution of allocated investment funding, and the underallocation of resources to routine and periodic maintenance. Addressing the first two of these issues would directly improve the finances of the implementing agencies. The third is rather different, as the effect of undermaintenance is to increase vehicle operating costs, so the benefits of addressing it would accrue to road users rather than to the implementing agencies.

A number of caveats are needed to qualify this apparently promising scenario:

- First, considerable uncertainty attaches to some unit costs, particularly of rehabilitation, partly because reliable data are difficult to obtain (see chapter 7).
- Second, the picture looks far less favorable if ODA is excluded from the calculation. This accounts for nearly 25 percent of the capital expenditure and about 12 percent of the total expenditure.
- Third, the picture varies enormously both among country groups and among individual countries. The deficits for many low-income countries and all low-income fragile states are much greater than the average, and the situation in many of these countries remains dire. Reallocation of funds among countries is likely to be an option only if a reallocation of ODA support is pursued.
- Fourth, the benefits of addressing the underallocation to periodic and routine maintenance, which would accrue primarily to infrastructure users, could improve road agency finances only if accompanied by some tax or user fee reforms.
- Fifth, the targets have already been scaled down overall in the "pragmatic" scenario, so the balance between finance and needs may seem unduly favorable for higher-income countries, which have higher current standards and aspirations.

These caveats emphasize that many countries will need to pursue additional ways of raising funds for transport infrastructure. The immediate prospects for finding these other sources are difficult to assess. Government is the main source of funding in most countries, but given the wide range of claims on the budget, the likelihood of significant increases in funding from this source seems low. Most funding has come from members of the Organisation for Economic Co-operation and Development. Other funding has come from Chinese sources associated with natural resource exploitation, from India, and from the Gulf states. Funding from sources other than the Organisation for Economic Co-operation and Development has been focused on the rail sector, and its robustness remains to be seen. Private capital flows have been volatile over time and have been focused mainly on middle-income, resource-rich countries, where they have gone to seaports and airports, as well as to rail concessions and a few toll roads. These flows are under stress during the global economic downturn. Local capital markets remain relatively weak, and the available maturities are often too short to be attractive for transport infrastructure investment.

That leaves ODA, which was already scaled up substantially between 2004 and 2007, and was set to increase further before the financial crisis of 2008. The main multilaterals—the African Development Bank, the European Commission, and the World Bank—secured record replenishment of concessional funding for three or four years from 2008. Attention to the possibility of reallocating ODA across countries would give impetus to the ongoing trilateral coordination of the African Development Bank, the World Bank, and the European Commission. While any discussion of a policy of redistribution of aid between countries would inevitably be politically charged, and might have to start at the level of the regional economic commissions, it could energize the prioritization of transport investments—the aim of the infrastructure plans of the New Partnership for Africa's Development and of the European Union-Africa Partnership on Infrastructure.

Bilaterals may be more squeezed, and because of their smaller portfolios, less able to implement a policy of redistribution than multilaterals. Overall, however, it remains critical to the continued development of transport infrastructure in Africa that the scaling up of ODA is sustained.

In sum, an agenda for African transport infrastructure finance might include the following steps:

- Consider what is sustainable—avoid excessively high network densities and design standards.

- Be cautious about "prestige projects"—that is where wasteful investments thrive.
- Invest only in what can be maintained—unsustainable investment is wasted.
- Decide which parts of existing networks are sustainable, and maintain those properly.
- Apply user fees to fund maintenance wherever possible.
- Embrace low-cost ODA funds—but only when they can be invested to yield a high social rate of return.
- Mobilize private capital for investment—but do not let it distort the investment program.
- Supplement private capital with public sector funds in public-private partnership schemes in cases where this is the best way to maintain social service provision.

That agenda for action is long and demanding. It requires changes in national institutions and attitudes as well as finance. So, while the international community can help, success in bringing Africa's transport infrastructure up to the best international standards can be achieved (in keeping with the philosophy of the New Partnership for Africa's Development) only through African leadership and commitment.

Notes

1. The Logistics Performance Index is based on a survey of worldwide operators (global freight forwarders and express carriers) providing feedback on seven characteristics of the logistics "friendliness" of 150 countries.
2. A port community system is a consultative association involving all principal stakeholders (public and private). Such systems have been very successful in some European ports, such as Rotterdam.
3. Development policy loans accounted for 50 percent of new lending by the World Bank in 2009 (World Bank 2009).

References

Bullock, R. 2009. "Railways in Sub-Saharan Africa." Africa Infrastructure Country Diagnostic Background Paper 17, World Bank, Washington, DC.

Drewry Shipping Consultants. 2009. *Annual Review of Global Container Terminal Operators.* London: Drewry Publications.

South African Department of Transport. 2007. "National Freight Logistics Strategy." Department of Transport, Pretoria, South Africa.

Transparency International. 2009. "Corruption Perceptions Index." Transparency International, Berlin.

World Bank. 2007. Logistics Performance Index (software). World Bank, Washington, DC.

———. 2009. "Development Policy Lending Retrospective." World Bank. Washington, DC.

———. 2010. Logistics Performance Index (software). World Bank. Washington, DC. http://go.worldbank.org/88X6PU5GV0.

Introduction

Appendix 1a   AICD Background Documents Relevant to the Transport Sector

The Africa Infrastructure Country Diagnostic (AICD) study covered all infrastructure sectors. In addition to the main summary report (Foster and Briceño-Garmendia 2009), the documentation included sets of background papers and working papers. The listing below (tables A1a.1 and A1a.2) includes both those that are specific to the transport sector and those that are of more general application. All papers are available for download from https://www.infrastructureafrica.org/aicd/.

Table A1a.1   Background Papers

No.	Category and title	Author(s)
	General	
2	"Access, Affordability, and Alternatives: Modern Infrastructure Services in Africa"	Sudeshna Banerjee, Quentin Wodon, Amadou Diallo, Taras Pushak, Helal Uddin, Clarence Tsimpo, and Vivien Foster
15	"Financing Public Infrastructure in Sub-Saharan Africa: Patterns, Issues, and Options"	Cecilia Briceño-Garmendia, Karlis Smits, and Vivien Foster
	Investment needs	
7	"Improving Connectivity: Investing in Transport Infrastructure in Sub-Saharan Africa"	Robin Carruthers and Ranga Rajan Krishnamani with Siobhan Murray
	Subsector reviews	
1	"Stuck in Traffic: Urban Transport in Africa"	Ajay Kumar and Fanny Barrett
8	"Beyond the Bottlenecks: Ports in Sub-Saharan Africa"	Mike Mundy and Andrew Penfold
11	"Railways in Sub-Saharan Africa"	Richard Bullock
14	"The Burden of Maintenance: Roads in Sub-Saharan Africa"	Ken Gwilliam, Vivien Foster, Rodrigo Archondo-Callao, Cecilia Briceño-Garmendia, Alberto Nogales, and Kavita Sethi
16	"Air Transport: Challenges to Growth"	Heinrich C. Bofinger
17	"Taking Stock of Railway Companies in Sub-Saharan Africa"	Mapapa Mbangala

Source: Author's compilation.

Table A1a.2   Working Papers

No.	Title	Author(s)
1	"Making Sense of Sub-Saharan Africa's Infrastructure Endowment: A Benchmarking Approach"	Tito Yepes, Justin Pierce, and Vivien Foster
3	"Infrastructure and Growth in Africa"	César Calderón
8	"Potential for Local Private Finance of Infrastructure in Africa"	Jacqueline Irving and Astrid Manroth
9	"Impact of Infrastructure Constraints on Firm Productivity in Africa"	Alvaro Escribano, J. Luis Guasch, and Jorge Pena
10	"A Tale of Three Cities: Understanding Differences in Provision of Modern Services"	Sumila Gulyani, Debabrata Talukdar, and Darby Jack
14	"Transport Prices and Costs in Africa: A Review of the Main International Corridors"	Supee Teravaninthorn and Gaël Raballand

(continued)

Table A1a.2   *(continued)*

No.	Title	Author(s)
15	"The Impact of Infrastructure Spending in Sub-Saharan Africa: A CGE Modeling Approach"	Jean-François Perrault and Luc Savard
17	"Fiscal Costs of Infrastructure Provision: A Practitioner's Guide"	Cecilia Briceño-Garmendia
19	"Crop Production and Road Connectivity in Sub-Saharan Africa: A Spatial Analysis"	Paul Dorosh, Hyoung-Gun Wang, Liang You, and Emily Schmidt

Source: Author's compilation.

Appendix 1b   Country Typology for Study Countries

Middle-income countries	Resource-rich countries	Low-income, nonfragile countries	Low-income, fragile countries	Other
Botswana	Angola	Benin	Burundi	Djibouti
Cape Verde	Cameroon	Burkina Faso	Central African Republic	
Lesotho	Chad	Ethiopia	Comoros	
Mauritius	Congo, Rep.	Ghana	Congo, Dem. Rep.	
Namibia	Equatorial	Kenya	Côte d'Ivoire	
Seychelles	Guinea	Madagascar	Eritrea	
South Africa	Gabon	Malawi	Gambia, The	
Swaziland	Nigeria	Mali	Guinea	
	Sudan	Mauritania	Guinea-Bissau	
	Zambia	Mozambique	Liberia	
		Niger	São Tomé and Príncipe	
		Rwanda	Sierra Leone	
		Senegal	Togo	
		Tanzania	Zimbabwe	
		Uganda		

Source: Foster and Briceño-Garmendia 2009.

Reference

Foster, V., and C. Briceño-Garmendia, eds. 2009. *Africa's Infrastructure: A Time for Transformation.* Paris: Agence Française de Développement; Washington, DC: World Bank.

Roads

Appendix 2a   Road Data Sources and Analysis

Primary Data Sources

The primary data on road infrastructure are drawn from three sources. The first is the Africa Infrastructure Country Diagnostic (AICD) road network survey. This includes an initial detailed survey of the nature, extent, and condition of road networks, performed in 21 of the 24 phase I AICD countries. In its second phase, the survey was extended to cover 40 countries. Where possible, statistics are based on the complete sample of 40; otherwise, the number of countries covered is specified. Fiscal data cover only the initial 21 countries surveyed. The AICD survey entailed consultant visits to the central road entity in each country to collect link-by-link information on the primary, secondary, and (when possible) tertiary networks. For each network link, the survey ascertained the class (primary, secondary, or tertiary), the surface type (concrete, asphalt, gravel, or earth), the condition (good, fair, or poor), and the traffic volumes (across a series of five bands corresponding to typical values for each class of the network).

The second data source is an institutional database maintained by the Sub-Saharan Africa Transport Policy Program (SSATP), which has tracked the development of institutional reforms in the African road sector in recent years, with emphasis on the design and adoption of road funds and road agencies.

The third main source is the AICD fiscal costs study, which collected detailed data on road expenditures in the 24 phase I AICD countries. The data allow for disaggregating road fund and non–road fund expenditures; capital and operating expenditures; and in some cases, expenditures on the main network and those on the rural network. But it is not possible to capture the budget allocations that local jurisdictions make to their rural network, and as a result, rural network spending is almost certainly underrecorded, though to varying degrees.

In addition to these three primary sources, chapter 2 draws extensively on work by the SSATP and on recent World Bank research on road freight transport operations in Sub-Saharan Africa. Throughout, the analysis distinguishes between the main road network—that is, those parts of the network under the jurisdiction of the central road entity—and the rest of the system. In most countries, the main network includes both the primary and the secondary networks, but in a handful of cases (including larger countries such as Nigeria and South Africa) it comprises the primary network only. The rural network comprises the remainder of the classified network. This categorization is adopted so that data on historical road expenditures (which can be split only between the main and rural network and not among primary, secondary, and tertiary networks) can be reconciled with data on road network conditions and future expenditure needs. Due to the lower quality of the available data on both rural network conditions and rural network expenditure, the analysis of the rural networks is necessarily more speculative than that of the main networks.

Methodology of the RONET Model
The Road Network Evaluation Tools (RONET) model is a tool for assessing the performance of road maintenance and rehabilitation policies and the importance of the road sector to the economy. The model is used to demonstrate to stakeholders the need for continued support of road maintenance initiatives. The length of the road network taken into consideration in the model may be the entire road system of the country (roads, highways, expressways, streets, avenues, and so forth), or a partial network—for example, the road network of a state or province of the country or the road network managed by the main road agency. Segments of the road network are classified according to (i) five network types, (ii) five surface types, (iii) five traffic categories, and (iv) five condition categories, for a total of 625 road classes (figure A2a.1).

Figure A2a.1   Matrix of Road Classes: Overall Network Evaluation

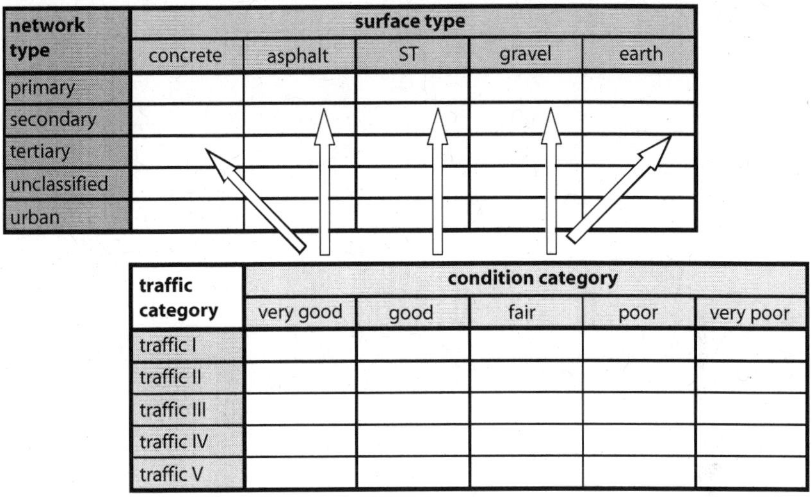

network type	surface type				
	concrete	asphalt	ST	gravel	earth
primary					
secondary					
tertiary					
unclassified					
urban					

traffic category	condition category				
	very good	good	fair	poor	very poor
traffic I					
traffic II					
traffic III					
traffic IV					
traffic V					

Source: Archondo Callao 2009.
Note: ST = surface treatment.

Each surface type is subdivided into five possible traffic categories. Table A2a.1 presents the default traffic level assigned to each combination of traffic category and surface type. Each network type, road type, and traffic category is further subdivided into five possible road condition categories defined as a function of the engineering assessment of the capital road works (periodic maintenance or rehabilitation works) needed to bring a road to very good condition. Routine maintenance road works are needed by all roads every year; therefore, they are not considered in the definitions of the road condition classes. The road condition classes are defined as follows:

Very good: Roads in very good condition require no capital road works.

Good: Roads in good condition are largely free of defects and require only some minor maintenance works, such as preventive treatment, crack sealing, or grading.

Fair: Roads in fair condition are roads with defects and weakened structural resistance, requiring resurfacing of the pavement (periodic maintenance) but not demolition of the existing pavement.

Poor: Roads in poor condition require rehabilitation (strengthening or partial reconstruction).

Table A2a.1   RONET Default Assignment of Traffic Levels

Surface type	Traffic category	Traffic level	Average annual daily traffic (vehicles per day)			Illustrative standards	
			Minimum	Maximum	Average	Geometry	Pavement
Earth	Traffic I	T1	0	10	5	1-lane warranted	Formation not warranted
	Traffic II	T2	10	30	20	1-lane warranted	Formation warranted
	Traffic III	T3	30	100	65	2-lane warranted	Gravel warranted
	Traffic IV	T4	100	300	200	2-lane warranted	Gravel warranted
	Traffic V	T5	300	1,000	650	2-lane warranted	Paved surface warranted
Gravel	Traffic I	T2	10	30	20	1-lane warranted	Formation warranted
	Traffic II	T3	30	100	65	2-lane warranted	Gravel warranted
	Traffic III	T4	100	300	200	2-lane warranted	Gravel warranted
	Traffic IV	T5	300	1,000	650	2-lane warranted	Paved surface warranted
	Traffic V	T6	1,000	3,000	2,000	2-lane warranted	Paved surface warranted
Paved	Traffic I	T4	100	300	200	2-lane warranted	Gravel warranted
	Traffic II	T5	300	1,000	650	2-lane warranted	Paved surface warranted
	Traffic III	T6	1,000	3,000	2,000	2-lane warranted	Paved surface warranted
	Traffic IV	T7	3,000	10,000	6,500	2-lane warranted	Paved surface warranted
	Traffic V	T8	10,000	30,000	20,000	4-lane warranted	Paved surface warranted

Source: Archondo Callao 2009.

Note: Standard given for illustrative purposes. Proper standards are country specific. Average annual daily traffic is for motorized vehicles with four wheels or more in two-way traffic.

Very poor: Roads in very poor condition require full reconstruction, almost equivalent to new construction.

RONET has one module that computes the network monitoring indicators based on the current condition of the network and another that does a performance assessment of the network under different road agency standards. The objective of the latter is to assess the consequences of applying different standards that represent different levels of expenditures on road works over time. The consequences are reflected in the road works requirements, including financial cost, road condition, asset value, and so on.

This module evaluates the performance of the network under different road works standards over a 20-year evaluation period. The standards that may be selected by users of the model are the following:

- Very high standard, which represents a scenario without budget constraints but with a high level of periodic maintenance and rehabilitation works
- High, medium, low, and very low standards, which represent scenarios of decreasing levels of road works expenditures
- Do-the-minimum standard, in which the only capital road work applied over the evaluation period is reconstruction at a very high roughness.
- Do-nothing standard, in which no capital road works are applied over the evaluation period
- Custom standard, in which one of the above standards is applied individually to each road network type
- Optimal standard, for which RONET evaluates each road class and identifies the standard that maximizes the net present value of social benefits at a given discount rate.

RONET was used to evaluate the preservation needs of the primary and secondary roads of 19 African countries. The total network length of the 19 countries is 991,567 kilometers (km), of which 293,039 km (30 percent) are main roads. The total network utilization of the 19 countries is 123,755 million vehicle-km, of which 117,905 million vehicle-km (95 percent) circulate on main roads. The median traffic volume on the main roads is 456 vehicles per day. RONET evaluated the current condition and traffic of the main roads and computed current monitoring indicators for each country. The median percentage of roads in good and fair condition is 75.6 percent, and the median average network roughness weighted per vehicle-km is 4.69 meters per kilometer. This is referred to as the International Roughness Index (IRI). The median current asset value as a share of the maximum asset value is 85 percent, and the median current asset value as a share of gross domestic product (GDP) is 17 percent.

RONET evaluated the performance of the main roads under different preservation standards to determine the optimal needs for recurrent maintenance, periodic maintenance, and rehabilitation road works. For each road class—characterized by functional classification, surface type, traffic, and condition—RONET identified the preservation standard that yields the highest net present value at a 12 percent discount rate and thus maximizes society's net benefits. The RONET evaluation assumed the following in all countries: (i) a traffic growth rate of 3 percent per year, (ii) discount rate of 12 percent, (iii) evaluation period of 20 years, (iv) average unit costs of road works based on the World Bank Road Works Costs Knowledge System, and (v) average unit road user costs based on the World Bank Road User Costs Knowledge System.

Appendix 2b   Basic Country Data for the Set of 40 Countries

Country	Land area (km²)	Population (millions)			GDP current prices (US$ billions)	Vehicle fleet (number of vehicles)
		Total	Rural	Urban		
Angola	1,246,700	18.0	7.8	10.2	83.4	691,192
Benin	110,620	8.7	5.1	3.6	6.7	229,536
Botswana	566,730	1.9	0.8	1.1	13.0	302,568
Burkina Faso	273,600	15.2	12.2	3.0	7.9	530,917
Burundi	25,680	8.1	7.2	0.8	1.2	61,271
Cameroon	465,400	18.9	8.2	10.7	23.4	31,627
Central African Republic	623,000	4.4	2.7	1.7	2.0	18,540
Chad	1,259,200	11.1	8.1	3.0	8.4	127,811
Congo, Dem. Rep.	2,267,050	64.2	42.4	21.8	11.6	321,134
Congo, Rep.	341,500	3.6	1.4	2.2	10.7	103,000
Côte d'Ivoire	318,000	20.6	10.5	10.0	23.4	362,560
Eritrea	101,000	5.0	4.0	1.0	1.7	62,674
Ethiopia	1,000,000	80.7	67.0	13.7	26.5	251,585
Gabon	257,670	1.4	0.2	1.2	14.4	20,600
Gambia, The	10,000	1.7	0.7	0.9	0.8	14,884
Ghana	227,540	23.4	11.7	11.7	16.1	959,591
Guinea	245,720	9.8	6.4	3.4	4.3	154,500
Kenya	569,140	38.5	30.2	8.3	34.5	1,034,370

(continued)

Country	Land area (km²)	Population (millions)			GDP current prices (US$ billions)	Vehicle fleet (number of vehicles)
		Total	Rural	Urban		
Lesotho	30,350	2.0	1.5	0.5	1.6	77,217
Liberia	96,320	3.8	1.5	2.3	0.9	11,419
Madagascar	581,540	19.1	13.5	5.6	9.0	203,920
Malawi	94,080	14.3	11.6	2.7	4.3	133,900
Mali	1,220,190	12.7	8.6	4.1	8.7	172,262
Mauritania	1,030,700	3.2	1.9	1.3	2.9	360,500
Mauritius	2,030	1.3	0.7	0.5	8.7	344,149
Mozambique	786,380	21.8	13.8	8.0	9.7	266,440
Namibia	823,290	2.1	1.3	0.8	8.6	246,800
Niger	1,266,700	14.7	12.2	2.4	5.4	78,343
Nigeria	910,770	151.3	78.1	73.2	212.1	7,828,000
Rwanda	24,670	9.7	7.9	1.8	4.5	62,830
Senegal	192,530	12.2	7.0	5.2	13.2	289,012
Sierra Leone	71,620	5.6	3.5	2.1	2.0	46,359
South Africa	1,214,470	48.7	19.1	29.6	276.8	9,514,701
Sudan	2,376,000	41.3	23.4	18.0	58.4	1,236,000
Swaziland	17,200	1.2	0.9	0.3	2.6	119,532
Tanzania	885,800	42.5	31.6	10.8	20.5	595,287
Togo	54,390	6.5	3.7	2.7	2.8	49,681
Uganda	197,100	31.7	27.5	4.1	14.5	374,568
Zambia	743,390	12.6	8.2	4.5	14.3	228,854
Zimbabwe	386,850	12.5	7.8	4.7	3.4	1,603,284
Total	**22,914,920**	**805.8**	**512.2**	**293.6**	**974.559**	**29,121,417**
Average	572,873	20.1	12.8	7.3	24.364	728,035
Median	364,175	12.3	7.9	3.2	8.696	229,195

Source: Calculations by Alberto Nogales based on AICD RONET summary outputs, June 2010.
Note: GDP = gross domestic product; km² = square kilometer.

Appendix 2c Classified Road Network Length for 40 Countries
(kilometers)

Country	Classified road network				Unclassified	Total including unclassified	Urban	Grand total including urban
	Primary	*Secondary*	*Tertiary*	*Classified*				
Angola	10,227	11,069	15,104	36,399	15,104	51,503	11,057	62,560
Benin	2,386	2,348	3,597	8,332	7,368	15,700	1,794	17,494
Botswana	4,028	4,705	9,002	17,735	5,668	23,403	4,749	28,152
Burkina Faso	6,705	3,526	4,971	15,202	7,108	22,310	1,889	24,199
Burundi	1,839	1,126	1,113	4,077	5,538	9,615	462	10,077
Cameroon	5,838	5,169	12,573	23,581	9,802	33,383	5,772	39,155
Central African Republic	5,037	4,952	7,623	17,612	7,623	25,235	3,544	28,779
Chad	7,064	5,891	15,283	28,238	5,162	33,400	3,202	36,602
Congo, Dem. Rep	19,451	8,850	5,634	33,934	5,238	39,172	9,123	48,295
Congo, Rep.	1,619	3,786	7,330	12,735	4,174	16,909	2,939	19,848
Côte d'Ivoire	5,752	7,539	12,267	25,558	516	26,074	5,887	31,961
Eritrea	2,171	2,241	1,400	5,812	2,373	8,185	1,190	9,375
Ethiopia	4,953	4,768	10,906	20,627	25,081	45,708	1,521	47,229
Gabon	2,954	1,713	4,317	8,984	3,100	12,083	3,733	15,816
Gambia, The	812	847	1,300	2,959	790	3,749	858	4,607
Ghana	3,564	7,613	17,452	28,628	11,634	40,263	5,574	45,837
Guinea	3,719	2,642	9,405	15,767	7,240	23,007	2,043	25,050
Kenya	5,532	16,809	34,609	56,951	6,314	63,265	4,237	67,502
Lesotho	1,483	1,521	2,295	5,299	641	5,940	702	6,642
Liberia	2,378	2,160	4,629	9,167	7,427	16,594	2,518	19,112
Madagascar	2,991	6,608	16,042	25,641	3,952	29,593	2,517	32,110

Malawi	3,444	6,692	3,147	13,283	2,208	15,491	1,702	17,193
Mali	7,017	11,203	15,852	34,072	12,667	46,739	2,258	48,997
Mauritania	5,303	1,796	2,831	9,930	2,505	12,435	2,791	15,226
Mauritius	896	592	527	2,015	42	2,057	591	2,648
Mozambique	4,909	4,900	12,689	22,498	6,740	29,238	3,321	32,559
Namibia	4,297	12,065	28,732	45,094	18,067	63,161	5,307	68,468
Niger	4,011	2,044	7,371	13,427	3,518	16,945	947	17,892
Nigeria	28,614	21,293	35,900	85,807	72,800	158,607	22,465	181,072
Rwanda	1,060	1,776	1,790	4,625	9,383	14,008	1,988	15,996
Senegal	2,920	1,860	10,891	15,671	2,392	18,063	1,898	19,961
Sierra Leone	2,312	2,091	4,152	8,555	444	8,999	3,000	11,999
South Africa	38,066	38,222	125,975	202,263	161,868	364,131	42,572	406,703
Sudan	10,122	6,682	8,199	25,003	5,542	30,545	6,829	37,374
Swaziland	1,467	1,647	1,192	4,306	569	4,875	388	5,263
Tanzania	7,010	21,720	20,000	48,730	5,727	54,457	6,433	60,890
Togo	1,852	992	1,834	4,678	2,842	7,520	1,127	8,647
Uganda	9,171	26,751	35,000	70,922	5,000	75,922	4,100	80,022
Zambia	3,290	3,763	11,232	18,285	18,958	37,243	2,282	39,525
Zimbabwe	5,270	6,758	7,772	19,800	18,984	38,784	5,000	43,784
Total	**241,536**	**278,730**	**531,938**	**1,052,203**	**492,109**	**1,544,312**	**190,311**	**1,734,623**
Average	6,038	6,968	13,298	26,305	12,303	38,608	4,758	43,366
Median	4,020	4,736	7,986	17,674	5,605	24,319	2,865	28,465

Source: Calculations by Alberto Nogales based on AICD RONET summary outputs, June 2010.

Appendix 2d Road Network Densities for 40 Countries

Country	Classified network length density			Total network length density			Network density per population	
	Per area (km/1,000 km²)	Per population (km/1,000 people)	Per vehicles (km/1,000 vehicles)	Per area (km/1,000 km²)	Per population (km/1,000 people)	Per vehicles (km/1,000 vehicles)	Tertiary network (km/1,000 rural people)	Urban network (km/1,000 urban people)
Angola	29	2.0	53	41	2.9	53	1.9	1.1
Benin	75	1.0	36	142	1.8	36	0.7	0.5
Botswana	31	9.3	59	41	12.3	59	11.7	4.2
Burkina Faso	56	1.0	29	82	1.5	29	0.4	0.6
Burundi	159	0.5	67	374	1.2	67	0.2	0.6
Cameroon	51	1.2	746	72	1.8	746	1.5	0.5
Central African Republic	28	4.0	950	41	5.7	950	2.8	2.1
Chad	22	2.6	221	27	3.0	221	1.9	1.1
Congo, Dem. Rep.	15	0.5	106	17	0.6	106	0.1	0.4
Congo, Rep.	37	3.5	124	50	4.7	124	5.2	1.3
Côte d'Ivoire	80	1.2	70	82	1.3	70	1.2	0.6
Eritrea	58	1.2	93	81	1.6	93	0.4	1.1
Ethiopia	21	0.3	82	46	0.6	82	0.2	0.1
Gabon	35	6.2	436	47	8.3	436	19.9	3.0
Gambia, The	296	1.8	199	375	2.3	199	1.8	0.9
Ghana	126	1.2	30	177	1.7	30	1.5	0.5
Guinea	64	1.6	102	94	2.3	102	1.5	0.6
Kenya	100	1.5	55	111	1.6	55	1.1	0.5
Lesotho	175	2.6	69	196	2.9	69	1.5	1.4
Liberia	95	2.4	803	172	4.4	803	3.1	1.1

Madagascar	44	1.3	126	51	1.5	126	1.2	0.4
Malawi	141	0.9	99	165	1.1	99	0.3	0.6
Mali	28	2.7	198	38	3.7	198	1.8	0.6
Mauritania	10	3.1	28	12	3.9	28	1.5	2.1
Mauritius	993	1.6	6	1,014	1.6	6	0.7	1.1
Mozambique	29	1.0	84	37	1.3	84	0.9	0.4
Namibia	55	21.3	183	77	29.9	183	21.5	6.8
Niger	11	0.9	171	13	1.2	171	0.6	0.4
Nigeria	94	0.6	11	174	1.0	11	0.5	0.3
Rwanda	187	0.5	74	568	1.4	74	0.2	1.1
Senegal	81	1.3	54	94	1.5	54	1.5	0.4
Sierra Leone	119	1.5	185	126	1.6	185	1.2	1.4
South Africa	167	4.2	21	300	7.5	21	6.6	1.4
Sudan	11	0.6	20	13	0.7	20	0.4	0.4
Swaziland	250	3.7	36	283	4.2	36	1.4	1.3
Tanzania	55	1.1	82	61	1.3	82	0.6	0.6
Togo	86	0.7	94	138	1.2	94	0.5	0.4
Uganda	360	2.2	189	385	2.4	189	1.3	1.0
Zambia	25	1.4	80	50	3.0	80	1.4	0.5
Zimbabwe	51	1.6	12	100	3.1	12	1.0	1.1
Average	**109**	**2.5**	**152**	**149**	**3.4**	**152**	**2.6**	**1.1**
Median	**57**	**1.5**	**82**	**82**	**1.7**	**82**	**1.2**	**0.6**

Source: Calculations by Alberto Nogales based on AICD RONET Summary Outputs, June 2010.

Note: km = kilometer; km² = square kilometer.

Appendix 2e Road Network Length by Surface Class and Network Type for 40 Countries

(kilometers)

Country	Paved road network				Unpaved road network			
	Primary	Secondary	Tertiary	Classified	Primary	Secondary	Tertiary	Classified
Angola	7,383	1,235	0	8,618	2,843	9,835	15,104	27,781
Benin	1,821	0	0	1,821	565	2,348	3,597	6,510
Botswana	4,028	2,268	645	6,942	0	2,436	8,356	10,793
Burkina Faso	2,640	23	7	2,670	4,065	3,502	4,965	12,532
Burundi	1,059	0	2	1,061	780	1,126	1,111	3,016
Cameroon	3,113	903	523	4,540	2,725	4,266	12,050	19,041
Central African Republic	654	0	0	654	4,383	4,952	7,623	16,958
Chad	908	78	0	986	6,156	5,813	15,283	27,252
Congo, Dem. Rep	2,269	0	4	2,274	17,181	8,850	5,629	31,661
Congo, Rep.	541	468	42	1,051	1,079	3,318	7,288	11,684
Côte d'Ivoire	3,973	1,643	73	5,689	1,779	5,896	12,194	19,869
Eritrea	817	28	0	845	1,354	2,214	1,400	4,968
Ethiopia	4,132	255	311	4,698	821	4,513	10,595	15,928
Gabon	941	164	34	1,139	2,013	1,549	4,283	7,845
Gambia, The	812	0	0	812	0	847	1,300	2,147
Ghana	2,204	3,157	753	6,114	1,360	4,456	16,699	22,514
Guinea	2,092	235	0	2,327	1,627	2,407	9,405	13,440
Kenya	3,787	3,470	725	7,982	1,744	13,339	33,885	48,968
Lesotho	847	191	3	1,041	636	1,330	2,292	4,258
Liberia	656	2	101	758	1,722	2,158	4,528	8,408
Madagascar	2,537	2,142	366	5,045	454	4,466	15,676	20,596

Malawi	2,486	423	96	3,004	958	6,270	3,051	10,278
Mali	3,873	602	71	4,545	3,145	10,601	15,782	29,527
Mauritania	1,900	37	14	1,951	3,403	1,759	2,816	7,979
Mauritius	896	592	527	2,015	0	0	0	0
Mozambique	4,360	880	458	5,698	549	4,020	12,231	16,800
Namibia	4,177	1,622	232	6,031	120	10,443	28,499	39,062
Niger	3,549	69	32	3,649	462	1,975	7,340	9,777
Nigeria	24,505	13,506	787	38,798	4,109	7,787	35,113	47,009
Rwanda	1,060	0	0	1,060	0	1,776	1,790	3,566
Senegal	2,700	1,191	189	4,080	219	669	10,702	11,591
Sierra Leone	905	46	0	951	1,407	2,045	4,152	7,604
South Africa	37,876	23,720	12,971	74,567	190	14,502	113,004	127,697
Sudan	2,068	161	0	2,229	8,055	6,520	8,199	22,775
Swaziland	1,043	80	6	1,129	424	1,567	1,186	3,177
Tanzania	3,297	1,033	0	4,330	3,713	20,687	20,000	44,400
Togo	1,591	15	0	1,606	261	977	1,834	3,071
Uganda	2,331	0	0	2,331	6,840	26,751	35,000	68,591
Zambia	3,290	2,058	1,111	6,459	0	1,705	10,121	11,826
Zimbabwe	5,270	2,652	0	7,922	0	4,106	7,772	11,878
Total	**154,392**	**64,947**	**20,084**	**239,424**	**87,143**	**213,782**	**511,854**	**812,779**
Average	3,860	1,624	502	5,986	2,179	5,345	12,796	20,319
Median	2,300	245	23	2,500	1,216	3,761	7,986	12,205

Source: Calculations by Alberto Nogales based on AICD RONET Summary Outputs, June 2010.

Appendix 2f   Average Annual Daily Traffic by Road Type for 40 Countries

Country	Road type Primary	Secondary	Tertiary	Classified
Angola	733	28	6	136
Benin	1,627	82	15	243
Botswana	1,381	386	41	284
Burkina Faso	401	49	30	130
Burundi	306	11	6	64
Cameroon	1,012	263	34	204
Central African Republic	55	26	6	23
Chad	159	35	6	44
Congo, Dem. Rep.	48	19	19	34
Congo, Rep.	251	93	24	55
Côte d'Ivoire	788	235	18	212
Eritrea	397	46	6	111
Ethiopia	555	153	92	100
Gabon	315	43	8	77
Gambia, The	375	31	6	83
Ghana	1,917	285	35	385
Guinea	635	140	6	117
Kenya	1,306	233	26	182
Lesotho	1,789	567	70	559
Liberia	317	33	10	54
Madagascar	937	299	13	160
Malawi	628	77	32	167
Mali	326	75	8	70
Mauritania	253	10	7	100
Mauritius	7,482	600	200	2,750
Mozambique	1,053	163	73	224
Namibia	1,644	221	31	160
Niger	415	64	33	118
Nigeria	2,310	746	40	469
Rwanda	913	125	6	84
Senegal	1,286	431	42	256
Sierra Leone	503	75	7	122
South Africa	6,596	126	26	676
Sudan	284	24	13	93
Swaziland	1,997	299	7	656
Tanzania	1,276	247	13	244
Togo	2,054	666	8	526
Uganda	870	37	13	121
Zambia	1,424	203	56	163
Zimbabwe	1,294	161	13	190
Average	**1,198**	**185**	**28**	**261**
Median	**829**	**126**	**14**	**148**

Source: Calculations by Alberto Nogales based on AICD RONET Summary Outputs, June 2010.

Appendix 2g   Distribution of Networks by Traffic Level for 40 Countries

(percent)

Country	T1 0–10 AADT	T2 10–30 AADT	T3 30–100 AADT	T4 100–300 AADT	T5 300–1,000 AADT	T6 1,000–3,000 AADT	T7 3,000–10,000 AADT	T8 >10,000 AADT
Angola	4	0	0	18	18	42	25	0
Benin	2	0	1	8	13	35	33	12
Botswana	1	0	1	21	22	23	35	0
Burkina Faso	4	8	12	9	26	47	0	0
Burundi	12	0	0	22	54	12	12	0
Cameroon	2	0	1	14	28	30	29	0
Central African Republic	55	22	8	60	0	0	0	0
Chad	14	3	29	27	33	6	0	0
Congo, Dem. Rep.	58	0	0	63	16	0	0	0
Congo, Rep.	4	29	0	13	66	5	0	0
Côte d'Ivoire	2	0	4	14	28	50	8	0
Eritrea	4	2	23	11	18	48	0	0
Ethiopia	8	1	12	25	40	18	0	0
Gabon	8	0	0	19	37	54	0	0
Gambia, The	10	0	3	41	47	12	0	0
Ghana	3	5	9	4	16	52	94	0
Guinea	4	2	8	12	30	25	6	18
Kenya	4	3	5	11	12	36	31	0
Lesotho	0	2	5	8	14	5	24	43
Liberia	10	13	12	19	16	48	0	0
Madagascar	3	4	3	12	23	11	21	25

(continued)

Country	T1 0–10 AADT	T2 10–30 AADT	T3 30–100 AADT	T4 100–300 AADT	T5 300–1,000 AADT	T6 1,000–3,000 AADT	T7 3,000–10,000 AADT	T8 >10,000 AADT
Malawi	1	11	7	12	31	41	0	0
Mali	9	3	6	20	42	22	2	0
Mauritania	6	0	0	31	23	50	0	0
Mauritius	0	0	0	3	5	5	50	39
Mozambique	1	9	5	11	12	55	10	2
Namibia	2	8	6	8	13	14	41	11
Niger	4	5	7	23	49	14	0	0
Nigeria	1	0	2	3	12	33	35	15
Rwanda	7	0	1	23	25	55	0	0
Senegal	2	0	1	11	24	45	19	0
Sierra Leone	6	5	3	23	4	10	57	0
South Africa	1	5	0	3	2	7	29	59
Sudan	5	15	1	16	14	60	0	0
Swaziland	0	0	6	12	6	27	43	5
Tanzania	1	6	11	13	15	17	26	14
Togo	1	0	1	7	23	24	0	46
Uganda	3	7	10	13	15	13	32	10
Zambia	1	7	2	18	14	16	41	6
Zimbabwe	3	1	2	12	21	41	24	0
Average	**7**	**4**	**5**	**17**	**23**	**28**	**18**	**8**
Median	**3**	**2**	**3**	**13**	**20**	**24**	**11**	**0**

Source: Calculations by Alberto Nogales based on AICD RONET Summary Outputs, June 2010.

Note: The columns cover ranges of AADT (average annual daily traffic), increasing from T1 to T8, which comprehensively cover the whole range of flows. Each row thus totals 100 percent (subject to rounding error).

Appendix 2h   Vehicle Utilization of Roads by Surface Class and by Passenger and Freight for 40 Countries

Country	Vehicle utilization in vehicle-km (millions)			
	Primary	Secondary	Tertiary	Classified
Angola	2,737	113	33	2,882
Benin	1,417	71	20	1,507
Botswana	2,030	662	133	2,826
Burkina Faso	981	63	54	1,098
Burundi	205	4	3	212
Cameroon	2,156	496	154	2,806
Central African Republic	102	47	17	165
Chad	410	74	34	518
Congo, Dem. Rep.	338	61	40	439
Congo, Rep.	148	128	64	340
Côte d'Ivoire	1,654	647	80	2,381
Eritrea	315	38	3	356
Ethiopia	1,002	267	367	1,637
Gabon	340	27	12	379
Gambia, The	111	10	3	124
Ghana	2,494	793	224	3,511
Guinea	862	135	21	1,018
Kenya	2,637	1,429	329	4,396
Lesotho	969	315	58	1,342
Liberia	275	26	17	318
Madagascar	1,023	720	78	1,821
Malawi	789	187	37	1,013
Mali	835	307	47	1,189
Mauritania	490	7	7	504
Mauritius	2,447	130	38	2,615
Mozambique	1,887	292	340	2,518
Namibia	2,579	972	329	3,880
Niger	607	48	90	745
Nigeria	24,123	5,794	522	30,439
Rwanda	353	81	4	438
Senegal	1,371	292	169	1,832
Sierra Leone	424	57	11	492
South Africa	91,648	1,763	1,194	94,605
Sudan	1,049	60	40	1,149
Swaziland	1,069	180	3	1,252
Tanzania	3,265	1,954	95	5,314
Togo	1,389	241	5	1,635
Uganda	2,914	363	166	3,443
Zambia	1,710	279	231	2,220
Zimbabwe	2,489	396	36	2,921
Total	**163,644**	**19,530**	**5,106**	**188,280**
Average	4,091	488	128	4,707
Median	1,036	183	43	1,425

Source: Calculations by Alberto Nogales based on AICD RONET Summary Outputs, June 2010.

Appendix 2i Classified Road Network Condition by Network Type for 40 Countries

(percent)

Country	Primary network			Secondary network			Tertiary network			Classified network		
	Good	Fair	Poor	Good	Fair	Poor	Good	Fair	Poor	Good	Fair	Poor
Angola	42	30	28	23	21	55	20	20	60	27	23	50
Benin	33	25	43	7	74	18	23	43	34	21	46	32
Botswana	68	22	10	68	16	16	31	34	35	49	27	24
Burkina Faso	75	21	4	72	11	17	63	28	9	70	21	9
Burundi	50	24	26	40	20	40	40	20	40	44	22	34
Cameroon	42	26	32	39	28	34	32	26	41	36	27	37
Central African Republic	60	19	20	56	16	29	40	20	40	50	19	31
Chad	35	43	22	28	27	44	39	20	40	36	27	37
Congo, Dem. Rep.	14	15	71	31	17	51	30	21	49	21	17	62
Congo, Rep.	4	23	73	4	2	94	24	12	65	15	10	74
Côte d'Ivoire	16	63	21	4	91	5	29	30	41	18	56	26
Eritrea	32	30	37	5	35	61	40	20	40	24	29	47
Ethiopia	61	25	15	28	38	34	32	25	43	38	28	34
Gabon	40	20	40	40	20	40	40	20	40	40	20	40
Gambia, The	20	40	40	20	20	60	20	25	55	20	28	52
Ghana	45	37	18	41	29	30	51	36	13	48	34	18
Guinea	19	21	60	8	10	82	40	20	40	30	18	52
Kenya	51	31	18	51	23	26	49	11	40	50	16	34
Lesotho	19	39	42	25	32	43	31	24	45	26	30	43
Liberia	21	61	19	1	35	64	40	20	40	26	34	40
Madagascar	64	22	14	25	31	44	10	5	85	20	14	66
Malawi	43	47	11	39	51	11	44	42	14	41	48	12

Mali	45	29	26	34	31	35	39	22	39	39	26	35
Mauritania	41	38	21	42	19	39	40	19	41	41	29	30
Mauritius	77	20	3	77	20	3	77	20	3	77	20	3
Mozambique	58	30	12	26	52	21	21	35	44	30	38	32
Namibia	56	36	8	44	42	14	33	25	43	38	30	32
Niger	47	42	12	33	33	34	31	24	45	36	31	33
Nigeria	38	37	24	14	38	48	31	33	36	29	36	35
Rwanda	41	48	11	7	21	73	0	0	100	12	19	69
Senegal	33	12	55	26	26	48	21	18	61	24	18	58
Sierra Leone	41	16	42	32	31	36	34	18	48	36	21	44
South Africa	90	8	2	31	34	35	31	24	45	42	23	35
Sudan	31	34	35	21	20	59	20	22	58	25	27	49
Swaziland	71	22	7	47	41	13	40	20	40	53	29	18
Tanzania	59	32	9	30	51	20	31	24	45	34	37	29
Togo	23	6	70	0	1	99	40	20	40	25	11	65
Uganda	14	73	13	0	11	89	40	20	40	22	23	55
Zambia	55	16	29	31	21	48	16	30	54	26	26	48
Zimbabwe	30	50	20	24	26	50	25	29	47	26	33	41
Average	**43**	**31**	**27**	**29**	**29**	**42**	**33**	**23**	**43**	**34**	**27**	**39**
Median	**41**	**29**	**21**	**29**	**26**	**39**	**32**	**21**	**41**	**32**	**27**	**36**

Source: Calculations by Alberto Nogales based on AICD RONET Summary Outputs, June 2010.

Note: For each network category, the percentages for the three road conditions add to 100 percent (subject to rounding error).

Appendix 2j   Road Accident Rates for Countries in Africa

In 2009, the World Health Organization published a study entitled "Global Status Report on Road Safety: Time for Action." It was based on a self-administered survey on road safety undertaken in 172 participating countries in 2008. For each country, a national data coordinator, assisted by a team of six to eight key respondents, prepared and checked the survey response. This included statistical data on the number of reported deaths and injury accidents, as well as institutional and administrative data on the approach to road safety in the country. Forty African countries were included in the survey. The data collected included recorded deaths, population, number of registered vehicles, and average per capita income (see table A2j.1).

The survey results showed the great difficulties of determining the road safety situation in Africa. Sixteen of the countries, while presenting statistics for deaths in 2008, were unable to give statistics for the trend in accidents. While injury accidents are always notoriously difficult to record and assess in all countries, the vast majority of African countries were also judged to underrecord deaths, in many cases by a factor of 3 or 4 and in one case by a factor of 10.

The World Health Organization adjusted the raw fatalities data in two ways. First, using the factors adopted by the European Conference of Ministers of Transport to secure consistency for a 30-day period, an adjustment was made to secure consistency in the definition of a traffic-related fatality. Second, information on the completeness of reporting was obtained from previous World Health Organization surveys. For countries with a high reporting level, a negative binomial model was calibrated explaining the death rates as a function of a set of independent variables described as exposure factors (E_j), risk or preventive factors (R_j), mitigating factors (M_j), and national income (I_j). Thus, $Y_j = f(R_j, M_j, E_j, I_j)$.

Despite the efforts to adjust for underrecording, the figures are still problematic. The estimated death rates per 10,000 people published in the report showed a very narrow range, between 23 in Burundi and 48 in Eritrea. Most values fell in the high 20s or low 30s. That might not be too strange, as the countries share the characteristics of relatively low income and poor policy provision for accident prevention; however, applying the same number of deaths to the registered vehicle populations in the various countries showed fatality rates per vehicle ranging from just over 2 to over 200 per 1,000 vehicles. Such a pattern of variation is hardly credible

Table A2j.1   Reported and Estimated Deaths from Road Accidents, 2008

Country	Population 2007	GNP per capita	Number of registered vehicles	Reported deaths	Estimated deaths	Death rate per 1,000 population	Death rate per 1,000 vehicles
Angola	17,024,084	2,560	671,060	2,358	6,425	38	9.5744047
Benin	9,032,787	570	222,850	653	2,815	31	12.631815
Botswana	1,881,504	5,840	293,755	482	636	34	2.1650695
Burkina Faso	14,784,291	430	515,453	804	4,595	31	8.9144888
Burundi	8,508,232	110	59,486	63	1,989	23	33.436439
Cameroon	18,549,176	1,050	312,259	1,069	5,206	28	16.672057
Cape Verde	530,437	2,430	54,158	49	133	25	2.4557775
Central African Republic	4,342,735	380	5,834	569	1,399	32	239.80117
Chad	10,780,571	540	124,088	814	3,696	34	29.785314
Congo, Rep.	3,768,086	1,540	100,000	207	1,084	29	10.84
Congo, Dem. Rep.	62,635,723	140	311,781	365	20,183	32	64.734541
Eritrea	4,850,763	230	60,849	81	2,350	48	38.620191
Ethiopia	83,099,190	220	244,257	2,441	29,114	35	119.19413
Gambia	1,708,601	320	14,450	54	625	37	43.252595
Ghana	23,478,394	590	931,642	1,856	6,942	30	7.4513601
Guinea-Bissau	1,695,043	200	57,839	152	583	34	10.079704
Kenya	37,537,716	680	1,004,243	3,760	12,198	34	12.146463
Lesotho	2,007,833	1,000	—	402	537	27	—
Liberia	3,750,261	150	11,086	—	1,235	33	111.40177
Madagascar	19,683,358	320	197,981	594	6,641	34	33.543623
Malawi	13,925,070	250	130,000	839	3,614	26	27.8

(continued)

431

Table A2j.1   (continued)

Country	Population 2007	GNP per capita	Number of registered vehicles	Reported deaths	Estimated deaths	Death rate per 1,000 population	Death rate per 1,000 vehicles
Mali	12,336,799	500	167,245	711	3,959	32	23.671859
Mauritania	3,123,813	840	350,000	262	1,109	36	3.1685714
Mozambique	21,396,916	320	258,680	1,952	7,432	35	28.730478
Namibia	2,074,146	3,360	239,612	368	594	29	2.4790077
Niger	14,225,521	280	76,061	570	5,357	38	70.430313
Nigeria	148,092,542	930	7,600,000	4,532	47,865	32	6.2980263
Rwanda	9,724,577	320	61,000	308	3,077	32	50.442623
São Tomé and Príncipe	157,638	870	1,219	20	52	33	42.657916
Senegal	12,378,532	820	280,594	345	4,023	33	14.337441
Sierra Leone	5,865,872	260	39,038	68	1,661	28	42.548286
South Africa	48,576,763	5,760	9,237,574	16,113	16,113	33	1.7442891
Sudan	38,560,488	960	1,200,000	2,277	13,362	35	11.135
Swaziland	1,141,427	2,580	116,050	235	300	26	2.5850926
Togo	6,585,147	360	48,234	613	1,851	28	38.37542
Uganda	30,883,805	340	3,673,658	2,838	7,634	25	2.0780377
Zambia	11,921,999	800	222,188	1,645	3,056	26	13.754118
Zimbabwe	13,349,434	131	1,556,586	1,348	3,669	28	2.3570815

Source: World Health Organization 2009.
Note: — = Not available.

and probably reflects a number of factors, including underrecording of vehicle numbers in extreme cases (such as the Central African Republic).

Despite misgivings about the spread of results, some fairly strong conclusions can be drawn. First, the average death rates in Africa are very high in comparison with world averages, matched only by rates in parts of South Asia. Second, where trends were recorded over time, death rates were rising in 13 countries, variable or static in 9, and falling in only 2. This pattern is contrary to the experience in most parts of the world, even in countries where vehicle stock is increasing.

Appendix 2k Road Maintenance Initiative Institutional Indicators, September 2007

Country	Transport policy[a] Cabinet adopted	Transport policy[a] Adoption date	Long-term road investment program Adopted	Long-term road investment program Period covered	Date of creation	Has a board?	Board with private majority?	Staff size (number)	Share of road fund resources from user charges (%)[c]	Share of road user charges from fuel levy (%)	Coverage of routine maintenance needs from all sources (%)	Coverage of total maintenance needs (%)[d]	Fuel levy[e] (U.S. cents/litre petrol)
Benin	yes	1993	yes	1996	1996	yes	no	12	24	52	100	59	5 5
Burundi	no	—	no	—	2001	yes	yes	14	85	60	28	40	4 4
Cameroon	yes	1996	no[f]	—	1998	yes	no	13	99	94	60	37	8 10
Central African Republic	yes	1990	yes	1990–2005	2000	yes	yes	21	91	90	75	20	10 10
Chad	yes	1999	yes	1999	2000	yes	yes	13	100	59	60	72	26 15
Congo, Rep.	no[f]	—	no[f]	—	2004	yes	no	20	—	—	60	95	—
Côte d'Ivoire	yes	1998	no	—	2001	yes	no	15	25	100	80	80	8 2
Djibouti	no	—	yes	2006	1999	yes	no	76	95	0	70	20	—
Ethiopia	yes	1997	yes	1997	1997	yes	no	35	7	99	100	65	9 7
Gabon	yes	1997	no	—	1997	yes	no	15	0	0	100	70	—
Ghana	yes	1996	yes	2001	1985	yes	yes	12	97	87	100	70	6 6
Guinea	yes	1999	yes	2003	2000	yes	no	21	54	100	41	67	2 2
Kenya	no	—	no	—	1999	yes	yes	48	99	96	50	55	8 8
Lesotho	yes	1995	yes	1995	1995	yes	no	10	92	67	50	35	3 3
Madagascar	no[f]	—	no	—	1997	yes	no	23	76	100	80	30	4 3
Malawi	yes	2001	no[f]	—	1997	no	no	—	100	90	40	50	8 6
Mali	yes	1998	yes	2002	2000	yes	yes	11	33	75	67	40	3 3
Mozambique	yes	2002	yes	2002	2003	yes	yes	23	93	87	100	60	12 1
Namibia	yes	1995	yes	2003	1999	yes	yes	16	75	96	80	65	16 1

Niger	yes	2004	yes	2005	1999	yes	6	96	92	88	35	6	6
Rwanda	yes	2005	yes	2005	1998	yes	10	65	67	21	25	4	4
Tanzania	yes	2003	yes	2001	1998	yes	10	89	94	29	76	8	8
Togo	yes	1996	no	—	1997	yes	10	100	100	56	56	7	7
Zambia	yes	2000	yes	2003	1994	yes	11	16	100	100	30	5	5
Zimbabwe	yes	2005	no	—	2001	no	15	98	98	30	70	3	3
Average							19	71	79	57	53	7	6

	% of direct channeling of road user charges	Allocation of RMF resources (%)				Established	Road agency			Road network conditions[b]		Audits	
		Main roads	Rural roads	Urban roads	RMF overheads		Date of creation	Has a board?	Private majority?	% in good	% in bad	Technical	Financial
Country													
Benin	10	96	13	0.3	2	no	—	—	—	41	7	yes	yes
Burundi	100	70	30	0	5.7	no	—	—	—	10	60	yes	yes
Cameroon	75	65	12	10	2.5	no	—	—	—	23	35	yes	yes
Central African Republic	100	75	—	5	10	no	—	—	—	—	—	no	no
Chad	100	82	0	15	3	no	—	—	—	48	—	yes	yes
Congo, Rep.	0	20	15	10	5	no	—	—	—	—	—	yes	yes
Côte d'Ivoire	25	90	0	10	0	yes	2001	yes	no	20	50	no	yes
Djibouti	0	50	0	20	30	no[f]	—	—	—	30	10	no	yes
Ethiopia	100	65	25	10	0	yes	1997	yes	no	37	35	yes	yes
Gabon	0	62	—	30	2	no	—	—	—	—	—	yes	yes
Ghana	100	37	30	25	1.5	yes	1974	yes	no	34	40	yes	yes
Guinea	59	49	24	22	9	no	—	—	—	22	38	yes	yes
Kenya	95	57	28	10	3	no	—	—	—	18	33	yes	yes
Lesotho	93	—	—	—	3.5	no	—	—	—	20	20	yes	yes

(continued)

Country	% of direct channeling of road user charges	Allocation of RMF resources (%)				Established	Road agency			Road network conditions[b]		Audits	
		Main roads	Rural roads	Urban roads	RMF overheads		Date of creation	Has a board?	Private majority?	% in good	% in bad	Technical	Financial
Madagascar	100	72	14	12	2	no[f]	—	—	—	25	25	yes	yes
Malawi	100	45	25	10	5	yes	1998	yes	yes	30	36	yes	yes
Mali	0	70	20	10	2.5	yes	2004	yes	no	50	20	yes	yes
Mozambique	13	35	25	10	1	yes	2003	yes	yes	55	28	yes	yes
Namibia	100	55	33	4.5	1.5	yes	1999	yes	yes	13	12	yes	yes
Niger	0	64	—	12	4.7	no	—	—	—	30	28	yes	yes
Rwanda	100	26	10	61	3	no[f]	—	—	—	20	40	no	yes
Tanzania	100	70	30	—	—	yes	1999	yes	yes	33	31	yes	yes
Togo	100	74	12	10	4	no	—	—	—	5	32	yes	yes
Zambia	0	50	25	25	—	yes	2004	yes	no	57	22	yes	—
Zimbabwe	100	28	28	14	6	yes	2002	yes	no	50	45	yes	—
Average	63	59	18	15	5	—	—	—	—	31	31	—	—

Source: SSATP 2007.

Note: RMF = road maintenance fund; — = not available or not relevant.

a. Transport policy document may be for roads alone or may be broader.

b. Denotes public road networks as a whole.

c. Road user charges = fuel levy + road tolls + transit + overloading fees.

d. Total maintenance denotes all maintenance works (routine and periodic) excluding rehabilitation.

e. This is the fuel levy actually collected (not amount legislated).

f. In preparation.

Appendix 2I   Selected Standards by Network Type, Surface Class, and Traffic Level for 40 Countries

(percent)

Country	Paved roads in the primary network with 10,000 AADT or more	Paved roads in the primary network with 300 AADT or less	Unpaved roads in the primary network with more than 300 AADT	Paved roads in the secondary network with 300 AADT or less	Unpaved roads in the secondary network with more than 300 AADT	Unpaved roads in the tertiary network with 300 AADT or less
Angola	0	42	0	100	0	100
Benin	1	10	34	0	2	95
Botswana	0	23	0	72	60	100
Burkina Faso	0	26	1	45	1	74
Burundi	0	47	0	0	0	100
Cameroon	0	16	36	49	18	94
Central African Republic	0	100	0	0	0	100
Chad	0	25	0	0	1	100
Congo, Dem. Rep.	0	86	0	0	0	100
Congo, Rep.	0	0	0	0	0	99
Côte d'Ivoire	0	24	3	30	7	93
Eritrea	0	36	0	100	0	100
Ethiopia	0	32	40	0	6	74
Gabon	0	10	0	52	0	99
Gambia, The	0	65	0	0	0	100
Ghana	0	13	0	26	0	72
Guinea	1	27	8	80	9	100
Kenya	0	26	3	37	4	89
Lesotho	10	44	18	27	18	65
Liberia	0	32	0	100	0	100
Madagascar	1	37	0	60	0	97

(continued)

Country	Paved roads in the primary network with 10,000 AADT or more	Paved roads in the primary network with 300 AADT or less	Unpaved roads in the primary network with more than 300 AADT	Paved roads in the secondary network with 300 AADT or less	Unpaved roads in the secondary network with more than 300 AADT	Unpaved roads in the tertiary network with 300 AADT or less
Malawi	0	22	13	87	0	81
Mali	0	48	0	59	3	100
Mauritania	16	82	15	100	0	100
Mauritius	0	0	0	0	0	0
Mozambique	0	34	7	72	2	40
Namibia	2	27	0	73	1	82
Niger	0	53	24	0	0	73
Nigeria	3	5	27	23	20	80
Rwanda	0	31	0	0	6	100
Senegal	0	9	0	34	0	77
Sierra Leone	0	69	8	73	1	100
South Africa	20	11	0	100	0	100
Sudan	0	19	2	100	0	100
Swaziland	1	5	62	4	24	100
Tanzania	2	10	27	25	10	100
Togo	6	19	76	0	44	99
Uganda	4	12	26	0	0	100
Zambia	2	41	0	86	6	80
Zimbabwe	0	16	0	90	5	100
Average	**2**	**31**	**11**	**43**	**6**	**89**
Median	**0**	**26**	**0**	**36**	**1**	**100**

Source: Calculations by Alberto Nogales based on AICD RONET summary outputs, June 2010.

Note: AADT = annual average daily traffic.

The thresholds used in these calculations broadly represent current engineering judgment on the minimum traffic levels necessary to progress from one standard to a higher one.

Appendix 2m Preservation Requirements for Securing the Custom Standard over a 20-Year Period for 40 Countries

| Country | Total classified (US$ millions) | Total including unclassified (US$ millions) | Grand total including urban (US$ millions) | Distribution by network type of grand total (%) | | | | |
| | | | | Classified | | | Unclassified | Urban |
				Primary	Secondary	Tertiary		
Angola	2,597	2,630	3,345	61	14	3	1	21
Benin	647	663	779	75	5	3	2	15
Botswana	1,613	1,625	1,932	45	31	7	1	16
Burkina Faso	1,044	1,059	1,181	70	13	5	1	10
Burundi	338	350	389	74	11	2	3	10
Cameroon	1,369	1,390	1,763	54	16	8	1	21
Central African Republic	783	799	1,028	41	31	4	2	22
Chad	725	737	944	51	17	9	1	22
Congo, Dem. Rep.	2,973	2,984	3,575	59	18	6	0	17
Congo, Rep.	647	663	779	75	5	3	2	15
Côte d'Ivoire	1,694	1,695	2,076	57	21	4	0	18
Eritrea	403	408	485	62	19	2	1	16
Ethiopia	1,817	1,871	1,970	51	20	22	3	5
Gabon	395	402	644	47	10	4	1	38
Gambia, The	296	298	353	62	19	2	0	16
Ghana	1,866	1,891	2,835	22	30	15	1	33
Guinea	908	924	1,056	64	17	5	1	13
Kenya	2,950	2,963	3,238	33	42	16	0	8
Lesotho	494	495	540	54	29	8	0	8

(continued)

Country	Total classified (US$ millions)	Total including unclassified (US$ millions)	Grand total including urban (US$ millions)	Distribution by network type of grand total (%)				
				Classified			Unclassified	Urban
				Primary	Secondary	Tertiary		
Liberia	367	383	546	45	16	7	3	30
Madagascar	1,459	1,468	1,631	33	42	14	1	10
Malawi	954	959	1,069	52	34	4	0	10
Mali	1,666	1,693	1,839	54	30	7	1	8
Mauritania	588	593	774	68	6	2	1	23
Mauritius	330	331	438	47	22	6	0	24
Mozambique	1,721	1,794	2,009	50	18	18	4	11
Namibia	2,066	2,105	2,448	36	35	14	2	14
Niger	1,026	1,034	1,095	71	11	11	1	6
Nigeria	11,305	11,462	12,916	55	30	3	1	11
Rwanda	271	291	420	53	11	1	5	31
Senegal	1,185	1,190	1,313	59	21	10	0	9
Sierra Leone	503	504	704	46	21	5	0	28
South Africa	14,696	15,044	17,802	39	29	14	2	15
Sudan	1,471	1,483	1,925	54	20	3	1	23
Swaziland	414	415	441	62	30	2	0	6
Tanzania	2,701	2,714	3,130	34	49	4	0	13
Togo	741	747	820	75	14	1	1	9
Uganda	2,710	2,721	2,986	41	44	7	0	9
Zambia	1,710	1,751	1,899	43	31	16	2	8
Zimbabwe	2,409	2,450	2,773	51	31	5	1	12
Total	**73,851**	**74,976**	**87,888**					
Average	1,846	1,874	2,197	53	23	7	1	16
Median	1,114	1,124	1,247	53	20	5	1	14

Source: Calculations by Alberto Nogales based on AICD RONET summary outputs, June 2010.

Note: The "custom" standard applies the same required standard to each road network type, with primary roads maintained to good standard and secondary only to fair standard. For the "optimal" standard, RONET evaluates road classes defined in terms of both engineering characteristics and traffic volumes and identifies for each road class the standard that maximizes the society benefits Net Present Value, at a given discount rate.

440

Appendix 2n Preservation Requirements for Securing the Optimal Standard over a 20-Year Period for 40 Countries

Country	Total classified (US$ millions)	Total including unclassified (US$ millions)	Grand total including urban (US$ millions)	Distribution by network type of grand total (%)				
				Classified			Unclassified	Urban
				Primary	Secondary	Tertiary		
Angola	1,208	1,276	1,609	63	8	4	4	21
Benin	525	558	612	78	5	3	5	9
Botswana	894	919	1,062	34	42	9	2	13
Burkina Faso	656	688	745	60	16	12	4	8
Burundi	162	187	206	65	11	3	12	9
Cameroon	1,105	1,149	1,323	59	17	8	3	13
Central African Republic	495	529	636	38	34	5	5	17
Chad	468	491	588	55	13	12	4	16
Congo, Dem. Rep.	1,443	1,467	1,742	52	21	10	1	16
Congo, Rep.	525	558	612	78	5	3	5	9
Côte d'Ivoire	1,149	1,152	1,329	58	24	5	0	13
Eritrea	261	271	307	65	18	2	3	12
Ethiopia	1,171	1,283	1,329	29	25	34	8	3
Gabon	248	262	375	52	9	6	4	30
Gambia, The	167	170	196	62	20	3	2	13
Ghana	1,498	1,563	2,469	19	21	21	3	37
Guinea	650	682	744	63	18	6	4	8
Kenya	2,264	2,292	2,420	26	42	25	1	5
Lesotho	461	464	485	46	36	13	1	4
Liberia	240	273	349	44	16	8	10	22
Madagascar	820	838	914	21	53	16	2	8

(continued)

Country	Total classified (US$ millions)	Total including unclassified (US$ millions)	Grand total including urban (US$ millions)	Distribution by network type of grand total (%)				
				Classified			Unclassified	Urban
				Primary	Secondary	Tertiary		
Malawi	682	692	744	42	42	8	1	7
Mali	834	891	959	40	36	11	6	7
Mauritania	179	190	275	54	7	5	4	31
Mauritius	246	248	259	82	11	2	1	4
Mozambique	1,206	1,370	1,470	31	18	33	11	7
Namibia	1,615	1,696	1,856	23	37	26	4	9
Niger	524	540	569	50	16	26	3	5
Nigeria	9,045	9,373	10,050	52	33	4	3	7
Rwanda	143	186	245	44	12	2	17	24
Senegal	873	884	941	63	21	9	1	6
Sierra Leone	344	346	440	47	26	6	0	21
South Africa	8,705	10,166	11,695	40	20	14	12	13
Sudan	1,044	1,069	1,274	60	15	7	2	16
Swaziland	339	341	353	54	40	2	1	3
Tanzania	2,491	2,517	2,711	26	59	7	1	7
Togo	651	664	698	72	20	1	2	5
Uganda	2,113	2,135	2,259	50	29	14	1	5
Zambia	1,178	1,349	1,418	33	27	23	12	5
Zimbabwe	1,512	1,598	1,748	51	27	8	5	9
Total	**50,136**	**53,331**	**60,016**					
Average	1,253	1,333	1,500	50	24	10	4	12
Median	751	765	829	51	20	8	3	9

Source: Calculations by Alberto Nogales based on AICD RONET summary outputs, June 2010.

Note: The "custom" standard applies the same required standard to each road network type, with primary roads maintained to good standard and secondary only to fair standard. For the "optimal" standard, RONET evaluates road classes defined in terms of both engineering characteristics and traffic volumes and identifies for each road class the standard that maximizes the society benefits Net Present Value, at a given discount rate.

Appendix 2o   Custom Standard 20-Year Preservation Needs by Work Type for 40 Countries

(US$ millions)

Country	Average annual grand total	Average annual		Distribution by work type		
		Years 1–5	Years 6–20	Road rehabilitation	Periodic maintenance	Recurrent maintenance
Angola	167	281	129	83	42	43
Benin	39	78	26	25	5	9
Botswana	97	148	79	50	22	24
Burkina Faso	59	58	59	21	19	18
Burundi	19	28	17	9	5	6
Cameroon	88	187	55	55	12	21
Central African Republic	51	68	46	15	17	19
Chad	47	78	37	18	13	17
Congo, Dem. Rep.	179	312	134	72	55	52
Congo, Rep.	39	78	26	25	5	9
Côte d'Ivoire	104	176	80	47	33	24
Eritrea	24	39	19	10	8	7
Ethiopia	98	143	84	20	55	23
Gabon	32	66	21	19	4	9
Gambia, The	18	34	12	10	4	4
Ghana	142	201	122	48	58	36
Guinea	53	108	35	29	11	13
Kenya	162	237	137	57	62	43
Lesotho	27	48	20	11	10	6
Liberia	27	42	22	11	8	9
Madagascar	82	147	60	42	19	21

(continued)

Country	Average annual grand total	Average annual		Distribution by work type		
		Years 1–5	Years 6–20	Road rehabilitation	Periodic maintenance	Recurrent maintenance
Malawi	53	67	49	19	16	18
Mali	92	124	81	38	25	29
Mauritania	39	56	33	20	7	11
Mauritius	22	22	22	7	9	5
Mozambique	100	146	85	43	33	25
Namibia	122	165	108	45	41	37
Niger	55	73	49	25	16	14
Nigeria	646	1,228	452	274	238	133
Rwanda	21	32	17	11	4	6
Senegal	66	151	37	43	9	13
Sierra Leone	35	63	26	16	9	10
South Africa	890	1,450	703	424	240	226
Sudan	96	159	75	38	30	29
Swaziland	22	29	20	4	12	6
Tanzania	157	195	144	45	61	51
Togo	41	94	23	23	11	7
Uganda	149	262	112	61	45	44
Zambia	95	190	63	55	20	20
Zimbabwe	139	223	111	63	44	32
Total	**4,394**	**7,284**	**3,431**	**1,929**	**1,338**	**1,127**
Average	110	182	86	48	33	28
Median	62	116	52	27	17	19

Source: Calculations by Alberto Nogales based on AICD RONET summary outputs, June 2010.

Note: The "custom" standard applies the same required standard to each road network type, with primary roads maintained to good standard and secondary only to fair standard. For the "optimal" standard, RONET evaluates road classes defined in terms of both engineering characteristics and traffic volumes and identifies for each road class the standard that maximizes the society benefits Net Present Value, at a given discount rate.

Appendix 2p   Optimal Standard 20-Year Preservation Needs by Work Type for 40 Countries

(US$ millions)

| Country | Average annual grand total | Average annual | | Distribution by work type | | |
		Years 1–5	Years 6–20	Road rehabilitation	Periodic maintenance	Recurrent maintenance
Angola	80	145	59	41	22	18
Benin	31	65	19	21	4	6
Botswana	53	79	45	26	16	11
Burkina Faso	37	36	38	11	15	12
Burundi	10	14	9	4	3	3
Cameroon	66	140	42	45	9	12
Central African Republic	32	27	34	4	15	12
Chad	29	37	27	9	10	10
Congo, Dem. Rep.	87	91	86	17	47	23
Congo, Rep.	31	65	19	21	4	6
Côte d'Ivoire	66	128	46	36	18	13
Eritrea	15	25	12	6	6	3
Ethiopia	66	80	62	16	33	17
Gabon	19	37	13	12	2	4
Gambia, The	10	15	8	6	2	2
Ghana	123	167	109	40	55	29
Guinea	37	74	25	22	8	7
Kenya	121	151	111	38	51	31
Lesotho	24	41	19	10	10	4
Liberia	17	23	16	6	6	5
Madagascar	46	82	34	25	11	9
Malawi	37	53	32	16	12	9
Mali	48	55	46	14	18	15
Mauritania	14	17	13	6	3	5

(continued)

Country	Average annual grand total	Average annual		Road rehabilitation	Distribution by work type	
		Years 1–5	Years 6–20		Periodic maintenance	Recurrent maintenance
Mauritius	13	17	12	2	8	3
Mozambique	74	105	63	33	25	16
Namibia	93	133	79	33	35	24
Niger	28	38	25	13	8	7
Nigeria	502	980	343	249	172	82
Rwanda	12	14	12	7	2	3
Senegal	47	115	24	34	6	7
Sierra Leone	22	31	19	10	7	5
South Africa	585	872	489	259	198	128
Sudan	64	104	50	25	23	16
Swaziland	18	20	17	3	11	4
Tanzania	136	175	122	38	66	31
Togo	35	77	21	20	11	4
Uganda	113	170	94	38	50	25
Zambia	71	145	46	45	14	11
Zimbabwe	87	148	67	40	30	17
Total	**3,001**	**4,790**	**2,404**	**1,302**	**1,048**	**651**
Average	75	120	60	33	26	16
Median	41	75	34	20	11	10

Source: Calculations by Alberto Nogales based on AICD RONET summary outputs, June 2010.

Note: The "custom" standard applies the same required standard to each road network type, with primary roads maintained to good standard and secondary only to fair standard. For the "optimal" standard, RONET evaluates road classes defined in terms of both engineering characteristics and traffic volumes and identifies for each road class the standard that maximizes the society benefits Net Present Value, at a given discount rate.

References

Archondo Callao, R. 2009. "RONET—Road Network Evaluation Tools: User Guide, Version 2.0." Sub-Saharan Africa Transport Policy Program Working Paper 89A, World Bank, Washington DC.

SSATP (Sub-Saharan Africa Transport Policy Program). 2007. "Road Maintenance Indicators Matrix." World Bank, Washington, DC.

World Health Organization. 2009. "Global Status Report on Road Safety: Time for Action." World Health Organization, Geneva.

APPENDIX 3

Rail Transport

Appendix 3a   Rail Networks in Africa

Country	Railway operator	Lines (kms)		Network density		Gauge[a]
		Total	Operating	km/1,000 km²	km/million pop.	
Angola	Amboin	123	0	—	—	3
	CFB	1,348	246	2.3	222	1
	CFL	510	181	—	—	1
	CFM-Angola	907	425	—	—	1
Benin	OCBN	579	438	5.1	66	2
Botswana	BRC	882	882	1.5	443	1
Burkina Faso/Côte d'Ivoire	Sitarail	1,250	1,250	2.0	35	2
Cameroon	CAMRAIL	1,100	1,016	2.3	58	2
Congo, Dem. Rep.	CFMK	366	366	1.9	—	1
	CFU	1,028	0	—	—	3
	SNCC	3,641	2,200	2.1	73	1
Congo, Rep.	CFCO	795	610	2.3	198	1
Djibouti/Ethiopia	CDE	781	781	1.0	100	2
Eritrea	ERA	117	0	1.0	21	3
Gabon	SETRAG	649	649	2.4	428	4
Ghana	GRC	947	947	4.0	40	1
Guinea	Bauxitelines	383	—	—	—	4
	ONCFG	662	0	4.3	104	2
Kenya	KRC	1,894	1,894	3.8	57	2
	Magadi	171	—	—	—	2
Liberia	Bong	77	77	—	—	4
	LAMCO	267	0	3.8	124	4
	NIOC	84	—	—	—	1
Madagascar	FCE	236	0	—	—	2
	Madarail	650	650	1.5	43	2

Country	Company					a
Malawi	CEAR	797	710	6.7	56	1
Mali	RNCFM	57	0	—	—	—
Mali/Senegal	Transrail	1,229	1,229	5.4	77	2
Mauritania	SNIM	704	—	0.7	225	4
Mozambique	CCFB	987	317	3.9	144	1
	CDN	872	611	—	—	1
	CFM-Mozambique	1,269	1,129	—	1,129	1
Namibia	TransNamib	2,382	1,683	2.9		1
Nigeria	Central Railways	52	0	—	—	4
	NRC	3,505	3,505	3.8	23	1
Senegal	Sefincs	—	—	—	—	2
	SNCS	408	40	—	—	2
	TrainBleu	—	—	—	—	2
Sierra Leone	MMR	84	0	1.2	13	1
South Africa	Coalex	574	574	—	—	1
	Metrorail	1,318	1,318	—	—	1
	Orex	880	880	—	—	1
	Spoornet	18,793	18,793	17.7	440	1
Sudan	SR-Sudan	4,680	2,252	—	—	1
Swaziland	SR-Swaziland	301	301	17.3	268	1
Tanzania	TRC	2,722	2,722	3.8	87	2
Tanzania/Zambia	TAZARA	1,860	1,860	—	—	1
Togo	CFTB	522	—	9.2	87	2
Uganda	URC	1,244	261	5.3	38	2
Zambia	RSZ	1,273	1,273	3.2	203	1
Zimbabwe	BBR	150	150	—	—	1
	NRZ	3,077	2,759	8.3	283	1

Source: Bullock 2009.
Note: — = not available. For full names of railway companies, see list following appendix 3e.
a. 1 = Cape; 2 = Metre; 3 = Narrow; 4 = Standard.

Appendix 3b Production Structure of African Railways, Average 1995–2005

Country	Railway operator	Transport task (million units)		Proportion of total task (%)		Average haul (km)	
		Passenger-km	Net tonne-km	Passenger	Freight	Passenger	Freight
Angola	CFM-Angola	89	472	16	84	91	146
Benin	OCBN	18	24	43	57	153	462
Botswana	BRC	94	631	13	87	237	342
Burkina Faso/Côte d'Ivoire	Sitarail	25	670	0	100	140	899
Cameroon	CAMRAIL	308	1,119	22	78	292	639
Congo, Dem. Rep.	CFMK	3	57	5	95	91	345
	SNCC	70	444	14	86	195	382
Congo, Rep.	CFCO	167	264	39	61	266	379
Djibouti/Ethiopia	CDE	82	97	0	100	253	404
Gabon	SETRAG	87	2,208	4	96	399	563
Ghana	GRC	64	224	22	78	30	123
Kenya	KRC	380	1,553	20	80	780	783
Madagascar	FCE	7	1	88	13	65	111
	Madarail	1	84	1	99	106	341
Malawi	CEAR	20	39	34	66	44	163
Mali	RNCFM	196	271	42	58	356	709
Mali/Senegal	Transrail	113	409	22	78	991	965
Mozambique	CCFB	3	172	2	98	13	277
	CDN	80	123	39	61	143	564

Namibia	TransNamib	45	1,247	3	97	450	636
Nigeria	NRC	174	77	69	31	73	819
Senegal	SNCS	173	485	26	74	34	168
South Africa	Spoornet	991	109,721	1	99	320	602
Sudan	SR-Sudan	40	766	3	97	625	606
Swaziland	SR-Swaziland	0	680	0	100	—	170
Tanzania	TRC	421	1,107	28	72	696	916
Tanzania/Zambia	TAZARA	241	937	20	80	219	1,483
Togo	CFTB	—	150	—	—	—	—
Uganda	URC	0	186	0	100	152	219
Zambia	RSZ	69	433	14	86	358	382
Zimbabwe	NRZ	457	1,404	25	75	250	360

Source: Bullock 2009.

Note: — = not available. For full names of railway companies, see list following appendix 3e.

Appendix 3c Rail Passenger Traffic

Country	Railway operator	Passenger (number / year)		Passengers as % of total transport task	Traffic unit, passengers (million passenger-km)		Traffic density, passengers (1,000 passenger-km/route-km)	Trip length per passenger (km/passenger)	
		2000	2005		2000	2005	2005	2000	2005
Angola	CFM-Angola	1,469	975	16	52	89	188	35	91
Benin	OCBN	577	118	43	100	18	119	173	153
Botswana	BRC	310	396	13	75	94	118	242	237
Burkina Faso/Côte d'Ivoire	Sitarail	300	0	0	126	—	46	420	—
Cameroon	CAMRAIL	1,266	1,053	22	384	308	318	303	292
Congo, Dem. Rep.	CFMK	155	33	5	16	3	11	103	91
	SNCC	1,307	359	14	188	70	60	144	195
Congo, Rep.	CFCO	546	628	39	84	167	195	154	266
Djibouti/Ethiopia	CDE	710	—	0	145	—	160	204	—
Gabon	SETRAG	237	218	4	95	87	139	401	399
Ghana	GRC	844	2,134	22	83	64	73	98	30
Kenya	KRC	422	487	20	311	380	176	737	780
Madagascar	Madarail	—	11	1	—	1	0	—	—
Malawi	CEAR	381	452	34	25	20	38	66	44
Mali	RNCFM	682	0	42	204	—	—	299	—
Mali/Senegal	Transrail	—	114	22	—	113	92	—	991
Mozambique	CCFB	540	229	2	18	3	44	33	13
	CDN	886	561	39	60	80	103	68	143
Namibia	TransNamib	154	—	3	66	45	33	—	—

Nigeria	NRC	2,610	2,399	69	170	174	31	65	73
Senegal	SNCS	2,783	0	26	143	—	—	51	—
South Africa	Spoornet	4,216	3,100	1	1,370	991	60	—	320
Sudan	SR-Sudan	410	64	3	129	40	26	315	625
Tanzania	TRC	631	605	28	428	421	163	678	696
Tanzania/Zambia	TAZARA	1,543	1,100	20	517	241	148	335	219
Uganda	URC	0	0	0	0	0	0	—	—
Zambia	RSZ	623	193	14	147	69	92	236	358
Zimbabwe	NRZ	1,691	—	25	565	—	166	—	—
Low-income, fragile		196	20	—	37	124	—	186	—
Low-income, nonfragile		415	33	—	122	158	—	231	—
Middle-income		1,165	15	—	282	1,962	—	310	—
Resource-rich		790	29	—	133	151	—	169	—
State-owned railways		862	30	—	202	780	—	200	—
Non-state-owned railways		310	22	—	108	95	—	315	—
Africa		586	27	—	145	569	—	226	—

Source: Bullock 2009.

Note: — = not available. For full names of railway companies, see list following appendix 3e. Passengers as percentage of total transport task is shown for 2005, where available; otherwise, for 2000.

Appendix 3d   Pricing and Institutions

Country	Railway operator	Freight average yield, 2000–05 (U.S. cents/net tonne-km)	Passenger average yield, 2000–05 (U.S. cents/passenger-km)	Concessioned company (1 = concessioned, 0 = nonconcessioned) 2005	Private company (1 = private, 0 = nonprivate) 2005
Angola	CFM-Angola	—	—	0	0
Benin	OCBN	5.8	2.0	0	0
Botswana	BRC	2.4	1.3	0	0
Burkina Faso/Côte d'Ivoire	Sitarail	5.5	3.3	1	0
Cameroon	CAMRAIL	5.2	2.2	1	0
Congo, Dem. Rep.	CFMK	13.7	4.2	0	0
	SNCC	12.5	3.1	1	0
Congo, Rep.	CFCO	10.7	5.6	1	0
Djibouti/Ethiopia	CDE	12.5	3.1	1	0
Gabon	SETRAG	2.5	8.6	1	0
Ghana	GRC	4.4	2.4	1	0
Kenya	KRC	3.8	0.6	1	0
Madagascar	Madarail	5.1	—	1	0
Malawi	CEAR	5.8	1.0	1	0
Mali	RNCFM	—	—	0	0
Mali/Senegal	Transrail	3.3	2.2	1	0
Mozambique	CCFB	3.3	0.5	1	0
	CDN	5.4	0.9	1	0
Namibia	TransNamib	—	—	0	0
Nigeria	NRC	—	—	1	0

Senegal	SNCS	—	—	0
South Africa	Spoornet	—	—	0
Sudan	SR-Sudan	—	—	0
Tanzania	TRC	4	1.6	0
Tanzania/Zambia	TAZARA	3	1.1	0
Uganda	URC	15.2	2.3	1
Zambia	RSZ	3.9	0.8	1
Zimbabwe	NRZ	—	—	0
Low-income, fragile		11	4	—
Low-income, nonfragile		5	1	—
Middle-income		7	2	—
Resource-rich		6	4	—
State-owned railways		7	3	—
Non-state-owned railways		5	2	—
Africa		6	2	—

Source: Bullock 2009.

Note: — = not available. For full names of railway companies, see list following appendix 3e.

Appendix 3e   Factor Productivity

Country	Railway operator	Employees (no.)		Labor productivity (1,000 traffic units per employee)		Carriage productivity (1,000 passenger-km per carriage)		Locomotive productivity (million traffic units per locomotive)		Wagon productivity (1,000 net tonne-km per wagon)	
		2000	2005	2000	2005	2000	2005	2000	2005	2000	2005
Angola	CFM-Angola	6,492	967	43	580	1,793	4,045	10	30	263	950
Benin	OCBN	1,204	1,040	157	40	5,263	900	13	3	273	74
Botswana	BRC	1,177	1,004	945	722	—	—	—	—	—	—
Burkina Faso/Côte d'Ivoire	Sitarail	1,712	1,393	379	481	4,500	—	32	35	682	1,020
Cameroon	CAMRAIL	2,711	2,367	477	603	5,053	4,738	18	26	783	868
Congo, Dem. Rep.	CFMK	2,945	1,950	57	221	1,527	3,212	14	27	104	300
	SNCC	3,401	3,359	29	18	291	64	16	10	215	257
Djibouti/Ethiopia	CDE	15,266	13,619	41	38	764	275	7	4	302	317
Gabon	SETRAG	1,400	1,291	1,284	1,778	2,065	1,891	30	39	749	902
Ghana	GRC	4,376	3,425	57	84	539	416	6	7	320	458
Kenya	KRC	9,700	9,500	170	203	948	1,159	20	24	187	218
Madagascar	Madarail	—	—	0	0	—	—	—	—	—	449
Malawi	CEAR	642	—	165	0	1,389	1,176	6	—	186	—
Mali	RNCFM	1,475	—	269	0	5,368	—	17	—	745	—
Mali/Senegal	Transrail	—	1,540	—	339	—	—	—	40	—	804

Mozambique	CCFB	5,859	623	42	281	818	750	14	13	263	476
	CDN	2,692	286	78	710	3,158	3,333	12	25	560	260
Namibia	TransNamib	2,213	—	440	0	—	—	21	—	568	—
Nigeria	NRC	14,507	6,748	17	37	566	737	8	13	62	59
Senegal	SNCS	1,490	—	455	0	1,324	—	15	—	713	—
South Africa	Spoornet	40,808	33,467	2,646	3,308	649	—	33	—	921	—
Sudan	SR-Sudan	14,021	—	96	0	772	—	12	—	282	—
Tanzania	TRC	8,947	5,900	195	259	3,035	3,264	23	25	968	583
Tanzania/Zambia	TAZARA	4,652	3,346	279	352	5,744	2,770	15	13	655	551
Uganda	URC	1,566	1,193	134	156	—	—	8	9	165	144
Zambia	RSZ	3,400	1,000	205	502	1,986	3,286	11	25	95	377
Zimbabwe	NRZ	9,536	—	408	0	—	—	—	8	—	—
Low-income, fragile		—	13,619	—	38	—	257	—	7	—	—
Low-income, nonfragile		—	4,387	—	240	—	1,610	—	19	—	—
Middle-income		—	32,443	—	3,258	—	—	—	136	—	—
Resource-rich		—	1,428	—	982	—	2,518	—	32	—	810
State-owned railways		—	31,195	—	3,118	—	1,664	—	25	—	708
Non-state-owned railways		—	3,530	—	387	—	2,945	—	24	—	510
Africa		—	2,9578	—	2,998	—	1,994	—	38	—	632

Source: Bullock 2009.

Note: — = not available. For full names of railway companies, see list following appendix 3e.

Railway Names

Country	Railway acronym	Railway full name
Angola	CFB	Caminho de Ferro de Benguela
Angola	CFL	Caminho de Ferro de Luanda
Angola	CFM-Angola	Caminho de Ferro de Moçâmedes
Benin	OCBN	Organisation Commune Benin-Niger des Chemins de fer et des Transports
Botswana	BRC	Botswana Railways
Burkina Faso/ Côte d'Ivoire	Sitarail	Société Internationale de Transport Africain par Rail
Cameroon	CAMRAIL	Cameroon National Railway
Congo, Dem. Rep.	SNCC	Société des Chemins de Fer du Congo
	CFMK	Chemins de Fer Matadi Kinshasa
	CFU	Chemin de Fer Urbain
Congo, Rep.	CFCO	Chemin de Fer du Congo Océan
Djibouti/Ethiopia	CDE	Chemin de Fer Djibouti-Ethiopien
Eritrea	ERA	Eritrean Railway
Gabon	SETRAG	Société d'Exploitation du Transgabonais
Ghana	GRC	Ghana Railway Company
Guinea	ONCFG	Office National des Chemins de Fer de Guinee
Kenya	KRC	Kenya Railways Corporation
Liberia	LAMCO	Liberian-American-Swedish Minerals Company
Liberia	NIOC	National Iron Ore Company of Liberia
Madagascar	FCE	Fianarantsoa Côte Est
Madagascar	Madarail	Private company
Malawi	CEAR	Central East African Railways
Mali	RNCFM	Réseau National des Chemins de Fer Malgache
Mauritania	SNIM	Société Nationale Industrielle et Minière de Mauritanie
Mozambique	CCFB	Campanhia dos Caminhos de Ferro da Beira
Mozambique	CDN	Corredor de Desenvolvimento do Norte
Mozambique	CFM-Mozambique	Portos e Caminhos de Ferro de Moçambique
Nigeria	NRC	Nigerian Railway Corporation
Senegal	SNCS	Société Nationale de Chemins de Fer du Senegal
Sierra Leone	MMR	Expected to be reopened soon
Sudan	SR-Sudan	Sudan Railways Corporation
Swaziland	SR-Swaziland	Swaziland Railway

(continued)

Country	Railway acronym	Railway full name
Tanzania	TRC	Tanzania Railways Corporation
Tanzania/Zambia	TAZARA	Tanzania-Zambia Railway Authority
Togo	CFTB	Chemin de Fer du Togo
Uganda	URC	Uganda Railways Corporation
Zambia	RSZ	Railway Systems of Zambia Limited
Zimbabwe	BBR	Beitbridge Bulawayo Railway
Zimbabwe	NRZ	National Railways of Zimbabwe

Reference

Bullock, R. 2009. "Railways in Sub-Saharan Africa." Africa Infrastructure Country Diagnostic Background Paper 17, World Bank, Washington, DC.

Airports and Air Transport

Appendix 4a   Data Sources for Air Transport Analysis

Air traffic analysis is highly data intensive. Unfortunately, because of limitations in both budget and capacities, those countries most in need of development aid are also those that have the most difficulties collecting and reporting vital data.

The standard source for traffic data collected by airlines or airports is the International Civil Aviation Organization (ICAO). Yet passenger counts from African airlines are often kept on paper ledgers with no computerization and, in many cases, are never submitted to ICAO. For many African countries, the gaps in reporting can be greater than five years; therefore, alternative sources of data must be tapped.

An excellent approximation of air traffic is the capacity offered. If one assumes that no airline would, over time, fly an aircraft with too few passengers to make the flight economically feasible, at any given point, 50 percent to 70 percent of the seat capacity offered on a route closely approximates the actual traffic. In addition, even with changes in load factor, the overall time trend of seat capacity approximates traffic trends. Hence, data published by airlines in reservation systems could substitute for travel data. Such data are readily available, are highly granular, and provide a wealth of information not only on the seat capacity, but also on the type of aircraft, the frequency of the routes, and the scheduled times of the flight.

Today, there are two main sources of these data: the Official Airline Guide and Seabury's Airline Data Group (ADG). Both sources depend on airlines to report their routes, and both have captured 99 percent of scheduled airline data, with about 900 to 1,000 airlines participating. Though the Official Airline Guide is the more established collector, both companies enjoy excellent industry reputations and are endorsed by the International Air Transport Association.

For the studies on Africa undertaken by the World Bank, ADG's data were used. A total of 12 snapshots in time was assembled, 4 each for the years 2001, 2004, and 2007. In order to ensure the capture of seasonal trends, the four samples for each year consisted of data for one week in the months of February, May, August, and November. To annualize these figures, the total of the four observations for one year was multiplied by 13.

The data consist of one record of each flight occurring during the sampled week, with relevant entries for the origin and destination airports, the changeover airport in the case of one-stop flights, the number of kilometers for the flight, the duration of the flight, the number of seats available on the flight, the number of times the flight occurred during the week, which weekdays the flight was scheduled, the aircraft type, the marketing operator as well as the actual operator, and various other flags of potential analytical utility.

Using Microsoft Access, the data were normalized and linked to other relevant tables (some of which were from other sources) to develop a relational database for summarization and querying. One important additional adjustment was made: flights going from one airport to another final destination with one or more stops in between had their capacity allocated evenly between each leg. This implies that a flight from airport A to airport C via airport B would have only half the capacity going from airport A to C, while the other half would deplane at airport B. This methodology prevents double counting of capacity for multilegged flights.

For assurance that the approximations used were reasonably accurate, some of the airport aggregates were compared to actual data when available from ICAO. The ratio of seats versus reported traffic hints at a load factor of about 65 percent to 69 percent for those routes tested—a sound figure supporting the credibility of the data.

The data are particularly helpful in capturing trends in city and country pairs, fleet renewal (in most cases the type of aircraft is provided, down to the series number, such as Boeing 737-100 versus 737-800), and airline market share. Nevertheless, the data reflect only scheduled and advertised services. An airline with no reservation system that issues paper tickets at the airport and provides a schedule only via a chalkboard or a printed flyer would not be captured. For example, the ADG data show virtually no older, Eastern-bloc-built aircraft operating in Africa, yet anecdotal evidence and accident statistics offer evidence of such operations. The overall portion of this market is suspected to be relatively small, though it has a high profile where incidents and accidents are concerned.

Since central data collection in Africa is still in a developmental stage, data had to be drawn from diverse sources. A questionnaire with extensive details on such things as civil aviation budgets, airport charges, and the number of employees within the civil aviation authority was sent to all 54 African countries. Twenty countries returned the questionnaires, with various levels of completion as their resources allowed. When a true comparative sample set was derived from the questionnaires, it has been applied in this report. However, since the questionnaire was large, and many sections were not completed by the civil aviation authorities, the sample size per answer was often very small.

In terms of air navigation and air traffic control infrastructure, reports provided by the Air Navigation Bureau of ICAO provided the most comprehensive inventory. Spot checks with data returned from the questionnaires agreed with data from the Air Navigation Bureau.

Data regarding airport infrastructure were gleaned from various sources. Satellite images from a commonly available satellite image service provided information regarding overall airport and runway condition. All airports receiving scheduled services were surveyed, and roughly 66 percent had images of sufficient quality to draw conclusions. Expert, on-the-ground observational inputs for a sample of 23 airports confirmed the general conclusions drawn from the satellite images. Additional information for each airport was researched using common data sources, including Jeppesen.

Since ICAO does not keep a central database regarding airport terminal capacity, data collected by http://www.azworldairports.com, a publisher in the United Kingdom that provides self-reported information from the largest African airports, were used.

Appendix 4b   Airports

Country	Airports with scheduled, advertised service (number)			Scheduled passenger carriers based in country (number)[a]	Total airports (number)[a]
	2001	2004	2007	2007	2007
Angola	2	11	13	2	24
Benin	1	1	1	7	7
Botswana	4	4	4	1	101
Burkina Faso	2	2	2	2	25
Burundi	1	1	1	1	3
Cameroon	9	6	3	3	38
Cape Verde	7	7	7	2	7
Central African Republic	1	1	1	0	38
Chad	1	1	1	1	40
Comoros	2	4	5	2	4
Congo, Dem. Rep.	8	8	8	53	239
Congo, Rep.	2	6	2	2	33
Côte d'Ivoire	1	1	1	3	25
Equatorial Guinea	1	1	2	5	2
Eritrea	1	1	1	1	4
Ethiopia	29	26	6	1	41
Gabon	12	3	8	5	30
Gambia, The	1	1	1	4	1
Ghana	1	1	4	2	8
Guinea	1	1	1	0	14
Guinea-Bissau	1	1	1	2	1
Kenya	13	12	10	9	172
Lesotho	—	1	1	0	10
Liberia	1	2	2	1	10
Madagascar	40	36	12	1	56
Malawi	5	3	3	1	23
Mali	6	2	1	5	26
Mauritania	8	8	1	0	20
Mauritius	2	2	2	1	2
Mozambique	8	12	12	1	21
Namibia	11	8	7	1	25
Niger	2	2	1	1	18
Nigeria	4	5	14	7	46
Rwanda	1	1	1	2	7
São Tomé and Príncipe	1	1	1	1	2
Senegal	3	4	4	2	13
Seychelles	1	2	2	1	14

(continued)

Country	Airports with scheduled, advertised service (number)			Scheduled passenger carriers based in country (number)[a]	Total airports (number)[a]
	2001	2004	2007	2007	2007
Sierra Leone	1	1	1	8	8
Somalia	5	3	7	0	14
South Africa	10	21	20	13	195
Sudan	12	11	11	5	44
Swaziland	1	1	1	5	11
Tanzania	16	11	12	3	72
Togo	1	1	1	1	7
Uganda	6	2	4	1	12
Zambia	8	6	6	1	69
Zimbabwe	5	3	4	3	129
Low-income, fragile	9.6	8.5	5.6	2.6	34.3
Low-income, nonfragile	2.1	2.0	2.4	5.3	33.3
Middle-income	8.1	7.9	7.2	3.3	36.9
Resource-rich	5.7	5.6	6.7	3.4	36.2
Africa	6.4	6.0	5.3	3.7	35.0

Source: Africa Infrastructure Country Diagnostic (AICD) data.
Note: — = not available.
a. Data are not available for 2001, 2004.

Appendix 4c   City Pairs Served

Country	Domestic (number)			International (number)		
	2001	2004	2007	2001	2004	2007
Angola	12	17	21	20	17	21
Benin	—	—	—	20	14	20
Botswana	4	6	4	7	9	8
Burkina Faso	1	1	1	12	14	13
Burundi	—	—	—	5	3	5
Cameroon	17	10	3	33	30	25
Cape Verde	14	11	10	20	16	29
Central African Republic	—	—	—	11	5	3
Chad	—	—	—	17	9	8
Comoros	1	4	7	18	24	19
Congo, Dem. Rep.	13	17	25	24	19	24
Congo, Rep.	4	8	1	31	22	21

(continued)

	Domestic (number)			International (number)		
Country	2001	2004	2007	2001	2004	2007
Côte d'Ivoire	—	—	—	42	30	29
Equatorial Guinea	—	—	1	13	9	18
Eritrea	1	—	3	10	10	14
Ethiopia	76	50	45	46	47	52
Gabon	18	11	9	25	24	13
Gambia, The	—	—	—	12	10	14
Ghana	—	—	5	35	26	30
Guinea	—	—	—	14	9	10
Guinea-Bissau	—	—	—	9	2	3
Kenya	25	18	15	60	66	77
Lesotho	—	—	—	1	1	1
Liberia	—	—	—	9	8	11
Madagascar	133	97	63	16	21	32
Malawi	9	8	3	15	20	12
Mali	15	1	—	24	19	18
Mauritania	8	10	1	15	10	10
Mauritius	1	1	1	32	32	34
Mozambique	22	25	30	13	22	32
Namibia	22	13	8	15	13	14
Niger	—	—	—	18	14	9
Nigeria	17	6	22	50	41	51
Rwanda	3	—	—	10	6	7
São Tomé and Príncipe	1	—	—	5	3	5
Senegal	4	4	4	33	34	43
Seychelles	1	1	1	16	16	12
Sierra Leone	—	—	—	8	9	11
Somalia	9	6	9	14	13	19
South Africa	48	48	36	101	100	115
Sudan	22	18	13	33	35	32
Swaziland	—	—	—	4	4	4
Tanzania	44	21	19	41	44	38
Togo	—	—	—	18	14	12
Uganda	8	1	4	21	10	19
Zambia	18	9	9	17	16	16
Zimbabwe	7	2	5	31	20	23
Low-income, fragile	28.8	21.2	17.8	30.6	30.0	36.2
Low-income, nonfragile	5.3	7.3	9.8	15.3	11.9	13.5
Middle-income	22.2	18.4	14.7	51.5	50.9	54.8
Resource-rich	15.4	11.3	9.9	26.6	22.6	22.8
Africa	20.4	16.5	14.0	30.7	28.8	32.1

Source: AICD data.

Note: — = not available.

Appendix 4d   Installation of Ground-Based Navigational Aids in Africa

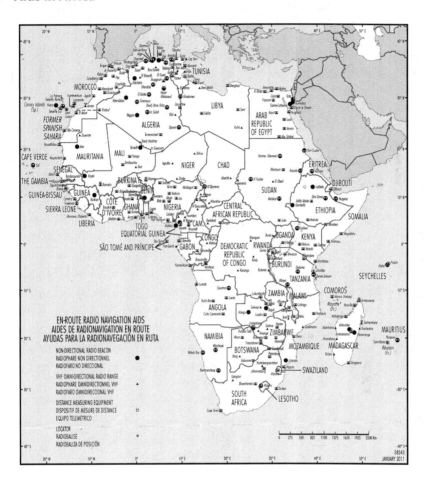

Appendix 4e   Total Capacity Supplied

Country	Annual seats, domestic (number)			Annual seats, intercontinental (number)			Annual seats, total (number)		
	2001	2004	2007	2001	2004	2007	2001	2004	2007
Angola	115,960	888,160	1,199,016	304,365	354,016	588,978	817,999	1,634,414	2,272,173
Benin	—	—	—	170,653	103,233	99,268	572,433	440,222	422,400
Botswana	193,648	212,784	241,696	—	—	—	569,634	664,794	677,404
Burkina Faso	28,362	30,622	20,245	113,707	113,698	147,095	383,656	372,975	412,061
Burundi	—	—	—	—	—	6,864	142,983	160,011	270,227
Cameroon	640,220	641,177	105,742	470,461	467,071	398,034	1,784,023	1,752,045	975,865
Cape Verde	994,179	750,889	575,120	418,349	526,617	538,094	1,620,918	1,471,323	1,168,759
Central African Republic	—	—	—	26,869	10,738	23,842	144,991	74,074	44,503
Chad	—	—	—	77,175	75,166	88,608	252,926	214,829	197,682
Comoros	27,720	94,475	111,258	183,447	223,009	336,540	351,020	466,811	571,879
Congo, Dem. Rep.	477,438	381,511	327,988	112,801	163,618	193,414	1,008,707	902,805	989,619
Congo, Rep.	512,564	806,822	443,634	52,390	106,093	117,962	953,186	1,281,700	913,478
Côte d'Ivoire	—	—	—	509,492	280,523	297,891	1,730,391	1,319,873	1,148,893
Equatorial Guinea	—	—	17,446	105,664	189,746	214,708	208,628	289,020	321,585
Eritrea	31,200	—	94,146	222,317	272,289	268,736	365,701	388,141	451,588
Ethiopia	932,616	887,332	728,797	745,396	1,030,439	2,004,704	2,324,225	2,879,530	4,570,648
Gabon	808,184	596,761	374,400	212,732	195,832	122,720	1,492,461	1,276,834	769,912
Gambia, The	—	—	—	95,069	66,183	126,061	378,853	229,697	252,270
Ghana	—	—	144,183	673,485	837,785	832,895	1,401,638	1,419,812	1,886,897
Guinea	—	—	—	118,460	107,354	111,462	411,925	309,764	317,378
Guinea-Bissau	—	—	—	29,744	39,910	20,280	117,468	73,684	66,846
Kenya	2,166,121	2,344,949	2,093,416	1,551,097	1,957,904	2,755,352	6,059,931	6,843,545	7,993,551
Lesotho	—	—	—	—	—	—	45,240	63,336	85,592
Liberia	—	—	—	35,681	11,440	40,040	113,165	88,712	161,485

Madagascar	1,333,890	1,324,447	1,291,284	340,535	466,665	574,379	1,865,735	2,019,011	2,147,009
Malawi	188,071	174,373	167,007	20,358	14,235	3,842	559,130	547,404	605,880
Mali	76,811	18,720	—	207,398	198,536	165,776	831,800	822,355	730,231
Mauritania	268,437	311,792	20,475	78,600	97,708	148,928	518,561	632,853	404,257
Mauritius	232,128	321,984	502,892	1,993,050	2,085,538	2,235,545	2,675,485	2,822,664	3,282,799
Mozambique	660,417	628,793	1,144,644	61,100	74,022	91,637	1,026,731	1,059,270	1,819,116
Namibia	148,980	123,409	84,162	157,820	222,300	242,736	948,086	1,224,613	1,204,710
Niger	—	—	—	38,428	33,800	41,717	215,703	179,930	170,131
Nigeria	1,059,292	1,996,592	9,304,568	1,220,923	1,492,170	2,437,702	3,479,787	4,432,305	13,116,014
Rwanda	5,434	—	—	16,181	18,304	18,304	225,013	279,398	485,507
São Tomé and Príncipe	11,856	—	—	14,300	50,505	16,478	61,152	68,328	45,725
Senegal	80,219	109,538	127,244	817,893	851,897	1,231,358	1,640,869	1,803,805	2,618,012
Seychelles	651,040	680,550	712,530	331,773	392,548	424,008	1,188,031	1,218,354	1,277,562
Sierra Leone	—	—	—	36,504	30,186	48,893	132,097	165,793	228,522
Somalia	91,035	35,549	126,633	28,752	4,485	50,005	198,179	134,414	350,701
South Africa	22,240,929	22,782,903	31,767,537	5,856,431	6,443,168	7,707,063	32,352,734	34,332,229	45,789,157
Sudan	507,429	471,575	610,263	906,861	1,200,747	1,571,891	1,899,138	2,167,423	3,099,328
Swaziland	—	—	—	—	—	—	63,934	100,854	141,388
Tanzania	1,155,362	1,567,908	1,871,255	442,514	494,587	585,763	2,413,840	3,257,388	3,728,170
Togo	—	—	—	135,714	106,808	76,856	461,747	331,373	296,361
Uganda	73,983	28,392	70,980	185,484	212,940	493,740	1,059,435	929,600	1,543,057
Zambia	175,539	108,511	437,658	63,180	78,624	113,217	953,082	841,685	2,010,641
Zimbabwe	479,080	393,120	237,835	200,360	157,456	182,585	2,011,848	1,412,844	1,530,406
Low-income, fragile	769,396	876,134	930,370	638,779	772,262	1,239,498	1,848,947	2,079,351	2,834,134
Low-income, nonfragile	186,388	226,164	179,572	124,965	108,893	119,996	508,682	408,422	448,427
Middle-income	4,293,495	3,599,684	4,729,884	2,828,044	3,031,996	3,962,775	6,164,366	5,906,664	7,737,390
Resource-rich	545,598	787,085	1,561,591	379,306	462,163	628,202	1,315,692	1,543,362	2,630,742
Africa	1,607,628	1,603,779	2,052,968	891,106	986,941	1,338,270	2,437,573	2,454,204	3,327,081

Source: AICD data.

Note: — = not available. Intercontinental flights exclude those between North Africa and Sub-Saharan Africa.

Appendix 4f   Costs of Airport Construction versus Rehabilitation

a. Estimated basic construction costs of a new airport with a 3,000-meter runway

Area	Length	Width	Area	Unit of measure	Costs (US$)	Running total (US$)
Terminal (2 floors)	100	100	20,000	Meters squared	53,819,552	53,819,552
Overall land requirement	n.s.	n.s.	6.63	Kilometers squared	n.i.	n.i.
Apron	n.s.	n.s.	85,760	Meters squared	18,462,259	72,281,811
Taxiway to apron	250	21	5,250	Meters squared	1,412,763	73,694,574
Runway	3,000	21	n.s.	Meters	17,716,535	91,411,110
Parallel taxiway	3,000	21	63,000	Meters squared	13,562,527	104,973,637

b. Estimated costs of rehabilitating an airport with a 2,000- by 30-meter runway, extending to 3,000 meters, and adding a parallel taxiway

Item	Unit cost per meter (US$)	Cost
Rehab 2,000 meters of asphalt	5,506	11,011,788
Add 1,000-meter extension	8,000	8,000,000
Add full-length taxiway	4,593	13,779,528
Total		**32,791,316**

Source: Per-unit costs are from Florida Department of Transportation, http://www.dot.state.fl.us/planning/policy/costs/Airports.pdf.

Note: n.s. = not specified; n.i. = not included. The per-unit costs have been cross-checked with estimates on currently proposed airport projects in Africa. Data do not include land acquisition costs. Also missing are other significant costs, such as a control tower, an instrument landing system, fuel facilities, vehicles, a fire station, parking facilities, landside access, and so on.

Appendix 4g   Domestic Air Transport Markets in Africa, 2007

Country	Estimated seats (millions)	Estimated seat-kilometers (millions)	Annual growth seat-kilometers (%)	Airlines (number)	City pairs, November 2007	Net city-pair change, 2004–07
South Africa	15.9	14,309.96	11.8	12	36	−8
Nigeria	4.7	2,235.54	66.8	7	19	13
Mozambique	0.6	492.62	19.7	3	28	9
Kenya	1.0	408.13	−3.7	4	15	−3
Tanzania	0.9	386.24	−1.8	5	16	−3
Madagascar	0.6	335.71	3.7	2	24	−61
Angola	0.6	309.64	10.0	2	21	4
Sudan	0.3	256.69	12.9	3	13	−5
Congo, Dem. Rep.	0.2	170.91	−5.7	2	9	−7
Mauritius	0.3	150.47	16.0	2	1	0
Ethiopia	0.4	129.87	−6.5	1	8	−42
Congo, Rep.	0.2	83.85	−18.1	4	1	−7
Zambia	0.2	65.82	57.7	2	6	0
Botswana	0.1	64.53	6.3	1	3	−3
Cape Verde	0.3	56.01	−7.9	1	10	−1
Zimbabwe	0.1	48.12	−16.4	1	5	3
Gabon	0.2	46.51	−9.4	1	9	−2
Somalia	0.1	45.22	54.5	4	5	2
Namibia	0	22.21	−12.1	1	7	−6
Malawi	0.1	20.28	−1.1	1	3	−3
Ghana	0.1	18.67	—	1	4	—
Senegal	0.1	17.38	4.0	1	3	0
Cameroon	0.1	16.90	−49.0	3	3	−7
Seychelles	0.4	15.45	1.5	1	1	0
Uganda	0	12.71	33.6	1	4	3
Comoros	0.1	10.94	11.9	3	7	6
Eritrea	0	9.33	—	1	—	—
Mauritania	0	3.38	−62.0	1	—	—
Burkina Faso	0	3.38	−12.9	1	1	0
Equatorial Guinea	0	2.09	—	1	1	—

Source: Analysis of data provided by Seabury ADG.
Note: — = not available. Countries are listed from highest to lowest number of estimated seat-kilometers. During the year, airlines may have stopped servicing a city pair—that is, although the Republic of Congo may show four airlines for 2007, in November 2007, there were, in fact, only two. Significant are the very high growth rates in Nigeria, Mozambique, and Zambia. Although Somalia is also growing at a very high rate, the domestic market is roughly only one-tenth the size of Kenya's, for example. Countries with missing growth rates represent new data where previous services in 2001 either did not exist or were not published.

Appendix 4h   Market Concentration, 2007

Country	Herfindahl Index, domestic and international markets	Herfindahl Index, domestic market	Herfindahl Index, international market
Angola	0.3	0.7	0.3
Benin	0.1	—	0.1
Botswana	0.6	1.0	0.5
Burkina Faso	0.2	1.0	0.2
Burundi	0.3	—	0.3
Cameroon	0.1	0.4	0.1
Cape Verde	0.6	1.0	0.4
Central African Republic	0.5	—	0.5
Chad	0.4	—	0.4
Comoros	0.4	0.5	0.5
Congo, Dem. Rep.	0.2	0.6	0.2
Congo, Rep.	0.3	0.9	0.2
Côte d'Ivoire	0.1	—	0.1
Equatorial Guinea	0.1	1.0	0.1
Eritrea	0.2	1.0	0.3
Ethiopia	0.7	1.0	0.7
Gabon	0.4	1.0	0.2
Gambia, The	0.1	—	0.1
Ghana	0.1	1.0	0.1
Guinea	0.2	—	0.2
Guinea-Bissau	0.5	—	0.5
Kenya	0.4	0.6	0.3
Lesotho	1.0	—	1.0
Liberia	0.2	—	0.2
Madagascar	0.7	1.0	0.3
Malawi	0.3	1.0	0.2
Mali	0.1	—	0.1
Mauritania	0.2	1.0	0.2
Mauritius	0.3	0.5	0.3
Mozambique	0.3	0.5	0.2
Namibia	0.4	1.0	0.4
Niger	0.2	—	0.2
Nigeria	0.1	0.2	0.1
Rwanda	0.3	—	0.3
São Tomé and Príncipe	0.3	—	0.3
Senegal	0.1	1.0	0.1
Seychelles	0.7	1.0	0.4
Sierra Leone	0.2	—	0.2

(continued)

Country	Herfindahl Index, domestic and international markets	Herfindahl Index, domestic market	Herfindahl Index, international market
Somalia	0.3	0.4	0.3
South Africa	0.2	0.2	0.1
Sudan	0.2	0.7	0.1
Swaziland	0.7	—	0.7
Tanzania	0.2	0.3	0.1
Togo	0.2	—	0.2
Uganda	0.2	1.0	0.2
Zambia	0.2	0.7	0.1
Zimbabwe	0.3	1.0	0.2
Low-income, fragile	0.3	0.8	0.2
Low-income, nonfragile	0.3	0.7	0.3
Middle-income	0.5	0.8	0.4
Resource-rich	0.2	0.7	0.2
Africa	0.3	0.8	0.3

Source: AICD data.
Note: — = not available.

Appendix 4i   Trends in Aircraft Age (seat-kilometers as percentage of total)

Country	Aircraft of unknown age (% of total)			Old aircraft (% of total)			Recent aircraft (% of total)		
	2001	2004	2007	2001	2004	2007	2001	2004	2007
Angola	18.6	57.8	40.2	14.1	0.2	0.1	67.3	41.9	59.7
Benin	13.1	3.6	4.2	32.0	13.7	7.4	54.9	82.7	88.5
Botswana	0.9	0.4	0.0	11.6	0.0	0.0	87.6	99.6	100.0
Burkina Faso	2.3	3.6	0.0	16.6	23.3	6.6	81.2	73.1	93.4
Burundi	37.7	13.8	0.0	46.8	65.7	12.7	15.5	20.5	87.3
Cameroon	13.2	10.2	0.3	16.4	1.5	7.9	70.4	88.3	91.8
Cape Verde	0.0	2.7	0.9	0.6	1.8	0.0	99.4	95.5	99.1
Central African Republic	15.1	72.5	0.0	27.9	0.0	0.0	57.0	27.5	100.0
Chad	0.0	13.8	0.0	9.9	0.0	0.5	90.1	86.2	99.5
Comoros	14.4	8.3	0.6	31.1	46.6	19.7	54.5	45.1	79.7
Congo, Dem. Rep.	10.2	6.5	0.6	50.1	48.6	24.7	39.7	44.9	74.7
Congo, Rep.	20.4	34.4	5.0	28.5	10.1	21.7	51.1	55.5	73.3

(continued)

Country	Aircraft of unknown age (% of total)			Old aircraft (% of total)			Recent aircraft (% of total)		
	2001	2004	2007	2001	2004	2007	2001	2004	2007
Côte d'Ivoire	0.6	4.0	0.5	9.0	14.6	8.7	90.4	81.4	90.8
Equatorial Guinea	3.9	1.7	1.7	1.4	0.1	0.0	94.7	98.1	98.3
Eritrea	12.2	7.7	1.5	22.1	0.0	10.7	65.7	92.3	87.8
Ethiopia	5.6	1.2	0.5	3.2	2.7	0.9	91.2	96.1	98.5
Gabon	41.1	33.3	0.8	6.7	4.1	1.2	52.3	62.6	98.1
Gambia, The	0.9	3.0	0.0	71.6	84.0	5.5	27.5	13.0	94.5
Ghana	0.7	3.9	0.6	47.3	39.7	2.6	52.0	56.4	96.8
Guinea	0.8	7.4	0.0	12.1	12.6	4.9	87.1	80.0	95.1
Guinea-Bissau	18.1	0.0	0.0	11.8	0.0	0.0	70.1	100.0	100.0
Kenya	6.5	11.2	14.1	9.8	8.8	5.7	83.7	79.9	80.2
Lesotho	0.0	0.0	0.0	0.0	0.0	0.0	100.0	100.0	100.0
Liberia	0.0	19.7	0.0	52.4	33.2	67.1	47.6	47.0	32.9
Madagascar	15.4	1.8	0.4	14.6	23.8	21.6	70.0	74.4	78.0
Malawi	5.4	1.9	0.0	56.2	64.8	20.6	38.3	33.3	79.4
Mali	2.8	9.1	0.7	10.1	9.3	3.7	87.1	81.5	95.6
Mauritania	0.0	1.2	0.0	33.7	24.2	10.5	66.3	74.7	89.5
Mauritius	18.3	0.9	5.5	0.8	0.8	0.7	80.9	98.2	93.8
Mozambique	32.9	25.8	26.7	3.9	8.1	16.3	63.2	66.0	57.0
Namibia	27.2	56.2	19.9	22.0	3.7	1.1	50.8	40.0	79.0
Niger	0.0	0.0	0.0	18.1	4.0	5.7	81.9	96.0	94.3
Nigeria	9.9	12.8	8.6	18.9	3.3	20.0	71.2	83.9	71.4
Rwanda	6.5	7.2	0.0	45.1	13.7	4.2	48.4	79.1	95.8
São Tomé and Príncipe	14.7	6.6	16.4	3.0	0.0	0.0	82.3	93.4	83.6
Senegal	12.6	0.5	0.3	3.8	5.0	1.4	83.7	94.5	98.3
Seychelles	3.0	2.1	0.0	5.7	0.4	2.9	91.3	97.4	97.1
Sierra Leone	6.1	19.6	0.0	93.9	52.2	45.1	0.0	28.2	54.9
Somalia	86.4	77.1	77.3	12.5	17.8	21.7	1.1	5.2	1.0
South Africa	18.6	13.1	14.0	18.5	5.4	2.2	62.9	81.6	83.8
Sudan	8.4	22.5	14.6	17.3	4.0	8.8	74.4	73.5	76.7
Swaziland	3.8	0.0	0.0	0.0	26.5	23.3	96.2	73.5	76.7
Tanzania	8.2	5.6	3.6	25.7	32.8	17.1	66.1	61.6	79.3
Togo	3.9	1.4	0.2	64.1	5.9	0.4	32.0	92.6	99.5
Uganda	12.9	6.3	1.2	17.3	23.3	25.7	69.9	70.4	73.2
Zambia	39.1	17.7	16.4	23.2	13.0	19.8	37.7	69.3	63.8
Zimbabwe	6.5	9.1	13.0	41.2	21.6	15.5	52.3	69.4	71.4
Low-income, fragile	7.9	5.4	3.4	21.4	18.7	9.4	70.7	76.0	87.2
Low-income, nonfragile	15.2	17.1	7.3	36.7	26.9	15.8	48.2	56.0	76.9
Middle-income	11.7	10.6	7.6	9.9	7.3	4.1	78.4	82.1	88.3
Resource-rich	17.2	22.7	9.7	15.2	4.0	8.9	67.7	73.3	81.4
Africa	12.5	12.9	6.6	21.8	15.7	9.8	65.7	71.4	83.6

Source: AICD data.

Appendix 4j   Trends in Aircraft Size (seat-kilometers as percentage of total)

Country	Aircraft of unknown size (% of total)			Large aircraft (% of total)			Medium-sized aircraft (% of total)			Smaller-sized aircraft (% of total)		
	2001	2004	2007	2001	2004	2007	2001	2004	2007	2001	2004	2007
Angola	1.0	1.6	0.1	91.3	81.8	86.0	7.7	16.6	13.9	0	0	0
Benin	2.1	0	0	53.4	66.8	57.9	42.1	29.3	41.2	2.3	3.9	0.9
Botswana	0	0	0	0	0	0	0	0	0	100	100	100
Burkina Faso	0	3.6	0	81.2	60.3	45.7	11.7	17.3	46.7	7.1	18.8	7.6
Burundi	0	0	0	0	0	29.2	90.9	61.8	64.5	9.1	38.2	6.3
Cameroon	0	0	0	77.0	71.8	65.7	20.6	28.0	31.9	2.4	0.2	2.4
Cape Verde	0	0	0	75.0	56.8	6.4	17.2	37.9	88.1	7.9	5.3	5.5
Central African Republic	5.1	7.1	0	55.3	27.5	76.5	37.9	65.5	23.5	1.8	0	0
Chad	0	13.3	0	81.7	55.7	6.4	17.3	31.0	93.6	1.0	0	0
Comoros	0	0	0	51.7	29.7	70.5	45.8	65.3	25.3	2.5	5.0	4.2
Congo, Dem. Rep.	1.2	4.0	0	51.3	49.8	57.5	46.8	45.9	39.3	0.7	0.3	3.2
Congo, Rep.	12.4	26.1	0	48.4	27.3	48.2	27.4	45.8	50.5	11.9	0.7	1.3
Côte d'Ivoire	0	0.3	0	83.6	60.3	47.7	15.3	31.6	46.8	1.1	7.8	5.5
Equatorial Guinea	0	0	0	27.6	39.9	19.2	72.1	59.6	80.7	0.4	0.5	0.2
Eritrea	10.7	0	1.5	57.3	77.1	63.7	32.1	22.9	34.8	0	0	0
Ethiopia	0.4	0.4	0.1	46.7	46.5	58.6	42.8	47.3	39.7	10.0	5.7	1.5
Gabon	0	7.4	0	68.4	65.4	62.1	29.9	24.6	27.6	1.7	2.6	10.3
Gambia, The	0	0	0	70.6	74.2	9.2	10.5	15.2	88.2	18.8	10.5	2.5
Ghana	0.2	0.1	0	95.0	93.6	84.3	4.3	6.1	14.4	0.5	0.1	1.3
Guinea	0.8	4.8	0	72.7	44.8	61.4	25.1	45.8	37.8	1.4	4.5	0.8
Guinea-Bissau	0	0	0	62.3	46.6	78.7	22.3	44.7	0.0	15.4	8.7	21.3

(continued)

Country	Aircraft of unknown size (% of total)			Large aircraft (% of total)			Medium-sized aircraft (% of total)			Smaller-sized aircraft (% of total)		
	2001	2004	2007	2001	2004	2007	2001	2004	2007	2001	2004	2007
Kenya	0	1.5	0.1	78.1	73.1	76.7	19.1	22.2	20.8	2.8	3.2	2.4
Lesotho	0	0	0	0	0	0	0	0	0	100	100	100
Liberia	0	5.9	0	88.8	47.0	8.4	11.2	47.1	90.0	0	0	1.5
Madagascar	0	0	0	68.2	70.9	69.9	25.6	21.8	20.7	6.1	7.3	9.4
Malawi	0	0	0	12.6	5.6	21.1	76.2	84.3	71.1	11.2	10.1	7.8
Mali	1.0	8.5	0	71.9	47.0	45.9	22.7	42.0	51.8	4.4	2.5	2.3
Mauritania	0	1.2	0	52.9	17.5	0	16.6	72.3	98.1	30.5	9.0	1.9
Mauritius	0	0.9	0	95.5	89.0	92.1	2.6	8.0	6.3	1.9	2.1	1.6
Mozambique	0	0	0	52.3	55.8	43.3	37.1	33.1	42.5	10.6	11.1	14.2
Namibia	0	0	0	56.3	64.8	64.1	31.6	26.0	28.3	12.0	9.1	7.6
Niger	0	0	0	75.6	52.1	49.4	23.7	43.0	44.9	0.7	4.9	5.7
Nigeria	0.2	3	0	90.6	84.1	70.4	9.2	12.5	27.6	0.0	0.4	2.0
Rwanda	0	0	0	30.4	25.3	26.0	54.0	73.6	72.0	15.6	1.1	2.0
São Tomé and Príncipe	0	0	0	80.4	27.3	80.7	14.7	72.7	16.4	4.9	0	2.9
Senegal	1.1	0	0	85.2	60.1	60.7	11.0	36.9	38.1	2.7	3.0	1.2
Seychelles	0.9	0	0	89.5	80.4	87.4	8.1	18.5	11.5	1.5	1.1	1.1
Sierra Leone	0	0	0	0	45.6	30.5	95.6	49.3	67.1	4.4	5.1	2.4

Somalia	82.4	77.1	77.3	0	0	0	12.5	0	21.7	5.1	22.9	1.0
South Africa	0	0.3	0	70.7	69.1	67.1	26.4	26.9	29.0	2.9	3.6	3.8
Sudan	3.1	4.5	1.0	72.3	47.2	61.2	23.5	46.8	36.7	1.1	1.4	1.1
Swaziland	0	0	0	0	0	0	0	0	0	100	100	100
Tanzania	0	0.5	0	53.7	40.1	51.4	36.6	47.7	37.4	9.7	11.8	11.2
Togo	0	0	0	75.6	83.9	58.9	22.1	11.8	40.7	2.3	4.4	0.4
Uganda	3.7	1.0	0	58.7	52.9	70.9	35.1	45.0	27.9	2.5	1.1	1.2
Zambia	0	0	0.2	18.7	51.5	37.0	66.2	39.2	50.6	15.1	9.3	12.2
Zimbabwe	0	0	5.4	62.5	58.0	47.9	34.7	39.7	42.7	2.8	2.2	4.0
Low-income, fragile	0.6	1.2	0	58.5	49.4	48.7	33.5	43.6	46.8	7.4	5.9	4.5
Low-income, nonfragile	6.7	6.6	5.6	54.1	44.8	48.1	34.5	41.3	42.6	4.7	7.3	3.7
Middle-income	2.9	1.2	1.1	44.2	39.6	35.6	25.6	33.6	38.1	27.4	25.6	25.2
Resource-rich	1.8	6.2	0.2	64.0	58.3	50.7	30.4	33.8	45.9	3.7	1.7	3.3
Africa	3.1	3.6	1.9	54.7	47.2	45.6	31.3	38.8	43.3	10.9	10.4	9.1

Source: AICD data.

Appendix 4k   Safety Assessments, 2007

Country	Country has registered carriers on EU blacklist (1 = yes, 0 = no)	FAA IASA safety audit status (1 = passed, 2 = failed)	Known carriers based in country having passed IATA IOSA audit (% of total)
Angola	1	0	0
Benin	0	0	0
Botswana	0	0	0
Burkina Faso	0	0	0
Burundi	0	0	0
Cameroon	0	0	0
Cape Verde	0	1	50
Central African Republic	0	0	0
Chad	0	0	0
Comoros	1	0	0
Congo, Dem. Rep.	1	2	0
Congo, Rep.	0	0	0
Côte d'Ivoire	0	2	0
Equatorial Guinea	1	0	0
Eritrea	0	0	0
Ethiopia	0	1	100
Gabon	0	0	0
Gambia, The	0	2	0
Ghana	0	2	0
Guinea	0	0	0
Guinea-Bissau	0	0	0
Kenya	0	0	11.1
Lesotho	0	0	0
Liberia	0	0	0
Madagascar	0	0	100
Malawi	0	0	0
Mali	0	0	0
Mauritania	0	0	0
Mauritius	0	0	100
Mozambique	0	0	100
Namibia	0	0	100
Niger	0	0	0
Nigeria	0	0	28.6
Rwanda	1	0	0
São Tomé and Príncipe	0	0	0
Senegal	0	0	50
Seychelles	0	0	100
Sierra Leone	1	0	0

(continued)

Country	Country has registered carriers on EU blacklist (1 = yes, 0 = no)	FAA IASA safety audit status (1 = passed, 2 = failed)	Known carriers based in country having passed IATA IOSA audit (% of total)
Somalia	0	0	0
South Africa	0	1	53.8
Sudan	1	0	20
Swaziland	1	2	0
Tanzania	0	0	33.3
Togo	0	0	0
Uganda	0	0	0
Zambia	0	0	0
Zimbabwe	0	2	33.3
Low-income, fragile	n.a.	n.a.	28.8
Low-income, nonfragile	n.a.	n.a.	2.2
Middle-income	n.a.	n.a.	46.2
Resource-rich	n.a.	n.a.	5.4
Africa	n.a.	n.a.	21.6

Source: AICD data.
Note: EU = European Union; FAA = Federal Aviation Administration; IASA = International Aviation Safety Assessment; IATA = International Air Transport Association; IOSA = IATA Operational Safety Audit.
n.a = not applicable.

Ports and Shipping

Appendix 5a   Annual Traffic

Port	Container				General cargo		
	Vessel calls (number)	Exports (TEU)	Imports (TEU)	Total handled (TEU)	Vessel calls (number)	Exports (noncontainerized tons)	Imports (noncontainerized tons)
Abidjan, Côte d'Ivoire	—	—	—	500,119	—	—	—
Apapa, Nigeria	—	26,348	184,047	336,308	—	1,712,793	1,666,070
Beira, Mozambique	50	—	—	50,000	—	486,032	345,729
Bissau, Guinea-Bissau	—	—	—	50,000	—	—	—
Calabar, Nigeria	—	—	—	—	—	173	48,058
Cape Town, South Africa	1,037	190,904	153,924	690,895	389	336,103	223,499
Conarky, Guinea	410	—	—	753,827	—	—	—
Cotonou, Benin	856	—	—	158,201	155	113,910	1,032,268
Dakar, Senegal	478	39,719	109,362	331,191	675	1,895,000	4,214,000
Dar es Salaam, Tanzania		107,107	91,365	198,472	289	645,223	1,328,529
Djibouti, Djibouti	—	—	—	195,000	—	—	—
Douala, Cameroon	—	—	—	190,700	—	—	—
Durban, South Africa	1,174	469,694	619,942	1,899,065	849	3,660,167	3,562,000
East London, South Africa	56	15,954	21,166	49,338	10	104,239	295,978
Harcourt, Nigeria	—	110	5,961	7,900	303	71,465	810,536
Lomé, Togo	—	—	—	460,000	—	—	—
Luanda, Angola	272	180,407	196,700	377,208	425	—	—
Luderitz, Namibia	—	—	—	6,154	—	—	—

Malabo, Equatorial Guinea	—	—	—	—	80	—	—
Maputo, Mozambique	—	—	—	44,000	—	—	—
Mindelo, Cape Verde	—	10,000	10,000	150,000	380	139,000	1,009,000
Mombasa, Kenya	491	94,120	193,223	436,671	302	—	—
Monrovia, Liberia	—	—	—	50,000	200	—	—
Onne, Nigeria	—	2,475	60,922	86,290	—	97,833	1,531,983
Owendo, Gabon	—	—	—	15,942	—	—	—
Pointe Noire, Congo, Rep.	549	102,800	102,800	369,759	—	—	—
Port Elizabeth, South Africa	—	53,930	167,282	—	86	481,111	367,807
Port of Banjul, Gambia, The	—	—	—	100,000	—	—	—
Rades, Tunisia	1,230	—	—	380,000	—	—	—
Richards Bay, South Africa	4	3,489	1,020	5,179	230	4,203,367	145,427
Saldanha, South Africa	—	—	—	—	87	1,219,448	—
Suakin, Sudan	—	—	—	—	—	50,000	102,000
Sudan, Sudan	406	170,858	25,536	328,690	409	7,686,009	1,584,181
Takoradi, Ghana	—	—	—	51,000	—	—	—
Tema, Ghana	—	—	—	420,000	—	—	—
Toamasina, Madagascar	308	12,404	26,837	92,529	168	235,067	2,071,800
Walvis Bay, Namibia	145	3,220	21,312	71,456	—	855,007	270,373

Source: Africa Infrastructure Country Diagnostic (AICD) Database.
Note: — = not available, TEU = twenty-foot equivalent unit.

Appendix 5b   Institutional Characteristics

Port	Port has potential as cargo transshipment hub (0 = no; 1 = yes)	Landlord model is used (0 = no landlord model; 1 = landlord model)	Concessions present in terminal operations (0 = no, 1 = yes)	Management contracts present in infrastructure (0 = no, 1 = yes)
Abidjan, Côte d'Ivoire	1	1	1	0
Apapa, Nigeria	1	1	1	0
Bata, Equatorial Guinea	0	0	0	0
Beira, Mozambique	0	1	1	0
Boma, Congo, Dem. Rep.	0	0	0	0
Buchanan, Liberia	0	0	0	0
Calabar, Nigeria	0	—	—	—
Cap Lopez, Gabon	0	0	0	0
Cape Town, South Africa	1	0	0	0
Conarky, Guinea	1	0	1	0
Cotonou, Benin	1	0	0	0
Dakar, Senegal	1	0	0	0
Dar es Salaam, Tanzania	1	1	1	0
Douala, Cameroon	1	1	1	0
Durban, South Africa	1	0	0	0
East London, South Africa	0	0	0	0
Gamba Terminal, Gabon	0	0	0	0
Gentil, Gabon	0	1	1	0
Kamsar, Guinea	1	1	1	0
Kpeme, Togo	0	0	0	0
Kribi, Cameroon	0	0	0	0
Lomé, Togo	1	1	1	0
Luanda, Angola	1	0	0	0
Luba, Equatorial Guinea	0	0	0	0
Luderitz, Namibia	0	0	0	0
Majajanga, Madagascar	0	0	0	0
Malabo, Equatorial Guinea	0	0	—	0
Maputo, Mozambique	0	1	1	0
Matadi, Congo, Dem. Rep.	0	0	0	0
Mindelo, Cape Verde	1	0	0	0
Mombasa, Kenya	1	0	1	0
Monrovia, Liberia	0	1	0	0
Onne, Nigeria	1	1	1	0

(continued)

Port	Port has potential as cargo transshipment hub (0 = no; 1 = yes)	Landlord model is used (0 = no landlord model; 1 = landlord model)	Concessions present in terminal operations (0 = no, 1 = yes)	Management contracts present in infrastructure (0 = no, 1 = yes)
Owendo, Gabon	0	1	1	0
Pepel, Sierra Leone	0	0	0	0
Pointe Noire, Congo, Rep.	1	0	0	0
Port Elizabeth, South Africa	0	0	0	0
Port of Banjul, Gambia, The	0	0	0	0
Port St. Louis, Mauritius	0	—	—	—
Rades, Tunisia	0	0	0	0
Richards Bay, South Africa	0	1	1	0
Saldanha, South Africa	1	—	—	—
Sherbro, Sierra Leone	0	1	0	0
Suakin, Sudan	1	0	0	0
Sudan, Sudan	1	0	0	0
Takoradi, Ghana	1	1	1	0
Tema, Ghana	1	1	1	0
Toamasina, Madagascar	1	1	1	0
Walvis Bay, Namibia	1	1	0	0

Source: AICD Database.
Note: — = not available.

Appendix 5c Infrastructure Facilities

Port	Total berths (number)	Total length of container berths (meters)	Water depth of container berths (meters)	Container handling capacity (TEU per year)	Container gantry cranes (number)	Total length of general cargo berths (meters)	Average length of general cargo vessels (meters)	Mobile harbor cranes (number)
Abidjan, Côte d'Ivoire	26	—	34.5	600,000	4	—	—	2
Apapa, Nigeria	29	1,000	10.5	500,000	3	2,307	·114	25
Bata, Equatorial Guinea	9	—	—	—	—	682	—	1
Beira, Mozambique	9	645	11	100,000	2	—	93	2
Bissau, Guinea-Bissau	5	—	—	100,000	—	400	—	—
Boma, Congo, Dem. Rep.	3	—	—	—	0	480	92	3
Buchanan, Liberia	7	—	—	—	—	334	—	0
Calabar, Nigeria	10	—	—	—	—	860	—	1
Cap Lopez, Gabon	1	—	—	50,000	—	—	—	—
Cape Town, South Africa	34	2,234	10.7	950,000	5	2,706	138	—
Conarky, Guinea	13	269	10.5	—	—	830	—	50
Cotonou, Benin	11	220	10	400,000	0	990	115	1
Dakar, Senegal	52	1,273	10	400,000	0	1,245	120	3
Dar es Salaam, Tanzania	11	550	12.2	400,000	3	1,464	123	—
Djibouti, Djibouti	18	400	11	350,000	4	1,032	—	—
Douala, Cameroon	18	660	8.5	270,000	2	150	—	0
Durban, South Africa	57	2,128	12.8	1,450,000	9	200	120	—
East London, South Africa	13	253	10.7	90,000	0	1,303	120	—
Freeport, Liberia	7	819	9.76	—	—	—	—	—

Gamba Terminal, Gabon	1	—	—	—	—	—	—	—
Gentil, Gabon	3	—	10	100,000	—	375	—	—
Harcourt, Nigeria	8	—	—	—	—	1,107	—	—
Kamsar, Guinea	3	—	—	—	—	116	—	—
Kpeme, Togo	2	—	—	—	—	—	—	—
Kribi, Cameroon	1	250	11.5	250,000	0	250	105	—
Lomé, Togo	8	448	10.5	400,000	—	367	—	2
Luanda, Angola	11	—	—	—	0	825	120	—
Luba, Equatorial Guinea	1	—	—	—	—	290	—	—
Luderitz, Namibia	8	—	—	—	—	339	—	—
Majajanga, Madagascar	5	—	—	—	—	700	—	0
Malabo, Equatorial Guinea	2	—	—	—	—	—	—	1
Maputo, Mozambique	—	300	10.3	100,000	2	1,200	135	3
Matadi, Congo, Dem. Rep.	10	520	—	200,000	0	772	98	—
Mindelo, Cape Verde	8	315	11.5	50,000	0	700	120	0
Mombasa, Kenya	29	964	10.36	600,000	6	950	108	7
Monrovia, Liberia	8	600	9.15	100,000	0	600	—	0
Onne, Nigeria	6	250	13.5	100,000	—	1,590	—	—
Owendo, Gabon	3	500	9.8	100,000	0	500	—	—
Pepel, Sierra Leone	—	—	—	—	—	—	—	—
Pointe Noire, Congo, Rep.	15	250	7.6	150,000	0	—	88.5	0
Port Elizabeth, South Africa	15	635	12.2	500,000	4	1,900	144	0
Port of Banjul, Gambia, The	6	300	13	150,000	—	120	—	3
Port St. Louis, Mauritius	—	—	—	—	—	—	—	0
Rades, Tunisia	11	530	7.5	400,000	—	—	—	—

(continued)

Port	Total berths (number)	Total length of container berths (meters)	Water depth of container berths (meters)	Container handling capacity (TEU per year)	Container gantry cranes (number)	Total length of general cargo berths (meters)	Average length of general cargo vessels (meters)	Mobile harbor cranes (number)
Richards Bay, South Africa	21	—	—	—	0	1,244	130	2
Saldanha, South Africa	7	—	—	—	—	—	136	0
Sherbro, Sierra Leone	0	—	—	—	—	—	—	—
Suakin, Sudan	6	—	—	—	—	392	—	1
Sudan, Sudan	—	420	12.6	400,000	3	2,011	115	16
Takoradi, Ghana	13	—	—	—	—	714	105	0
Tema, Ghana	14	383	11.5	375,000	3	2,196	92	30
Toamasina, Madagascar	6	307	11	500,000	—	526	98	3
Walvis Bay, Namibia	9	—	10.6	100,000	0	1,426	104	1
Low-income, fragile	98	2,758	15	1,400,000	4	4,019	95	63
Low-income, nonfragile	201	6,495	11	3,890,000	22	10,850	127	3
Resource-rich	109	3,528	10	2,070,000	8	11,339	109	45
Middle-income	150	4,642	11	2,875,000	16	9,985	110	46
Africa	558	17,423	11	10,235,000	50	36,193	114	157

Source: AICD Database.
Note: Country type numbers are either totals or simple averages, as appropriate. — = not available, TEU = twenty-foot equivalent unit.

Appendix 5d   Cargo-Handling Performance Indicators

Port	Container crane, productivity gross average (containers per hour)[a]	Container vessel berth, productivity average (containers per hour)[b]	General cargo vessel berth productivity average (tonnes per hour)[b]
Abidjan, Côte d'Ivoire	18	35	—
Apapa, Nigeria	12	28	28
Beira, Mozambique	10	20	—
Boma, Congo, Dem. Rep.	—	6	10
Cape Town, South Africa	18	36	—
Cotonou, Benin	—	—	60
Dakar, Senegal	—	10	—
Dar es Salaam, Tanzania	20	19.8	22.6
Djibouti, Djibouti	17	68	—
Douala, Cameroon	18.5	37.5	12
Durban, South Africa	15	45	—
East London, South Africa	8	10	—
Freeport, Liberia	—	8	—
Harcourt, Nigeria	—	—	26
Kribi, Cameroon	—	—	5.5
Lomé, Togo	—	14	—
Luanda, Angola	6.5	7	16
Luderitz, Namibia	—	7.5	—
Majajanga, Madagascar	—	—	18
Malabo, Equatorial Guinea	—	—	11
Maputo, Mozambique	11	22	22.5
Matadi, Congo, Dem. Rep.	6.5	10	11
Mindelo, Cape Verde	6.5	13	13.5
Mombasa, Kenya	10	10	20.8
Onne, Nigeria	—	14	26
Pointe Noire, Congo, Rep.	6.5	6.5	13.5
Port Elizabeth, South Africa	14.95	15	45
Port of Banjul, Gambia, The	—	1.5	—
Rades, Tunisia	—	10	—
Richards Bay, South Africa	—	10	25
Suakin, Sudan	—	—	15
Sudan, Sudan	8	20	24.5
Takoradi, Ghana	—	—	30
Tema, Ghana	13	39	40
Toamasina, Madagascar	—	17.6	27
Walvis Bay, Namibia	—	7.5	31

(continued)

Port	Container crane, productivity gross average (containers per hour)[a]	Container vessel berth, productivity average (containers per hour)[b]	General cargo vessel berth productivity average (tonnes per hour)[b]
Low-income, fragile	12.3	12.4	10.5
Low-income, nonfragile	13.2	22.2	28.6
Resource-rich	10.3	18.8	16.5
Middle-income	12.8	19.8	30.1
Africa	12.2	18.9	22.1

Source: AICD Database.
Note: Country type numbers are reported as simple averages. — = data not available.
(a) Containers loaded and unloaded per single crane working hour.
(b) Containers loaded and unloaded alongside berth.

Appendix 5e Port Access and Landside Quality

Port	Adequate road access (0 = no, 1 = yes)	Working rail access (0 = no, 1 = yes)	Container dwell time, average (days)	Container vessel pre-berth waiting time, average (days)	Container vessel stay, average (hours)	Cargo vessel pre-berth waiting time, average (hours)	Cargo vessel stay, average (hours)	Truck processing time for receipt and delivery of cargo, average (hours)
Abidjan, Côte d'Ivoire	—	1	12	1	1	2.9	2.2	2.5
Apapa, Nigeria	0	1	42	12	24	36	40.8	6
Bata, Equatorial Guinea	—	—	—	—	—	6	—	—
Beira, Mozambique	1	1	20	7	24	8	48	6.8
Bissau, Guinea-Bissau	1	1	21	2.5	—	—	—	—
Boma, Congo, Dem. Rep.	0	0	—	—	—	108	84	—
Buchanan, Liberia	1	1	—	—	—	—	—	—
Calabar, Nigeria	0	0	—	—	—	26.4	55.2	—
Cap Lopez, Gabon	—	—	12	2	1	2	—	—
Cape Town, South Africa	0	1	6	3	24	3	36	4.8
Conarky, Guinea	0	1	15	2.5	2	—	2.7	—
Cotonou, Benin	0	1	12	24	36	48	48	6
Dakar, Senegal	0	1	7	18	24	24	60	5
Dar es Salaam, Tanzania	1	0	7	24	24	6	62.4	5
Djibouti, Djibouti	1	—	8	1	1	1.5	—	12
Douala, Cameroon	—	—	12	1.6	3.2	—	—	12
Durban, South Africa	0	1	4	5	32	2	60	5
East London, South Africa	1	1	7	0	24	6	48	2

(continued)

493

Port	Adequate road access (0 = no, 1 = yes)	Working rail access (0 = no, 1 = yes)	Container dwell time, average (days)	Container vessel pre-berth waiting time, average (days)	Container vessel stay, average (hours)	Cargo vessel pre-berth waiting time, average (hours)	Cargo vessel stay, average (hours)	Truck processing time for receipt and delivery of cargo, average (hours)
Freeport, Liberia	—	—	15	2	1	2.5	3	5
Gamba Terminal, Gabon	—	—	—	—	—	—	—	—
Gentil, Gabon	1	—	10	1.5	—	2	2.5	—
Harcourt, Nigeria	0	1	—	—	—	38.4	45.6	—
Kamsar, Guinea	1	1	—	—	—	—	—	—
Kpeme, Togo	—	1	—	—	—	—	—	—
Kribi, Cameroon	1	0	—	—	—	24	72	—
Lomé, Togo	0	1	13	1	1	—	—	4
Luanda, Angola	0	1	12	96	48	144	60	14
Luba, Equatorial Guinea	1	—	—	—	—	—	—	—
Luderitz, Namibia	1	—	8	0	2	0	—	3
Majajanga, Madagascar	0	—	—	—	—	24	67.2	—
Malabo, Equatorial Guinea	1	—	—	—	—	7	2	—
Maputo, Mozambique	1	1	22	3	24	12	55.2	4
Matadi, Congo, Dem. Rep.	0	0	25	—	48	108	84	18
Mindelo, Cape Verde	1	0	16	24	48	36	72	6
Mombasa, Kenya	0	1	5	12	36	36	48	4.5
Monrovia, Liberia	1	—	15	1.5	1	2.5	—	5.5
Onne, Nigeria	0	0	30	4	32	6	38.4	24

Owendo, Gabon	—	1	10	1.5	1	2	—	—
Pepel, Sierra Leone	—	1	—	—	—	—	—	—
Pointe Noire, Congo, Rep.	0	1	18	38.4	48	43.2	60	12
Port Elizabeth, South Africa	1	1	6	3	24	5	48	4.5
Port of Banjul, Gambia, The	0	0	2	2	1.5	3	—	2.5
Port St. Louis, Mauritius	0	0	—	2.5	2	1.5	2	—
Rades, Tunisia	1	1	10	0	24	2	36	6
Richards Bay, South Africa	1	1	—	—	—	2	28.8	0
Saldanha, South Africa	1	1	—	—	—	2	28.8	—
Sherbro, Sierra Leone	—	—	—	—	—	—	—	—
Suakin, Sudan	0	1	28	2.1	45.6	28.8	57.6	24
Sudan, Sudan	0	1	—	—	—	28.8	52.8	—
Takoradi, Ghana	0	1	25	12.35	32	3	52.8	8
Tema, Ghana	0	1	8	12	12.25	9.6	48	3.5
Toamasina, Madagascar	0	1	8	0	48	24	52.8	3
Walvis Bay, Namibia	1	1	8	—	0	0	57.6	—
Low-income, fragile	—	—	14.8	1.8	7.9	37.8	35.2	6.3
Low-income, nonfragile	—	—	8.1	3.9	22.9	5.4	43.2	4.6
Resource-rich	—	—	19.3	17.7	22.6	28.2	44.3	15.3
Middle-income	—	—	13.3	14.0	26.5	19.5	54.2	5.4
Africa	—	—	13.9	9.5	20.6	21.3	45.5	7.3

Source: AICD Database.

Note: Country type figures are reported as simple averages. Vessel stay is equivalent to turnaround time. — = data not available.

Appendix 5f   Average Port Costs and Charges (US$/unit)

Port	Container cargo handling charge per TEU	General cargo handling charge per ton	Bulk dry handling charge per ton	Bulk liquid handling charge per ton
Abidjan, Côte d'Ivoire	260	13.5	5	—
Apapa, Nigeria	155	8	—	1
Bata, Equatorial Guinea	185	17	8	—
Beira, Mozambique	125	6.5	2.5	0.75
Boma, Congo, Dem. Rep.	—	10	—	4
Cap Lopez, Gabon	280	14	—	—
Cape Town, South Africa	258.2	—	6.3	0.4
Cotonou, Benin	180	8.5	5	—
Dakar, Senegal	160	15	5	4
Dar es Salaam, Tanzania	275	13.5	4.5	3.5
Djibouti, Djibouti	135	7.5	4	1.25
Douala, Cameroon	220	6.5	6	—
Durban, South Africa	258.2	8.4	1.4	—
East London, South Africa	—	8.4	6.3	—
Freeport, Liberia	—	8	5.5	3.3
Gentil, Gabon	280	11	—	—
Harcourt, Nigeria	—	8	—	1
Kribi, Cameroon	—	12	—	—
Lomé, Togo	220	9	5	—
Luanda, Angola	320	8.5	5	—
Luderitz, Namibia	90	12	5	3
Majajanga, Madagascar	—	6	—	—
Malabo, Equatorial Guinea	185	17	—	—
Maputo, Mozambique	155	6	2	0.5
Matadi, Congo, Dem. Rep.	120	10	8	2
Mindelo, Cape Verde	100	10	5	2.5
Mombasa, Kenya	67.5	6.5	5	—
Monrovia, Liberia	200	10.5	4	—
Onne, Nigeria	145	6.5	—	—
Owendo, Gabon	340	16	—	—
Pointe Noire, Congo, Rep.	140	5.5	2.75	—
Port Elizabeth, South Africa	258.2	8.4	1.4	—
Port of Banjul, Gambia, The	210	13	5	—
Rades, Tunisia	—	9	4.5	—
Richards Bay, South Africa	—	—	1.4	—

(continued)

Port	Container cargo handling charge per TEU	General cargo handling charge per ton	Bulk dry handling charge per ton	Bulk liquid handling charge per ton
Suakin, Sudan	—	—	3	1
Sudan, Sudan	150	10	3	1
Takoradi, Ghana	—	7	2.5	1.5
Tema, Ghana	168	10	3	1.5
Toamasina, Madagascar	—	6	3	—
Walvis Bay, Namibia	110	15	5	2
Low-income, fragile	210	10.1	4.9	3.3
Low-income, nonfragile	172.8	9.8	4	1.8
Resource-rich	226	11.2	5	1
Middle-income	161.5	8.5	3.6	2
Africa	191.7	9.9	4.3	1.9

Source: AICD Database.
Note: Country type figures are reported as simple averages. Charges are ship to gate or rail. — = data not available, TEU = twenty-foot equivalent unit.

APPENDIX 6

Expenditure Needs

Appendix 6 Costs of Achieving Targets of Pragmatic Scenario, by Expenditure Purpose (US$, millions/year)

Country	OPEX	CAPEX Improve condition	CAPEX Upgrade category	CAPEX Expand capacity	Total CAPEX	Total spending
Angola	140	39	57	5	101	241
Benin	33	15	23	0	39	72
Botswana	47	12	12	0	24	72
Burkina Faso	60	3	41	0	45	105
Burundi	17	9	4	0	13	30
Cameroon	97	19	78	2	99	196
Cape Verde	3	3	0	3	6	9
Central African Republic	69	8	82	0	91	160
Chad	102	3	79	53	135	237
Congo, Rep.	55	22	21	8	52	106
Congo, Dem, Rep.	352	45	350	129	524	876
Côte d'Ivoire	130	27	56	2	84	215
Equatorial Guinea	19	8	3	17	27	46

(continued)

Country	OPEX	CAPEX Improve condition	Upgrade category	Expand capacity	Total CAPEX	Total spending
Eritrea	13	7	2	0	10	23
Ethiopia	127	12	73	21	106	233
Gabon	52	23	36	1	60	112
Gambia, The	15	17	3	1	20	36
Ghana	98	43	40	3	87	184
Guinea	77	19	55	3	77	154
Guinea-Bissau	13	8	2	0	10	23
Kenya	130	66	40	11	117	247
Lesotho	11	3	2	0	5	16
Liberia	38	8	45	8	61	99
Madagascar	154	18	73	8	99	252
Malawi	34	9	16	0	26	60
Mali	83	16	36	18	70	153
Mauritania	39	16	8	16	40	80
Mauritius	14	8	13	6	27	40
Mozambique	167	21	78	5	104	271
Namibia	67	39	18	0	57	124
Niger	67	9	10	6	24	91
Nigeria	373	151	67	61	279	652
Rwanda	11	3	3	3	9	20
Senegal	49	20	15	3	38	87
Sierra Leone	32	9	17	6	32	64
South Africa	421	182	60	46	288	710
Sudan	221	17	146	148	311	532
Swaziland	29	4	10	3	16	46
Tanzania	223	26	135	16	178	401
Togo	18	12	10	25	47	65
Uganda	55·	14	57	3	74	130
Zambia	134	21	32	0	53	186
Zimbabwe	69	23	16	1	40	110
Resource-rich	1,192	302	520	294	1,116	2,307
Low-income, nonfragile	1,329	293	648	114	1,056	2,385
Low-income, fragile	844	192	642	174	1,009	1,853
Middle-income	593	251	115	59	425	1,018
Africa	3,958	1,039	1,925	641	3,605	7,563

Source: Carruthers, Krishnamani, and Murray 2009
Note: OPEX = operating expenditure; CAPEX = capital expenditure.

APPENDIX 7

Financing

Appendix 7a Transport Spending and Finance Sources, by Country (annualized flows)

| Country | GDP share (%) | | | | | | | US$ millions/year | | | | | | |
| | O&M public sector | Capital expenditure | | | | | Total spending | O&M public sector | Capital expenditure | | | | | Total spending |
		Public sector	ODA	Non-OECD financiers	PPI	Total CAPEX			Public sector	ODA	Non-OECD financiers	PPI	Total CAPEX	
Benin	0.97	0.37	1.07	0.14	0.00	1.58	2.55	41	16	46	6	0	68	109
Botswana	1.01	1.33	0.00	0.09	0.00	1.42	2.43	106	140	0	9	0	149	256
Cameroon	1.06	0.19	0.32	0.08	0.00	0.59	1.64	175	32	53	13	0	98	273
Cape Verde	6.04	2.30	4.45	0.14	0.00	6.89	12.92	61	23	45	1	0	69	130
Chad	0.08	0.23	0.39	0.09	0.00	0.72	0.79	4	14	23	5	0	42	46
Congo, Dem. Rep.	0.43	—	0.77	0.02	0.00	—	0.43	30	—	55	2	0	—	30
Congo, Rep.	1.47	2.29	0.28	0.20	0.00	2.77	4.23	89	139	17	12	0	168	258
Côte d'Ivoire	0.04	0.80	0.02	0.06	0.08	0.97	1.00	6	131	3	10	14	158	164
Ethiopia	0.43	1.74	1.70	0.16	0.00	3.61	4.04	53	215	209	20	0	444	497
Ghana	1.19	0.47	1.11	0.08	0.01	1.66	2.85	127	50	119	8	1	178	305
Kenya	1.50	0.42	0.77	0.07	0.12	1.38	2.88	280	79	144	13	22	259	539
Lesotho	0.80	0.59	1.29	0.32	0.00	2.21	3.01	11	8	18	5	0	31	43
Madagascar	2.41	0.64	2.60	0.08	0.16	3.48	5.89	122	32	131	4	8	175	297
Malawi	1.74	0.87	1.01	0.08	0.00	1.97	3.72	50	25	29	2	0	56	106

Mali	0.18	0.80	1.49	0.45	0.09	2.82	3.00	10	42	79	24	5	150	159
Mozambique	1.06	0.73	1.61	0.25	0.85	3.44	4.50	70	48	106	16	56	226	296
Namibia	0.98	0.22	0.37	0.08	0.00	0.67	1.65	61	14	23	5	0	42	103
Niger	0.23	0.47	0.89	0.28	0.00	1.63	1.86	8	16	30	9	0	54	62
Nigeria	0.10	0.69	0.02	0.48	0.38	1.57	1.67	112	780	26	537	422	1,765	1,877
Rwanda	0.27	0.14	1.06	0.14	0.00	1.34	1.61	6	3	25	3	0	32	38
Senegal	0.08	0.86	0.54	0.26	0.05	1.71	1.79	7	75	47	23	5	149	156
South Africa	1.93	0.76	0.00	0.00	0.18	0.94	2.87	4,661	1,843	0	0	444	2,287	6,948
Tanzania	1.37	0.58	0.82	0.05	0.06	1.52	2.89	194	82	117	7	9	214	408
Uganda	0.51	0.07	0.86	0.02	0.26	1.21	1.71	44	6	75	2	22	106	150
Zambia	1.35	1.79	0.93	0.11	0.04	2.86	4.21	99	132	68	8	3	210	309
Middle-income	1.88	0.78	0.03	0.01	0.16	0.98	2.86	5,081	2,103	88	22	444	2,657	7,738
Resource-rich	0.32	0.74	0.11	0.34	0.21	1.39	1.72	720	1,646	234	745	469	3,095	3,815
Low-income, nonfragile	0.98	0.67	1.12	0.22	0.12	2.13	3.11	1,084	737	1,241	242	128	2,347	3,431
Low-income, fragile	0.16	0.56	0.61	0.13	0.04	1.33	1.49	60	214	234	49	14	511	571
Africa	1.20	0.74	0.28	0.16	0.16	1.34	2.54	7,701	4,724	1,797	1,059	1,055	8,635	16,336

Appendix 7b   Potential Efficiency Gains

	GDP share(%)				US$ millions/year			
Country	Undercollection	Capital execution	Tariff cost recovery	Total	Undercollection	Capital execution	Tariff cost recovery	Total
Benin	0.00	0.00	0.01	0.01	0	0	0	0
Botswana	—	0.26	—	0.26	—	27	—	27
Cameroon	0.20	0.06	0.00	0.26	33	9	0	43
Cape Verde	—	0.30	—	0.30	—	3	—	3
Chad	0.14	0.04	0.25	0.43	8	2	15	25
Congo, Dem. Rep.	—	0.00	—	0.00	—	0	—	0
Congo, Rep.	0.00	0.54	0.08	0.62	0	33	5	38
Côte d'Ivoire	—	0.23	0.20	0.42	—	37	32	59
Ethiopia	0.22	0.38	0.30	0.91	28	47	37	112
Ghana	0.32	0.00	0.39	0.71	34	0	42	76
Kenya	0.00	0.10	0.14	0.24	0	19	25	44
Lesotho	0.08	0.00	0.67	0.75	1	0	10	11
Madagascar	0.00	0.19	0.52	0.71	0	10	26	36
Malawi	—	0.31	0.79	1.10	—	9	22	31
Mali	—	0.00	—	0.00	—	0	—	0
Mozambique	0.47	0.21	0.19	0.87	31	14	13	57

Namibia	0.56	0.13	0.46	1.16	35	8	29	72
Niger	0.17	0.07	0.59	0.83	6	2	20	28
Nigeria	—	0.20	—	0.20	—	223	—	223
Rwanda	0.00	0.04	0.16	0.20	0	1	4	5
Senegal	—	0.25	—	0.25	—	21	—	21
South Africa	0.34	0.23	0.00	0.23	—	553	0	553
Tanzania	—	0.19	—	0.53	48	27	—	75
Uganda	—	0.02	—	0.02	—	2	—	2
Zambia	0.00	0.48	0.27	0.75	0	35	20	55
Middle-income	0.01	0.23	0.01	0.25	36	613	38	688
Resource-rich	0.08	0.20	0.07	0.35	170	455	163	788
Low-income, nonfragile	0.15	0.15	0.19	0.49	169	162	211	541
Low-income, fragile	—	0.16	0.12	0.28	—	61	46	107
Africa	0.08	0.20	0.09	0.37	497	1,298	574	2,368

Source: Derived from Foster and Briceño-Garmendia 2009.
Note: — = not available.

Appendix 7c   Agency and Total Social Benefits of Timely Road Maintenance

The financial analysis in chapter 8 attempted to identify the extent to which shortfalls in the financing of maintenance and investment in transport infrastructure, and roads in particular, might be overcome by more efficient policies. It has been widely recognized for many years that inadequate funding of current and periodic maintenance might both increase total road agency costs (because of the extra burden of rehabilitation and reconstruction expenditure that it caused) and substantially reduce road user welfare (by increasing vehicle operating costs). Most traditional research on the topic has concentrated on the total social benefit (the sum of user benefits and agency benefit), while the balance between these two types of benefits has been given less attention. The importance of that balance in the present context is that any agency benefits from changed policies accrue directly to the public budget, and the potential saving to road users is available to finance the policy change only if part or all of the benefits can be captured for the public purse by changes in road user charges.

To examine this balance more closely, we compared the total life-cycle costs of two possible maintenance and rehabilitation road agency alternatives for a typical road class in Africa. The road agency alternatives that were evaluated are to (i) perform annual routine maintenance and rehabilitate the road when its condition becomes poor and (ii) perform annual routine maintenance and proper periodic maintenance. The evaluation was done using the Highway Development and Management Model (HDM-4) using representative vehicle fleet characteristics for Africa.

Sixteen road classes were evaluated, corresponding to two climate/terrain types, four traffic levels, and two road condition types. The two climate/terrain types evaluated were dry and flat roads and wet and hilly roads. The four traffic levels were 500, 1,000, 3,000 or 6,000 annual average daily traffic (AADT). Roads with 500 and 1,000 AADT were considered surface treatment roads, and roads with 3,000 and 6,000 AADT were considered asphalt concrete roads. Each road was designated as being in either good or fair condition.

For the surface treatment roads, the following road agency alternatives were evaluated:

- *Rehabilitation:* Perform annual routine maintenance and rehabilitate the road to a surface treatment standard when the road roughness reaches International Roughness Index (IRI) value of 10 m/km[1]

- *Periodic maintenance:* Perform annual routine maintenance and periodic maintenance corresponding to 12 millimeter (mm) reseals done every seven years. If during the evaluation period the road roughness reaches 10 IRI, m/km, the road is rehabilitated to a surface treatment standard.

For the asphalt concrete roads, the following road agency alternatives were evaluated:

- *Rehabilitation:* Perform annual routine maintenance and rehabilitate the road to an asphalt concrete standard when the road roughness reaches 10 IRI, m/km.
- *Periodic maintenance:* Perform annual routine maintenance and periodic maintenance corresponding to 50 mm overlays done when the road reaches 4 IRI, m/km.

Table A7c.1 presents the unit cost of road works adopted on the evaluation that corresponds to representative figures for Africa.

The performance of each road class under the two possible alternatives was evaluated with HDM-4 for a 20-year evaluation period, and the resulting road agency costs and total transport costs (road agency costs plus road user costs) were calculated, both undiscounted and discounted using a 12 percent discount rate. Table A7c.2 shows that the ratio between the undiscounted costs of total rehabilitation and the undiscounted costs of periodic maintenance varies from 0.42 to 2.92. The table also shows that when all costs are discounted to a present value at 12 percent a year, the ratio between the rehabilitation alternative costs and the periodic maintenance alternative costs varies from 0.49 to 1.85.

Table A7c.2 considered only the road life-cycle agency costs in financial terms. Table A7c.3 presents the present value, at a 12 percent

Table A7c.1   Unit Cost of Road Works

Surface type	Type of road work	Unit cost (US$/km)
Surface treatment	Routine maintenance	2,600
	Periodic maintenance (reseal 12 mm)	24,150
	Reconstruction surface treatment pavement	273,000
Asphalt or concrete	Routine maintenance	2,600
	Periodic maintenance (overlay 50 mm)	73,500
	Reconstruction asphalt or concrete pavement	315,000

Source: World Bank Rocks Database.

Table A7c.2 Comparison of Road Agency Costs for Various Roads and for Rehabilitation vs. Periodic Maintenance

Road class	Alternative	Undiscounted value of road agency costs (US$/km)	Undiscounted rehabilitation/ periodic maintenance ratio	Present value agency costs (US$/km)	Present value rehabilitation/ periodic maintenance
Dry/flat 500 AADT	Rehabilitation	325,000	2.61	53,448	0.87
ST road fair condition	Periodic maintenance	124,450		61,767	
Dry/flat 1,000 AADT	Rehabilitation	325,000	2.61	91,823	1.49
ST road fair condition	Periodic maintenance	124,450		61,767	
Dry/flat 3,000 AADT	Rehabilitation	367,000	1.84	102,604	0.94
AC road fair condition	Periodic maintenance	199,000		108,679	
Dry/flat 6,000 AADT	Rehabilitation	367,000	1.84	148,974	1.39
AC road fair condition	Periodic maintenance	199,000		107,240	
Wet/hilly 500 AADT	Rehabilitation	325,000	0.82	100,232	0.99
ST road fair condition	Periodic maintenance	397,450		101,528	
Wet/hilly 1,000 AADT	Rehabilitation	325,000	0.87	132,011	1.17
ST road fair condition	Periodic maintenance	373,300		112,686	
Wet/filly 3,000 AADT	Rehabilitation	367,000	1.84	135,343	1.21
AC road fair condition	Periodic maintenance	199,000		112,095	
Wet/filly 6,000 AADT	Rehabilitation	367,000	1.84	164,241	1.47
AC road fair condition	Periodic maintenance	199,000		112,095	

Dry/flat 500 AADT ST road good condition	Rehabilitation	52,000	0.42	21,751	0.49
	Periodic maintenance	124,450		44,457	
Dry/flat 1,000 AADT ST road good condition	Rehabilitation	325,000	2.61	53,448	1.20
	Periodic maintenance	124,450		44,457	
Dry/flat 3,000 AADT AC road good condition	Rehabilitation	367,000	2.92	67,629	1.58
	Periodic maintenance	125,500		42,881	
Dry/flat 6,000 AADT AC road good condition	Rehabilitation	367,000	2.92	79,300	1.85
	Periodic maintenance	125,500		42,881	
Wet/hilly 500 AADT ST road good condition	Rehabilitation	52,000	0.42	21,751	0.49
	Periodic maintenance	124,450		44,457	
Wet/hilly 1,000 AADT ST road good condition	Rehabilitation	325,000	2.61	66,283	1.49
	Periodic maintenance	124,450		44,457	
Wet/hilly 3,000 AADT AC road good condition	Rehabilitation	367,000	2.92	67,629	1.58
	Periodic maintenance	125,500		42,881	
Wet/hilly 6,000 AADT AC road good condition	Rehabilitation	367,000	1.84	102,604	1.77
	Periodic maintenance	199,000		57,814	

Source: Calculations by R Archondo Callao using HDM4.

Note: ST = surface treatment; AC = asphalt concrete.

Table A7c.3 Total Economic Costs Discounted at 12 Percent

Road class	Alternative	Total value of agency costs (US$/km)	Rehabilitation/ periodic maintenance ratio	NPV (US$/km)	NPV/PV of agency costs
Dry/flat 500 AADT ST road fair condition	Rehabilitation	658,946	1.04	24,586	0.40
	Periodic maintenance	634,360			
Dry/flat 1,000 AADT ST road fair condition	Rehabilitation	1,851,305	1.04	69,264	1.12
	Periodic maintenance	1,782,041			
Dry/flat 3,000 AADT AC road fair condition	Rehabilitation	3,589,946	1.08	277,785	2.56
	Periodic maintenance	3,312,161			
Dry/flat 6,000 AADT AC road fair condition	Rehabilitation	6,952,731	1.07	436,891	4.07
	Periodic maintenance	6,515,840			
Wet/hilly 500 AADT ST road fair condition	Rehabilitation	761,213	1.00	3,771	0.04
	Periodic maintenance	757,442			
Wet/hilly 1,000 AADT ST road fair condition	Rehabilitation	2,080,735	1.01	18,177	0.16
	Periodic maintenance	2,062,558			
Wet/hilly 3,000 AADT AC road fair condition	Rehabilitation	4,027,216	1.07	264,184	2.36
	Periodic maintenance	3,763,031			
Wet/hilly 6,000 AADT AC road fair condition	Rehabilitation	7,937,865	1.07	502,055	4.48
	Periodic maintenance	7,435,810			

Category	Treatment				
Dry/flat 500 AADT ST road good condition	Rehabilitation	561,097	0.97	−19,450	−0.44
	Periodic maintenance	580,547			
Dry/flat 1,000 AADT ST road good condition	Rehabilitation	1,695,824	1.02	41,015	0.92
	Periodic maintenance	1,654,809			
Dry/flat 3,000 AADT AC road good condition	Rehabilitation	3,341,756	1.04	114,690	2.67
	Periodic maintenance	3,227,066			
	Periodic maintenance	6,405,968			
Wet/hilly 500 AADT ST road good condition	Rehabilitation	646,004	0.98	−15,981	−0.36
	Periodic maintenance	661,984			
Wet/hilly 1,000 AADT ST road good condition	Rehabilitation	1,935,770	1.02	34,134	0.77
	Periodic maintenance	1,901,636			
Wet/hilly 3,000 AADT AC road good condition	Rehabilitation	3,776,335	1.03	111,081	2.59
	Periodic maintenance	3,665,253			
Wet/hilly 6,000 AADT AC road good condition	Rehabilitation	7,481,304	1.02	145,671	2.52
	Periodic maintenance	7,335,633			

Source: Calculations by R Archondo Callao using HDM4.
Note: ST = surface treatment; AC = asphalt concrete.

discount rate, of the total economic costs (sum of road agency costs and road user costs) as well as the net present value (NPV) of the periodic maintenance alternatives and the ratio between the NPV and the present value of financial agency costs. The NPV is the difference between the present value (PV) of total society costs of the base alternative (rehabilitation) and the project alternative (periodic maintenance).

The optimal alternative from an economic point of view is the one with the lowest present value of total society costs. The periodic maintenance alternative is the recommended alternative if the rehabilitation/periodic maintenance ratio is higher than 1.0. The study shows that only for the two roads with traffic of 500 AADT and in good condition is the recommended alternative to perform routine maintenance and rehabilitation, but no rehabilitation is needed during the evaluation period in both cases. For all other cases, proper periodic maintenance is the recommended alternative.

These results can be interpreted as follows. First, performing timely periodic maintenance is likely to save on agency costs if no discounting is applied, except where traffic volumes are as low as 500 vehicles per day. When discounting is applied at 12 percent, timely routine maintenance may or may not reduce total agency costs, depending on the combination of climate/terrain, traffic volumes, and initial surface condition. When user costs are taken into account, however, the only circumstance in which there is a net loss from timely maintenance is when traffic volume is low and the initial condition is good; clearly this circumstance will change as surface conditions deteriorate from good to fair. Moreover, only a small proportion of roads meet those criteria. While the cases included in this examination represent only a small set of the very wide range of possible situations, it can be safely concluded that timely periodic maintenance, whether or not it reduces road agency costs, will yield high net social benefits, which may be up to five times the extra expenditures on maintenance of the more heavily trafficked roads.

Appendix 7d Closing the Gap (US$ millions/year)

Country	Infrastructure spending needs	Total spending in sector	Total gain	Gain from raising capital budget execution	Gain from cost recovery through fuel levy	Gain from ending undercollection	Financing gap or surplus
Benin	116	105	0	0	0	0	(11)
Botswana	107	107	27	27	—	—	27
Cameroon	328	220	43	9	0	33	(65)
Cape Verde	19	19	3	3	—	—	3
Chad	364	46	25	2	15	8	(292)
Congo, Dem. Rep.	1,474	87	0	0	—	—	(1,387)
Congo, Rep.	163	163	38	33	5	0	38
Côte d'Ivoire	341	164	69	37	32	—	(107)
Ethiopia	393	298	112	47	37	28	17
Ghana	307	301	76	0	42	34	71
Kenya	474	474	44	19	25	0	(44)
Lesotho	25	25	11	0	10	1	11
Madagascar	377	297	36	10	26	0	44
Malawi	85	85	31	9	22	—	31
Mali	236	154	0	0	—	—	(83)
Mozambique	395	296	57	14	13	31	(41)
Namibia	154	103	72	8	29	35	21

(continued)

Country	Infrastructure spending needs	Total spending in sector	Total gain	Gain from eliminating inefficiencies			Financing gap or surplus
				Gain from raising capital budget execution	Gain from cost recovery through fuel levy	Gain from ending undercollection	
Niger	139	62	28	2	20	6	(50)
Nigeria	1,222	842	223	223	—	—	(157)
Rwanda	36	29	5	1	4	0	(2)
Senegal	141	94	21	21	—	—	(25)
South Africa	7,971	6,948	553	553	—	—	(470)
Tanzania	619	408	75	27	0	48	(136)
Uganda	221	150	2	2	—	—	(70)
Zambia	280	239	55	35	20	0	14
Middle-income	8,430	7,738	688	613	38	36	(4)
Resource-rich	3,810	3,113	788	455	163	170	91
Low-income, nonfragile	3,797	3,266	541	162	211	169	10
Low-income, fragile	3,155	571	107	61	46	—	(2,477)

Source: derived from Foster and Briceño-Garmendia, 2009 and Carruthers, Krishnamani, and Murray 2009.
Note: — = not available.

Note

1. The International Roughness Index, IRI, is a measurement of the accumulated deviation of an actual surface from a true planar surface. A value of 10 meters per kilometer represents a very badly damaged pavement with many shallow and some deep depressions.

Index

Boxes, figures, maps, notes, and tables are indicated with *b*, *f*, *m*, *n*, and *t* following the page number.